D1008660

the SOULFUL
DIVAS

the SOULFUL DIVAS

*Personal portraits of over a dozen divine divas, from
Nina Simone, Aretha Franklin, & Diana Ross to
Patti LaBelle, Whitney Houston, & Janet Jackson.*

DAVID NATHAN

Foreword by Luther Vandross

Billboard Books
An imprint of Watson-Guptill Publications/New York

Dedication

For the angels, watching over me:

Mother and Father, Eric B., Gary W., John S., Hayden S., Fred M., Steve H., George H., Darryl C., Murvyn D., Aunt Phoebe, and a heavenly-but-earthy choir of singin' sisters that includes Big Maybelle, Billie Holiday, Lorraine Ellison, Laura Nyro, Esther Phillips, and Phyllis Hyman.

David Nathan, a reissue producer and accomplished writer of liner notes, is an award-winning freelance journalist who has written for *Billboard*, *USA Today*, *Blues & Soul*, Amazon.com, and *Launch*. He is on the Board of Trustees of the Rhythm & Blues Foundation and is a Governor of the Los Angeles chapter of NARAS. He lives in Los Angeles.

Unless otherwise stated, all interview quotes originally appeared in *Blues & Soul* magazine and are used with the kind permission of the publisher, Blues & Soul Ltd. For further information about the publication, please write: 153 Praed Street, London W2 1RL, England.

Picture credits:
Half-title page: (top to bottom, left to right) David Corio, Michael Ochs Archives/Venice, CA; Archive Photos/Monitor; Michael Ochs Archives/Venice, CA; Reuters/Romeo Ranoco/Archive Photos; Nick Elgar UNE/London Features International © 1990; CBS Television/Archive Photos; Michael Ochs Archives/Venice, CA; Buddah promotional shot/Frank Driggs Collection; Photofest; Archive Photos/Scott Harrison; Archive Photos; Reuters/Gary Cameron/Archive Photos

First published in 1999 in New York by Billboard Books,
an imprint of Watson-Guptill Publications, a division of BPI Communications,
1515 Broadway, New York, NY 10036

Library of Congress Cataloging in Publication Data

Nathan, David.
      The soulful divas : personal portraits of over a dozen divas, from Nina Simone, Aretha Franklin & Diana Ross to Patti LaBelle, Anita Baker & Natalie Cole / David Nathan.
        p.   cm.
      Includes index.
      Contents: Dionne Warwick — Nina Simone — Aretha Franklin — Esther Phillips — Doris Troy — Diana Ross — Gladys Knight — Chaka Khan — Patti LaBelle — Millie Jackson —Natalie Cole — Phyllis Hyman — Roberta Flack — Anita Baker — Whitney, Janet, and Toni, the young divas.
      ISBN 0-8230-8425-6
      1. Singers—United States—Biography.   2. Afro-American women singers—Biography. I. Title.
ML400.N28   1999
782.42164'092'396073—dc21
[B]

                                      98-45684
                                      CIP
                                      MN

Manufactured in the United States

1 2 3 4 5 6 7 8 9/07 06 05 04 03 02 01 00 99

Senior Editor: Bob Nirkind

Editor: Liz Harvey

Production Manager: Hector Campbell

Designer: Mirko Ilić Corp.

CONTENTS

ACKNOWL

There are so many, many people I have to thank for the contributions they have made to my life and thus to the eventual creation of this book. First and foremost, it was two people with the same initials who encouraged me to develop the idea: the late entertainment-industry attorney Barry Rosenthal who loved the concept way back in 1991 and who saw the vision for what it could be. Then, in 1997 when I was having a momentary career "crisis," it was my "Rhythm & Blues Foundation" partner in crime and, I can proudly say, friend Bonnie Raitt who suggested I write a book to help me get out of the "I'm-in-a-rut" blues. For that and all your encouragement and assistance, Bonnie, I am so very grateful.

I have been blessed to have two women whose support and love have been essential: my truly inspiring sister and lifelong friend Sylvia, a wonderful creative artist who has shared my love for the divas way back to those drama-filled days in London when I played early Dionne Warwick albums 'till I knew every vocal lick and run; and Stephanie Jourdan, my hypnotherapist, my astrologer extraordinaire, my champion, and my friend. Two wonderful spirits who have seen me through the highs and lows of life!

So many others have endured my "insanity" over the last few years, and they have each contributed to my evolution: the one and only Mr. A., incorrigible, unique, who has shown me the value of never quitting; my constant "inner circle," Byron Motley, Michael Lewis, Ralph Glenmore, Sharon Rosenfield, Rudy Calvo, Art Arellano, Forrest D. Wilson, Jay Jacobsen, and Jane Halsey, always there and always caring. And my wonderfully feline companion, Nefer, a constant opportunity to reflect what love's all about! Thank you.

To the two "D's"—Dionne and Doris—whose love and friendship have been so enduring: all the angels ain't in heaven! To Luther Vandross for being kind enough to read this tome and add his thoughtful insight and comments: I guess you could still beat me at gin rummy if I let you! And to the great Dr. Nina Simone, whose influence on me went way beyond her music: thank you for instilling in me the importance of telling it like it is and being forever real. Many thanks to Andy McKaie for encouragement, inspiration for the title, and the opportunity to create the wonderful "Soulful Divas" CD series on Hip-O!

I have been blessed with many folks who may not been daily

contacts but whose friendship and wisdom have been a constant: Chuck Smith, Nestor Figueroa, Jeff Forman, Terrence Morris, Johnny Butler, A. Scott Galloway, Vernal Scott, Patricia Phillip, Jeff Bennett, Ron & Roberto, Hassan Haghani, Janine Coveney, J.R. Reynolds, Dan Willis, Jeff Lorez, Dave Godin, Wayne Edwards, Brenda Russell, Sharon Heyward, Nelson George, Mabel John, Jeffrey Hersh, Barbara Shelley, Harriette Lessner, Reggie Hosea, Ronald Simmons, Sid Johnson, Percy Bryant, Michael Critchley, Kenn Reynolds, Gene Shelton, Bob Jones, Miguel Baguer, Yvette Noel-Schure, Will Downing, Dyana Williams, Devre Jackson, James Mtume, Thom Bell, Glenda Gracia, Aly Adnan, Tom Cartwright, Aaron Walton, Herbert Price, Kevin Wafford, Sadie Doherty, Bill Glazer, Vicki Wickham, Victor Washington, Lee Bailey, Karen Kennedy, Imhotep Gary Byrd, Toni Patillo, Altheal Ware, Steven Ivory, David Ritz, Stix Hooper, Gary Taylor, Pat (P.P.) Arnold, Greg Edwards, Glen Davis, Carlos Jones, my cousin Hilary Collins, Kevin Tong, Kashif, David Cole, Patti Austin, and Eric Burns, among many others. Much appreciation to my accountant and friend, Marty Merrill; to my attorney and buddy, Kendall Minter; and to my computer wiz team, Dale and Joyce Robertson.

To the teachers and healers who have kept my spirit, mind, and body intact, I am eternally grateful. Their ranks have included Maurice White, Werner Erhard, Harry Rosenberg, Joan Rosenberg, Dr. Phillip Eng, Dr. Steven Lewis and Roberta, Gwen Wycoff, Rev. Allen Page, Dennis Brady, Eileen Hamza Henry, Sheilaa Hite, Laurel Scheaf, Armand DiCarlo, Tirzah Cohen, Gale LeGassick, Jerome Downes, Richard Condon, Tracy Goss and Sheila Reed, Aaron Christeaan, "Michael," Dr. Kirk Wright, Dr. Pearl McBroom, Bishop Carl Bean, Reverend Michael Beckwith, Rickie Byars, members of my Agape family, multiple fellow Landmark seminarians, Forum and seminar leaders and staff members, the written work of Deepak Chopra, some great masseurs, and all my brethren with whom I have party-ed from 1967 at Le Deuce to the Paradise Garage in 1977, the Catch One in 1987, and, every once in a great while, Fridays at the El Rey in 1998!

I am indebted to so many folks in the music industry through my twenty-plus years as a journalist, compilation producer, liner-notes writer, and interview coach. Forgive any omissions but the long list includes Barbara Harris, Simo Doe, Irene Gandy, Win Wilford, Gary

Stewart, James Austin, David McLees, Ted Myers, Harry Weinger, Jean Riggins, Beverly Paige, Sandra Trim DaCosta, Anita Samuels, Gene Sculatti, Hedi Butler, Billy Pierce Jr., Sidney Miller, Graham Armstrong, Mike Farrace, David Gritten, Kenny Gamble, John Brown, Brenda Andrews, Sylvia Rhone, Eddie Pugh, Tom Draper, Ruth Innis, Ruben Rodriguez, Sheila Eldridge, Daniel Markus, Lisa Jefferson, Wendy Washington, Diana Baron, Jamie Foster Brown, Lorraine Sanabria, Ken Levy, Doreen D'Agostino, Janet Williams, Ray Harris, Ron Carter, Michael Mitchell, Kelly Halley, Tony Anderson, Juanita Stephens, Bob Merlis, Tony Johnson, Bobbi Cowan, Bruce Garfield, Audrey Strahl, Kathy Aquaviva, Ron Shapiro, Mike Stefanik, Tee Alston, Henry Carr, Marie Byars, Howard Bloom, Mary Moore, the late Elliott Horne, Bernard Jacobs, Ramon Hervey, Bill Hammond, Jaime Ikeda, Laverne Perry, Louil Silas, Benny Medina, Kurt Nishimura, Primus Robinson, Jackie Rheinhart, Tony Anderson, Gwendolyn Quinn, Bob Fisher, Ruth Bowen, Nancy Pitts, Danyel Smith, Ron Brewington, Ruth Robinson, Audrey Bernard, Michael Paoletta, Marie Moore, Ike Williams, Jam & Lewis, L.A. & Babyface, Teddy Pendergrass, Brian Chin, Didier Deutsch, Sandra St. Victor, Reve Gipson, Linda Haynes, Jerry Wexler, and Violet Brown. Special thanks to Janis Hazel and my colleagues at the Rhythm & Blues Foundation, and Angelia Bibb-Sanders and the Los Angeles chapter of NARAS.

I owe big props to John Abbey for giving me a gig back in 1970; I might never have become a bona-fide music journalist for *Blues & Soul*. My thanks also to the magazine's publisher Roy Daniell and editor Bob Killbourn for keeping *Blues & Soul* as now, the longest-running publication on black music anywhere in the world and for allowing me to continue to contribute to it. Thanks to the ever soulful Ms. Dee Dee Warwick for granting my first interview; and to Nick Ashford & Valerie Simpson for the first interview I conducted in the U.S. back in 1974.

My gratitude to Billboard executive Ken Schlager for the introduction to Bob Nirkind at Billboard Books, who said "yes" to this book without so much as a blink. Finally, *The Soulful Divas* is for all the women featured in this book whose music has provided me with the tapestry for my life, and to my parents, Frances and Mark, for bringing me into the world so I could experience all that it is to be human, bumps, bruises, and all!

David Nathan
Los Angeles, August,1998
e-mail:dnathsoul@aol.com
websites: http//www.soulfuldivas.com,
http://www.davidnathan.com

FOREWORD

As I've stated many times in the past, my musical influences have included some of the divas that David Nathan writes about in this book, so its premise was something that interested me right away. What a rich legacy these women have given all of us, and I got much insight into each diva's personal traits through his memories and recollections. I was very curious to read about women I didn't know like Nina Simone and the late Esther Phillips, and I read the chapter on the young divas (Whitney, Janet, and Toni) twice! Being friends with some of the subjects included here, I've gotten to see one side of the divas that maybe David hasn't seen; that said, I found this book fascinating, and I hope the divas themselves understand and know David's full intention to tell the real stories, be they happy, sad, or otherwise.

I read most of the book while flying to do some concerts in South Africa, so I had plenty of time to be a "voyeur" and, through David's invaluable memories and recollections, to gain insight into the personality traits of each diva. I remember how I used to sit in school and wonder whether or not Dionne Warwick and Diana Ross were friends, or whether Barbra Streisand and Aretha Franklin ever ate lunch together! Through David's objective approach, I gained insight into how many of the divas relate to each other. And, as the former president of the Patti LaBelle & The Bluebelles' fan club, it was wonderful to read inside scoops about one of my favorite girl groups.

I'm someone who tends to read very slowly so as not to miss any nuance or inflection, and there were so many things that I found fascinating as I turned these pages: for instance, I never knew what caused Aretha's fear of flying. As I read about David's experiences in her kitchen, I wanted to call her and say, "Dear Aretha, when I came to your house we 'rehearsed'! You see, I forgot my peach-cobbler takeout bag— so I'll see you when I come back to Detroit! Oh and by the way, Aretha, peach cobbler or no, I love you to death—you know that don't you?"

To find out that Diana Ross loves Rosko's chicken and waffles—with extra gravy, no less—was the first thing that put a tear in my eye. I just knew there was a reason I loved the Supremes! It was so insightful to hear my friend Patti LaBelle speak about her proximity to other female artists in terms of success; at times in my career, I, too, could relate to what she felt about her own struggle for mainstream recognition. After reading David's observations on her, I wanted to pick up the phone and say, "Patti, I'll tell you what I told an interviewer once: 'If there was an intergalactic singing competition, I would suggest that Earth sends Patti LaBelle!'"

Many of the divas in the book mean so much to me not just musically but personally. I read about Natalie Cole; I couldn't help remember the night my sister passed away and how she called and talked to me until five o'clock in the morning, something I will never forget.

Naturally, I was curious to see how David, a longtime friend of mine, would characterize my "feud" with Anita Baker. Well, no matter what he heard or what he said about it in his chapter on Ms. Baker, one thing has always remained very clear about me and Anita, and that's that I have total respect for her voice and talent.

What I found particularly great about this collection of portraits is the way David approached his writing for this project: I myself have done countless interviews with him, and I must say that I have never read one sentence he wrote about me that was untrue or unjustly slanted, so I trust these accounts of his encounters with these divas. Of course, now that I've finished reading, I'll be picking up the phone to call David . . . to find out which emergency room he's in after some of the divas read this book!

But seriously, David, you've given us a book that is both informative and entertaining. Congratulations, and when you write about the men divas, make sure I see it before it comes out!!! Oh, in case I forget all those times we sat and played cards when we were neighbors back in the day . . . you're still a lousy gin-rummy player!

Luther Vandross
September, 1998

INTRODUCTION

I learned a whole lot during the process of writing this book—about myself, my love for music, my love for life, and the emotional impact the women included here have had on me, in some cases for more than thirty years. But as I think about it, what I discovered above all else was the incredible courage, tenacity, belief in themselves, and faith it takes to survive as a public black woman in the world of music, a world essentially run by white men. Of course, I realize that it hasn't been easy for female entertainers to make it, regardless of skin tone. But as Gladys Knight said in a song a few years ago, "There are two strikes against me when I come up to bat, one strike for being female and one for being black." That could well have been the subtitle for this book.

I first thought about doing a book on selected African-American female entertainers back in the early 1990s. A conversation with the late Barry Rosenthal, a popular attorney and manager, when we were both in Puerto Rico for a U.S. Armed Forces show led to a standard book proposal, and Barry kindly set me up with a literary agent. I made the rounds of publishers, and editors were interested but no one took the bait back then, mostly because I wasn't interested in writing a sensational, "tell-all," gossip-and-hearsay kind of book. Thankfully, the success of a couple of autobiographies, specifically Patti LaBelle's *Don't Block the Blessings and Gladys Knight's* Between Each Line of Pain and Glory, made books on popular African-American female entertainers a little more salesworthy. So when I revisited my book proposal in 1997, I knew there would be a market for this work.

The first question I know folks are going to ask is why I haven't included a whole slew of deserving divas, such as Tina Turner, Etta James, Ruth Brown, and a whole cadre of other superbly talented women. The answer is very simple: I wanted to write from my own experience of my subject matter. I've interviewed all of the women in this book time and time again, and that was my criterion, plain and simple.

Of course, some women I've written about extensively would have made the cut if this were a massive tome, such as Nancy Wilson, Brenda Russell, Patti Austin, Teena Marie, Angela Bofill, Stephanie Mills, Jody Watley, Mavis Staples, Mable John, Randy Crawford, Valerie Simpson, Vesta, Dianne Reeves, America's own P.P. Arnold (a U.K. resident since the 1960s when we met), and Dee Dee Warwick, my very first interview subject. If there's a Volume 2, girls, you got it!

You might question—even with the parameters I created for the book—how some women qualify for inclusion, specifically Millie Jackson, Esther Phillips, and Doris Troy. So let me clear that one up right away. Millie represents the kind of downhome, salt-of-the-earth, hard-working women who have no pretensions about being "sophisticated" ice princesses. Musically and personally, she is a no-shit truth-teller. Esther, with her raw mouth and "don't-fuck-with-me" attitude, was much the same, a little sharper than Millie in her approach, but just as real. And Doris is here because she represents all the many, many R&B women who have survived with, comparably, the bare minimum of chart success and yet have managed to sustain themselves. Even though she had just one hit single with 1963's "Just One Look," Doris is a trooper of the first order.

Some people might wonder what Whitney Houston, Janet Jackson, and Toni Braxton are doing in such illustrious and legendary company. When I originally planned this book, I thought that some reference should be made to a future generation of divas. Once again, I used my own personal experience as the guide to my choices, which is why other talented women who have emerged in the last few years, such as Erykah Badu, Sandra St. Victor, Lauryn Hill, and Dionne Farris, aren't included here.

I approached writing this book from the desire to give respect to and express my appreciation to the women included here who have had such a major impact on my life and on the lives of millions of people the world over. It wasn't meant to be a fawning adoration because I know the importance of accepting that each diva here is no more or less human than you or me. I don't subscribe to the showbiz myth that entertainers, by virtue of their "creativity," have some "divine right" that excuses any rudeness or disrespect they might show to others. And while each of the women here has surely shown her "other side" more than once to people in and out of the industry, I don't buy the reasoning that being "stars" gives them carte blanche to treat anyone with any less respect and courtesy than they themselves would like to be accorded.

I sequenced the book in the specific order in which I first met these ladies of soul. There are many quotes from those interviews, which first appeared in Britain's *Blues & Soul* magazine. (In fact, any quote without an attribution in this book originally appeared in that magazine.) This publication gave me my start in music journalism and continues, nearly thirty-five years after its creation, as the oldest publication in the world dedicated to R&B and soul, now balanced with a heavy dose of rap and hip-hop. I hope the quotes will give further insight into the personalities of each of the women included here.

The glue for each chapter was a career retrospective, and from the outset, I knew it would be impossible to include every event in each woman's career within the confines of single chapters. Diehard fans will, I hope, forgive me for a certain amount of arbitrary selection. I tried to make sure the milestones in each career were duly noted. In advance, I apologize for any "glaring" omissions that hardcore fans might notice.

I will say that in writing each chapter, I found common links. Almost without exception, each woman here went through some kind of personal revelation or transformation at some stage in her life. For some it was learning to love themselves fully and completely; for others, learning to love others. Beyond their ability to bring life to words and melodies, to reference their own dramas, traumas, and highs and lows, and share their experiences with us through their music, it is the universal lesson of loving and being loved in return that each of these gifted women has to offer us.

And, ooh child, can they s-a-a-n-g!

David Nathan
(a/k/a "The British Ambassador of Soul")
May, 1998
e-mail: dnathSoul@aol.com

DIO
WAR
black

NNE

WICK

pearl

Dionne Warwick
performing
Credit: Archive Photos

Dionne Warwick wasn't happy, and I understood why. It was early 1998, and we were discussing an article that had appeared in *Vibe* magazine a month or so beforehand. Aside from using an ancient photograph of the singer from around 1969, the piece was based on testimony that Dionne had given to the United States Congress a few years earlier when she was commenting on, among other things, the demeaning verbiage used by various rappers to describe young women.

The writer of the article had met Dionne briefly at a press conference held to celebrate the release of a single that featured Dionne and soul man Chuck Jackson, a longtime friend and a 1960s labelmate when both artists had been with Scepter Records. As Dionne recounted, "She never once asked about anything related to the project Chuck and I were doing. . . ." Instead, it seems, the writer had developed something of an "attitude" when Dionne didn't want to speak at length about her then-involvement with now-bankrupt Psychic Friends Network and its popular infomercial. The result was a *Vibe* article that painted a picture of a woman who was clearly angry about a whole bunch of things, including the constant comic jabs that had resulted from her work as the host of the infomercial. To cap it all off, the headline read "Psychic Enemy."

Three-and-a-half decades before she would become the butt of those quips and jokes, on everything from "The Wayans Brothers" television show, to the 1997 hit movies *Men in Black* and *My Best Friend's Wedding*, Dionne Warwick revolutionized the pop music scene. It looked as if segments of the entertainment industry were suffering from collective amnesia when it came to the singer.

Sure, the first time I saw Dionne on the infomercial myself, I was surprised but not shocked; I'd long known of her interest in the area of psychic phenomena. But for longtime Warwick aficionados like me, the constant ridicule at the mere mention of her name reached intolerable proportions in 1997. The discovery that a whole generation of young television watchers barely knew that she'd had a long and glorious career as a recording artist and performer was more than a little disconcerting. After all, Dionne had been the first black female to capture a pop audience with a vocal style she herself once described as "raw silk and satin mixed together." Before Aretha Franklin finally gained a national audience after years as a superstar-waiting-to-happen and before Diana Ross left the Supremes for a golden solo career, the barely-out-of-her-teens singer from New Jersey had made it to the hallowed halls of London, Paris, and Rome with a natural soulfulness tempered by years of gospel training and a formal musical education.

Flashback to the 1960s when British groups like the Beatles, the Rolling Stones, and the Who threatened to take over the American pop music charts. Armed with brilliantly crafted, tailor-made tunes from producer/songwriters Burt Bacharach and Hal David, Dionne was establishing an undeniable presence with "Don't Make Me Over," "Anyone Who Had a Heart," "Walk On By," "Reach Out for Me," and "Message to Michael."

Long before Luther Vandross (who has often acknowledged Dionne as one of his prime musical inspirations) had "adopted" "A House Is Not a Home"—a song written for a movie of the same name starring Shelley Winters that was actually about a brothel—as his nightly show-stopper, Dionne Warwick laid down the definitive version of the song. The Carpenters pop duo exploded into national consciousness in the early 1970s with "(They Long to Be) Close to You," a song recorded as a demo that ended up as a track buried on her third album, *Make Way for Dionne Warwick*. And before Aretha Franklin earned her seventh gold single with "I Say a Little Prayer" in 1968 and 1990s newcomer Diana King "reggae-fied" it for the movie *My Best Friend's Wedding* in 1997, it was Dionne who had turned the infectious ditty into her first gold record.

When I asked Dionne about the negative comments surrounding her involvement with the Psychic Friends Network during an interview we did for *Billboard* in 1995, Dionne replied, "I'm not a psychic myself but—as do millions of others—I find the subject fascinating, and I admit it. I've heard all the jokes, and I just remember what my grandfather told me many years ago: 'While people run their mouths, run your business.' And that's what I'm doing. . . ." Indeed, as the host of what became the most successful infomercial of its kind, Dionne amassed enough money to buy a house in a luxury section of Rio de Janeiro, making Brazil her second home in 1997.

Getting to the mansion, which sports a bird's-eye view of the famous statue of Jesus Christ in ritzy Rio, from the quiet, tree-lined suburb of East Orange, New Jersey, took a lot for the girl with the high cheekbones and the golden voice. She was born Marie Dionne Warrick on December 12, 1940 (or 1941, depending on who you believe!) to parents Mancel, a former train porter and chef who later worked as a gospel-music promotions man for Chess Records, and Lee, a member of a renowned gospel group, the Drinkard Singers (whose ranks included Lee's sister Emily, nicknamed Cissy, the mother of Whitney Houston). The oldest of three children (late brother Mancel Jr. and sister Delia, nicknamed Dee Dee, a fine recording artist and performer in her own right), Dionne was singing at her local church by the age of six, learning to play the piano shortly afterward, and graduating to occasional spots with the Drinkard Singers. In a 1979 interview in *Blues & Soul*, she laughingly recalled, "I wasn't always the best kid on the block!" but her obvious natural musical talent was increasingly being nurtured by her parents.

With sister Dee Dee, Dionne formed her own teen group, the Gospelaires. During a visit to see her mother sing with the Drinkard Singers at the famed Apollo theater in Harlem, Dionne got her first "professional" break. When word came backstage that a producer was looking for a group to do a background session in Newark for saxophone player Sam "The Man" Taylor for Savoy Records, Dionne, clearly an ambitious go-getter as a teenager, volunteered the Gospelaires. The next night, the Warrick sisters and friend Carol Slade were chirping away behind Taylor on "(Won't You) Deliver Me," marking Dionne's professional musical debut.

Getting paid for the session was an immediate incentive. Soon after that first session, Dionne boarded the bus from Newark to Manhattan on the weekends and during school breaks to sing background for a host of future stars (such as Little Eva, Garnet Mimms & the Enchanters) and more than a few already-established hit-makers, including Dinah Washington, Brook Benton, Ray Charles, and the Drifters.

With their gospel-infused harmonies, sisters Dionne and Dee Dee along with Doris Payne (who later became Doris Troy of "Just One Look" fame) and others [including their Aunt Cissy (Houston) and adopted sister Judy Clay] quickly earned a reputation in and around New York's Tin Pan Alley. As a member of what became affectionately known as "The Group," Dionne earned enough money to put herself through college, the Hartt School of Music in Hartford, Connecticut. She might have gone on to fulfill an early ambition to teach music if it hadn't been for a 1961 session for the Drifters.

The Atlantic Records' date was produced by Leiber & Stoller, who had already given the Drifters and labelmates the Coasters a hit or two. One of the songs being cut was "Mexican Divorce," written by fledgling tunesmith Burt Bacharach and his then-partner Bob Hilliard. The ruggedly handsome Bacharach was on hand and heard a voice that would definitively alter his own destiny: ". . . She was singing louder than everybody else, so I couldn't help noticing her," Bacharach told *Ebony* magazine in 1968. "She had a very unique look—pigtails and sneakers, just a certain quality about her," Bacharach is later quoted as saying. A few weeks later, when he needed a vocalist to work on an instrumental single he was recording ("Move It on the Backbeat"), he tracked her down. In short order, Bacharach and Hal David, his new songwriting partner, began using Dionne as the main vocalist for demos.

When a demo of the song "It's Love That Really Counts" landed on the desk of Scepter Records' owner Florence Greenberg, intended for the Shirelles, the company's primary hit-makers, she called writers Bacharach and David. She hated the song, she declared, but she loved the singer: Dionne Warrick. Dionne, by now signed to the duo's production company, became a Scepter artist in a heartbeat.

A rainy August night in 1962 at Bell Sound Studios in midtown Manhattan was the scene of Dionne's recording debut as a solo artist: a dramatic, defiant plea for acceptance, the emotionally charged "Don't Make Me Over" didn't seem like an obvious hit to label owner Greenberg. But it was different enough that radio stations picked up on it, and through a typographical error on the original record label, Dionne Warrick became Dionne Warwick—and a bona fide chart-maker just a couple of weeks after her twenty-first birthday in December, 1962.

What immediately distinguished Dionne Warwick's early hits from those of her black female contemporaries was the union of the intricate arrangements and ambitious musical construction of Bacharach's melodies, the sensitive and heartfelt lyricism of Hal David, and her own soulful yet sophisticated vocal style. "I sang [many of those songs] with a certain lightness," she said in a 1991 interview. This combination got an immediate response not just from R&B radio stations but also from their pop counterparts, and until she started making regular television appearances, some music buyers didn't know whether she was black or white.

At the time that "Don't Make Me Over" began its chart ascent, Dionne hadn't been focusing on a potential career in the music industry. "I really didn't know what a hit was," she told John Abbey in a 1982 interview for *Blues & Soul*. "I was still in college, and I really didn't care because I was more concerned with my education. But ["Don't Make Me Over"] was such a totally different record from what I was hearing on the radio at the time that maybe that was the real reason for its success...." It didn't take too much to convince the budding singer that dedication to a musical career might pay off. "I knew it took a lot of hard work to be more than just a recording artiste," she noted in a 1979 interview that she and I did. "That's what I've done—worked damn hard and sung my ass off!"

Destiny was certainly on her side. Producer Bacharach happened to have another gig when he wasn't in the studio with Dionne. As the musical director for the movie legend and entertainer Marlene Dietrich, he managed to get Dionne a slot as a special guest on the eccentric Dietrich's show at the prestigious Olympia theater in Paris in late 1963. Dionne was just coming off a series of one-nighters on what was commonly known as "the chitlin' circuit," playing venues like the Regal in Chicago, the Howard in Washington, DC, and Brooklyn's own Fox theater with the likes of such soul stars as Sam Cooke, Jackie Wilson, the Shirelles, Chuck Jackson, and Esther Phillips. Crisscrossing the country, often with her mother as a chaperone, Dionne encountered hardcore racism head-on during southern dates. In essence, the grueling tours had introduced Dionne firsthand to black audiences who would remain supportive for years to come.

No sooner had Dionne arrived in Paris than Dietrich decided to take the singer under her wing—and instantly on the rounds of French designers like Pierre Cardin and Yves St. Laurent. Whatever gowns Dionne had brought for her European debut were unceremoniously tossed aside, and at Dietrich's insistence, Dionne donned some of the designers' best. Years later, openly bisexual Dietrich's early sponsorship of the young singer fueled completely unfounded rumors in gay and lesbian circles that the association extended beyond professional realms. As Dionne became more and more successful with her special brand of pop'n'soul, rumormongers would later imply that her relationship with the dashing Bacharach also extended beyond the studio into the bedroom. Decades after she rose to prominence, I asked Dionne point blank if there was indeed any truth to the rumors. She threw back her head, laughed, and replied that while Bacharach had been one of the most important men in her life, there wasn't an iota of truth to the suggestion that they'd been lovers.

Bacharach's role was, however, pivotal in Dionne's career. By persuading Dietrich to introduce her to Parisian audiences, he had in essence launched her internationally, making her the first black female solo contemporary music artist to achieve stardom in Europe. Following in the footsteps of women like Josephine Baker, who had captivated the French with her talent, Dionne was a resounding success with her Olympia gig. The French press dubbed her "The Black Pearl," and Dionne's soulful, gospel-honed voice won the hearts of the audiences at the Olympia—and the ears of one Brian Epstein, the manager of the Beatles, who happened to be in the audience during her first run at the prestigious venue. At the time, she was introducing a newly recorded Bacharach & David song, "Anyone Who Had a Heart." Epstein was so taken with the song that he bought a copy, returned to London, and promptly booked a recording session for another of his clients, Liverpudlian singer Cilla Black. When Black's version was rushed for release in Britain, Scepter Records' British licensee Pye Records brought Dionne Warwick in to promote her original recording. That event not only started what would be a long-term love affair between Dionne and British audiences, but changed my own life forever.

I'd been a staunch Cilla Black fan. During my teenage years in London, she'd become the object of my adolescent fantasies and in my world, the best singer I'd ever heard. My bedroom wall was adorned with multiple photographs of the redheaded thrush. In school, I defended Cilla's version of "Anyone Who Had a Heart" until it got me into a few fistfights.

That all changed when Pye Records released Dionne's follow-up single in April, 1964. I played "Walk on By" until my mother and sister begged me to stop! In love not just with Cilla but also with real-life high-school student Marilyn Wolfe, I understood every nuance, every ounce of pain, hurt, and anguish that Dionne infused into what would become essentially a timeless classic and my own lifelong No. 1 favorite recording. When I heard "Don't Make Me Over" one evening on my beat-up red radio while taking a hot bath, I burst into tears. Somehow, this woman I didn't know was saying in song exactly what it was I wanted to tell my parents. Adolescence hadn't been easy for me, and the Nathan household wasn't exactly a nurturing haven for love and compassion. I literally begged my mother for pocket money to buy *Presenting Dionne Warwick*, the first album issued by Pye Records by my newfound musical friend. That LP has gone with me everywhere I've been ever since that day in 1964. As it would turn out, Dionne's music not only served as my introduction to the world of African-American artists, but also literally gave me the blessed life and wonderful career I've had in the music industry for the past three decades.

Needless to say, down came the photographs of Cilla, and up went the photographs of the svelte Ms. Warwick, whose exotic features made her the most beautiful woman in my world. It didn't take long for me to discover that Dionne had a fan club in the U.K. The fan club, initially founded for the Shirelles by a perky woman by the name of Gloria Marcantonio, had expanded to include Dionne and other artists like

Maxine Brown and Chuck Jackson who recorded for Scepter and its sister label Wand Records. To say that I continually bugged Gloria would be an understatement: I was determined to meet Dionne. An opportunity finally arose when Gloria banded a group of us together to meet Dionne at the airport on one of what would become her frequent visits to the U.K. Flushed beet red and so embarrassed, I stumbled over my words as I handed Dionne a bouquet of flowers. I was struck by her elegance and her smile. Seeing her on television and on album covers, I imagined her to be very tall and statuesque, and the illusion lingered during that first meeting as she walked through the airport to a waiting limo. Only years later, after we became professional colleagues and friends, did I realize that Dionne was in fact only an inch or so shorter than me . . . closer to 5'5", and not some wispy 5'10"goddess!

Dionne might not have been a physical giant, but she was certainly well on her way to becoming a towering musical presence as 1964 came to an end. Indeed, she'd established herself on both sides of the Atlantic, and she was enjoying life on the road. As she recalled in a 1983 interview, "I have some wonderful memories of those days! It was at a time we referred to . . . as the "British Musical Invasion" because groups with the names of every bug . . . you could name (the Beatles, the Animals, and so on) were hitting the charts and taking over. I was fortunate to carve my own niche within all of that and also get the recognition in Britain. . . . I toured with the Searchers, the Zombies, the Springfields, the Seekers, and got to meet some of the people who became legendary in this business. It was fun—because we were all young and crazy and we didn't mind spending 97 hours on a bus traveling across the country—we loved it!"

My own admiration for Dionne had grown with each of those early albums. Her first album to be released in Britain did in fact include songs from her first two U.S. LPs, *Presenting Dionne Warwick* and *Anyone Who Had a Heart*, suitably named after a song that is arguably one of the most soulful unrequited love ballads she ever sang.

For me, there was magic on every track, from the infectious "Shall I Tell Her," to the oh-so-poignant "Mr. Heartbreak." I learned every one of those songs by heart, and in my pursuit of true love, Dionne's music offered solace, consolation, and a frame of reference. As I heard her emote on songs like "I Cry Alone" and "I Could Make You Mine," I found someone else who understood the pangs of adolescent puppy love I was experiencing, which was truly real for me.

The love affair continued through other albums. *Make Way for Dionne Warwick* showed Scepter Records' then-bestselling artist looking sophisticated and provocatively sexy on its cover, and the musical contents were glorious. Dionne had taken a song originally recorded by Lou Johnson, a New York-based artist who'd cut a couple of other Bacharach-David tunes before she did. "The Last One to Be Loved" verbalized my own sentiments; "In the Land of Make Believe" was dreamily romantic, as was "You'll Never Get to Heaven (If You Break My Heart)," one of the many hits that Dionne was racking up as a consistent pop'n'soul chartmaker.

Of all the albums from those early years, my favorite is quite possibly *The Sensitive Sound of Dionne Warwick*, a 1965 release. With my musical heroine looking suitably wistful on the cover, it included some of the finest songs Bacharach and David ever wrote, many of which have been heard only by the most fervent of Dionne Warwick fans. Never released as singles, tunes like the emotionally wrenching "How Many Days of Sadness"; the gorgeous "Forever My Love," which evoked the feel of a scene from some epic like *South Pacific*; and the stirring "Is There Another Way to Love You?" might have been lost forever were it not for the miracles of modern technology, which have brought them back to life via compact disc. Back then, high above the London street in my playroom two stories on top of my Dad's fish-and-chip shop, I swooned and sighed as I played the album night after night, introducing its contents to the then-current object of my affections, Bernice.

I was still smitten when Scepter released the 1965 album *Here I Am*, which also contained other Bacharach-David gems, such as "Don't Go Breaking My Heart," "In Between the Heartaches," and "If I Ever Make You Cry," alongside a rousing reminder of Dionne's gospel roots via the traditional spiritual "This Little Light." The album also featured a moving version of "I Loves You Porgy," the song that first brought the wondrous Nina Simone, one of Dionne's favorite artists, to the public's attention some years before.

Subsequent albums that Dionne recorded for Scepter never quite had the same consistent magic for me. I could always find great songs— mostly written by Bacharach and David—on each of them. They included 1966's *Here Where There Is Love*, her first gold album; and two 1967 releases, *On Stage and in the Movies* and *The Windows of the World*, which was named after a plaintive ballad that was one of Dionne's personal all-time favorite recordings, reflecting a desire for peace when public sentiment against the conflict in Vietnam was starting to reach a boiling point. I continued to enjoy her work through three later albums: 1968's certified gold album *Valley of the Dolls*, with its beautifully poignant title track, and *Promises, Promises*; and Dionne's final pair of Scepter albums, *I'll Never Fall in Love Again* and *Very Dionne*, both released in 1970.

By the time Dionne scored her first gold record with "I Say a Little Prayer" in the early months of 1968, she'd already racked up seventeen consecutive hit singles and seven best-selling albums, including a "live" album recorded in Paris at the Olympia, the sight of her earlier triumph. She shared the stage in 1966 with French heartthrob Sacha Distel, then romantically involved with actress Brigit Bardot, who, in a reported confrontation with Dionne, expressed her anger at the more "personal" relationship that seemed to exist between the two singers. Dionne never went on record publicly to confirm or deny the exact nature of her friendship with Distel, but the two remained close through the years, forming a mutual admiration society. This "admiration" was fully evident when I was present for a brief reunion when they met up in London in 1983 during a time when Dionne was promoting her successful *Heartbreaker* album. I observed that there was a real chemistry between them, and I took a barely disguised hint from Lee Valentine, her longtime guitarist, to make myself scarce! I was also smart enough not to ask Dionne too many questions about the French singer.

While I was enjoying so much of Dionne's music 3,000 miles from where it was being recorded, back at home, Dionne could do no wrong. "Trains and Boats and Planes," "I Just Don't Know What to Do With Myself," and her version of "Alfie" (which, ironically, was first recorded by Britain's Cilla Black for the film of the same name) catapulted her to the heights. Gigs at hot nightspots like New York's Copacabana and London's Savoy Hotel made her the toast of the supper-club crowd, but Dionne was also adamant about performing for her R&B base, frequently returning to New York's Apollo theater for standing-room-only engagements. Her roots in R&B were fully evident in 1968 when she recorded a best-selling album entitled *Soulful*, a collection of tunes popularized by Otis Redding, Aretha Franklin, the Righteous Brothers, and the Impressions.

During the mid-1960s, Dionne went through her share of personal changes. She met drummer-turned-actor Bill Elliott and married him in 1963, divorced him a year later, and remarried him a year after that. The marriage appeared to be happy, and in 1969, she gave birth to her first son, David, shortly after completing *Slaves*, her first major movie, which costarred Ossie Davis and Stephen Boyd. Four years later son Damon was born, and in 1975 the couple finally separated. Bill Elliott passed away in 1983, and Dionne has always remained publicly tight-lipped about the reasons for the split.

Markedly guarded when broaching any subject she deems too personal, Dionne has never been one to open up to prying journalists, and on occasions when she feels that her privacy is being compromised, she becomes noticeably cool. I've seen this reaction a couple of times, and it is clear that she doesn't suffer fools gladly. Her eyebrows arch, and wise folks will think before venturing on. Not recognizing the signs, some of my more intrusive journalistic colleagues have tested the boundaries, walking away with the impression that she is aloof to the point of being an ice goddess. I consider myself fortunate in gaining Dionne's trust by respecting her desire to stay away from subjects that she considers off-limits. However, that didn't stop her from being remarkably candid in a 1979 interview we did for *Blues & Soul*. On the verge of a career renaissance with a first best-selling album for Arista Records, Dionne was ready to talk: "It was only after my divorce—and I hesitate to actually say this—that I really got to know myself and like myself. Now that's a heavy statement for anyone to make about themselves, but it's quite true. Because, frankly, for a lot of those years, I didn't like me. I knew there was a person in there somewhere, but I was always thinking about being Mrs. Somebody, never thinking about the real *me* in there. . . ."

Thoughts of separation and divorce were likely far from her mind as the 1960s came to a close. But within a couple of years, Dionne was facing a professional split that was to have far-reaching effects. With a solid decade of hits behind her, it was hardly surprising that Dionne was being wooed by various major record companies as her contract with Scepter was up for renewal. Leaving was not easy for several reasons. Label president Florence Greenberg had been more than just a company head. She had become a friend, almost like a second mother to the woman who had become the independent record label's top international best-selling artist. Dionne had also bonded with the Shirelles, even joining the group for a hot minute when lead singer Shirley Alston was pregnant and Chuck Jackson, whom Dionne referred to as her show-biz "big brother." Staff producer Luther Dixon; and Greenberg's son Stan Green and son-in-law Sam Goff had all worked with Dionne on very early recordings after she signed with the label in 1962. Scepter's in-house personal manager Paul Cantor had become Dionne's personal manager by 1964 and remained so until the early 1980s; and Dionne met Marie Byars, originally a Scepter employee who began working as her personal secretary, a position Byars has held ever since.

When Warner Brothers Records came to the table with a big-money offer, Greenberg couldn't match it, so she gave Dionne her best wishes as she lost her most consistent hit-maker. The original 1971 deal included

Dionne and the golden team of Bacharach & David, and while the final years at Scepter hadn't been as musically inspiring as the first few had been, Warner Brothers clearly felt that it was getting a great package. For all intents and purposes, they were. The first album produced by the "trio" for its new recording home was one of its best, including great new Bacharach & David songs like "Be Aware" and "I Just Have to Breathe," as well as a remake of "(They Long to Be) Close to You" and a version of "One Less Bell to Answer," a song Dionne claimed to have done the original demo for years before the Fifth Dimension made it into a major hit record.

On the advice of astrologer Linda Goodman, Dionne—who had always shown an interest in psychic matters, attending a seance or two in London according to British fan-club secretary Gloria Marcantonio back in the mid-1960s—had added the letter "e" to her last name in 1971. Instead of bringing her good fortune, the added vowel had the completely reverse effect: "Anyone who's into astrology will tell you, Linda Goodman is one of the finest astrologers . . . however, she is a horrible numerologist! She did my name numerologically and said that I needed to come up with one more letter to have right vibrations in my name. . . . That's the story. . . . And I got rid of that (extra "e") as quickly as I could!"

Apparently not quickly enough: no sooner had Dionne finished recording her Warner's debut than she read in a newspaper that Bacharach and David were no longer talking and no longer working together. The impact was devastating, and Dionne felt betrayed. Accepting that the pair had split was one thing; reading about it in the papers was another matter. Without the two men who had been such an essential part of her musical career for so long, she was left to her own devices. Warner Brothers suggested that she hook up with Eddie Holland, Lamont Dozier, and Brian Holland, the trio that had created a string of hits at Motown for the Supremes, Martha & the Vandellas, and the Four Tops, and others, before starting their own labels, Hot Wax and Invictus.

With their own company, H-D-H (Holland-Dozier-Holland) graced the charts through such artists as Freda Payne, Chairmen of the Board, Laura Lee, and the Honeycone. Dionne Warwicke was another proposition. Although the resulting album, *Just Being Myself*, was a notable change of flavor for the singer, the public responded with little interest, hardly helped by a lack of enthusiasm on the part of Warner Brothers. "Working with the guys was different," Dionne said during a 1973 interview for *Blues & Soul*. ". . . I have to be honest and say that I was not personally satisfied with the finished product, or my part of it. . . . The material was good for the Invictus artists but somehow it just wasn't right for me. . . ."

Attempting to remedy the situation, Warner Brothers teamed Dionne with Nick Ashford and Valerie Simpson. The results (including the song "No One Else Gets the Prize," later recorded by Diana Ross for her 1980 best-seller *The Boss*), according to all concerned, were fine but never saw the light of the day. According to the Warner tape logs, there was an abortive session with Bacharach alone, and an extensive recording date with producer Tony Camillo, which yielded no releases. In the midst of trying to figure out how to salvage her recording career, Dionne was going through a great deal of personal trauma. Her father passed away suddenly in 1977, and her mother suffered a stroke the next day. Her relationship with Bill Elliott was coming apart at the seams. All of a sudden, her life was in turmoil.

A hookup with Philadelphia's master producer Thom Bell, who was responsible for hits with the Delfonics and the Stylistics, provided a respite. Dionne had been touring with the Spinners and Bell, who had given the group a string of hits at Atlantic Records beginning in 1972 with "I'll Be Around." The Detroit-based quintet had scored six back-to-back Top 10 R&B singles with Bell by the time they entered the studios with Dionne to record the song "Then Came You." Released in 1974, the gold single gave Dionne her first ever No. 1 pop hit and should have been the catalyst for a turnaround in her recording career.

Dionne didn't do an entire album with the Spinners, but "Then Came You" became the title track for an album produced by Jerry Ragavoy, best known for his work with soul stalwarts like Garnet Mimms, Lorraine Ellison, Howard Tate, and the writer of some of rock star Janis Joplin's biggest hits. While the musical combination worked well, Warner Brothers failed to bring the album home. Worse still, the album *Track of the Cat*, an excellent collaboration with Bell released at the end of 1975, did little to remedy matters. Although considered Dionne's best work for the Burbank-based company, it didn't achieve anything like the success it deserved. Tracks like "Jealousy" and "One More Time" were hardly heard. One song in particular, "His House and Me," was a standout, and it was obvious to anyone who knew Dionne well that the song was written for her in the aftermath of her recent divorce from Bill Elliott. Bell later confided to me that Dionne had burst into tears when she first tried recording the song, a tale of a woman who is left alone in the home she once shared with her husband.

Even though Warner Brothers ultimately never brought the album to the attention of mainstream audiences, Dionne and Thom were excited and enthusiastic about the project. Their promotional work together afforded me an opportunity to catch up with the pair. The three of us traveled from New York to Washington, DC, together on an Amtrak train. Originally I was supposed to conduct an interview with Dionne onboard the train. I felt pretty much left out of the proceedings when Dionne and Thom turned their backs on me and talked to each other.

As it turned out, I did my interview with Dionne in the limo that took us to her hotel—but not before I had seen her "in action" at the train station. "Excuse me, miss, aren't you Diana Ross?" the black Amtrak porter asked as we stepped off the train in DC. Dionne stopped dead in her tracks. Fuming, she swung around, looked him straight in the face, and snapped, "No, I'm not!!" The chilled air that followed was evident throughout that ride to the hotel. Sitting next to the woman whose music had been my salvation, I tried to tailor my questions to fit the prevailing mood. Responding to a question about whether she expected her career to take off initially, Dionne veered toward the egotistical: ". . . It's like no one else is doing what I'm doing, no one else does what I do the way I do it. I never looked at anyone else as competition . . . in as much as I don't sound like anyone else, I'm just me—I knew no one else would do things I'm doing. . . ."

Being mistaken for Diana Ross had hardly added luster to Dionne's day back then, although years later when Dionne and I were sharing a moment or two of conversation pertaining to a proposed autobiography, she mentioned how Diana showed up one day when she was in a Las Vegas hospital. Dionne relayed, with a hearty laugh, how she awoke from sleep to find Diana standing in the room and began "thinking to myself, 'Oh-oh, she's finally come to murder me!'" In truth, Dionne maintained a cordial relationship with Diana, which suggests that any rivalry between the two was more a media invention than a fact.

During a telephone chat in 1998, Dionne and I talked a little about her relationship with Diana: "We recently ended up on the Concorde going to London together, and we both wondered how much longer we'd be able to do this road stuff! There have been times when we were together, and we both giggled about how people always thought we were rivals. . . . I'm not sure where it began. Perhaps it was something someone at Motown started. . . . Who knows? She's been to my house; we've talked, joked. No, we're not hang-out buddies like I am with, say, Gladys Knight, but Diane—I call her that because that's her name—and I are all right with each other. . . ."

Back in 1978, as the decade came to a close, comparisons with other soulful divas weren't exactly Dionne's main preoccupation. Her relationship with Warner Brothers was rapidly deteriorating; the label released one final album, *Love at First Sight*, but a clear lack of promotion meant that the record made little impact. The album had the distinction of containing not even one charted single, a first for Dionne since virtually all of her albums (aside from obvious compilations) had yielded at least one or two hits. A one-off single, "I Didn't Mean to Love You" (taken from sessions with Joe Porter, a former Motown staffer), spent an unglorious three weeks on the R&B charts.

Although her records weren't selling, Dionne's shows continued to attract a solid audience, and in the absence of current hits of her own, she would frequently reveal her innate interpretive ability by performing tunes associated with others. Her renditions of Roberta Flack's "Killing Me Softy With His Song," Elton John's "Sorry Seems to Be the Hardest Word," and Diana Ross's hit "Touch Me in the Morning" were flawless—and reminders of why she was one of the most skillful lyrical interpreters of her generation. When looking back on her early years in the business, she often recalled that it was doing demos for up-and-coming songwriters and publishers of the day had given her the training in pop music that would prove to be such an asset in terms of her own career. Tackling the hits of others but finding new meaning in the lyrics was clearly one of Dionne's fortes.

A joint tour with Isaac Hayes tagged "A Man and a Woman" had produced not only glowing reviews and great audience reaction, but also a double album that captured the excitement of the duo's concerts together. The tour also sparked show-biz scuttlebutt that the two were an item. However, Dionne's ability to keep a public lid on her private life meant that such speculation never made it into print.

Still, in terms of Dionne's recording career, the music press knew without question that the writing was on the wall: it was time for a change. "I actually thought about quitting a couple of times during the 1970s," Dionne told me in the aftermath of her stay with Warner Brothers. "I considered going back to my original career plan to be a music teacher. . . . To be honest, I didn't understand it because [Warner Brothers] paid a small fortune for me to sign with them. We made some damn good records during those years, and the company just lost them. The company wasn't being realistic—they didn't see that they signed the singer, Dionne Warwick, not Bacharach & David songs."

Fortunately relief was just around the corner as 1978 turned into 1979. Music-industry executive Clive Davis had already shown his ability to pick hit after hit for pop artists like Barry Manilow, Melissa Manchester, and Eric Carmen. Davis had taken the New York-based Bell Records and

Dionne Warwick
rehearsing in the 1970s
Credit: Photofest

transformed it into Arista Records in 1974 after being unceremoniously dismissed from Columbia Records, where he'd helped nurture the careers of such giants as Earth, Wind & Fire, Janis Joplin, and Sly & the Family Stone. He was ripe for a challenge when he signed Dionne to Arista, knowing that he had the opportunity to turn a fine recording artist from "cold" to "hot." Davis used his shrewd instincts to find the right songs and the right material for Dionne's all-important debut. And after a planned recording session with the late Marvin Gaye as producer never materialized, he talked with his new signing about working with pop superstar Manilow.

"When [Clive Davis] first came to me with the idea . . . I said a flat 'no' because I didn't feel a producer/artist would be able to capture me," Dionne reflected in a 1979 interview just weeks after the release of what would be her first platinum-selling LP. "I didn't want to come out like Dionne Manilow! I just didn't see how it would work. Well, Clive went back to Barry and told him that, but he insisted that we meet. . . . When I realized that Barry adopted different attitudes as a producer and as an artist, I felt more comfortable and I agreed."

The Will Jennings-Richard Kerr ballad "I'll Never Love This Way Again" was the massive Top 5 hit that brought Dionne back to the charts, opening up new doors for her that included a stint as hostess for the highly popular music show "Solid Gold." She tearfully accepted no fewer than two Grammy Awards in February, 1980, one of which was for "Best Female R&B Vocalist" for "Déjà Vu," a tune she'd gotten from recent tour mate Isaac Hayes.

The change in fortunes in her recording career had also helped usher in a change in Dionne's attitudes about herself and her life. Asked about how she perceived herself during our 1979 chat, she grinned, "A sophisticated lady, a mother, and sexy! You see, I never really wanted to feel that I was sexy but guess what, I found out that I am!" What had happened, she stated, was "that I reevaluated my life, decided what I wanted for the future, and determined to make up for what I'd been missing—which was quite a lot!" Her divorce from Bill Elliott had had an obvious effect: ". . . I was lucky because I had my work and my children to keep me busy, so it took me a lot less time to adjust to it. But it's given me a whole different perspective on people and relationships. If I ever remarry, I'd make it clear that if things didn't work out, there wouldn't be any bitterness . . . it would be about saying goodbye without any recriminations. . . ."

While Dionne's name was seldom publicly linked with any other entertainers after her divorce—apart from those occasional inferences about Dionne and Isaac Hayes—the rumor mill did some overtime work two years after her Arista album was released. The object of Dionne's affection was said to be one of the most popular black male vocalists of the 1970s and early 1980s. I asked the very sexy, handsome Teddy Pendergrass about his relationship with Dionne in a 1981 interview for *Blues & Soul*: "We've been friends for some time, more like distantly associated you might say. So we talked about that, like how come we don't stay in touch. She said, "I don't know.' I said, 'I don't know,' so we decided to stay in contact with each other. She's a fantastic human being and a good, good friend—and that's all I'm saying! After all, you never know what the future holds, what might be lurking around the corner," Pendergrass said with a broad grin, refusing to be drawn into any other comments on the subject!

One song on the *Dionne* album said a great deal about how she was feeling as she reflected on the previous eight years of her life, which had included the death of her father, her divorce from Elliott, and her breakup with Bacharach & David. Manilow's "All the Time" had in fact been tough for Dionne to record, and she reportedly left the session in tears when she first attempted the song because the lyrical content— about someone who discovers her own inner beauty and self-worth— was too close to home. ". . . I'm doing things I've never done before," she said with a mischievous grin, "and my sister [Dee Dee] keeps calling me a 'late bloomer'—and maybe that's just what I am!"

The "blooming" continued through the first few years of the 1980s. Dionne's performance schedule became much heavier after the first Arista LP took off. Her second album for the label, 1980's *No Night So Long*, did well without achieving the same kind of response as its predecessor, prompting Arista to record Dionne live in concert in 1981 for a double entitled *Hot! Live and Otherwise*, the fourth side of which contained new studio recordings. The absence of a hit single meant lukewarm sales; in an attempt to remedy the situation, she teamed up with producer Jay Graydon for the 1982 set *Friends in Love*. The title track, a duet with Johnny Mathis, one of Dionne's longtime musical heroes, did well on the charts. Although the album contained some great tunes, such as the Stevie Wonder-penned "With a Touch" and "Never Gonna Let You Go," and covers of "Betcha By Golly Wow" and "Can't Hide Love," it failed to take off. Not until label president Davis hooked her up with Barry Gibb of the Bee Gees did her career get another boost. *Heartbreaker* was a much bigger success internationally than domestically, and Dionne's long love affair with Britain was renewed when the album's title track and the song "All the Love in the

World" became huge hits in the U.K. in late 1982 and early 1983.

Around this time Dionne and I began talking about collaborating on an autobiography. I can remember one of our first meetings at Arista's offices in New York. I explained that in order to get started on the research for the project, I would need to get a small advance. "How much do you need?" Dionne asked. I came up with what I thought was a reasonable figure for my immediate services, and she simply opened up her purse and peeled off several hundred bills!

A three-month stint in Los Angeles at her expense afforded me the opportunity to spend a lot of time with her. Sitting in the den of the vast Beverly Hills mansion that had been her home virtually since her move to California in the early 1970s, I was struck by her warmth, honesty, and sense of humor. More often than not our conversations took place in the kitchen or in the library, and our friendship blossomed to the point where she invited me to Christmas dinner at her home in 1982. Along with a dozen or so others (including the late Yvonne Fair—an earthy singer in her own right and the wife of Sammy Strain of the O'Jays—who had become her wardrobe mistress and personal assistant on the road), I partook of Dionne's cooking. Her coconut cake had to be the best I'd ever tasted! I insisted on taking not one but two pieces home with me! "Did you make all of this yourself?" I asked incredulously as I looked at the amazing spread of food that was beginning to fill the kitchen table. "Been up all night!" Dionne grinned, as she stirred a big pot of greens.

Working together intermittently gave me the chance to see different sides of Dionne. One particularly memorable night, we agreed to get together when we were both in New York to talk about the prospects for our projected collaboration. It was late, and Dionne was ready to retire. She greeted me at the door in her dressing gown and asked if I minded us talking while she took off her makeup. Somehow, the conversation drifted toward philosophical matters. "Do you ever wonder what you're really here for?" I asked her. "Well," Dionne paused, "I guess I think that I'm here as a global communicator. I think that's what God put me here for," she said almost shyly. "Not just through music . . . but through whatever I can do to make a difference with people. . . ."

Dionne and I never ventured too far into conversations that were too personal, and I could sense when her guard was up. It wasn't that way during a meeting we had in New York at the Waldorf-Astoria with a prospective publisher for our book. Dionne's plane had been delayed, so the publisher had long since left when she arrived in the hotel lobby. We headed to the bar for a quick drink, and I was astonished when Dionne commented on an attractive man sitting at the next table.

"Wow, he sure is handsome," she quipped, and before I could blink, the legendary Dionne Warwick had turned to him. "You know, you're a really handsome man," she flirted. "Where are *you* from?" In pretty good English, he shyly stated that he was from Havana, Cuba, and it was obvious from his response that he had no idea who he was talking to! After the brief flirtation, Dionne resumed our conversation. I was nonplused! "I can't believe you did that!" I laughed. "Well, hey, it looks like they have more than just great cigars in Havana!" she replied. "I guess I'm going to have to make a trip down there soon!"

In the early 1980s, Dionne made no secret of the fact that she was involved in a relationship with Gianni Russo, a Las Vegas businessman and restaurant owner. As part of the preliminary research for our collaborative writing effort, Dionne had arranged for me to meet Gianni in Vegas. During the second half of the conversation, which I taped, he talked about Dionne's pro-black stance, intimating that from his standpoint, she was quite militant in her attitude. Russo's comments seemed less than complimentary. Naturally, Dionne wanted to hear the tape as soon as I got back from Vegas. As it turned out, by some quirk of fate, the side of the tape with Russo's unflattering comments was miraculously blank! As it turned out, I need not have worried since their relationship ended not too long afterward.

On the recording front, Dionne's records were doing fairly well, without breaking wide open. An album produced by Luther Vandross promised a great deal, and while some of the ballads (including a rare Warwick composition, "Two Ships Passing in the Night") were fine, Dionne didn't sound comfortable with upbeat Vandross ditties like "Got a Date," the second single from the 1983 release. In concert at the time of the album's release, she would quip how that particular song was her "Tina Turner number!" The next project that followed, *Finder of Lost Loves*, reflected some important musical matches for Dionne. Aside from a new session with Barry Manilow, she'd also brought Stevie Wonder in to work on the soundtrack for the Gene Wilder film "The Woman in Red." the result: an international smash, a Grammy Award for "I Just Called to Say I Love You," and a couple of duets by Dionne and Stevie on the tunes "Weakness" and "It's You."

But more than anything else, the album brought Dionne back together with a man she hadn't spoken with for close to a decade. "When the producers [of the short-lived Aaron Spelling television show "Finder of Lost Loves"] heard the theme song, they asked the writer if he'd called me yet about singing it. He told them he hadn't but that he would. Now I don't know if he really wanted me to because we hadn't spoken in ten years," Dionne recounted in a 1985 interview we did. The man in question was Burt Bacharach, and he did indeed call. 'Hi. This is Burt,' he said. 'Burt who?' was my response. It wasn't until he used a particular nickname that I realized who it was. He said, 'It's me, Charlie!' and I knew it could only be one man." Bacharach stopped by that evening, and Dionne recalled, ". . . I felt like someone out on a blind date. I didn't know just how that first meeting would be. But as it turned out, we spent four-and-a-half hours giggling, laughing, and getting reacquainted. It was as if our friendship never ended, just like we'd been on this little ten-year hiatus. . . ."

The first result of their new collaboration, a duet between Dionne and R&B vocalist Glenn Jones, received little attention. But their next session proved to be a milestone for everyone involved. Bacharach and his then-wife and musical partner Carole Bayer Sager had written a song for the 1982 film *Night Shift*. "That's What Friends Are For," which was originally recorded by British rock star Rod Stewart immediately resonated for Dionne. Hardly known as a partygoer in Hollywood circles—in 1979 she referred to Los Angeles as "Gollywood—all make-believe!"—she'd established a close circle that included fellow entertainers like Leslie Uggams and Nancy Wilson. On a personal level, she was regarded by those who knew her as a loyal friend who could be trusted and who offered real support to those she cared for. Indeed, when my mother passed away in 1984, Dionne was one of the first people I called.

"The lyrics of the song are such that I thought it would be a great idea to call up Stevie (Wonder) and Gladys (Knight) and ask them to sing on it with me. Then, Clive (Davis) spoke with Elton (John), who was here in Los Angeles on vacation, about participating with us," Dionne said. "The session was one of the most emotional I've ever done. It puts the exclamation point at the end of the word 'friendship' for me. Naturally, I felt great about having all three of them be part of the record. It was like we were living the words of the song itself. . . ."

The recording would probably have been a major hit for Dionne and her friends regardless. But when actress Elizabeth Taylor, a friend of Bacharach's, stopped by the session, she was so moved by the emotional content of the song that she suggested that the record could be used to support her fund-raising efforts on the part of AmFar, the American Foundation for AIDS Research.

Dionne was no stranger to the tragedy that AIDS had wrought on the lives of thousands of people the world over. Aside from the initial high incidence of the disease in Africa, AIDS struck deep into the heart of the gay community in the U.S. in the early 1980s, and it struck close to home. By her own account, she had lost a number of friends, including one of her valets, to the killer virus. Back in 1985, she commented, "I have only recently become fully aware of the effects the disease is having. . . . I know we all have to make a determined effort to beat it, and you can bet that I'm committed to making sure that happens. . . ." Several years later, after Vernal Scott, a friend of mine in London, asked me to approach her, Dionne agreed to open a health clinic in the city for those with HIV. She didn't hesitate to make time to do so, bringing the same kind of hands-on attention to the situation in England as she'd been doing back home in the States.

As it turned out, "That's What Friends Are For" ended up generating more than a million dollars for AmFar, but the release of the record brought with it the first upset in my relationship with Dionne. I'd set up an interview with her for *The Herald Examiner*, a local Los Angeles newspaper, through her then-publicist Tim Barker. As always, the session itself was cordial and warm. Unbeknownst to me, the paper was set to run the story a few days before the record hit the streets—and a few days before a press conference Liz Taylor was planning to announce its official release on Arista. The stuff hit the fan after the story appeared! Not only did *The Examiner* add ten years to Dionne's age, but the breaking of the story literally upstaged Taylor's plans. According to publicist Barker, Dionne was furious with me. Apparently, Taylor's now-deceased publicist Sam Chin was madder than hell and had passed on the actress's anger to Barker and thus to Dionne. From the outside looking in, it appeared that Dionne had purposely given the interview to get a jump on the publicity she knew the story would create. I was crestfallen, especially since I had no idea what I'd done simply by submitting the article. No matter what I said to Barker, he was adamant that Dionne's reaction when I called to say how sorry I was had fallen on deaf ears. Trying to soften what he intimated had been said, Tim told me coldly, "Dionne Warwick wishes you would go . . . somewhere!"

It took a while for the dust to settle. Just before she was being honored with a star on the Hollywood Walk of Fame, I wrote her an impassioned letter, telling her how sorry I was for all that occurred, recounting the real facts—which I feared had gotten lost in translation between Barker and herself—and letting her know how much I wanted to attend the ceremony. All was forgiven. And even though I felt just a tad nervous, I was there to watch her receive her due acclaim for work as an entertainer, recording artist, and humanitarian.

Indeed, "That's What Friends Are For" was the beginning of a period

37

of several years in which Dionne became closely associated with efforts to end the deadly scourge. She worked consistently with the Minority AIDS Project, an organization created by longtime friend and former gospel singer Bishop Carl Bean, an openly gay minister who had recorded a popular 1970s disco classic, "I Was Born This Way." Dionne actively participated in the project's fundraising activities, including a yearly concert "Coming Home for Friends," which often featured some of Dionne's show-biz buddies. One year, the bill included Dionne, Stevie Wonder, Gladys Knight, Patti LaBelle, Natalie Cole, Cissy Houston, and gospel greats Tramaine Hawkins and the late Reverend James Cleveland. Dionne was named the U.S. Ambassador of Health in 1987.

In a 1989 interview Dionne commented on her involvement with charitable causes, noting that her own public visibility in the area had begun in 1984 when she was one of the participants in the "We Are the World" multi-artist session, and continued with her appearance at the Live Aid concert. In addition to her work with the Minority AIDS Project, she'd created the Dionne Warwick Foundation in 1989 and hosted three days of events designed to raise awareness and funds for AIDS organizations.

To the consternation and surprise of many of Dionne's loyal friends and supporters, ABC-TV ran a piece on Dionne's charitable work during one of its news shows, suggesting that funds hadn't ever reached their designated targets. The broadcast prompted a rebuttal from Dionne when Geraldo Rivera invited her to respond to the allegations and, speaking in her defense, Bishop Bean was included on the show. Dionne spoke to all the accusations, including suggestions that Guy Draper, a longtime music business associate who had essentially run the day-to-day operations of Dionne's foundation, was a less-than-upstanding businessman. While adamant in her denials of any impropriety, the whole episode left Dionne's public persona briefly tarnished.

Whatever change in the public's perception of her that had occurred as a result of the ABC-TV story was further compounded when Dionne began appearing as hostess for the Psychic Friends Network, a gig that had started as a sideline. By the mid-1990s, Dionne had become the target of constant jabs. And while she admitted privately that she found some of the references funny, others angered her. But she always told me that the hugely successful infomercial had her laughing all the way to the bank. Nonetheless, comics would jest, saying that she should talk to some of her psychic friends to find out when she was going to have another hit record.

While Dionne was quick to point out that she was merely the hostess and not a professional psychic herself, such comedic comments about her status as a hit-maker at the time weren't that far off the mark. Arista had begun taking its attention off one of their prize recording stars, devoting increasing time and energy to Dionne's cousin, diva Whitney Houston; to artists signed to producers L.A. & Babyface's LaFace Records; and to reigniting the recording career of another soulful diva, Aretha Franklin. *Reservations for Two*, a 1987 album with tracks produced by R&B hit-maker Kashif and a 1990 tribute to Cole Porter, went virtually unnoticed by all but Dionne's most devoted fans. What should have been an even more commercial proposition, the 1993 release *Friends Can Be Lovers* bombed in spite of an all-star lineup that included a duet with Whitney (co-written and produced by Dionne's son David, who had already co-penned the massive Luther Vandross smash "Here and Now" a few years before), as well as production work from Barry Eastmond (known for hits with Anita Baker, Freddie Jackson, and Billy Ocean) and from the British team responsible for success with another Arista signing, Lisa Stansfield.

The recording of that album also marked an incredible reunion: the first collaboration between Burt Bacharach and Hal David in twenty years. "I put the request into each of them separately. I told them, 'I want the two of you to write me a song again . . . and they did!" she revealed in a 1993 *Blues & Soul* interview. The result, "Sunny Weather Lover," was one of the standouts on the album but gained little attention in spite of Dionne's claims that she'd created a new working relationship with the company that had been her recording home for twelve years. "I feel that with the new album, I have a new relationship with Arista," she noted. "I felt that I had to make my presence felt with the company this time around. I know that I haven't done a lot of videos in the past and that may have something to do with the lack of success with some of my records . . . but what I want now is for the company to treat me as a new artist. There have been times in the past where I've had an album all ready to come out, and then they've signed a new act and the attention and focus has gone entirely on them. . . ."

Whatever Arista was focused on a year later in 1994, it wasn't Dionne's final work for the label. She'd begun a love affair with Brazilian audiences back in the 1960s, and her vocal style was the perfect vehicle for the country's homegrown music. Indeed, Dionne had become so enamored with the Brazil that she was considering moving to Rio. And as a step in that direction, Dionne had worked with a number of Brazilian producers and writers to put together *Aquarela do Brasil*, a tasteful set that showed another side of her talents. As it turned out, Arista had no clue about what to do with the record. Label president Clive Davis was totally devoted to creating hit singles for his current roster, which by now included the likes of Toni Braxton and TLC (both through LaFace) and the late Notorious B.I.G. (through Bad Boy Entertainment). Even though Davis had given Dionne the green light to do the project, there was a distinct lack of enthusiasm when it was finally released; privately, Arista staffers would say that it was the change in Dionne's image from sophisticated pop'n'soul star to "friend to the psychics" that had made selling the record a hard job.

Irrespective of the fate of Dionne's Brazilian album, the land of the Amazon become her second home. In fact, by 1998, she'd bought a house and used her skills as an interior designer with Bruce Garrick, a longtime partner in a design company she'd created to work on private homes and international hotels, to make it a tailor-made fit. I knew that Dionne obviously loved the music of Brazil and the friendly nature of its people, but remembering her flirtatious encounter in New York back in the early 1980s with the handsome man from Havana, I suspected that Dionne likely had a male admirer or two tucked away in Rio.

While Dionne and I were conducting an interview at her Beverly Hills office, I felt bold enough to ask her if she had any marriage plans! She grinned and turned to Henry Carr, who had been working with her for years, and asked him if he knew of any such plans; the two burst out laughing. We were having such a good time that I also decided to ask Dionne about the initials she'd given as the name for her company. It was called "KMBA," and through some weird reasoning, I'd made up that the "MB" had some connection to her secretary of thirty-four years, Marie Byars. Dionne gave me quite an astonished look. "Huh?" she asked. "You want to know what 'KMBA' stands for? Okay . . . well, I'll tell you. . . ." With a deadpan expression on her face, she slowly said the words with deliberation: "KMBA means . . . 'Kiss My Black Ass'!" I believe I might have blushed ever so slightly, but then I remembered that behind the cool sophistication and the superstar status was a warm, funny down-home girl from East Orange, New Jersey, who had never forgotten where she came from.

Indeed, Dionne had decided to revisit her musical roots in 1998 when she made her first album for a new label, River North. Titled *Dionne Sings Dionne*, it included new versions of her classic hits, including a stunning "Reach Out for Me" with the Emotions and El DeBarge and a salsa-flavored "Do You Know the Way to San Jose?" with Celia Cruz and Pete Escovedo. Just to counter the people who had claimed that Dionne was an "enemy" of rap, she hooked up with a whole crew of different stars to cut "What the World Needs Now Is Love," which charted briefly in the summer of 1998.

Dionne knew what she was doing by cutting the album. And I got a chance to sit in on some of the sessions. She was upbeat, having fun and in fine voice. As the work on the album ended, she packed up her house, finally leaving Los Angeles after almost thirty years and making good on her commitment to live in Brazil, while still maintaining an apartment back in her home state of New Jersey. Returning to Jersey brought Dionne full circle, as did her decision to revisit those early hits: her very first decade of hits at Scepter with Bacharach & David had guaranteed her longevity, and audiences in Europe and Japan in particular were always glad to see her in concert. Likewise, at home, she remained a constant "live" attraction, especially when she decided to hook up with Bacharach in concert. The combination was dynamic, and even though some critics would say that years of smoking had diminished her vocal range, Dionne was like a true songbird when she tackled such early classics as "Make It Easy on Yourself" and "Alfie" onstage. Many a night when I got an opportunity to see the Bacharach-Warwick team in action, I would be moved by the magnificence of it all, Bacharach playing piano and conducting while Dionne, head to the sky, sang her heart out. She was especially impressive on one occasion in 1997 when she'd been injured in a car accident just days before her performance at a benefit in Long Beach. Like the trooper she'd always been, she stepped out onstage and gave a sterling performance, a reminder to one and all that she'd survived through breakups; reunions; career births, deaths, and rebirths; media controversy; *and* the Psychic Friends Network!

NIN

SIMO

the
only high

NA ONE

one and priestess

"She scared the shit out of me the first time we were alone together!" I recalled in my liner notes for *The Colpix Years: Nina Simone Anthology*, which I compiled for Rhino Records in 1996. Anyone who has ever been face to face with this one-of-a-kind musical genius, this woman I described as "a regal African queen reincarnate, with a larger-than-life persona," knows that Nina didn't acquire the mid-1960s tag "The High Priestess of Soul" for nothing! And I found that out as the founder of her British fan club, a skinny, pimple-faced, Beatle-mopped, four-eyed, timid British teenager. At a television taping in London in 1965, she started raging in her dressing room when Blood, Sweat & Tears' version of "God Bless the Child" came over the loudspeakers. "Who the hell is this?" I recounted in my liner notes in 1996. "That's Billie's song, man!" she screamed, referring to the original by one of her own musical heroes, the equally unique Billie Holiday. Before I could proffer a response, Nina Simone, a mere 5'6" but a giant nonetheless, was in my face. "Do you believe in God?" she screeched as she flew around the tiny room, a witch without a broom! I meekly whispered a polite "yes," and Nina was satisfied. "Good, man, good. . . ." she replied, with a smile that few ever saw, a broad grin that could light up the very heavens.

Fast forward some twenty years to when I saw Nina in London, meeting her at a West Indian couple's home where she was seeking refuge from the madness of a life lived out of a suitcase. I'd always known that Nina lived in her own reality and in that reality, she was indeed a real African queen reincarnate. I came up with the term "bleedthrough" to describe the condition she was manifesting, a state in which people operate as if they are still in a past life. When I walked into the tiny room where Nina was staying and told her how I'd just returned from Cairo, she explained that she'd been there at the very same time, staying at the swanky Cairo Hilton. Then, with a broad grin, she bade me look at her feet. Her toenails were painted silver. She explained, matter-of-factly, "I painted them silver because that's what Nefertiti did ... and you know, I used to *be* Nefertiti in Egypt," she added without a trace of disbelief. Nina, I knew, wasn't kidding.

This was the same Nina Simone—born Eunice Waymon in the little town of Tryon, North Carolina, in February, 1933—who had already made her mark at home as a jazz-turned-folk-turned-pop-turned-who-knew-what-she-might-do-on-any-given-night diva. The liner notes for *In Concert*, her 1963 debut album for Philips Records asked if she was a witch or an avenging angel, and her audiences have debated the question for decades. Nina was known for her eccentric behavior, with a typically unsmiling demeanor that could cause grown men to quake and shrink into their own shadows and a fierce temperament born of the intense pain of being totally different, unique, and special that could lead in a drumbeat to an onstage temper tantrum. Her typical early 1960s audience was primarily white and well-to-do. But a few years later, all the rage and anger Nina had felt but had contained boiled over when she became one of the most important figures in the Civil Rights movement.

Nina's unequivocal call for justice and an end to prejudice didn't endear her to the American establishment. But it did help her gain a much stronger foothold among her own people, and she soon became the darling of an upwardly mobile black audience. Gone were the Euro-styled wigs and the evening gowns, replaced by corn rows and African garb; long before it was en vogue to do so, Nina was expressing her "Afrocentricity." All of a sudden, the supper-club chanteuse and pianist—whose repertoire included everything from Gershwin standards to Israeli folk songs, and from oldtime spirituals to African chants—was leading the pack with rallying cries like "Old Jim Crow," "Mississippi Goddam," and in 1969, "To Be Young, Gifted and Black." Perhaps because she sought refuge from the madness of the American music business by becoming a wandering soul who made her home at different times in the West Indies, West Africa, and finally Europe, she never got full credit for being one of the very first black female performers to speak out on social and political issues when it wasn't fashionable to. This, aside from my own reverence for her and for the impact she had on my life, is why she has a place of pride in this book.

Born the seventh child into a family of nine to barber-turned-handyman John and minister Mary Waymon, young Eunice was playing the piano at the ripe age of three and a half. By the age of six, she was traveling with her mother to local churches, accompanying Mary on the keyboards during the musical portion of the rousing services. At around the same time, Eunice began taking classical lessons from Muriel Massinovitch, a local tutor. At the age of eleven, a poised young Eunice, now well versed in the works of Bach, gave her first recital at Tryon's town hall. Her career path was essentially determined by her extraordinary natural gift as a pianist: the town set up a fund to ensure that she could continue studying with "Mrs. Mazzy," as the tutor became known. When it was time to complete school, the young musician had qualified for a scholarship to the renowned Juilliard School of Music in New York.

The move to New York was a big deal for a country girl in 1950, exposing Eunice to urban life—and to Harlem in particular. After a year at Juilliard, she was ready to take an examination whose successful completion would have gained her entry into the Curtis Institute of Music in Philadelphia. The whole Waymon family moved to the City of Brotherly Love, and Eunice was full of anticipation about her life as a student at the famed college. When news came that the Institute had rejected Eunice, she was forced to rethink her plans. To survive, she began giving piano lessons and working as an accompanist for local performers. During this period she began expanding a repertoire that had consisted mostly of gospel and classical music.

As it turned out, Eunice's exposure to jazz and pop standards came in very useful when she made what would be a fateful trip to Atlantic City, New Jersey. Looking to earn more money during the summer of 1954, she began playing at a local bar, changing her name to Nina Simone. As she explains in her 1991 autobiography, *I Put a Spell on You*, she chose "Nina" (Spanish for "little") because that was a nickname she'd gotten from a Hispanic boyfriend and "Simone" after the French actress Simone Signoret. After a first night during which Nina displayed her considerable talents at the piano, the owner asked why she hadn't sung. Nina was given an ultimatum: sing on the second night or go find a new job! She opted for the former, and her life was never the same.

Blending her classical piano style with an innovative approach to pop and jazz tunes made Nina an instant attraction among visitors to the Atlantic City boardwalk. As she notes in her autobiography, "... I used my voice as a third layer, complementing the other two layers, my right and left hands. When I got to the part where I used elements of popular songs I would simply sing the lyric and play around with it, repeating verses, changing the order of the words...."

The following summer, Nina was back in Atlantic City, and by this time, word had spread. Even though her mother was dismayed that her daughter had begun playing what she considered "devil's music," Nina was packing folks into the Midtown Bar & Grill, and upon returning to Philadelphia she started performing at clubs there. In her own mind, she was simply making money so she could continue her classical studies. But fate had other plans. A friend had dropped off a copy of a Billie Holiday album and asked Nina if she would include "I Loves You Porgy," one of the songs on the LP, in her show. The tune, from the Gershwin musical *Porgy & Bess*, became a permanent part of Nina's repertoire at the time, and its significance soon became apparent after she started playing at New York clubs.

It was at one such gig that Nina was approached by Sid Nathan (not, as far as I know, a distant relative of mine!), the owner of King Records and its sister label, Bethlehem. After agreeing to let Nina record material of her own choice, Nathan set up her first recording session, which ran for a marathon fourteen hours. Toward the end of 1958, Bethlehem released *Little Girl Blue*, Nina's official debut as a recording artist— official, that is, because someone had taped one of her club performances. And as she points out in her autobiography, "the first album I ever made was a pirate that I never got paid for," and the first of what would become a long series of bootleg albums to be issued throughout her career.

Nothing much happened with the album until a Philadelphia radio deejay started playing "I Loves You Porgy" three or four times in a row. The telephones began ringing off the hook, and before they knew it, Bethlehem and Nina Simone had a hit on their collective hands. After forcing the track from the album as a single, it reached the pop Top 20 in the summer of 1959 and made it all the way to the No. 2 slot on the R&B charts. Nina hadn't set out to become a pop star, and she made no bones of the fact that her heart still lay in classical music. But the die had been cast, and she'd started on a path that would lead to concert halls the world over.

While a twenty-six-year-old Nina was beginning to cope with being in the national limelight, she was also dealing with a personal life in crisis: she'd married a young, white beatnik named Don Ross in 1958. The marriage lasted for only a short time. "I had originally married Don so I'd never be alone, but after we had got married, I went home hoping he wouldn't be there," she recounts in her autobiography. She was back to being alone after walking out on Don; a divorce followed in 1959.

But Nina's attention was very much on a career that she'd never expected. In the wake of her success with "I Loves You Porgy," she was signed to Colpix Records, a division of Columbia Pictures. *The Amazing Nina Simone*, her first album for the label, contained the kind of diversity of material that earmarked her as a special talent but drove industry pundits and the music press crazy as they tried to categorize her. The cuts ranged from the foot-stompin' spiritual "Children, Go Where I Send You," to jazz standards like "Stompin' at the Savoy."

As interesting as Nina's Colpix debut might have been, an album recorded at New York's Town Hall in September, 1959, opened up the floodgates for her. With everything from "Summertime" to torch songs like "You Can Have Him" and "To the Other Woman" and a great example of her virtuosity as a pianist, a self-penned instrumental entitled "Under the Lowest," the record signified Nina's "arrival." the press went nuts, and in New York in particular Nina became the talk of the town.

This album also served as my personal introduction to La Simone. Six years after the album had been recorded, I was reading Nina's name in a British music paper. An interview with the reigning diva in my world, Dionne Warwick, revealed that Nina was one of Dionne's favorite artists. I knew I had to check her out. I was working in a record shop in London on Saturdays, trying to scrape together pocket money. And one Saturday afternoon when the mad rush had died done and I was feeling somewhat brave, I timidly asked Mr. Green, the formidable manager, if I could check if there were any albums available by the said Nina Simone.

Contrary to my own thoughts that she was likely some French chanteuse, he informed me, in a dismissive tone, that she was "some Negro jazz singer" and thought we might have some album by her. There it was—*Nina at Town Hall*. I stepped into one of the booths we had for customers to listen to their prospective purchases. As I began listening to "Black Is the Color of My True Love's Hair," Nina's highly personal reading of an old Norwegian folk song, tears welled up in my eyes. Who was this woman who could go from soprano tenderness to dark velvet in a millisecond? the photograph on the cover gave little clue, and there was virtually no information on the back of the album to tell me who I was listening to.

My appetite was whetted, but it took the British group the Animals to turn curiosity into a deep love that would last from 1965 to today. The outfit fronted by Eric Burdon had engaged in a common practice of the day: they'd covered a song that had originally been recorded by a black American artist. Released by Philips, "Don't Let Me Be Misunderstood" was a soulful song written especially for Nina by Benny Benjamin, a drummer at Motown, and its lyrical message resonated for me the same way that Dionne Warwick's "Don't Make Me Over" had done. Sung with intense feeling and with the kind of deep tones that gave her voice an almost androgynous quality, the record became my own personal anthem. It also meant that for the first time Nina's name got some coverage in the British music press, thanks to Burdon's acknowledgment of her as the artist who originally recorded the song.

The buzz about this mysterious Nina Simone also gave me the chance to become a part of the "in" crowd: everyone who was anyone in R&B circles had "adopted" a U.S. artist and formed a fan club for the individual or group. Ben E. King, Barbara Lynn, Doris Troy, Martha & the Vandellas, Inez & Charlie Foxx, the Shirelles, and Dionne Warwick all had fan clubs. Nina enabled me to set one up, too. To get permission, I promptly tracked down her U.S. manager, one Andrew Stroud, who unbeknownst to me was also her husband. Weeks later, I received my confirmation letter allowing me to set up a club for Nina in the U.K. No mere R&B act, I knew Nina deserved more than a fan club. So "The Nina Simone Appreciation Society" was officially born sometime in 1965, just months before she decided to cross the ocean for the first time.

At the airport I met Nina, who was shorter than I'd expected; Andy, a stocky, Buddha-like man with a keen business mind and a warm smile that belied his years as a New York cop; and little Lisa Celeste, all of three years young. As we drove together in the limo Philips Records provided, Nina looked at the rows of box-like, typically British semidetached houses below the highway as we headed into the heart of London's West End. "Are those *real* chimneys?" Nina demanded of me in a booming tone. I barely got out "Yes," still in awe that I was sitting next to this strange, animated woman whose behavior would deeply affect my own development as an adult. "Andrew," she said, drawing herself up in the regal manner that I would become accustomed to over the ensuing years, "those buildings look very strange. Do you think people really *live* in those places?" Andy, by now five years into living day in and day out with the many different moods of La Simone, proffered a "Yes, dear" accompanied by a big grin.

Days later, we were at the studios for "Ready, Steady, Go!", the nearest British equivalent to the television show "American Bandstand," produced by Vicki Wickham. This enterprising young woman would go on to co-write singer Dusty Springfield's big hit, "You Don't Have to Say You Love Me" and—a few years later as the group's manager— transform Patti LaBelle & the Bluebelles into the futuristic soul trio Labelle. After my previously mentioned one-on-one encounter with Nina face to face in her dressing room, we headed out to the set where my teen peers were grooving to a new song by Doris "Just One Look" Troy, another woman who was to play an important role in my life. "Do you dance, David?" Nina asked, in the warm, honeyed Southern—but nevertheless commanding—tone that always sounded so distinctive. "Uh, no, Nina." I responded. "Well, sugar, if you don't dance, you better be having sex!" she roared. Beet red, I timidly ventured that I was still a virgin, and Nina grinned. A couple of years later, over an intimate dinner, I revealed that I'd finally done "the nasty" and could dance, too! Nina just winked and smiled at the revelation. It seemed that smiling wasn't something that people expected from Nina. She had a tough "don't-fuck-with-me-or-I'll-put-a-spell-on-you-forever" manner in her dealings with industry types, and her level of tolerance for stupidity was zero. But I quickly found through my own interactions with her that there was an incredible warmth and humor in her persona; when Nina smiled, it was as if an angel flew round heaven.

But when disguised in human form, angels are frequently misunderstood, and the song "Don't Let Me Be Misunderstood" had not only "introduced" Nina to the British musical consciousness and become my mantra, it was also a plea from the heart for the woman herself. Nina had been through many changes since the September, 1959, concert immortalized on *At Town Hall,* the first Simone LP I'd purchased in 1965. Her recording career had begun in earnest with Colpix, which was now recording two albums a year with one of its main moneymakers. Because of the rapport she could establish with her growing audiences and the personal, spontaneous creative process that was so much a part of her onstage performances, Nina was best captured live. Albums like 1960's *Nina at Newport* and 1961's *At the Village Gate* reflected the dizzying diversity of her repertoire. It included everything from African chants like "Flo Me La," to "The House of the Rising Sun," a haunting folk tune about a woman of the night that the Animals had made into its first big hit in 1964. Nina was as at home with torch songs like Rodgers & Hart's "He Was Too Good to Me" as she was with the lyrical poetry of songwriter Oscar Brown Jr., whose evocative "Brown Baby" was an early indicator of Nina's desire to express her feelings about the trying times facing all African-Americans in the struggle for freedom and everyday justice in the early and mid-1960s.

In between taping her spellbinding shows—which featured Nina on piano, usually accompanied by longtime musical associate Al Schackman on guitar, Bobby Hamilton (or Montego Joe) on drums, and Chris White (and later Lisle Atkinson) on bass—Colpix sent her into the studio to record great albums like *Forbidden Fruit* (one of my personal favorites because it shows Nina's humor, pathos, and ability to understand the array of emotions involved in any personal relationship) and *Nina Sings Ellington.*

Occasionally, the company would make an attempt to go for a hit record for Nina; thus, recordings like "Come on Back, Jack," a 1961 "answer" song to Ray Charles's "Hit the Road, Jack"; a 1960 revival of Bessie Smith's "Nobody Knows You When You're Down and Out"; and a 1961 version of the blues tune "Trouble in Mind," both of which actually made it as singles to the R&B charts. But for the most part, Colpix recognized Nina's strength as an in-concert attraction and committed to tape amazing performances like *Nina at Carnegie Hall* in 1963 and *Folksy Nina*, which was released in 1964.

But Nina had become more than just a favorite among club and concert-goers by the time she left Colpix in 1963. As her popularity grew, she began associating with some of the political and artistic leaders of the day: writers like James Baldwin, Lorraine Hansberry, and Langston Hughes; activists like Malcolm X, Martin Luther King, Jr., and Dick Gregory; and fellow performers like Miriam Makeba and Odetta. Nina had been embraced by both the black intelligensia and hip, white jazz and folk audiences. And although she was known for her eclectic choice of material, only those engaged in the "struggle" (for civil rights) knew what Nina might have up her musical sleeve when she decided to go for broke.

Nina expressed all the fury, rage, and anger in several of the songs on *In Concert*, her first LP for Philips. Recorded in New York in April, 1964, the album left no one in doubt about Nina's stand for equality and basic human rights. Her own biting "Mississippi Goddam" (which earned her the dubious distinction of having her music banned in that then-bastion of ignorance and bigotry) had been written out of the anguish she felt when four little girls were killed in the infamous bombing of a church in Birmingham, Alabama. The song fit right alongside a rather dramatic, passionate reading of "Pirate Jenny," from German composer Kurt Weill's *Threepenny Opera*, a chilling tale of revenge transformed by Nina into a no-shit warning if blacks' demands were ignored. Another Simone original, "Old Jim Crow," was self-explanatory. With the release of *In Concert*, Nina staked her claim as a fearless musical leader for civil rights.

Nina's career now had a new focus, and she owed this change in part to her new manager. She'd dated and then married Andy Stroud in December, 1961, in spite of an incident of abuse (detailed in her autobiography) that could have served as a warning of what might lie ahead. A year later, Lisa Celeste was born, and Stroud had become Nina's full-time manager. He showed an aptitude for business and in particular for dealing with the twists and turns of the music industry, which would help take Nina to a new level of international recognition.

Part of Andy's strategy included Nina's first British trip. Accompanied by my father and an uncle (since I was still under age), I went to see her at her U.K. club debut at Annie's Room, a swanky nightspot owned by jazz vocalist Annie Ross (of Lambert, Hendricks & Ross fame). Nina was incredible, setting an intimate mood with "I Loves You Porgy" and ending the set with the hypnotic African chant "Zungo." When Nina left England for Antibes in the south of France, audiences raved. She was also a hit at the Montreux Jazz Festival. To the pride of myself and my younger sister Sylvia, who ran the Nina Simone Appreciation Society with me, our star had finally "arrived" in Europe.

Nina's visits to Europe became more regular, and with the release of each new Philips album, she became more and more popular on the continent, a factor that would be key in her life decades later. She followed her *In Concert* album with *Broadway-Blues-Ballads*, a fascinating collection that spanned everything from a revival of turn-of-the-century black performer Bert Williams's hit "Nobody," to "Something Wonderful" from *The King & I*. The title track for her next album was an eerie version of Screamin' Jay Hawkins's "I Put a Spell on You." She sounded so authentic that people wondered if plain ole' Eunice-Waymon-turned-Nina-Simone might not really be a practicing voodoo priestess—and the song even made it to the lower parts of the British charts. The album was stunning, with uplifting pieces like "Feeling Good" and "Tomorrow Is My Turn" juxtaposed with the raunchy "Gimme Some" and the provocative "Take Care of Business." Sex, I learned, was a subject that Nina approached head on! Subsequent albums included explicit tunes like Billie Holiday's turgid "Tell Me More and More and then Some" (on *Pastel Blues*), the sly "Chauffeur" (from *Let It All Out*) or the blues-y "I Want a Little Sugar in My Bowl" (from her 1966 RCA debut, *Nina Simone Sings the Blues*).

The stunning *Pastel Blues*, a second 1965 release, became one of my personal favorites, and I used Nina's stark reading of Billie Holiday's "Strange Fruit" in a school project to explain to my fellow Brits about the rampant racial injustice in America. The effect of Nina's chilling vocals on my classmates was stunning: there was absolute silence as Nina hit the song's climax and wild applause as it ended. Over the years, I witnessed that reaction time and time again. With her stranger-than-life, almost otherworldly vocal style, Nina had a way of reaching audiences of all sorts. She had a mesmerizing effect on listeners, and her innate sense of artistic integrity carried over into her live performances. Many times I watched as a devoted crowd would sit enraptured by her captivating presence. It didn't matter what she was using as a vehicle;

whether it was the rhythmic chant of her own "See Line Woman" or the plaintive ballad "Don't Smoke in Bed," Nina never held back, and paying customers loved her for it.

No matter what drama had taken place backstage, Nina almost always gave a great performance. Her willingness to do so was tested on one occasion during her first British tour. She was sharing the bill with comedian and friend Dick Gregory, and playing London and other large cities was fine. For whatever reason, the promoter had booked the team into a hall in the city of Bristol, not known as a hotbed for jazz or R&B lovers. There must have been about thirty people in the audience and when Nina sneaked a peek during Gregory's set, she was furious. She began yelling and screaming at Andy, who decided he couldn't deal with it. So he invited me to take a walk with him while he let off steam about how he felt conned by the promoter, and that had he known, he would never have agreed to play a venue where a full audience wasn't expected. By the time we got back, Nina had calmed down—somewhat. She hit the stage and rather than share how upset she was at the lack of attendance, she gave a wonderful performance. Those thirty-odd people were treated to what amounted to a private show, and Nina insisted that everyone move up to the front so she could see them. It was an unforgettable experience as she wound her way through "I Put a Spell on You," "Ne Me Quitte Pas" (a standout from the *Spell* album), and "Wild Is the Wind," the title track from her 1966 album for Philips.

That LP included "Four Women," her now-classic tale describing a quartet of different African-American females, which became an instant standout in her live performances. Like its predecessor, the 1966 album *Let It All Out* (which featured songs by everyone from Van McCoy of 1970s "Hustle" fame, to Bob Dylan), *Wild Is the Wind* was another specially concocted Simone potpourri. It included such time-honored standards as "If I Should Lose You" alongside pop/R&B ditties like the raging "Break Down and Let It All Out" and "I Love Your Lovin' Ways."

Nina's final album for Philips was equally eclectic, running the musical gamut from Chuck Berry's "Brown Eyed Handsome Man," to Duke Ellington's "Gal from Joe's." The album was aptly named *High Priestess of Soul*, and its release crowned a brief three-year, seven-album tenure with the label that helped cement Nina's presence as an international favorite. It was clear that this personally volatile, musically unpredictable woman was here to stay.

I got more chances to see the Simone persona up close. In my 1996 liner notes for the Rhino anthology, I related the story of her visit to the

Ram Jam, a tiny, hole-in-the-wall club in the heart of Brixton, home to the biggest community of West Indian immigrants in London. I'd told Nina that the venue would be filled with a primarily Jamaican audience, and she thought that was cool. Cool, indeed, but more like freezing! the club's heating system was woefully inadequate, so Nina took to the stage in a full-length fur. Stepping up to a piano that likely hadn't been tuned in years, Nina began her set. The amiable Jamaican crowd began yelling for their favorite Simone song almost immediately. It seems that a cover of a Frank Sinatra tune, "My Baby Just Cares for Me," recorded for Nina's first Bethlehem album, had become a rare single and a cult favorite among Jamaican audiences. They didn't care about Nina's newly released first album for RCA Records. "'My Baby Just Cares,' sing 'My Baby Just Cares,'" they yelled incessantly as Nina tried to do her thing. "Why are y'all yelling?" she screamed back, the anger visibly rising on her increasingly taut, unsmiling face. "I'm here to perform. Now shut up!" Nina's verbal interplay with noisy audience members had earned her a reputation as a tough, no-nonsense performer in the States. She was about to show her "other side" to this crowd. When the yelling got louder, she simply stopped, slammed down the piano lid, and stormed offstage to the boos and hisses of an audience that was getting out of control.

Backstage, all hell broke loose. Nina was screaming, Andy was trying to comfort her, and she turned to me. I was quaking in my boots. "What the fuck do they want, David?" she bellowed, inches from my face. "They want to hear 'My Baby Just Cares for Me,'" I replied. "That piece of shit! I ain't doing that! I don't even remember the goddam song!" she retorted. A few kind words from Andy and a swig from half a bottle of gin, and Nina was temporarily appeased. She relented and headed back to the stage, and from the moment she launched into an impromptu version of the song with the loping, ska-like beat, she could do no wrong. Almost as a way of saying thanks, she spotted me in the front of the crowd and asked me what I wanted to hear. I picked "Since I Fell for You," which had rapidly become my personal favorite from her RCA debut, *Nina Simone Sings the Blues*. Ironically, twenty years after that infamous night at the Ram Jam, "My Baby Just Cares for Me" became a massive British pop hit after being used for a television ad campaign in the fall of 1987, reigniting interest in Nina's career and producing her first charted single in almost two decades.

Watching Nina seek comfort with that bottle of gin was a telling sign: her reputation for eccentricity, for being "difficult," had now become part and parcel of her persona. But it wasn't hard to understand what was happening. While Andy had unquestionably helped give Nina's career the boost it needed, he also insisted, as her manager, that she work constantly. As she noted in a brief telephone interview we did in 1974, ". . . I haven't been working in concert or recording because I got tired of the whole thing. . . ." Certainly, her career had risen to new heights as the 1960s turned into the 1970s. Nina's albums for RCA were not only getting critical acclaim, they were selling. *Silk'n'Soul*, her second RCA album, contained her definitive version of Billy Taylor's "I Wish I Knew How It Would Feel to Be Free," along with such Simone gems as "You'll Go to Hell," John D. Loudermilk's "Turn Me On," and the Burt Bacharach-Hal David classic, "The Look of Love."

A live concert at the Westbury Music Fair on Long Island, New York, was recorded on April 7, 1968, for what would be her third album for the label. Tragically, the night before, Dr. Martin Luther King, Jr., a friend, a partner in the struggle, and, at that particular juncture, the country's most prominent civil rights leader, had been assassinated. Emotionally devastated, Nina went ahead with the show, performing "Why (the King of Love Is Dead)?" written the same day by Gene Taylor, her bass player, in tribute to the slain preacher. *'Nuff Said*, the album that contained her moving performance of the song, also included a version of "Ain't Got No-I Got Life," a medley of two tunes from the hit Broadway musical *Hair*. To the surprise of one and all, the song was released in the U.K. as a single, and as I lay in a hospital bed in London, with a life-threatening case of ulcerative colitis, I got a telegram from Andy informing me that Nina had entered the British charts at No. 45.

Yes, Nina had finally cracked the charts—the song went on to reach No. 2 on the pop charts in Britain—but that success brought with it a whole set of new problems. Nina felt that Andy was pushing her too much. She wanted time off to spend with a growing daughter, and she wanted to relax and to rest up. Instead of slowing down, everyone demanded more. More shows, more recordings, more hits, more smiles. The wear and tear began to show in Nina's behavior. At a concert before a packed London Palladium, she asked all the black audience members to stand up: "This show is for just you!" she stated from the stage, implying that the mostly white crowd need not have bothered coming. Backstage Andy was fuming, and even I felt uncomfortable at Nina's remarks. I accepted her politics, and I understood her anger after all the years of discrimination; she'd given me and countless others an education in the realities of life in the U.S. as an African-American growing up in the 1950s and 1960s. But that gave her no excuse for railing against a crowd of devotees who had paid their money to see a great artist, not to be dismissed for the color of their skin.

Nina's hectic recording and performing schedule continued unabated throughout the late 1960s. Andy knew that the British success of "Ain't Got No-I Got Life" was validation that his wife could be a contemporary hit-maker, and like all major record labels, RCA Records wanted to keep the momentum going. More albums followed. An artistic high point was the brilliant "And Piano!" which, as the title implied, featured Nina without any other accompaniment; on the album Nina laid down imaginative versions of tunes as varied as Jonathan King's "Everyone's Gone to the Moon," Randy Newman's "I Think It's Going to Rain Today," and Hoagy Carmichael's "I Get Along Without You." the common element, as always, was Nina's emotion-filled approach to each tune.

In 1969 RCA issued *To Love Somebody* (whose title track had been released as a follow-up single to Nina's Top 5 British hit at the suggestion of myself and my sister Sylvia, and had given Nina another chart hit), which visited material penned by Bob Dylan, Barry and Robin Gibb, Pete Seeger, and Leonard Cohen, along with Nina's own fast and furious "Revolution." Six months later, there was *Black Gold*, a live recording cut at New York's Philharmonic Hall that included Nina's classic "To Be Young, Gifted & Black," a tribute to her good friend, playwright Lorraine Hansberry. But all the constant recording and performing had left Nina feeling emotionally, creatively, physically, and mentally drained. In January, 1971, *Blues & Soul*, the magazine I'd been writing for since 1970, gave me a little treat by sending me to Amsterdam to see Nina in concert. She revealed that she'd split from Andy and that her younger brother Sam, who accompanied her on the trip, was now managing her affairs, as well as performing with her. Sam told me that his sister had done some key performances in 1970 at places like New York's Fillmore East and had been the subject of several notable magazine features during the second half of that year, at which time she'd decided to take her first vacation in a long while.

The Amsterdam show was interesting. Nina was the special guest for a television show, taped before a live-concert audience; however, she was having major problems with the local musicians who had opened the show and were supposed to provide backing. In typical Simone fashion, Nina, dressed to the hilt and looking every bit the reincarnated African queen that she believed she was, was getting irritated and as always, she wasn't hiding her emotions. She cut the program short and retreated backstage. Once again, as the former head of her U.K. fan club—the duties having been taken over by my sister Sylvia—I was asked for my input. "You're the head of the fan club, David," Nina imperiously demanded. "What the hell can I do now? You know my music, man. Give me some suggestion, goddam it!" I remembered how my teenage schoolmates had been stunned by her version of "Strange Fruit," the Billie Holiday classic. Why not do that, I suggested—just you and the piano. The idea resonated with Nina immediately, and she returned to the stage, promptly turning the entire audience on its head with one of the most moving and compelling performances I've ever witnessed. Ending with one of her perennial favorites, the mesmerizing, rhythmic crowd-participation number "See Line Woman," Nina left the stage triumphant once more. The High Priestess was still weaving her magic!

During 1971 Nina made two more albums for RCA. *Here Comes the Sun*, produced with master musician and arranger Harold Wheeler, has often been hailed as among her finest work from the RCA years and includes a great version of the Beatles' classic, as well as Nina's own excellent reading of "Ooh Child," a hit for the R&B group the Five Stairsteps. *Emergency Ward*, the other album, is a live set recorded in June that featured Hoyt Axton's "The Pusher" and George Harrison's "My Sweet Lord" and "Isn't It a Pity."

By Nina's own admission, she spent the next few years wandering the globe. She'd begun an affair with Earl Barrow, the then-prime minister of Barbados, and her divorce from Andy had been finalized. Since he'd been responsible for the details of managing Nina's career, her business affairs had fallen into disarray. She owed money to the IRS, whose attempts at collection later landed Nina in a New York courthouse where she pleaded not to be sent to jail for nonpayment. She'd finally left RCA, completing one more album, a strange concoction that featured Ike and Tina Turner's "Funkier Than a Mosquito's Tweeter," the old spiritual "Come By Here," and the classic "Mr. Bojangles." the LP was suitably entitled *It Is Finished*, and its cover depicted a stone-faced Nina, sitting apparently on some rocks and, I considered, looking somewhat stoned!

By the time the album was issued in 1974, Nina had been forced to sell the home she and Andy had shared in Mount Vernon. And with the many political changes that had taken place in the U.S. since the late 1960s, she felt that the organized struggle for civil rights had prematurely petered out without accomplishing many of its objectives. With the deaths of Malcolm X and Dr. Martin Luther King, Jr., the movement had lost some of its focus. From Nina's standpoint, however, America had given up some concessions, but the essential element of racism still pervaded everyday life—a notion that several decades later is the focus of much debate in wake of the controversy surrounding government-supervised affirmative action.

A May, 1974, celebration in Washington, DC, honoring Nina on Human Kindness Day reassured her temporarily that she was still much loved in her homeland, and we talked on the telephone for *Blues & Soul*. "I've been staying in Los Angeles," she'd confided and then went on to tell me about the changes in her life. "Nowadays, I'll do isolated performances when the time and money is right, but no more nonstop tours. I've also left RCA Records, and right now I've got no management. That is by my own choosing because right now I'm trying to decide exactly what I want to do with my life. I need some time to work it out, so I'm thinking of going down to the Caribbean to rest up and take time to consider everything. . . ."

A few months later Kwame Brathwaite, *Blues & Soul* magazine's New York man on the spot, reported on a concert at Lincoln Center. Nina was in rare form that night. Brathwaite noted, "Her comments were sharp and to the point, whether they related to the way America looks at black beauty. . . . She spoke of how the U.S. will let her get all the fame she wants, but no money." She was less than kind about fellow performers Diana Ross and Roberta Flack during the show, commenting that—according to Brathwaite—"Billie Holiday would turn in her grave" if she saw the way Ross had portrayed her, and that Flack's notion of playing Bessie Smith in a proposed movie on the blues singer's life was equally incredulous.

Roberta had unwittingly earned Nina's wrath years before. At some point in time, Nina had been approached by Atlantic Records to possibly sign with the company, but when pianist Les McCann had brought Roberta to the label's attention, Atlantic decided to sign her instead. It didn't help that she was also an accomplished pianist who accompanied herself; that certain tunes, such as the old spiritual "I Told Jesus," Bob Dylan's "Suzanne," and Jim Webb's "Do What You Gotta Do," had been in Nina's repertoire before Roberta had recorded them; or that Flack, another North Carolinian by birth, had also adopted Afrocentric styles of dress and appearance! Roberta had relayed to me in a 1970s interview in New York how Nina had called Atlantic executives threatening to blow the offices up with a bomb when she got word that they'd signed Roberta to the label! the resentment apparently hadn't diminished by the summer of 1974: when audience members requested an encore, Brathwaite reported, Nina retorted, "I'm not singing no more . . . You've got Roberta Flack . . . What more do you want?"

What audiences probably wanted was more music but as she

traveled the globe as a veritable nomad, making her home at various times in France, Liberia, Switzerland, Trinidad, the Netherlands, Britain, and Belgium, recording became less of a priority for Nina, who had been awarded an honorary doctorate and insisted on being called "Dr. Simone." She cut material for small labels in France and did the occasional concert, and after a show at London's Drury Lane in December, 1977, she was approached by Creed Taylor, a U.S. recording executive who owned CTI Records, long a home for Grover Washington Jr., Esther Phillips, Bob James, Hubert Laws, Patti Austin, and others.

Like others, Taylor was completely awestruck by Nina's eclectic performance and asked her about recording for CTI. By January, 1978, Nina was ensconced in Studio Katy in Brussels, Belgium, making her one and only album for the label. *Baltimore* was certainly her most contemporary record in years. It worked wonderfully, bringing together great musicians and material that was a perfect fit, including Hall & Oates' "Rich Girl," the Quincy Jones classic "Everything Must Change," the Randy Newman-penned title track, and "My Father," a Judy Collins song that had long been a Simone favorite, dedicated clearly to Nina's own father with whom she'd always enjoyed a strong bond.

But a few months after the album's release, Nina was back in London and speaking with my sister for *Blues & Soul*, revealed that she wasn't a happy woman. Rather than praise the *Baltimore* project, she admitted to being less than thrilled with the outcome: ". . . The material was not my personal choice . . . and it was all done before I could make any decisions." Through the years, I'd learned that Nina was prone to occasional exaggeration, and her comments on the album were a case in point. Not only had she arranged "Music for Lovers" herself, but "If You Pray Right" and "Balm in Gilead" were obvious nods to her early years in church in North Carolina that no producer could possibly have chosen for her!

Nina's mental state had understandably been affected by an event a few months earlier that had occurred during a spring trip to Britain. As she told Sylvia, ". . . during my visit, I was physically assaulted with the result that I have been in pain ever since. . . ." Seemingly, so-called "friends" hadn't helped matters, and Nina was bemoaning the turmoil she was experiencing: "All of my life, I've been protected in various ways, and after the breakup of my marriage, I had to try to manage on my own—to come to terms with the situation I found myself in . . . I trusted people—and now I've learned the hard way."

The CTI album did fairly well, but Nina's decision to remain virtually in exile meant that she did could do little to promote or publicize it, and when I saw her a year later in New York, she wasn't in a good place mentally or emotionally. I noted that at a performance at the Grand Finale, she seemed erratic, and her voice hoarse. She jumped from song to song, from Bob Marley's "No Woman, No Cry," to her own "Pirate Jenny," and promised she would end the show with "Young, Gifted & Black" and "Where Can I Go Without You." Instead she delivered "Baltimore," "Everything Must Change," and "He Was Too Good to Me," an old torch song from her Colpix days.

By the mid-1980s, Nina was still globe-trotting, living a gypsy-like existence, performing when she needed money. She was in London in 1984, talking once again, more candidly than ever, with my sister Sylvia for *Blues & Soul*. Speaking of her obvious distaste for the music business, she noted, ". . . I've spent my life working, writing, recording, and the only people who got rich out of my sweat were the fat cats in the record companies. They got rich while I continued to work myself into the ground to survive. I should be able to relax a little now and take things easy but I still have to fight for what's mine." She had nothing nice to say about ex-husband Andy: ". . . I put my complete trust in him, and he used me . . . everyone tries to use me . . . but he was my husband and I believed he really cared but in the end, he turned out like all the others, so I continue to pay . . . I always pay in the end, either with my voice or with my soul—sometimes both!" Nina acknowledged that she had reputation: "They say I'm crazy but they just don't know the real me. . . . No one bothers to look behind the mask. I am a human being, too. I hurt and feel as you but the public sees me as a performer and not as a person. . . .What they fail to realize is that I'm lonely and I have no one to care, except my brother Sam so I cannot go on stage and sing of love. . . . I have no one to love and no one to love me. I am alone. When and if I have someone to love then maybe I'll sing of love . . . who knows?"

During the mid-1980s, Nina spent more and more time in and around Los Angeles, which had become my home in 1984. She'd purchased a condominium in Hollywood, and out of the blue she called one day, asking if I knew anyone who could be her assistant. I suggested that my good friend Byron Motley, who had been making a name for himself as a singer and songwriter in his own right, might be able to help out for a week or so. I warned Byron that Nina was unpredictable and eccentric but nonetheless a warm and lovable woman. I was unprepared for the daily stories of drama that followed! Nina had taken on a new manager and was recording a new album, her first in years. While pleading poverty, she'd allowed Byron to see a money belt she wore, which was packed with dollars! "They think I'm poor, man, but I got money," she laughed. Indeed any conversation with Nina was always peppered with comments on how the music business had ripped her off. True, her then-husband Andy had taped many of her shows and licensed the material to countless companies, and Nina hadn't received a dime from any of them. Also, her original contract with Bethlehem hadn't exactly been a fair one. But companies like RCA and Philips were continually reissuing her music and because of the dealings of her astute attorney, she'd finally been receiving regular payments. But Nina wasn't fessing up publicly and still pleaded poverty.

Needless to say, Byron's stint with Nina didn't end well. She cursed him out once too often, and he threw her out of his car on an unusually rainy day in Los Angeles, even though she still owed him a few days back pay. When she called me up the next day, screaming about why he hadn't turned up for work, I told her that I didn't know how to reach him. They finally came face to face again a few years later when Nina was performing at the Vine Street Bar & Grill, where she also recorded a live album for Verve Records entitled *Let It Be Me*. While I stood outside waiting for Byron, I saw Nina arrive and tried to approach her. She rushed past me, feigning nonrecognition. I was momentarily crestfallen, recalling the many years we'd spent together, with me, the worshipful fan club secretary, and Nina, my heroine. I couldn't face going backstage, but Byron braved it. "You come for your money?" she asked as he was ushered into the dressing room. "No, Nina, I just wanted to say hello," he responded with a smile. She was polite and gracious, but after he left the room all hell broke lose. "How did that motherfucker get in here?" she bellowed at her assistant.

Some five years passed before Nina and I were in each other's presence again. By the time I saw her in 1992, she'd enjoyed an amazing resurgence as a result of the European success with that old Bethlehem chestnut "My Baby Just Cares for Me." The perfume company Chanel had selected the song as its theme for a British national ad campaign, and Charly Records, which had licensed the tune from Salsoul, a company that had bought the Bethlehem masters years before, had released it as a single. The record took off—but not before Nina made it clear publicly that she hadn't received any royalties for the record!

Still, Nina's career seemed more settled than it had ever been. She was touring from time to time, and in 1992 alone she'd been to Australia, New Zealand, and Japan (for the first time in two decades). She'd also purchased a home in the south of France, in Aix-en-Provence, and was buying some more land in Ghana to use as her African retreat. She'd also signed a deal with Elektra Entertainment, her first such contract with a major U.S. company since her RCA contract had expired in 1974. In Los Angeles to begin the process of picking material for her debut album for the label, Nina had performed at the Hollywood Bowl the night before we met up.

At the Bowl, Nina had been simply magnificent. The crowd was awestruck. The mere mention of her name produced a standing ovation, and it became obvious that the reissue of her music on CDs had generated new interest in her career. That night her choice of material was a delight, ranging from "I Put a Spell on You," still sung with menace; to the torch song "You Can Have Him"; to the show-stopping "See Line Woman"; to the little-known Ellington number, "Hey, Buddy Bolden," which she'd recorded way back in 1962.

Usually punctual, I was running unceremoniously late from an appointment with my astrologer/hypnotherapist Stephanie Jourdan on the day of a *Blues & Soul* interview. I'd called Nina's assistant to let her know that I was on the way, but as it got later and later, I knew I had to do something to create a calm atmosphere when I finally did see "the good doctor" after years and years without a real sit-down, heart-to-heart chat. So I bought a big bouquet of flowers. When I finally entered Nina's condo a good hour late, she wasn't smiling. "You're late, man!" she berated me. I'd hidden the flowers behind my back, and when I proffered a sincere apology and gave her the bouquet, she beamed and leaned forward so I could kiss her on the cheek. Our relationship was restored, and I spent the next hour talking with Nina about both her plans to record and her reflections on her amazing life for the interview. "I can't seem to realize how much I've done sometimes," she confessed. "To be honest I'm very happy about my career, but sometimes it's not real to me. I mean, God gave me a talent and I used it . . . and although there have been times when I've had a 'love/hate' relationship with music, I find that I do get excited about music when I'm onstage. In fact, although I'm interested in everyday living and doing everyday things like swimming and playing tennis, as I grow older, I find myself wanting to be onstage more and more."

When I asked what kept her going through all the ups and downs of her life, Nina paused and mentioned "the liberation of my people around the world wherever they are." She then added, roaring, "I believe in music, in love, and in relationships, and in keeping good people around you . . . although I don't know so much about romantic relationships anymore! I used to want to get married again but . . . These days, people don't know what to do in bed!" Some twenty-seven years after our conversation about my own sexual naivete, I actually blushed once more!

It was obvious to me that Nina, now sixty and a little slower in her movements, was as razor-sharp, witty—and for those who had known for any length of time—warm and wonderful as ever. As she reflected on her own life back in 1992 at her Hollywood condo, I thought about her artistry and about her eccentricity, about the madness of genius and the wounded heart that might lie behind the outbursts, the volatility, the drama. As I wrote in my 1996 liner notes for Rhino Records, "In her very essence, Nina wanted nothing more than the freedom to be her full and glorious African-American, proud and dignified queenly self. "

Fortunately in recent years, a revival of interest fueled by the inclusion of much of her music in the soundtrack for the 1992 movie *Point of No Return*, Nina Simone is more of a "fashionable" diva this decade. There have been literally dozens of reissues of her work to the point where every album she has ever made for Colix, Philips, and RCA is now available on compact disc. Indeed, as recently as the fall of 1998, RCA found some incredible previously unreleased material that it included on a new compilation entitled *Sugar in My Bowl*. But, it should be noted, her U.S. audience remains primarily Caucasian. Perhaps when all is said and done, Nina is just too much for even the hippest African-Americans (save for gifted newcomers like Erykah Badu and Dionne Farris, and jazz great Dianne Reeves). It was gratifying to see that in 1997, two years after I'd first suggested to Danyel Smith of *Vibe* magazine that a "Props" piece on Nina might be appropriate, the publication did just that (but didn't, I might add, use the piece that I'd originally submitted!). It is still true that Nina's name isn't mentioned in the same context as other jazz legends like Ella Fitzgerald, Carmen McRae, or Sarah Vaughan, and that it isn't included among other soul singers like Aretha, Patti (a longtime admirer of Nina's work), or Gladys. Whatever the real reason, Nina is certainly one of the most soulful—possibly the most distinctive—divas to have graced the public consciousness this century. And at the time of this writing, she shows no signs of quitting! In 1997, she hit the headlines when she shot blank bullets at the rear end of a teenager who lived next door to her at her home in the south of France because he wouldn't stop making noise. The French court sentenced her to both psychological counseling and a fine, and I can only conjecture that after the counseling, the psychologist might have needed his or her own session!

It occurred to me only years later that Nina's outlandish personality might have its roots in the pain she might have experienced as a child prodigy and then as a young black woman seeking entry into the whiter-than-white world of classical music. I could only imagine how crushing it might have been for her to have been rejected by the Curtis Institute in Philadelphia and how she'd been forced to kiss goodbye to her dream of being a world-renowned classical pianist. Her attempts to break into an arena that was peopled with folks of a different color had been thwarted, and how she reacted deep down inside shaped much of her thinking as an adult.

As I considered all that Nina might have endured during her earliest years, I developed a better understanding for her eccentricity, for her "madness." This is not to suggest that her early traumas provided a blanket excuse for every act of rudeness Nina might have committed during her adult life—and there were enough horror stories from those who had dealt with her over the years to paint a less-than-favorable picture. But I'd been fortunate to see another side: I knew that beyond the icy stare or cold manner was a complex but loving individual whose heart was, underneath it all, in the right place. I knew that only a human being with great compassion or sensitivity could even perform some of the music she had, from the utter poignancy of "Ne Me Quitte Pas" (from her 1965 *I Put a Spell On You* album), to the despair of "My Man's Gone Now" (from the 1966 *Sings the Blues* album). While others might badmouth her for her off-the-wall outbursts and seemingly constant demand for attention, I understood that behind the fierce Nina Simone façade was little Eunice Waymon, struggling to make sense of the world into which she'd been born.

Even at the age of 65, Nina is still a grand dame, occasionally performing at different venues. She appeared in London in January, 1998, to glowing reviews and standing ovations. A British fan who had seen her show noted that she was "in a good mood." She doesn't make the trek across the Atlantic Ocean very often, and her last television appearance (on, of all things, "The Tonight Show With Jay Leno"!) was brief and from all accounts, quite eventful with Nina throwing a diva fit just prior to going on about—surprise, surprise—getting paid! In the fall of 1998, Nina appeared in Seattle and Newark before packed houses and earned customary reviews. I tried to reach her directly without success and sent flowers to express my personal gratitude for her contribution to my life.I knew that "the good doctor" Nina Simone would always be a one-of-a-kind high priestess, a diva of divas, mysteriously returned from other lives and other dimensions to tell it like it is!

AR

FRA

a

still c

THA
NKLIN

ose is
rose!

I was calling Aretha Franklin from a telephone booth at a subway station in Queens, New York. It must have been around 9 P.M. A promised "liaison" had gone awry, and I was on my way back to my Manhattan apartment, unfulfilled. There had been no "sock-it-to-me" action, and even though we both knew "who had zoomed who," no one had "rocked steady" that night. I paused at the station to check my answering machine, and lo and behold, my spirits were lifted. Miss Aretha Franklin had called to confirm that she and I were going to get together on August 11, 1980, for a one-on-one interview for *Blues & Soul* at her Los Angeles home. Aretha, then newly married to actor Glynn Turman, had just signed a recording contract with Arista Records at the end of a twelve-year association with Atlantic Records, where she'd racked up more gold records and Grammy Awards than any other black female performer.

Aretha wanted to talk, but I told her there was one condition. "You know, I've always heard so much about your cooking," I ventured bravely, "and I want to know when I get some of it?" Aretha giggled, "Well, I'll cook something special that day!" True to her word, that August evening, after I arrived at her Encino mansion and her son Teddy opened the gates for me, I was in the kitchen chowing down on the best peach cobbler I ever tasted! Aretha Franklin, the singular "Queen of Soul," had given me so much through her music through the years and as much as I loved her for it, I loved her even more for that melt-in-the-mouth, better-than-ever, to-the-bone, righteously soulful peach cobbler! As I had my second helping, I mused that Aretha obviously put as much soul into her cooking as she did into her singing.

Much has been both written and said about Aretha Louise Franklin over the thirty-plus years since she became a bona fide international superstar and, with the passing of time, a musical legend and African-American icon. I know, because I've written more about Aretha than anyone else in my career—or hers! I am truly thankful that our interviews have led to some serious milestones in my career: as a result of our meetings, I got my first cover story in *Blues & Soul*, my first feature in

Billboard, and my first *USA Today* article. I did my first VH-1 show with Aretha, and I take much pride in having written more about Aretha and her music than any other living journalist. Between the countless articles for *Blues & Soul*, *Billboard*, and various other publications, as well as liner notes for the reissues of almost all of her music, my name has appeared multiple times in association with my appreciation of her enduring contribution to my life and the lives of literally millions of people all over the world. I remember asking Aretha during that August, 1980, interview if she ever thought about the impact she'd had on so many people with her music. She smiled, almost embarrassed. "Hey, I just do my thing," she replied. " . . . I'll never stop singing because that's what I'm here to do."

Of all the divas I've met or written about, Aretha has been the one woman who always evokes questions from peers and fans alike who want to know more about "the Queen." Whether these are comments about her music, her private life, or her fashion sense, Aretha has been the topic of more conversations I've had on the subject of artists I've interviewed than anyone else. From buddies like Josh Pridgen who used to sit with me at the rehearsal studios in Manhattan where he worked and talk endlessly about Aretha, to artist manager Sid Johnson, to my Washington, DC, friend Johnny Butler's pal Clinton, a true Franklin devotee, chats about Aretha have become a staple in my life! I tell people that even with all the interviews we've done, which date back to the late 1960s, I don't "know" Aretha outside of the professional but personable relationship we've had. That said, over the years, we've shared some funny moments and some really good times. I can attest to her sassy sense of down-home humor, her quick wit, and her ability to get down with the pots and pans. I can also say that this is a woman who knows what she wants, is clear about who she is in the world of music, and has survived all manner of trends and fads to take her rightful place as a true original; she is an artist who literally began paving the way for a whole generation of female singers from the time she recorded her first ground-breaking album in 1960. She is also, as far as I know, the only recording artist whose first record hit the charts back in 1960 and found herself still on the charts in 1998!

If I were to sum up exactly what has made Aretha a pioneer, I would go back to 1960, seven years before she became a household name, to that first Columbia album entitled simply *Aretha*. I would go back there because it is within those twelve songs that an eighteen-year-old girl with the life experience of a woman twice her age brought to the studio a totally unique skill. She was, without a doubt, the first black female to bring the essence of her gospel roots to a range of tunes that spanned

Billie Holiday ("Who Needs You"), *The Wizard of Oz* ("Over the Rainbow"), *Porgy & Bess* ("It Ain't Necessarily So"), blues ("All Night Long"), and soul ("Won't Be Long").

Aretha's phrasing was unlike anyone else's: she fused the emotion of the church with a touch of jazz and added a heavy dose of blues. The result made her a lasting original. Even if she'd never made another album, that 1960 record would have marked her as a once-in-a-lifetime artist. And even though it became popular to criticize her work for Columbia after she became a musical superstar with Atlantic, her early records for that label speak volumes about her remarkable artistry.

As I sat listening to those early records in my room in London as a teenager, I never dreamed that I would get to meet, let alone interview, the amazing woman behind the music. But life, like love, is strange, and I've been privileged to check out the artist whose music—through everything from "Skylark" to "Baby, Baby, Baby"—touched the depths of my own soul. But describing the personal side of the woman who, for years, people in the music business called "difficult" because she most decidedly sets her own rules and works on her own schedule is no easy task. At different times, Aretha definitely had a reputation within the industry for unpredictability, although this has changed with her self-generated increased visibility over the last five years or so. I've never seen the brooding "lady of deep sorrow," as a longtime producer described her. And if there are moments when she expresses personal sadness about events in her life—such as the loss of her father; Cecil, her brother and longtime manager; and Carolyn, her younger sister, all in the space of a few years—her reactions are no different from those who have undergone loss and grief. True, Aretha will seldom proffer any deeply private information: in all the years we've talked, she has never made any direct reference to the men in her life. Also, a kind of coolness becomes apparent once you enter territory she considers off-limits.

One time, during a memorable 1978 interview session in Encino, at what was then her home in Los Angeles, I summoned up the nerve to comment on her dress sense, tactfully noting that her onstage attire sometimes gave rise to adverse comments. Aretha bristled, sat straight up in her chair, and gave a no-nonsense response: "I like what I wear, and I design a lot of the clothes myself," she replied stiffly. "Sometimes I test things out for my family . . . and yes, I have tried a few things that didn't work so I didn't wear them in public." From that day on, I figured any further discussion about Aretha's taste in clothes was a no-no, even though her occasional penchant for cleavage-revealing gowns has given her multitude of fans much cause to talk throughout the years!

But the "lady next door," as she has described herself, emerges when she feels comfortable enough to "dish the dirt," or, as she did during another interview session at the home she had in 1985 in the suburbs of Detroit, share photographs of some of the people who have been part of her life. She proudly pointed to one picture of a guy "who I had a crush on way back in school!" This was someone she'd subsequently had a chance to meet again since returning to the city during the time her late father had lapsed into a coma after being shot during a burglary at his home in 1983. After fixing me a plate of spaghetti with a meatless sauce once she discovered I was a vegetarian, we relaxed in the kitchen, exchanging comments on some of the music of the day: "I like the things Tina Turner is doing," she commented, referring to *Private Dancer*, Tina's comeback album, "but Patti LaBelle's *New Attitude*? It's o-k-a-y," she ventured.

I had no idea that I would get to know soul music's "natural woman" one cold December day in 1966 in London when I picked up the telephone to call Detroit. "Excuse me, my name is David Nathan, and I'm calling from London. Can you tell me how I can reach Miss Aretha Franklin?" I asked somewhat timidly, speaking with her then-husband and manager Ted White. I'd gotten White's number from the bottom of a Columbia Records' publicity photograph. And since the Christmas treat at the record store I co-owned was to call anyone in the United States, I'd chosen Aretha. For a couple of years before dialing Detroit, I'd been writing "fan" letters to Aretha, mostly sent in care of her father's church, simply mailed to "The New Bethel Baptist Church, Detroit." Miraculously, Aretha had received them, and I was blown away when I got a reply in the early part of 1966.

Ten months later, I was excited about tracking Aretha down on the telephone. "Just one moment, please," replied the business-like White. The next voice I heard was that of a young woman whose music had been thrilling me for a couple of years. "Hi, this is Aretha," she said softly. I don't remember all that we said, but I do recall that she was excited about speaking with someone in Britain for the first time and equally happy to let me know that she'd just signed with Atlantic Records. "We're going to be going into the studio in a few weeks," she said with a speaking voice I would come to recognize instantly for many years after that first conversation. Little did Aretha—or the rest of the world, for that matter—have any idea what 1967, the year she broke through to international mainstream recognition, had in store for her. My first face-to-face encounter with the "natural woman" who became known the world over as "the Queen of Soul" took place just two years later when I went to Gatwick Airport to meet Aretha and give her a bunch of flowers. She stepped into the waiting area with Ted, her sister Carolyn, and other members of her entourage, arriving in London fresh from triumphant dates in Scandinavia for her eagerly awaited debut performances in Britain. Aretha was shorter than I expected, gracious and warm in her welcome. She introduced me and my sister Sylvia to Ted and Carolyn before fawning British Atlantic representatives whisked her away. Days later, I went to see her at London's Hammersmith Odeon, and I took my mother to one of the shows. Mom had been subjected to the constant playing of Aretha's Columbia albums for a couple of years, but nothing prepared her for the intensity, power, and passion that Aretha expressed that night. "She reminds me of that gospel singer, Mahalia Jackson," my very British mum observed, as she stood to her feet to give Ms. Aretha, a much-deserved standing ovation. An accurate observation on the part of Mrs. Nathan.

Aretha, the gospel prodigy who would become an R&B superstar, is the daughter of the Reverend C.L. Franklin, a much-revered orator and preacher at the aforementioned New Bethel Baptist Church in Detroit, as well as a recording star in his own right with dozens of albums on Chess Records. She'd received all her early training in gospel music, and Mahalia Jackson had been more than just an influence on her. She'd been a family friend, a visitor to the Franklin household along with other notable artists of the day including gospel star Clara Ward and the Reverend James Cleveland (who both provided further inspiration for the young Aretha), and jazz-and-blues star Dinah Washington.

As I detailed in an extensive five-part series on Aretha for Britain's *Blues & Soul* magazine in 1977, she was born on March 25, 1942, in Memphis, Tennessee, to Reverend C.L. and Barbara (nee Siggers) Franklin, one of six children. The family moved to Buffalo, and in 1948, Aretha's mother left the household, leaving her to receive further maternal care from Frances Steadman and Marion Williams, both members of the Clara Ward Singers. In a rare lengthy interview session for *Essence* magazine in 1973, Aretha recalled, "My mother died in 1952. I was young but I remember how warm and beautiful she was. I was very close to her and I can't say which, if either, of my parents was the greater influence on me. Both gave me something, as has each member of my family, which is why it has not been difficult remaining close to them."

Notwithstanding the trauma of her mother's departure, Aretha commented, "My childhood was pretty much a happy one. I was always falling out of trees, scraping my knees. A real tomboy. I liked school, and even though I dropped out, I was a pretty good student. But it was always music. That's what I remember most about my childhood. Music at home, music in church." Aretha's sister Carolyn, who passed away at the age of forty-three after a bout with cancer, recalled in the same 1973 interview session, "I could have killed Aretha sometimes! When I was a child, she'd take me to the rabbit field across the street from our house, place me in the middle and hide. I'd scream my head off in fright, darn near had a stroke screaming and crying while I'd hear Aretha laugh her fool head off behind some bush . . . [But] she was like mama lion with me. If anyone messed with me at school, they had Aretha to deal with!"

Certainly, Aretha's exposure to the great gospel figures of the 1950s had an impact on her. Legend has it that at the funeral for one of Aretha's aunts, the late Clara Ward was singing "Peace in the Valley" and got so caught up that she tore off her hat in the midst of her fervor and flung it to the ground. Aretha is variously quoted as saying that this was the reason for her desire to pursue a musical career and that this was when [she decided) to become a singer."

Whether or not Ward provided the real impetus for Aretha's ambitions, she was destined to sing if only because of the extraordinary gift she displayed once she became a featured soloist at her father's popular church. Because of the resonance and power of Reverend Franklin's own speaking voice, he'd gained a solid reputation as one of the nation's most effective preachers, and his influence on his young daughter was undisputed. Indeed, a study of the sermons that he gave reveals a distinct way of phrasing that might have had an impact on Aretha's own skills. Certainly, her earliest secular recordings for Columbia showed her amazing grasp of how to extract meaning from the most mundane lyric lines for a young woman still in her teens at the time.

Aretha gained fame for her amazing vocal skills during the years she spent on the road with her father. Staunch gospel audiences, not quick to heap praise on every singer who came to town, marveled at young Aretha's vocal power and mastery. It was no surprise that her reading of Thomas Dorsey's "Precious Lord, Take My Hand" became a favorite with the late Dr. Martin Luther King Jr., a longtime friend of Reverend Franklin's, who always requested Aretha sing the tune whenever she was in his presence.

But life on the road in the 1950s wasn't necessarily an easy thing for the young gospel star. As Aretha's brother Cecil pointed out during a *Rolling Stone* interview in 1974, "Driving eight or ten hours trying to make a gig, and being hungry and passing restaurants all along the way . . .

having to go off the highway into some little city to find a place to eat because you're black, that had its effect. . . ." For Aretha, the craziness of the road was compounded by a teenage, out-of-wedlock pregnancy. For the daughter of a famed preacher to give birth at the age of fourteen back in the 1950s must have caused a good degree of anguish and concern; in attempting to understand her personality, critics and commentators have tended to overlook what impact the birth of her first son, Clarence, might have had on the young girl.

But inspired and encouraged by the late Sam Cooke, an obvious object of her affections, Aretha wanted to pursue a career in secular music while raising Clarence. Rather than dissuade her, Reverend Franklin took Aretha to New York City with some demos to help her secure a recording contract. Although RCA, Cooke's label, made an offer, savvy Columbia Records A&R man John Hammond—who had been responsible for putting Bessie Smith and Billie Holiday on wax for the first time—actually signed her to the label in 1960.

This first Columbia album, entitled *Aretha*, offered the key to the essence of Aretha's art. Alongside her first Atlantic LP, *I Never Loved a Man (the Way I Love You)*, a 1967 release, and possibly the 2-record gospel set, *Amazing Grace*, Aretha's recording debut says as much about her role as a musical pioneer than almost anything she has ever recorded. The result of those first sessions for Columbia was awesome: with a basic quartet in back of her, forging her own arrangements on the piano, eighteen-year-old Aretha sang and played her heart out. And while it is never fully acknowledged as such, the resulting masterpiece crossed the bridges between blues, jazz, pop, and gospel.

The album met with critical acclaim without achieving massive sales success, a fate that was to befall much of Aretha's fine work for Columbia. Usually maligned in contrast to her hit records for Atlantic, her six years at the label were more than an apprenticeship for the young performer; in retrospect a close listen reveals Aretha's undisputed role as a pioneer. Albums like *Runnin' Out of Fools* (a splendid 1964 collection that focused mostly on pop and soul hits of the day like Dionne Warwick's "Walk on By," Brook Benton's "It's Just a Matter of Time," and Nancy Wilson's "How Glad I Am") and *Yeah!!!* (a tour de force of mostly pop standards like "More," "Misty," and "Love for Sale" given exquisite jazz interpretations) remain road maps for gospel-based vocalists singing secular material. And although these albums didn't sell in any appreciable quantities, they were remarkable because no other female performer of the day was utilizing the emotional power of her gospel training with such abandon, and at such a young age.

In their haste to dismiss Aretha's work for Columbia as schmaltzy pop, pundits have erroneously concluded that the lack of sales was a reflection on Aretha's recorded performances. In addressing the choice of material—which admittedly ran a somewhat strange gamut from Al Jolson favorites like "Swanee" and "You Made Me Love You," to soul gems like "(No, No) I'm Losing You" and "Until You Were Gone"—I must note that Aretha herself chose much of what she recorded during those years. As if to validate her own appreciation of older pop and show tunes, she stepped on to the stage of the Apollo Theater for a special series of "homecoming" concerts in early 1974, clad in top hat and tights, and opened the proceedings with Al Jolson's 1918 chart topper "Rock-a-Bye Your Baby With a Dixie Melody," which had actually been a Top 40 hit for Aretha back in 1961! She'd included the song in her nightclub act at venues like the Village Gate when she first began appearing in New York. In a 1978 interview for *Blues & Soul*, she revealed, ". . . I liked the *Soft & Beautiful* album—it had some nice standard things on it [like Streisand's "People" and "My Coloring Book," and Pat Boone's "Friendly Persuasion"] . . . and I dig that other Columbia album [1962's *The Tender, Moving, Swinging Aretha Franklin*]. . . ."

Not long after signing with Columbia, Aretha married Ted White. Pop folklore suggests that entertainer and later minister and 1990s television star Della Reese introduced her to him. After their marriage in 1961, in keeping with a tradition that was commonplace among female entertainers (including Nina Simone, deep soul diva Lorraine Ellison, Patti LaBelle, Gladys Knight, and Melba Moore), White took over the management of her career from Jo King, who had been Aretha's manager when she first arrived in New York. Clearly, his vision for Aretha wasn't necessarily in keeping with the powers that be at Columbia: interested in having Aretha perform at swanky supper clubs where the earning potential was clearly greater than on grueling chitlin'-circuit tours, he wanted Aretha to record jazz and pop material.

Although material like "Skylark," "If Ever I Would Leave You," and "Ol' Man River" hardly seemed befitting for a gospel-reared twenty-one-year old, Aretha always put her magic touch on it, even though the record-buying public's response was, not surprisingly, somewhat lukewarm. While youthful contemporaries in R&B like Mary Wells were singing "You Beat Me to the Punch" and Barbara Lewis was enchanting listeners with "Hello Stranger," Aretha was doing her best on "Sitting on Top of the World" and "That Lucky Ol' Sun," material that was miles away in mood from the perky hits of 1962 and 1963.

White had Aretha appearing at notable events like the Newport Jazz

Festival, and she always won rave reviews from audience and critics alike. A 1964 tribute to the late Dinah Washington, a friend of Aretha's father and thus a frequent visitor to the Franklin house who had tragically passed away in December, 1963, showed Aretha's brilliant way of meshing blues, gospel, and R&B into a soulful mix that put her head and shoulders above her contemporaries. The problem was, bereft of hit singles, such albums were great artistic accomplishments without gaining any sales success. Her reading of Washington's "Drinking Again," "This Bitter Earth," and "Evil Gal Blues" were remarkable, inspiring the likes of Bette Midler to claim in later years that listening to Aretha's *Unforgettable* album altered her whole way of relating to singing.

By now a mother of two more sons, Ted Jr. and Edward, Aretha never said much publicly about how she felt about her career at that time. In interviews after signing with Atlantic in 1966, she would always politely comment that she'd had some turntable hits (records that got lots of airplay without accompanying sales) without reaching mass audiences. Rumors were rife that Ted was forceful in his dealings with his wife, and in interviews over the years, insiders like producer/songwriter Clyde Otis intimated that the relationship was fragile at best. Aretha herself never commented directly on the subject, except to say in a lengthy 1973 interview with *Essence* magazine, ". . . Oh, I've had my bad times, but they're the same problems, aches and pains other people have; relationships that don't work and relationships that begin not to work. OK. That causes pain, but when I think back on my marriage, I only think of how beautiful it was . . . and then came the time when it wasn't."

In spite of Ted's insistence that Aretha make records that could reach the nightclub—read primarily white—crowd, a brief working association with Otis (who had been successful with artists like Dinah Washington and Brook Benton) yielded some R&B success. "Runnin' Out of Fools" was a Top 60 hit; the poignant "One Step Ahead," a Top 20 R&B chart single; and an Ashford & Simpson tune, "Cry Like a Baby," another Top 30 R&B contender in late 1966. An album from that same month, *Soul Sister* was a disjointed mishmash of material from "Swanee," to the upbeat soul slice "Can't You Just See Me," but it did contain the remarkable "Take a Look," an Otis-penned tune that was a cry for racial equality. Some twenty-seven years later, Natalie Cole revived it as the title for an album she made for Elektra in 1993.

By the time "Cry Like a Baby" was inching its way up the charts, Aretha and Ted were on the way out of Columbia. Philadelphia disc jockey Jimmy Bishop and his wife, Louise, were friends of both Aretha and Ted's and Jerry Wexler, one of the co-owners of Atlantic Records, a label that had been firmly entrenched in the R&B world thanks to hits with Ruth Brown, Lavern Baker, the Drifters, the Coasters, and of course, Ray Charles. Wexler had long admired Aretha's talent from afar. In a 1977 article on Aretha in *Blues & Soul*, he noted, "I knew Aretha was just the best black singer around at the time. I'd heard that voice throughout all the material she cut with Columbia. . . ." Atlantic circulated a photograph of a smiling Wexler with Aretha and Ted as she put her signature to the deal.

The story of what happened next has been told countless times in articles and on various television documentaries on Aretha. Wexler felt that she would really shine if she recorded an album in Muscle Shoals, Alabama, where gospel-influenced soul brothers like Wilson Pickett, Jimmy Hughes, and Percy Sledge were churning out hits. There was supposed to be an album, but after recording just one song, the glorious "I Never Loved a Man (The Way I Love You)," Aretha and Ted left the next day and headed back to Detroit.

As Wexler was quickly discovering, Ted was no easy man to deal with, and when he returned to New York, all the producer found was the finished recording of "I Never Loved a Man" and an incomplete track for a second song, "Do Right Woman—Do Right Man."

Aretha temporarily "disappeared" and was out of communication. Wexler was stuck: the initial response from various radio deejays to "I Never Loved a Man" was phenomenal, but he had no "B" side for the record, let alone a finished album. Aretha finally emerged from seclusion in early February, and with sisters Erma and Carolyn, she finished "Do Right Woman—Do Right Man," in itself a virtual R&B classic. "She [already] had a lot of songs for that first album . . . after we signed, she came out to my house [in Great Neck] and prepared the first session," Wexler said in 1977. "She played me a lot of things . . . [that were] ready to go that she played on the piano. . . ."

By the end of February 16, 1967, Aretha Franklin put the finishing touches on "Dr. Feelgood (Love Is a Serious Business)," a definitive commentary on the virtues of homemade lovin' , which Aretha and Ted penned. She sang her heart out while sitting at the piano, creating the essential arrangements as members of the Muscle Shoals rhythm section, flown to New York for the occasion, provided just right the amount of Southern funk. Her first Atlantic album was a wrap.

No one could have anticipated what would follow. All of a sudden, Aretha's career went into overdrive. No longer known just to music-industry insiders, smart journalists, and discerning music lovers, she was suddenly the hottest female artist in the country. By virtue of of her emotional workout on "I Never Loved a Man" followed by her reworking of Otis Redding's "Respect" and a first Atlantic album that is in retrospect one of the all-time classics in contemporary pop music, Aretha Franklin had—as the title for second LP for the label suggested—arrived.

It is almost impossible in hindsight to recreate the kind of impact Aretha had on the world in 1967. It is almost like you just had to be there. Her music became the everyday soundtrack for millions of black men and women and white listeners were bowled over by the sheer passion in Aretha's delivery. For African-American women, in particular, Sister 'Ree, as Aretha was known to close friends and family, provided musical salvation. They could identify with the pain of "Drown in My Own Tears," a Ray Charles tune that Aretha made over; with the joy in "Good Times," a song Aretha's close friend Sam Cooke wrote and recorded; with the hope in "Don't Let Me Lose This Dream"; and with the kind of comfort at the end of a hard workday that no one else could offer outside of her own "Dr. Feelgood." Not just another new LP, *I Never Loved a Man (The Way I Love You)*—the first of an incredible six gold Atlantic albums—was the voice of a young woman who knew life at its most basic, the mother of three sons who knew love, heartbreak, and triumph, first hand. Later in 1967, she would note, "I might be just 26 but I'm an old woman in disguise—26 goin' on 65!"

Commenting on her sudden rise to international fame, Aretha said in 1968, "I never thought it would happen. Well, you see I've always wanted a gold record. So badly. Well, I've finally got some!" Indeed, indeed. The performer who had early in her career sung to the floor because she felt uncomfortable having audiences looking at her was now on the road nonstop, appearing before thousands as her records tripped over each other on the way up the charts. Aretha had finally crossed the Atlantic for her first European dates in 1968, recording a live album at the famed Olympia Theater in Paris and stunning audiences with the intensity and passion she brought to each performance. During her visit to London, she'd asked Atlantic executives to check the store hours at Soul City, the record shop I co-owned with Britain's leading soul expert Dave Godin and a third partner, Robert Blackmore. We stayed open very late that night in hopes that Aretha and Ted White would come down for a private shopping spree, but it never happened.

Behind the scenes, away from the crowds, Aretha was dealing with very personal challenges: the late Big Maybelle, a blues singer who originated several tunes that Aretha recorded on her *Soul '69* album, recalled in her one and only visit to Britain in 1967 that she'd been on tour with Aretha, traversing the South with Wilson Pickett, Freddie Scott, and the Marvelettes among others. During this tour Aretha sustained a broken arm, and Maybelle implied that what the press called an accident might have had another source.

With Aretha's newfound success, details of her private life became the subject of comment and speculation. A *TIME* magazine cover story on her in 1968 did more to definitively alter Aretha's relationship with the press. The article mentioned how Ted had "roughed her up" in public at a National Association of Television and Radio Announcers (NATRA) convention at Atlanta's Hyatt Regency Hotel; the picture the article painted, using quotes from Mahalia Jackson and others close to Aretha, was less than pretty. A 1974 *Rolling Stone* article, referring to the *TIME* story made it pretty plain: ". . . the story said her husband beat her up and that is the one sentence that anybody remembers."

Suggestions of a marriage in trouble, of abuse, and of a woman whose music was an outer expression of inner pain created a public perception that stayed with Aretha for many, many years. Indeed, many Franklin fans from way back will admit that their appreciation and love for Aretha's music stemmed, right or wrong, from the notion that whatever Aretha was singing about was a reflection of whatever she was dealing with behind closed doors. In a 1978 interview, I noted, "People frequently wonder if your songs reflect your own personal situation when you write or record them." Aretha responded: "Well, sometimes they're personal and sometimes they're just based on a situation I might see. People seem to think that they're personal and that's up to them. It doesn't stop me from writing because I still feel comfortable doing that regardless of what people may see in the songs." All I knew was Aretha's voice offered comfort in the storm, solace for the lonely, and salvation for the brokenhearted. Her songs became the soundtrack for many lives, including my own. Her second Atlantic album, *Aretha Arrives*, ran the gamut of emotions that I was experiencing myself at the time. Yes, I knew about the "Night Life" even though I was just twenty years old. Yes, I spent many nights listening to "I Wonder" because that's just what I was doing. Yes, I felt like I, too, was "Going Down Slow" although I was determined not to let my heart get broken again. Aretha said it all with "Ain't Nobody Gonna Turn Me Around." But when you are young and in love, you want someone to "Prove It," and you pray that you can turn to the one who has captured your heart and say "Never Let Me Go." Yes, for me and for folks the world over, Aretha was killing us soulfully with her songs.

With the recording of further masterful albums, such as the gold LPs *Lady Soul* and *Aretha Now*, speculation continued as to whether

Aretha's song selection was based on events in her own life. When she poured her heart and soul into "Good to Me as I Am to You" (a bluesy opus written by Aretha and Ted and featuring Eric Clapton on guitar) or the massive 1968 hit "Chain of Fools," was she revealing her own personal feelings or merely recording great songs? Was "I Can't See Myself Leaving You" a musical message to Ted? Had younger sister Carolyn written the amazing "Ain't No Way" because she knew what Aretha was going through? And was the 1968 classic "Think" all about the state of a relationship or the increasingly vociferous cry of a people who had been oppressed, suppressed, and denied the justice and equality they were fighting for?

No doubt Aretha knew, but she wasn't saying. In an early 1970s recording, poet Nikki Giovanni expressed her thoughts on the matter on "Poem For Aretha," a piece that defended Aretha's right to privacy, implying that an entertainer's popularity didn't give the public license to know the intimate details of life away from the spotlight. Journalist Ritchie Yorke, who had written the liner notes for *Soul '69*, a masterful album that featured Aretha accompanied by some of the hottest jazz players of the day, observed: "In one of the pleasant middle class homes which line the long streets of northwest Detroit, passers-by often notice an attractive young woman dusting and rearranging objets d'art in the living room. If any of the pedestrians stopped to tie up a shoelace, they would catch the familiar sound of daytime t.v. soap operas. The situation is typical. The woman is not. . . . She finds fame and fortune difficult to comprehend and to justify. Aretha is reserved . . . there is no pretense. She has her feet firmly planted on the ground."

Twenty-two years later, during an interview she and I did, Aretha reaffirmed to me what she'd always maintained about herself: "The other side of the coin, when I'm not recording or performing, I like to be seen in a nontheatrical light as a woman, a lady, a good friend, an aunt, a sister. I like to cook, iron and I can wash as good as the next lady. . . . When I'm at home, I'm a domestic goddess—I can sew with the best of 'em but . . . I don't do windows!"

Much of Aretha's lasting appeal lay in the natural-woman persona that she presented when she occasionally did consent to talk to the press or appear on television in the late 1960s. It soon became clear that her relationship with Ted White was reaching its end as her first decade as a recording artist came to its conclusion in early 1970. There had been press reports of problems: an engagement in Las Vegas ended abruptly, Aretha missed a few shows, and the press were quick to jump on a short stay in a Detroit hospital as proof of a nervous breakdown. Longtime booking agent and friend Ruth Bowen of the Queen Booking Agency (named after Dinah Washington, Bowen's first major client) recalled in comments to *Essence* in 1973, "Aretha wasn't happy and it showed. Her personal problems often affected her health. She kept getting sick. Eventually, when she thought her performances were less than what she was capable of, we cancelled an entire year's booking. And why not? It takes a while to get over loving a man. . . ." Aretha herself added, in the same story, "I used to cry about things that I couldn't do anything about, but no more. What difference what things . . . just things . . . but no more crying over what was or what might have been."

Aretha began recording "This Girl's in Love With You," her seventh Atlantic album, in January, 1969, at Atlantic's studios in New York City with producers Jerry Wexler, Arif Mardin, and Tom Dowd, a trio that had been involved (initially in differing roles, with Mardin primarily as an arranger and Dowd as an engineer) with her since her arrival at the label three years earlier. She finally completed the record nine months later in Miami at Criteria Studios, which had become a location that Atlantic's Wexler had begun using for different sessions. It is said that the record was almost like a musical depiction of the end of her relationship with Ted White, particularly on songs like "It Ain't Fair," "Sit Down and Cry," and the self-penned ballad "Call Me," her eighth No. 1 R&B hit single. Aretha herself had a whole different take on that tune, a moving tale of two people who are parting company. While listeners speculated that it was Aretha's final ode to Ted, she told *Rolling Stone* in 1974, ". . . there were two people on Park Avenue (in New York City), a couple. And they were just getting ready to leave each other, going in different directions. And as he got across the street and she was on the other side, he turned around and said, 'I love yoooooo!' and she said, 'I love you tooooo!' He said, 'Call me! The moment you get there!' She said, 'I w-i-l-l!' And they just stopped traffic on Park Avenue and everybody was checking that out. Romance on Park Avenue!"

While she sounds vocally tired on the January sessions, by October Aretha was back in top form, and with the release of *Spirit in the Dark*, another 1970 album, she was looking and sounding great. She also made her second visit to the U.K. in late July, and we got a chance to catch up in person. After sending flowers to her London hotel, I received an invitation to visit with Aretha on the set of the popular British television show, "Top of the Pops," on which she was singing her new smash, "Don't Play That Song," a sparkling cover of the Ben E. King 1960s hit. I almost missed her when she walked through the lobby: slimmed down, with a neat Afro, I hadn't recognized her!

A very young
Aretha Franklin
Credit: Archive Photos/
Metronome Collection

I couldn't help but comment on Aretha's weight loss when we finally came face to face, and as I noted in a subsequent cover story—my first for *Blues & Soul*—Aretha admitted, "I've just had my baby, you know—a boy—and that has certainly helped! Although," she laughed, "I still love my food!" Most of our conversation centered around recent recording sessions in March that made up the bulk of her *Spirit in the Dark* album. She was happy with her new work and proud of her new son, Kecalf (pronounced "Kelf"), the result of her union with new companion, photographer Ken Cunningham. A few days later, she blew London audiences away with thrilling performances at the Hammersmith Odeon. Aretha had made it over . . . and new triumphs lay ahead.

In the fall of 1970, on her return to the States, Aretha was back in the studio. Among the songs she cut for what would be the *Young, Gifted and Black* album (released in 1972) was a version of "Brand New Me," a tune singer Jerry Butler penned with Philly producers Kenny Gamble and Thom Bell. In an interview with *Ebony* magazine in 1971, she stated, "That's one [song] that expresses actually what I felt when I recorded it and the way I actually feel right now—like a brand new woman. I'm feeling much brighter these days . . . it's just that I've gotten rid of a lot of things that were weighing me down . . . and I've gained a great deal of confidence in myself. I wonder how many people know that I once had this big problem actually about walking out on the stage . . . all those people out there looking at me, checking me out from head to toe! Wow! That really used to get to me but I've overcome most of that by just walking out on that stage, night after night, year after year."

Aretha got a chance to express that new pep in her step when Atlantic's Wexler arranged for her to perform at the Fillmore West in San Francisco, known as a hangout for the flower children of the 1960s. He had some trepidation about the event, but Aretha turned the place upside down in February, 1971, working with her longtime friends King Curtis, Billy Preston, and her own Sweethearts of Soul. It didn't hurt that brother Ray Charles stopped by to ad-lib with Aretha on her own "Spirit in the Dark." The resulting album became Aretha's fourth gold LP upon its release in June, 1971, and a year later, Aretha was back in California to lay down what would become yet another triumphant recording— one that I consider to contain some of the finest singing ever put on tape by any recording artist.

The occasion was a two-day special performance at the New Temple Missionary Baptist Church in Los Angeles, and Aretha was "back home" with the Reverend James Cleveland, one of her longtime mentors, and his Southern California Community Choir. Her father was on hand and made some appropriate comments; and Clara Ward, an early inspiration, was right there with her mother. The magic that happened during those nights was captured on the double album *Amazing Grace*, which not only became Aretha's all-time best seller but also holds the distinction of selling more albums in the gospel world than any other album since its release in 1972, racking up an unprecedented two million-plus sales. The glory and majesty of Aretha's singing were in full evidence as she revisited her roots, and when I listen to the album now, years later, it is clear that she never lost the very essence of the musical training she'd received in her father's church in Detroit. But beyond that voice, with its range and power, were the sheer intensity and the unbridled emotion and conviction that made her a truly remarkable, stand-alone artist.

On the private front, Aretha seemed happy. Years after she'd recorded them, she revealed that certain songs had a very direct personal connection for her. For example, 1971's "Daydreaming" was, it turns out, a tune she wrote after a romantic relationship with Dennis Edwards, who was then singing with the Temptations, while "First Snow in Kokomo" was a reference to her then-beau Ken Cunningham. She'd moved from Detroit to New York, purchasing a four-story brownstone on East 88th Street, just blocks away from Central Park on Manhattan's fashionable Upper East Side.

Aretha had been back to California to record an album with Quincy Jones, which was entitled *Hey Now Hey (The Other Side of the Sky)*, but it was different musically than previous work with her usual Atlantic team and the public response was lukewarm. Her sister Carolyn's tune "Angel" became Aretha's thirteenth No. 1 R&B single, followed just a few months later by the Stevie Wonder-penned "Until You Come Back to Me (That's What I'm Gonna Do)," her biggest pop hit in a few years.

Toward the end of 1973, Aretha and I spoke briefly when she was performing at the Apollo. She revealed that she'd "almost re-signed" with Atlantic and had been working on new material for a projected album for the company. She was exploring some movie possibilities, noting, "my companion [Ken Cunningham] is looking into that for me right now. . . ." She'd toned down her performance schedule to incorporate more extended club dates rather than one-nighters, and she was looking forward to a return trip to Europe.

As it turned out, the next few years would bring some upheaval in Aretha's world. After the album *Let Me in Your Life*, whose cover showed Aretha looking more glamorous than ever in a black mink stole, did well (bolstered by hits like "I'm in Love" and "Ain't Nothing Like the Real

85

Thing"), the follow-up, "With Everything I Feel in Me," did only moderate business. For better or worse, Aretha had become much more involved with producing her own albums, and she tended toward a certain vocal self-indulgence. This was best typified by album cuts like "You'll Never Get to Heaven" and "Don't Go Breaking My Heart." Her relationship with Cunningham ended, and she'd moved out to Encino, California, with her sons.

In concert, Aretha was trying some different things. I'd seen her during my first trip to New York in November, 1974, at Radio City Music Hall and was unprepared for her opening number. She literally emerged from the floor, dressed in a clown outfit, complete with red nose, singing "That's Entertainment"! Fortunately, what followed was an exceptionally soulful performance (taped for a possible future album release that never happened) that included spine-tingling versions of Stevie Wonder's "All in Love Is Fair" and her own composition, "Without the One You Love," a tune she'd recorded back in her Columbia days.

The move to Los Angeles meant a lot more television exposure, and Aretha appeared on all manner of programs, from "The Hollywood Squares" to "The Dinah Shore Show." In addition to picking up countless Grammy Awards over the years, she co-hosted the show in 1976, a task she undertook with occasional wit and humor, noting on one telecast that she couldn't read the teleprompter because some guy was blocking her vision!

In May, 1975, Aretha had recorded a new album in Glendale entitled *You*, her last with Atlantic's Wexler, and the cover depicted Aretha clad in a yellow bikini-type outfit, lying on what we can assume was her Encino home. The cover was enticing. Apparently, though, the record-buying public wasn't impressed with the music. By Aretha standards, it was a relatively poor seller, so when Curtis Mayfield invited Aretha to sing songs he'd written for the movie *Sparkle*, she headed out to Chicago in January, 1976. The result was a smash: Aretha sounded better than ever, the album went gold, and "Something He Can Feel," the lead single, was another No. 1 hit for the Queen of Soul.

The relative dip in Aretha's recording success had temporarily ended, but not before the press and industry insiders were suggesting that a new artist had finally come along to challenge Aretha for the crown. Natalie Cole, the daughter of Nat King Cole, had picked up her first Grammy for "This Will Be," her 1975 debut single, ending Aretha's lock on the Best R&B Female category after nearly a decade.

Aretha's last few albums for Atlantic met with a cool response because music itself had begun to change. Disco, a dance music form that had essentially begun in black gay clubs on the East Coast, went mainstream, and every diva worth her salt was trying to get in on the action. Thelma Houston, Esther Phillips, Cissy Houston, and others were caught up in disco madness, competing for chart action. In an extensive interview at Aretha's Encino home in the fall of 1978, I asked her how she felt about it. "I like it! I didn't think it would be as big as it is and I was kinda surprised that it was more than just a fad. . . ." Aretha even ventured that she'd been to a few clubs herself: "Sure! . . . I've been to Studio 54 in New York and The Speakeasy in L.A, and a disco down in Acapulco . . . it's good for us girls who want to shed a few pounds!" And, yes, she replied, she would consider doing a disco record herself!

The interview had been set to focus on Aretha's then-new album, *Almighty Fire*, her second musical union with Curtis Mayfield. We got to cover plenty of territory. Aretha spoke about some of her favorite performances (the Hollywood Bowl in 1973, a Madison Square Garden event with the late Dr. Martin Luther King Jr., her Radio City shows in 1974), her favorite music of the day (Barry White, Rufus, the Emotions, Earth Wind & Fire, the Four Tops, and friends Bill Withers, Stevie Wonder, and Marvin Gaye), Curtis Mayfield ("He's great once we get inside the studio"), and her famous response to questions about her sometimes "different" wardrobe ("You can't please everybody and as long as I'm comfortable with what I wear, that's what's important").

Then, of course, there was her new husband. Aretha had met actor Glynn Turman when she decided to take acting classes. They'd wed in 1978. Two years later, she revealed, ". . . I paid as much attention to the teacher as to the class!" And certainly Aretha had a few comments on the subject of marriage herself in 1978: "I don't feel that everyone has to deal with a piece of paper . . . personally, I agree with the tradition that love and marriage go together like a horse and carriage! I think, though, it's an individual thing, up to the people involved."

While her marriage to Glynn was working out, Aretha was understandably deeply affected when her father was shot in an attempted burglary at his Detroit home in the summer of 1979. He lapsed into a coma and never gained complete consciousness. Although she had some major decisions to make with an imminent parting from Atlantic Records, Aretha was understandably preoccupied with her father's health, and she began flying back and forth to Detroit on a regular basis.

Meanwhile, it was clear to Aretha that her recording career needed a major change even though she was in great form in concert. I'd seen her at New York's Avery Fisher Hall in April, 1980, and she was upbeat, happy, and joking with the audience about her new trim look. "Have I lost weight?" she quipped. "Well, I'm up here starvin', let me tell ya!" In addition to revisiting some golden gems like "Call Me," "Baby, Baby, Baby" and "Ain't No Way," Aretha did her own take on some of 1979's biggest hits, including Michael Jackson's "Don't Stop Til You Get Enough," Diana Ross's "The Boss," and the Commodores' "Still." She ended the show with Peter Allen's "I Go to Rio," complete with dancers and a parasol that wouldn't open! I had a chance to say hello backstage, and a few months later we were talking on the telephone about my coming to Los Angeles to do our interview-with-peach-cobbler-session.

The session was quite extensive, and much of the focus was on her new deal with Arista Records. "I liked the way the company did their thing—they've always appeared to be creative, progressive and a company that's making great strides," she commented. "And [Arista president] Clive [Davis] has great expertise and experience in the business. We met briefly while I was with CBS and then again around 1973 when we were re-negotiating with Atlantic and I was looking at some other situations . . . I'm really happy to be working with him and I am thrilled at the enthusiasm and excitement that the company has for the [first] album. It's exactly what I've been looking for—the kind of support that you need when you've put energy and creativity into a project."

It also didn't hurt that Davis had signed Dionne Warwick a couple of years before and literally returned her to the charts and a double Grammy win in 1979. Davis had used savvy in putting together Aretha's debut for the label: she'd reunited with Arif Mardin for a few songs, and she began working with Chuck Jackson, not the 1960s singer but one half of the team that had helped give Natalie Cole her run of 1970s hits. Aretha was excited about playing some of the tracks for me, including the lead-off single, the much underrated ballad "United Together," a revival of Otis Redding's "I Can't Turn You Loose" and a cover of the Doobie Brothers' "What a Fool Believes." The music sounded fresh and crisp, and Aretha's vocals were strong and powerful.

Of course, my hearing was somewhat affected by the Aretha Franklin, home-cooked peach cobbler that she began to serve. I concluded that if she ever decided to quit music, she would have no problem opening her own restaurant! As duly noted at the beginning of this chapter, the cobbler was indeed finger-lickin' good, and I badly wanted to ask for a doggie bag but didn't want to impose.

It was obvious that Aretha was happy. She seemed more relaxed than at any other time we'd met, and a recent appearance in the movie *The Blues Brothers* had given her new visibility. "Yes, I am surprised at just how people have reacted. I enjoyed working on the movie . . . although it was tough! All that getting up real early and spending hours on the set waiting to do your scene," Aretha stated. "Made me realize how hard Glynn works and how happy I am to be singing!" Glynn piped in that in his acting class (where their relationship had bloomed), ". . . she was about the only one who took notes! So when it came time to do the movie, I knew she'd be fine. Plus she did get a little extra coaching from me here at home!"

As the evening drew to a close, we watched British comedian Benny Hill on television; discussed new music by Diana Ross, Stephanie Mills, and Chaka Khan that Aretha liked; her love for boxing; a possible move to Connecticut; and an impending Royal Command Performance for the Queen of England. As Aretha was looking forward to her first release on Arista, she had no clue that almost twenty years later, she would be giving the company another hit record with her 1998 smash, "A Rose Is Still a Rose."

If the 1960s was a period of learning and laying a foundation and the 1970s was a time for reaping the rewards for dues paid, the 1980s offered Aretha a chance for self-affirmation. Certainly, the personal circumstances were tough: she and Glynn split up without any public word on the matter although the Hollywood gossip mill did overtime on what happened to cause the split. Neither party has ever commented on why what looked like a fairytale marriage ended after four years, but shortly after the split Aretha hightailed it back to Detroit with her children. Of course, she had good reason for going back home: her father remained in a coma, and Aretha wanted to be close at hand for what would be his final years. When Reverend Franklin passed away in July, 1984, his funeral was held at his own New Bethel Baptist Church, packed to the rafters with members of the congregation and leading dignitaries, such as family friend Reverend Jesse Jackson.

When Aretha first returned to Detroit, she still found time to perform and record. Her second set for Arista, *Love All the Hurt Away*, was actually one of her best for the label from a musical standpoint, boasting an amazing version of Diana Ross's "It's My Turn," which reeked of authenticity and honesty. But aside from the title track, a stone-to-the-bone duet with George Benson, there were no other hit singles on the album, and Aretha and Arista president Davis worked hard to come up with a new strategy.

Just a few years earlier, I'd been sitting in my neighbor Luther

Vandross's living room, listening to some of Aretha's Atlantic material and eating some good old Kentucky Fried Chicken. I remember particularly hearing *Aretha Arrives*, one of my all-time favorite Franklin albums. "One day, I want to produce Aretha," Luther declared boldly. "Oh, and Dionne and Diana. The three fabulous divas! Yes, that's what I'm gonna do!" he said, with a gleam in his eye.

Clive Davis made it his job to stay informed about new artists and producers who were creating a stir. He could hardly have ignored Luther, who had racked up three hit singles and two platinum albums in two years. When Davis read in an interview that Vandross would love the chance to produce Aretha, he arranged for the two to meet.

Jump to It was recorded in early 1982 at Media Sound Studios on West 57th Street, around the corner from the adjoining apartment buildings on West 56th Street that had made Luther and me neighbors. It brought Aretha her first gold album of the 1980s, and the infectious title track became her first No. 1 R&B hit for Arista. Packed with both punchy, hip tracks and delicious ballads, the LP was a validation of Aretha's ability to stay ahead of the game. In 1985 Aretha spoke to me at her home in the suburbs of Detroit: "When I first met Luther, he had me laughing like *crazy*!"

Unfortunately, though, the making of a second Franklin-Vandross collaboration didn't go as smoothly as the first. *Get It Right* should have been another smash album. Although the 1983 title track gave Aretha another No. 1 R&B chart topper, the rest of the record lacked the fire of its predecessor. There were reported tensions between producer and artist, and one observer (name withheld for future hiring concerns!) remembers Aretha picking up her fur and walking out of the studio, leaving the album incomplete. Supposedly, it took some mediation on the part of a renowned gospel and R&B singer in her own right to bring the two parties back together. But the magic was missing the second time around.

In concert Aretha seemed to be going through the motions. She wasn't in top form at a Madison Square Garden gig, appearing on a show with a number of major acts of the day including Ashford & Simpson and Stephanie Mills. The final act on a jam-packed bill, Aretha went on late. After a spectacular entrance in which a group of muscle-bound hunks carried her onto the stage, she vocally skated through the show. By the time she finally got to "Jump to It," inviting Luther Vandross to join her on stage for the song, some audience members had already left the Garden.

Understandably, Aretha's attention was focused on matters at home. After Reverend Franklin's passing in 1984, she took time off, finally returning to the recording studios in the fall. She and Arista's Clive Davis decided that her next album had to be the one that would bring her the pop crossover hit that had eluded her during her first few years with the record label.

The pair picked Narada (pronounced "Narda") Michael Walden, a former drummer, a recording artist in his own right, and the man who had given R&B vocalist Stacy Lattisaw a hit or two; he'd also worked with two other Arista divas, Angela Bofill and Phyllis Hyman. In a 1985 interview for *Blues & Soul*, Narada recounted how he'd sent some demos to Davis and then to Aretha: "She was delighted with what she heard—I sent her roughs on "Push," "Freeway of Love," and "Who's Zoomin' Who" . . . I really came up with a lot of the ideas lyrically from talking with Aretha on the phone. I'd ask her about what she'd do at home, how did she spend her time. She told me that one of the things she liked to do on occasion was go to a club and maybe she'd be checking out some guy who'd be checking her out too—that's where I got a lot of the ideas for 'Who's Zoomin' Who.' I discovered that Aretha had this great sense of humor, something I had no idea about before we started working together."

One Saturday afternoon in June, 1985, I arrived at Aretha's mansion in Bloomfield Hills. She was cordial, warm, and funny. Naturally, she wanted to talk about her latest album, which was due to come out about a month later: "I had decided I wanted to do a record that had a younger sound to it. I had been listening to some of the music on the radio and I really liked what I heard. Records by Eurythmics, John Waite, Van Halen, the Stones, as well as Tina [Turner], Lionel [Richie] and Luther . . . I figured to myself it was time for me to get out there and do something *serious*! . . . I wanted to come up with something for the kids. After all, I like to bop too!" Putting on a tape of the track "Push," a duet with Peter Wolf, she got up and starting bopping around as if to demonstrate! "Yeah, I really *like* this stuff. In fact, I think it's some of the best material I've done since the mid-'60s!" she continued.

With a high-flying video that showed a sassy Aretha getting out of the pink Cadillac referred to in the Top 5 pop and No. 1 R&B hit, "Freeway of Love," the collaboration with Narada did the trick. Aretha was back in stride and gaining a new young, hip audience. At our interview session, she donned pink shades and asked, "How do you like my punk look? Yeah, you could say this is my 'new wave' of hits!" Included in the new album was the anthem "Sisters Are Doin' It For Themselves," a spirited duet with Annie Lennox of Eurythmics. Aretha recalled, "I got to the session in what I thought was the right kind of outfit—I pulled out my 'rock' leather jacket with rhinestones and here I am, all punked out while Annie's there with this pair of chic, elegant pants on! A case of role reversal, you might say!"

Even though the circumstances of Aretha's return to Detroit were unfortunate, she seemed to be adjusting well to being back home. "I've been having a great time since I've been back . . . catching up with some friends I haven't seen since my school days. There's one guy who I had a crush on when I was all of 12 years old and when I told him that recently, he fell about laughing!" Aretha had been running into "some interesting guys. I'm really an old-fashioned girl—I like to be romanced. I don't think being 'jive' inspires love and devotion and I've met my share of guys between the ages of 30 and 45 who have insulted and assaulted my intelligence with their stories and games. When I met those kind of guys, I say hello and *goodbye!* I like a man who can rise to the occasion!" Aretha giggled as I pretended mock shock. "Aretha, are you sure you want me to print that?" I chuckled. "Sure!" she replied, as the telephone rang. It was Luther Vandross. Aretha began discussing his upcoming shows in Detroit and about getting him some home-cooked food while he is in the Motor City. "I have this girl who'll make you anything you want!" she laughed. Luther apparently informed her that he is more interested in getting some turkey wings than meeting the girl. Aretha hangs up the telephone, beaming. She returned to the discussion about Detroit's finest: "Now there are some men who have come through with flying colors. . . ." She mentioned a local Detroit businessman she'd been seeing "who's real hot! I get on the phone with my girlfriends [just like in my record "Jump To It"], and I tell them all the details! But I'm not ready to make any major commitments in that area. Of course, I never say never but for now, I'm not thinking about getting married again."

What Aretha was thinking about was hit records. About a year after "Who's Zoomin' Who" was barreling its way up the charts, Aretha was back with a self-titled album that featured the production credits of Narada Michael Walden. Once again, destined for pop success, the record's high points included a soaring version of the Rolling Stones' "Jumpin' Jack Flash" (produced by the Stones' Keith Richards), which had been used as the title song for a Whoopi Goldberg film. This prompted the actress to appear (along with Richards) in the companion video that depicted Aretha with a way-out, punk hairstyle and mauve lipstick! However, it was the duet "(I Knew) You Were Waiting For Me" with British pop icon George Michael that took Aretha to the very pinnacle of the pop charts in the early months of 1987.

In the summer of that year, Aretha decided to make a new gospel record. At Arista's expense, I was duly summoned to Detroit for the occasion, a two-day event at the New Bethel Baptist Church. Special guests included the Reverend Jesse Jackson, Joe Ligon of the famed Mighty Clouds of Joy, and fellow childhood road traveler Mavis Staples, who joined Aretha for a version of "Oh Happy Day." But it was clearly Aretha's night—and what a thrill to see her in her natural element! While the album never had anything like the sales impact of 1972's *Amazing Grace*, Aretha inspired everyone who was present with her intense performance. I was supposed to make a special presentation to her on behalf of *Blues & Soul*, but it never happened publicly; when I gave her the award backstage, she was gracious, polite, and warm.

Two more years would pass before we got back together. The occasion was Aretha's "return" to New York. She'd admitted during our 1985 interview that after twenty-three years of flying, she'd stopped as a result of a bad incident. She'd been a passenger in a small, four-seat plane when a thunderstorm struck Georgia and the plane literally went upside down. That was enough to put her off flying forever, and she'd barely ventured out of Detroit since. Ready to get back to performing in 1989, she had a special bus built nicknamed "The Legend"; it included a kitchen, telephone, state-of-the-art stereo system and VCR, and of course, a luxury sleeping section, complete with queen-sized bed! Aretha hit the road for her first major appearance in New York in the summer of 1989 as *Through the Storm*, her eighth Arista album, hit the streets.

Aretha herself hit the stage in a pink Cadillac and proceeded to wear out the audience with a powerhouse performance. Although Aretha's voice had lost some of its upper register as a result of years of chain smoking, she was in good shape that night. She asked Peabo Bryson to join her onstage for "I Knew You Were Waiting for Me" and "Tonight I Celebrate My Love." There was magic in the air. As she commented to the audience, "The last time I danced like that with a man, I ended up *marrying* him!" I'd known Peabo for years, and I couldn't help but tease him when we both arrived at a party in Aretha's honor. I even took the liberty of sitting next to the pair and was bold enough to make some sly little comments to Aretha about him. Days later, she called and asked me to send her copies of all the articles that had ever appeared in *Blues & Soul* on him! It seems that he'd performed at her birthday gathering that March, and she made no bones about how she felt about him . . . and his singing: "He really does it for me! I love him, the man *moves* me!" Whatever private "moves" might have taken place remains a matter of conjecture. Peabo got married not too long after to the former wife of boxer Sugar Ray Leonard, and Aretha made no further mention of him in subsequent conversations!

What had become apparent to me as Aretha and I got to know each other over the years was that she became more open about private matters; if she liked a guy, she wasn't afraid to say so. The woman who had sung about "Dr. Feelgood," about getting her props in "Respect," and about giving her guy something he could feel back in 1976 was upfront in her conversations about men and equally witty on record. A self-produced composition "He's the Boy" (from *Through the Storm*) provided more than a clue as Aretha ad-libbed, "The man is so tall, he wears those pants so well, that's what I like, just make you wanna . . . can I feel your thighs? Now, don't be blushing, just come on over here!" A spicy, fun-filled duet with Whitney Houston, "It Isn't, It Wasn't, It Ain't Never Gonna Be," gave Aretha a chance for some more "girl talk," and she admitted, "I love to talk trash!" Indeed from her little ad-libs on *Jump to It*, all the way through her lyrical asides on "The Woman," another self-penned tune on her 1998 album, Aretha was being as a real as she could be. Her offstage personality was finally merging with her public persona, and the result endeared her even more to loyal fans who had been following her career for years.

Of course, being real didn't mean being more accessible. Whether it was a calculated move or not, Arista's Clive Davis was intent on ensuring that Aretha's role as "the Queen Of Soul" was never forgotten. As the 1980s became the 1990s, it was impossible to see Aretha's name in print or on television without the reference to her legendary status. Years before, when I'd asked her how she felt about the tag, she'd smiled, shrugged, and said that she didn't think of herself as "the Queen" but as just an everyday woman who loved to sing. It became apparent that as the 1990s rolled on, she was now fully embracing all that it meant to be the undisputed monarch!

Along the way, "the Queen" had a couple of interactions with peers that kept the gossip mill busy. She and childhood friend and fellow gospel traveler Mavis Staples had a falling out following quotes attributed to Mavis that appeared in a *Vanity Fair* article on Aretha. Mavis said that after she and Aretha went into the studio to do some doctoring on the recording of "Oh Happy Day" they'd done at New Bethel in 1987, Aretha had cut out a sustained note Mavis had sung. Mavis made the mistake of recounting the story to a journalist doing the feature on Aretha. After the article appeared in print, Aretha made a veiled comment to Donnie Simpson in a BET interview, confirming that in a planned autobiography, she would set the record straight on the subject.

A few years later, on the occasion of talk-show host Oprah Winfrey's fortieth birthday, Aretha appeared with Gladys Knight and Patti LaBelle on the show, and it was obvious that there were some tensions. Aretha clapped politely while remaining seated as everyone gave Gladys Knight a standing ovation. In her 1997 autobiography, *Between Each Line of Pain and Glory*, Gladys mentions the aloofness and distance she felt Aretha projected toward her for years, prompting a "I don't know what you mean" response from Aretha in *Jet* magazine.

While she never admitted it publicly, Patti LaBelle also referred to how hurt she had been by the attitude of a legendary artist toward her in an *Ebony* article in the late 1990s, and it didn't take a brain surgeon to figure out who she meant. When Aretha was being an excellent Mistress of Ceremonies at the Rhythm & Blues Foundation Pioneer Awards in 1997, foundation chairman Jerry Butler announced onstage that Aretha would be appearing with Patti LaBelle at the organization's annual festival in Newport some months later. "Huh? Me and Patti LaBelle? What's that all about, Jerry?" Aretha asked over the mike. "I don't know anything about me and Patti LaBelle doing anything together!" Maybe it was just as well that the two divas appeared on separate nights that summer.

I never had a face-to-face problem with Aretha, although circumstances conspired to make my visit to Detroit in December, 1996, at her request less than fulfilling. I was thrilled that Aretha had insisted that Arista fly me to the Motor City for a concert she was doing at the New Bethel Baptist Church, which would be recorded for her own World Class Records label. The concert was originally supposed to be done for a Showtime television special, but that didn't happen—neither did my proposed interview with Aretha.

I later found out about some of the pressures Aretha had been dealing with that day: the church's officials had scheduled not one but two funerals for the day of Aretha's show. More tickets had been sold than were available seats, and all in all everything hadn't gone as smoothly as she'd hoped.

Still, a live album was cut, featuring Aretha and special guests Vanessa Bell Armstrong, Bobby Jones, and Billy Preston. I did get a chance to ask Aretha about its release, as well as other questions, when I attended an international press conference held in February, 1998. This event came just two days after she'd blown the world away when substituting for opera legend Luciano Pavarotti on the Grammy Awards telecast (see next page). She recognized me when I stood up to ask a few questions, and I'd be lying if I didn't say how special I felt in a room filled with international journalists to be personally addressed by "the Queen"!

The press conference was convened so Aretha could talk about her 1998 album *A Rose Is Still a Rose*. The release was her first in seven years, and I certainly wasn't alone in considering that it was much stronger than her 1991 album *What You See Is What You Sweat*. I'd loved her 1994 song "Willing to Forgive," her first big hit of the 1990s, from a "Greatest Hits" collection Arista had released. But the 1998 album was confirmation that Aretha could still deliver the goods nearly forty years after making her first secular album.

Aretha seemed in good spirits at the press conference just as she had a year earlier when she was spectacular as the Mistress of Ceremonies at the Pioneer Awards in February, 1997, telling funny little stories and anecdotes as she introduced some of her 1960s peers, including Gene Chandler, the Four Tops, and the Spinners. I told her how much I enjoyed them, and she thanked me, noting that I could expect a lot more in her autobiography that she was working on with author David Ritz.

In the wake of *A Rose Is Still a Rose*, Aretha made a number of key television appearances in order to promote the album, which included production by Lauryn Hill, Jermaine Dupri, Dallas Austin, Sean 'Puffy' Combs, Michael J. Powell, Narada Michael Walden, and Aretha herself. She seemed truly happy, rightfully basking in the acclaim she was receiving for her longevity as one of the few contemporary performers who could justifiably be called a legend. But no television spot could equal the showstopping performance she'd given at the Grammys on the night of February 26, when she performed the classical aria "Nessun Dorma" in place of Luciano Pavarotti, who had canceled at the last minute due to throat problems. I watched the show in my New York hotel room with my journalist friend Michael Paoletta. When Aretha finally finished, I jumped up from the bed and screamed, "Go ahead, girl, you better sing! Shit, you better sing!"

If I'd had a hat I might have flung it down the way a young Aretha had many years before when she heard Clara Ward sing and realized that she wanted to do the same thing. All I knew was that in that one performance on the Grammys, she'd silenced anyone who considered her reign as "the Queen of Soul" to be over, and she'd reinforced her status as one of the most incredibly talented artists of our time. It is great to see that Aretha seems genuinely happy as her career continues its fourth glorious decade, in her prime and at her peak, receiving across-the-board industry recognition for her accomplishments.

For me, all that could top her current renaissance now would be a nice acoustic album with Aretha at the piano, as it was in the old days, working with a tight rhythm section on her interpretations of jazz and blues tunes. Over the past few years, she has provided her fans with a few all-too-brief samples of that, during a BET interview taped in her living room, on a Motown fortieth-anniversary special and a couple of other television appearances. I'd even given up the chance of some peach cobbler for that album! Now that she has her own record label (World Class), Aretha diehards, including myself, just might be lucky. In the meantime, we celebrate her longevity, her ability to survive ever-changing times, and her musical majesty.

ESTI
PHIL
better
be

HER
LIPS

ware !

Blues singer Esther Phillips
performing in Los Angeles
Credit: Archive Photos

Esther Phillips was one soulful diva who you didn't want to fuck with. She had an unforgettable vocal sound, naturally blues-y, as tart as a sour apple but as warm as a hot toddy on a winter's night. It was a razor-edged voice you either loved or loathed. I loved it. I had only a few rough encounters with her myself; indeed, most of my memories of the "I-don't-pull-no-punches" sister from Texas are wonderful. But the story of how she got a check from Creed Taylor's CTI Records back in the mid-1970s gives a clue as to why she earned a reputation for being one of the toughest women in the business.

Esther had been recording for CTI's Kudu label for a few years and had done pretty well with her albums. Like many of the other R&B stars who had grown up in the music business in the 1950s and early 1960s, she was used to being ripped off, and if she suspected that she wasn't being given her full due, she had her own special "remedies"! One winter day, she decided to take matters into her own hand. Clad in a full-length mink, Esther made her way up to the swanky offices of CTI, situated in the heart of Manhattan's Rockefeller Plaza. She was on a mission, and when she got there, she made it perfectly clear.

"I wanna see Creed!" she demanded in her best nasal-toned, "don't-even-try-it" manner. The secretary/receptionist had met Esther before and was somewhat prepared. "Ms. Phillips, he's not available," she replied, barely bothering to see if he was in his office. "You didn't hear me!" Esther roared. "I said I wanna see Creed, and I want a fuckin' check!" "Okay, Ms. Phillips, let me see if he's here," the receptionist responded. A moment later, she said, "I'm sorry, Ms. Phillips, he's not available." Esther wasn't having it! "Listen, bitch," she screamed, opening her coat to reveal a baseball bat, "If you don't get me a fuckin' check now, I'm gonna break this place up! . . . I pay the rent on this fuckin' office, bitch. My records pay your wages ... and I'm not leavin' till I get a goddam check!" In abject terror, the receptionist—who years later would become a publicist at the label before moving on to Atlantic Records to perform the same duties—called back to the inside office. "I think someone better come out and see Ms. Phillips now!" she said timidly. Moments later, another CTI employee came out, check in hand. "Yeah, motherfuckers, you better pay me!" Esther exited, baseball bat firmly tucked under her mink, and headed for the bank to make sure the check was good before any conniving executive could put a stop on it!

I was all of two years old when Esther Mae Jones from Galveston, Texas, was climbing the charts with "Double Crossing Blues," the biggest of ten Top 10 R&B hits she had during a life that took her from the dizzying heights of international fame to the depths of drug-induced despair, and back again. Of all the divas that have passed on, Esther Phillips—"Little Esther" as she was known during her years as a child star—is the one I miss most. She died tragically on August 7, 1984, of liver and kidney failure and—as I comment in the liner notes for *The Best of Esther Phillips 1962-1970*, released by Rhino Records in 1997--"heartbreak, and the highs and lows of a life lived on the edge. Historians [may] have painted a picture of a tragic druggie who only knew despair and depression, and that may indeed have been part and parcel of the complex lady I grew to know and love over an eighteen-year period. . . ."

But when I think of Esther, all I hear is her hearty laugh, and I see that wink in her eyes, that sassy grin. And, of course, there was her highly distinctive, naturally bluesy voice, with its bittersweet, sometimes tart nasal vibrato and echoes of her childhood idol Dinah Washington, a voice like no other that was instantly and immediately recognizable in R&B circles. I might have seen the woman behind the diva, who could cuss better than almost anyone else I've ever met, but others, less fortunate, have a different recollection of the woman who transformed the Beatles' "And I Love Him" into an extraordinary soul opus and Dinah Washington's "What a Diff'rence a Day Makes" into a frenzied disco ditty. Short in stature but mighty, mighty in voice and manner, Esther had the kind of sharp tongue that could freeze an entire room. As veteran producer and Atlantic Records' producer Jerry Wexler recounts in the liner notes I did in 1997, "Esther Phillips was great to work with. Funny, and so sly, so hip. She'd give you that knowing look, like, 'I know where you're comin' from, whitey ... so don't bullshit me, papa! I loved her."

Now, Esther could be really nasty if she didn't know you (as I found out in the 1970s) or if she thought she was being ripped off or, as was often the case, she just didn't want to be bothered. At different times when our paths crossed, I saw that side of her. I also got a chance to get to know the sly, funny, sensitive side of a woman who was the salt of the earth, a down-home mama who pulled no punches and started more than a few fights in her all-too-short-but-action-packed forty-eight years on this earth.

Anyone who knew about Esther's early life as a child star would have some compassion in comprehending why she developed a "reputation" for being tough to deal with, as well as why the drug addiction that plagued much of her adult life had such a crippling effect on her behavior. After all, Esther had no adolescence to speak of, and like so many kids thrown into the limelight without the opportunity to develop "people" skills, she was forced to grow up quickly.

Author Barney Hoskins states in his liner notes for *Better Beware*, a 1990 Charly Records' compilation of Esther's 1950s recordings, she grew up singing in her grandmother's sanctified church, living at different times in Galveston and Houston with her father. She spent her summers in Los Angeles with her mother, finally moving to the city in 1949. Esther's knack for singing was evident to members of her family; Marianna, her sister, had taken her to the Largo theater to perform in a local talent contest.

Esther told Didier Deutsch, the publicist at CTI Records during Esther's stint with the New York-based label, "My older sister and her best friend fixed me up to look much older and took me to this club. At the time, everybody in Watts was digging on a drink called 'White Port and Lemon Juice.' She and her girlfriend wanted some, but they didn't have any money. So they entered me in the contest, and I won ten dollars. They gave me one dollar, and they kept the rest [to buy drinks]."

That night, according to Norbert Hess, a noted German music historian and photographer, as well as a good friend to Esther during her trips to Europe in the 1970s, bandleader Johnny Otis was in the audience when Esther Mae Jones won the contest, singing Dinah Washington's 1949 hit "Baby Get Lost." He invited Esther to come down to his Barrelhouse Club in the Watts section of Los Angeles a few days later. A sharp musician and a shrewd businessman, Otis loved the maturity in Esther's voice and her sheer gutsiness, and asked her mother's permission to take her under his musical wing. Hess recalls in his liner notes for *Set Me Free*, a retrospective of Esther's Atlantic recordings released in 1986, that he'd taken Esther to RPM/Modern Records to cut some tunes but nothing came of the situation.

Having just signed with Savoy Records himself, Otis was producing a vocal group known as the Robins for the label, and Esther, all of thirteen years young, tagged along. Not content to observe the proceedings, she bugged Otis for a chance to record. She got her shot at the end of the session, when there were twenty minutes left to spare. Otis teamed her with Bobby Nunn from the Robins, and they cut an impromptu, unnamed tune. Young Esther's career might have taken a few more years to get going if "Broadway Bill" Cook, a local deejay, hadn't dropped by the offices of Savoy owner Herman Lubinsky. After Cook heard the song that Otis had recorded with Bobby and Esther, he started playing it on the air. He held a contest to give the tune a name, and "Double Crossing Blues," as it became known, was released in the early months of 1950. It climbed to the top of the R&B charts, where it stayed for nine weeks, spending a total of almost eight months on the best-seller lists of that year.

Over the course of the next twelve months, Little Esther's name appeared on the charts no fewer than six more times, making her undeniably the hottest recording artist of 1950. In duet mode with Mel Walker, who was another Johnny Otis "discovery," Esther hit the top with "Mistrustin' Blues" and "Cupid Boogie." She became a national teen star long before she was old enough to vote. Years later, Esther told Didier Deutsch, "The wear and tear of the road was pretty hard on me at that age. Look, it was not a normal life for a young girl. I was the only kid on the tour, so I didn't have any playmates. What I would do is play with the switchboards in the hotels we stayed in. That was my only toy!"

But as Esther spent more and more time on the road and in the company of other artists, the switchboard wouldn't be the only toy. Drugs were easily available to itinerant musicians, and while no one has ever fessed up publicly as to who gave Esther her first shot of heroin, author Barney Hoskyns speculates in his 1990 liner notes, "It may have been [duet partner] Mel Walker, who subsequently died of an overdose of the drug, who turned her on to it." Whoever was responsible, the high-flying days of alcohol, marijuana, and harder narcotics were taking their toll on the teen star. "[I did drugs] just because it was there, it was available," was her comment on the subject in her interview with Deutsch in the late 1960s.

It didn't help matters that Esther wasn't getting a proper education. "I had a tutor up to the time I was supposed to graduate. I never graduated. She gave me a piece of paper; I think they paid her to give me that paper. I really didn't learn anything. I couldn't!" she revealed to Deutsch. "We were traveling on a bus, doing one-nighters and dance halls, and concerts. . . . When we finished a job, we had 600 miles to travel. We slept on the bus and traveled all night. I couldn't deal with any books with all the noise that was going on, anyway. Everybody else was laughing and talking and practicing music. I actually did take some books along with me on the bus, and I really tried . . . but I just couldn't do it!" Years later, Esther reflected, "I never had any childhood, and I've always missed that!"

Not that life was dull for the buxom teenager. Esther's success with Savoy Records made her a prize artist and in a sly move that had some suspect business practices attached to it, the newly formed Federal

Records (a subsidiary of King Records) spirited her away in 1951. She stayed with the label for two years, recording about eighteen tunes but making chart inroads with just one song, "Ring-a-Ding-Doo," a final duet with Mel Walker in the early months of 1952.

Esther's name didn't appear on the charts for another ten years. According to writer Hess, she had a falling out with Johnny Otis during the early part of her stint with Federal Records. As I note in my 1997 liner notes for the Rhino Records anthology, "the main attraction on the bandleader's highly popular revue, her nose was no doubt put out of joint when Willie Mae 'Big Mama' Thornton joined the show. She even recorded her own version of Thornton's "Hound Dog" the same year as Thornton had a hit with it in 1953. A dispute over money reportedly ended the relationship. . . ." Left to deal with the vagaries of the cutthroat aspects of the music business and still in her teens, Esther floated from record deal to record deal, signing with Decca for a quick minute, going back to Savoy for a few years, cutting tunes for a small label called Warwick in 1960, and trying to resuscitate a career that was rapidly fading into oblivion.

Esther had checked into what writer Hoskins called "Kentucky's infamous Lexington Hospital" in an attempt to overcome her drug addiction and was playing dives on the chitlin' circuit where, she told Deutsch, "[there was] just a sink and a toilet, and it was often small and dirty. . . . I had a few rough years just trying to keep my head above water. . . ."

Esther returned to Texas to live with her father; the move to Houston would prove fortuitous. Singing in and around town, she was performing one night in 1962 with a then-unknown Kenny Rogers at Paul's Sidewalk Café, according to writer Hess. The country/pop singer was so impressed with Esther's blues-y delivery on Charlie Rich's "No Headstone on My Grave" that he called his brother, Lelan, who was working in the music industry at the time, to check her out. With partner Bob Gans, Rogers started Lenox Records, and Esther became the label's first recording artist. The new recording deal also brought a name change: "I got the name [Phillips] from the boarding of a Phillips '66 gas station," she told writer Norbert Hess. "I was tired of being 'Little Esther' because I was little no more!"

In a brief conversation in early 1997, Lelan Rogers recounted that the first night Esther stepped into Bradley's recording studio in Nashville was magical. A recording vet at the ripe old age of twenty-seven, Esther poured her entire heart and soul into fourteen, country-and-western songs. The result was awesome. With some of Nashville's top musicians, famed Anita Kerr Singers, and a full orchestra, the diminutive singer laid down definitive versions of such tunes as "Am I That Easy to Forget?"; "I've Forgotten More Than You'll Ever Know About Him"; and a tune that was to become her biggest record as an adult performer.

"Release Me" had been a country hit for Ray Price, Jimmy Heap, and Kitty Wells. Esther's version was the epitome of a great musical fusion, instilling the lyrics with deep soul feeling, and it was right on time. Just months before the great Ray Charles had enjoyed a massive hit with "I Can't Stop Loving You," another country classic. And in 1961, soul man Solomon Burke had done well with his soul-filled version of "Just Out of Reach," another of the gems that Esther recorded for her first chart-making album. Clearly, music buyers and radio listeners alike were open and receptive to hearing the marriage of country and R&B music.

Esther's recording of "Release Me" hit the No. 1 slot on the R&B charts in the early months of 1963, giving her a Top 10 pop smash in the process. All of a sudden, Esther was back in the game—and winning. Even though Lenox Records didn't survive (the company was sold to Atlantic Records), its demise brought her to a label that would appreciate her amazing ability to bring her unique style to a whole range of musical genres.

"Getting a hit on Esther was no easy thing," Atlantic executive Jerry Wexler recalled in our 1997 telephone interview. "We figured she had capabilities in a number of musical areas, so why not try different things with her?" Jack Hooke, who had known Esther since her teen years and had started managing her in the wake of her success with "Release Me" added his own comments to the liner notes for "Set Me Free," Atlantic's 1986 reissue: "Atlantic tried very hard with Esther. They recorded her in lots of different settings. . . ."

Atlantic chief Ahmet Ertegun and Hooke (rumored to be more than just Esther's manager, he was her main love interest for many years) supervised sessions for an album of standards, with tunes like "People," "The Girl from Ipanema," and "Makin' Whoopee." The obvious aim was to get Esther positioned as a supper-club attraction, an artist who could play jazz spots and nightclubs, taking her out of the chitlin' circuit and into more money-making venues. Esther added her own special soulfulness to the songs, and at the very end of the session Ertegun played her another song he wanted her to record. According to Hooke, ". . . she looked at him like he was crazy. She said, 'What does this have to do with me?' Ahmet said to her, "I want you to just sing the melody.' She couldn't understand what it was all about but she did it. . . ."

The song was "And I Love Him," a Lennon-McCartney tune that the

Beatles had recorded as "And I Love Her" earlier in 1964 and that was included in the movie *A Hard Day's Night*. Esther's reading of the song was magnificent. After its release in the spring of 1965, it began its ascent on the charts, giving her a Top 10 R&B hit and a Top 60 pop single. The LP, *And I Love Him! Esther Phillips Sings Great Love Songs*, preceded the single's release, and in a sign of the racist times, it had two different covers. One was a headshot of Esther, complete with a wig and a smile; the other, designed for pop buyers, in the South in particular, was a woven tapestry with a Cupid-like figure that had no relevance to Esther or her singing style. Although no one would admit to it publicly, the bottom line was that Esther looked "too black" with her strong African features, and Atlantic (known primarily as an R&B and jazz company) was afraid that her image would deter white record buyers from purchasing the LP. So much for tolerance.

Esther's success with "And I Love Him" led to her first trip to Britain in November, 1965. As I recount in the liner notes for *The Best of Esther Phillips* in 1997, I formed the Nina Simone Appreciation Society months before, and in one of our first newsletters Esther had been "voted" runner-up to Nina for best artist. This was a good excuse to arrange to meet Esther, and through Tony Hall, a longtime R&B fan and label manager for Atlantic in the U.K., I set up an interview session with her a few days after she arrived in London.

Although I knew that Esther had been "off the scene" for a few years during her attempts at conquering her drug addiction, I really didn't understand that she'd already been a hit-maker in her teens or that although she was just thirty years old, she'd lived a full, often trauma-ridden life. After all, I was just seventeen, still in high school, and prepped for diva encounters only through my first meetings with Nina Simone a few months before.

I met Esther at the Cumberland Hotel, a favorite haunt for visiting American artists. She turned out to be gracious and quite pleasant, if a little guarded. She seemed flattered that people knew her music and was blown away that she'd come in second in the Simone Appreciation Society's readers' poll. Of course, she had no way of knowing that the fan club consisted of all of twenty members, but it mattered little. Esther thought it was "a gas!" to be in England. The Beatles—undoubtedly the hottest group in the business at the time—had been so impressed with her reading of their song that they'd invited her to be a special guest on a television show they were taping.

Esther answered my questions politely, dragging on a cigarette and smiling as she spoke. I asked her about some of her own current favorites of the day, and she was quick to mention labelmate Wilson Pickett's "In the Midnight Hour." With a broad grin, she said the song had particular significance among black listeners. "Baby, we just know all about that midnight hour!" she laughed with the kind of sassiness that I would come to understand many years later.

We hit it off, me, the teenage schoolboy, and Ms. Esther, the former-child-star-but-still-young-earth-mama. She invited me to come see her at a taping for the popular British television show "Ready Steady Go!" Ember Records, an independent U.K. label, had issued Esther's country album and decided to put out "Release Me" as a single. Esther decided to perform the song on the show, and her appearance was so dynamic that she was rewarded with her first British Top 50 pop hit. She asked me to ride back to her hotel with her after the taping, and once in her room she relaxed on her bed and called manager Jack Hooke in New York. "Hooke, I wanna stay here and work, man!" Esther pleaded. "These people really dig my music, and I know I can get some dates here. I don't want to come back and do those rinky-dink dives, man." Hooke was having none of it. He'd booked Esther to open for none other than Britain's own Tom Jones in Bermuda, and more dates were in the offing.

Esther hung up the telephone, angry, pouting, and not in the mood for conversation. While she'd been begging Hooke to let her stay in Britain, I'd been staring at an object on the dresser. I couldn't figure out what it was; it didn't look like anything I'd ever seen before. I just had to ask Esther what I was looking at, so I summoned up all the schoolboy nerve I could. "What?" she snapped. "I just want to know what this thing is," I said meekly, considering that I hadn't chosen the moment well. Esther sat straight up on the bed and burst out laughing. "That's my wig, sugar! You ain't never seen one before?" Indeed, I hadn't seen anything remotely similar to the blonde wig perched carefully on its stand. Blushing every color of crimson, I proffered a proper British apology. "Oh, I'm sorry!" I gushed, while Esther tried to compose herself. "Hey, no problem, baby!" she replied, grinning as I got up to leave.

I saw Esther one more time before she left London. Tony Hall had invited me to stop by on the day of her departure. Esther had another visitor on that last day: a U.S. singer who hadn't had much stateside success but who had made her home in the U.K. She was there to say goodbye but she was decidedly frosty when we were introduced. I didn't understand why and was even more confused when Esther asked me to step outside for a moment, leaving her and her friend alone. Only years later did I understand that her "friend" had brought along a "gift" for Esther. I'd never encountered anyone with a drug habit, but I knew something was "different" when I re-entered the room. Feeling decidedly uneasy, I made a hasty exit.

In the seven or so years until Esther and I came face to face again, she went through many changes. As the 1960s went on, Esther was dealing with a monkey on her back; she was having a tough time kicking her drug habit. Singer Etta James, a self-confessed addict, recalls in her autobiography how she and Esther had started a check-cashing scheme as way to get dope: "bouncing from hotel to hotel, we kept ourselves high for weeks." Esther was known throughout the New York music business as quite a character. Atlantic labelmate Doris Troy remembers Esther's behavior on one particular night: "(British singer) Dusty Springfield was opening for the first time at a club in New York City. I knew Dusty from my visits to Britain, and she was really cool and soulful. Well, who knows why, but Miss Esther Phillips insisted on talking real loud all the way through Dusty's set! We tried to keep Esther quiet, but she just wouldn't shut up! That was Esther for you ... always real!"

After the initial burst of interest surrounding "And I Love Him," Atlantic had a difficult time selling Esther's records. *Esther*, a second LP, put her fairly and squarely in a jazz setting with big-band arrangements alternating with tracks that had a more intimate, "late-night" feel. The highlights included a wonderful version of "As Tears Go By," a song popularized by British chanteuse Marianne Faithfull; the bossa nova-like "You Can't Go Home Again"; and the plaintive "I Could Have Told You," transformed from a Frank Sinatra ballad into a heartbreaking torch song by La Phillips. Although the album didn't produce any hits, an "answer" song to Percy Sledge's smash "When a Man Loves a Woman" put Esther back onto the charts in 1966. The story goes that she and Sledge got together at a party after his first appearance at the Apollo in Harlem and sang the tune for hours!

The following year, in an attempt to cash in on the success of British singer Engelbert Humperdinck's version of "Release Me," Atlantic reissued Esther's single. After it made a brief chart appearance in 1967, the label reissued her Lenox LP under the name *The Country Side of Esther Phillips*, with a photograph depicting her wearing the blonde wig that had led to my embarrassing encounter with her two years earlier.

Recording-wise nothing seemed to be working: Esther recorded more material in a jazz vein and kept trying for R&B hits with an assortment of great singles, including "Try Me," "When Love Comes to the Human Race," and "I'm Sorry," but none made any chart noise. It didn't help matters that her drug use had increased. When Atlantic finally dropped her from the label in 1968 amid rumors that she was missing and canceling gigs, it was obvious that Esther was at a crossroads.

According to Norbert Hess in his 1986 liner notes, she joined Synanon, described as "a re-education community founded in 1958 to provide an answer for people who seek a more fulfilling way of life and find it in Synanon's totally integrated, non-violent and drugfree community." It was a no-nonsense rehabilitation program, and although Esther never spoke about the experience publicly, it clearly affected her: during her stay there, she recorded a gospel tune,"I Will Greatly Rejoice," for a special album entitled *Prince of Peace* that Epic Records did at Synanon.

Esther also landed a new deal with Roulette Records and cut three singles, one of which, a version of the Glen Campbell song "Too Late to Worry, Too Blue to Cry," made the charts and reunited her with Lelan Rogers from her "Release Me" days. Finally out of Synanon in September, 1969, Esther headed to Los Angeles to consider her options. A conversation with a longtime friend, famed sax player King Curtis, led to a new contract with Atlantic. Esther had begun doing gigs in Los Angeles, performing at a club owned by comedian Redd Foxx and getting rave reviews. A date at Freddie Jett's Pied Piper Club, a popular jazz and blues venue, provided the perfect opportunity for Esther to showcase her wares. And with King Curtis in charge of production, she cut an amazing album called *Burnin'*," which featured hits like "And I Love Him" and "Release Me" alongside her blues-drenched readings of classics like Percy Mayfield's "Please Send Me Someone to Love" and "I'm Getting 'Long Alright," an old tune Big Maybelle did many years before.

Esther's opening rap for that tune was particularly telling: "I'd like to do this song for all my lady friends because we always have the blues, you see. They're usually created by the menfolk, especially on Friday, when the eagle flies and they don't wanna give up the money to pay the folks for the televisions and stereos. . . ." As I point out in the liner notes for the 1997 Rhino anthology, "Depicting a hard-core reality that came from years of givin' and not gettin,' Esther's tell-all take on everyday ghetto life, seen through the eyes of black women everywhere, was on the money. She was no-shit, tellin' it, straight up, uncut . . . the rap on this tune speaks volumes about the woman and her life. . . ." Showing another side of her persona, Esther recorded "Long John Blues," a raunchy old blues tune associated with her musical inspiration, Dinah Washington. The song ended up on *Confessin' the Blues*, an LP released by Atlantic. "Long John Blues" was the tale of a girl who went to visit her "dentist" to get her cavity filled, a saucy song filled with delightful double entendres that Esther sang with the kind of sassy wit that I later learned was very much a part of her real-life personality.

Atlantic had a special party to celebrate the album's release at the end of the year, and the LP did good business. Meanwhile, after she completed the recording of *Burnin'*, 1970 continued with a reunion with Johnny Otis at the old Barrelhouse Club, the scene of Esther's original "discovery" by bandleader Otis. This performance was televised. Esther continued the year with appearances on "The Tonight Show with Johnny Carson" and comedian Bob Hope's "Honor America" show, as well as at the Monterey Jazz Festival, again with Otis. Even before releasing the live album, Atlantic had decided to send Esther down to Miami, Florida, to record with a group of musicians known as the Dixie Flyers. She cut a whole album that included versions of the Van Morrison tunes "Crazy Love" and "Brand New Day," along with a version of "Set Me Free," a song originally recorded by soul man Clarence Carter. Manager Jack Hooke recalled, "[The song] was picked out for her by [Atlantic executive] Jerry Wexler. . . . I loved the way she did that, and I thought we had a sure hit. But we didn't have any luck with it."

Esther wasn't too happy with the results of her Miami sessions, and apparently neither was Atlantic: ". . . we just couldn't seem to find the right material; they wanted to try some real pop kinda things, so one day, they called me and said, 'Look, we've lost quite a bit cutting things on you,' and they gave me a release from my contract," Esther recounted during a telephone interview in 1972, our first contact since our meeting in London in 1965. Her next move proved to be the most significant in her career as an adult performer, finally giving her the kind of recognition she'd long deserved.

Veteran jazzman Creed Taylor had formed two labels, CTI and Kudu, in late 1971, and according to Esther, "Disc jockeys round the country put Kudu on to me—they told them I was free from contracts, so we signed a deal for one album. . . ." That LP, *From a Whisper to a Scream*, was so musically strong that no less a diva than Aretha Franklin gave Esther the 1972 Grammy Award she'd received for *Young, Gifted & Black* because she considered Esther's album to be more deserving. Over tight tracks that featured such stellar musicians as Richard Tee, Cornell Dupree, Eric Gale, Gordon Edwards, Hank Crawford, and Airto Moreira, Esther gave some exceptional performances on tunes like "Baby I'm for Real," the Allen Toussaint-penned title track, and the blues-y "Scarred Knees." But the knockout track was "Home Is Where the Hatred Is," a song about the life of a junkie, penned by poet/artist Gil Scott-Heron.

111

"Creed Taylor asked me to do the song but, naturally, I went through quite a lot of emotional changes before I agreed to do it," Esther revealed during our telephone chat in late 1972 on the occasion of the release of *Alone Again Naturally*, her second Kudu LP. "After all, although everyone knew about the problems I'd faced, singing the song was just like being interviewed about it all in public. I really don't want to do it—fact is, I continually postponed recording it, and it was the very last song we did for the album. . . ."

The three albums that followed *From a Whisper to a Scream* did well without becoming hardcore best-sellers, and each had special moments. Certainly, *Alone Again Naturally* was a standout and included a brilliant cover of the Gilbert O'Sullivan hit, a funky read of Bill Withers's "Use Me," and the unforgettable "Georgia Rose," Esther's way of paying tribute to black women. *Black-Eyed Blues*, the follow-up set, was a personal favorite, featuring the blues opus "You Could Have Had Me Baby," the Ellington classic "I Got It Bad and That Ain't Good," and "Too Many Roads," penned by Aretha Franklin's sister Carolyn. *Performance*, a 1974 LP, was no great shakes, but it did include a fine version of Dr. John's "Such a Night" and Gene McDaniels's thought-provoking "Disposable Society."

As important as best-selling albums night be, Esther, who was now living in Los Angeles, was nonetheless working more than ever. She'd performed on several shows with other labelmates, such as Grover Washington Jr., and had started playing European jazz festivals. Her career seemed to be on track. This didn't mean that she'd lost any of the personal "bite" that still made her tough for some folks to handle. I got my own taste of the sharper side of her personality when she finally returned to London in June, 1973. Pye Records, the U.K. licensee for CTI, had arranged a special press event for her opening night at Ronnie Scott's club. This proved to be a big mistake: Esther had been unable to bring her own musicians, and in spite of rehearsals she was clearly unhappy with the level of playing that the British band was providing. It was obvious that she wasn't in a particularly good mood when we were reintroduced. I don't remember what she said, but she was curt, cold, and unresponsive. It was if we'd never met before, and I could see that the conversation was going nowhere, so I backed off. With her dissatisfaction with the band apparent during the show, the main highlight was "Cry Me a River Blues," which afforded the audience a chance to see her play the piano—and she played her ass off!

Apparently, I was far from the only one with whom Esther could be less than friendly. As former CTI executive Didier Deutsch reflects in his liner notes for *The Best of Esther Phillips*, a 1990 CD release, "Esther was a most difficult woman. She had acquired such a reputation while she was under contract at CTI that staff members studiously avoided answering the phone when they knew she was calling. . . ." In his essay for the reissue of *From a Whisper to a Scream*, Deutsch recalls, ". . . she was mostly known as a terror, likely to make long-distance phone calls from Los Angeles . . . and be extremely abusive to whomever picked up the phone when she couldn't get what she had called about in the first place. . . ." Thankfully, it was a mutual friend that brought Esther and me together in a more harmonious way in the wake of Esther's success with "What a Diff'rence a Day Makes," her 1975 remake of the Dinah Washington 1960s hit.

The idea for putting Esther in a more contemporary, dance-oriented setting came from an A&R man at CTI, and from the very beginning she'd been less than happy at the prospect. Thanks to Doris Troy, Esther and I got a chance to talk after her opening at New York's Bottom Line club in the summer of 1975. She told me straight up, "If you're okay with Doris Troy, you're okay with me!" and from that moment until the last conversation we had in 1983, she stayed true to that statement.

Talking with me about the new album she'd made with guitarist Joe Beck, she confessed, ". . . the album was cut in a totally different way to how I usually work. We all work on the material—I submit songs, Creed does. . . . Usually, I go into the studios and cut my vocal with the rhythm section at the same time, but this time Creed wouldn't let me—he finished the tracks beforehand! The reason? Well, he says I have a tendency to co-produce, which is true! I'll go in there and say, 'Let's try it like this' or whatever. But this time he put his foot down. . . . And I must say, it was tough for me. . . . So, I just went in there and did my best!"

One of the funnier aspects surrounding the album was the photo shoot for the cover. It depicted Esther with boa constrictor! ". . . When I got to the studio, everyone was getting ready, and I noticed people started to get cagey, nervous. . . . then I saw it! [The photographer] Alan had a boa constrictor wrapped around his waist. Eventually, they got me to hold it. . . . It was after I had a Colt 45! Well, I decided to touch it and found it was nothing like I'd expected. . . . Eventually, we got to take the pictures and then Connie (the boa) decided she was nervous and wet all over the floor! Don't ask me how I smiled [for the album cover]. I guess I just had one more Colt 45 to give me the courage!"

Esther clearly did have the courage to face the new challenge of having a massive hit record. "What a Diff'rence a Day Makes" became a monster international pop, R&B, and dance smash, and she was happy about the whole project: "I feel like we've been picking up momentum all the time. . . . You know, when you're classified as an R&B act, you can only draw a certain element (of the population). I feel that maybe this (new) album is gonna be the one to 'release me'! . . . But, you know, it's very hard to work without a record, and that's why I'm so happy to see the reaction we're getting on this one." Obviously, Esther was experiencing a whole new level of recognition and found herself literally crisscrossing the country and traveling overseas: "My mother asked me if it was really worth it all—all the traveling about, everything. And I called her the other day to tell her that I had a hit record—so it was worth it all!"

The fact that the song had been previously recorded by one of Esther's musical heroes hadn't gone unnoticed by critics, who often compared her vocal style to that of the woman known as "The Queen." But Esther wasn't fazed: "I always take that as a compliment, you know. I really didn't listen to any other singer up until I was fourteen years old so naturally I tended to adapt her style. But I think people don't realize that although I did that, our ranges, for instance, are very different. . . . But, you know, I'm so happy because "What a Diff'rence" has drawn people's attention back to Dinah. . . . This was the first song I'd ever recorded of Dinah's because when she died, a lot of people came out with tributes . . . and I felt that it was like capitalizing on her death. . . ."

That Esther's career was moving into high gear was quite obvious: I saw her at the famous Coconut Grove in Los Angeles in October, 1975, and she turned it out, eliciting standing ovations in a packed room for a performance that included tunes that showcased her blues-y style, as well as key tracks from her then-current hit LP. A year later Esther was still enjoying the impact of the success of "What a Diff'rence a Day Makes," even though *For All We Know*, a follow-up album, might have gone too far in trying to turn her into a disco queen and did only moderately well for her.

I saw Esther perform at New York's Bottom Line in the summer of 1976 just after the release of *For All We Know*. She seemed happy and content before the show, but the events that followed quickly brought on a change of mood. Apparently, the good old Internal Revenue Service (IRS) had been after her for some tax money she owed and, unbeknownst to Esther, had put a lien on her fee for the night. Without telling her, the club manager simply handed over her fee. In the tradition of many R&B stars from the 1950s and 1960s, Esther had asked for the money before going onstage; the manager broke the news to her then. "Well, y'all," Esther angrily stated as she took to the stage after a long warm-up by her band, "This is the Bottom Line, and the bottom line is, you better enjoy this show 'cause I ain't gonna be back here again! The motherfuckin' club manager gave my money to the fuckin' IRS. But I'm gonna sing for y'all anyway—you're just gettin' a free fuckin' show!" And what a show it was, filled with emotion and intensity: Esther had channeled all her rage and anger into her performance and gave it all she had.

Indeed, even with the success Esther was having, she could still be a trip; however, the time I saw her at a black radio convention in the summer of 1976, her reaction to the events that took place was justified. The organization in question was NATRA (National Association of Television & Radio Announcers), which had been in existence for twenty-one years when the powers that be had decided to hold the annual meeting on the Caribbean island of Antigua. As I noted in the report I filed for *Blues & Soul* in September, ". . . the logistics and problems involved in transporting 750 people from the States to Antigua and accommodating them on an island which is not used to such 'invasions' are innumerable. . . ." After a number of delays while we waited for various artists, including Esther, to board our chartered plane, we finally left New York at 2 A.M. and arrived on the tiny island only to find that all the hotel reservations hadn't been made, and several travel-weary industry types were less than thrilled at the ensuing delays.

I recalled one of the true high points of the trip in liner notes for Rhino's *Best of* anthology in 1997: "Organizers of the event—an excuse for radio programmers and jocks to hang with promo men and women from different labels and strike all manner of (under-the-table) deals—had flown Esther in from a gig in Italy for the occasion. She was to be honored as "Best Female Jazz Artist," but things didn't go according to plan. . . ."

"Two storm-drenched days had made the hastily constructed outdoor stage unusable. Monday night and Tuesday night were washouts, so Esther and other acts like the Spinners, Donald Byrd, and Brass Construction were unable to perform. . . . Wednesday was awards night, and in typical fashion the event started late and dragged on. Some brave soul broke the news to Esther that she would be able to sing only one song. "I have something to say!" were the first words out of her mouth. "I am no one-song singer!" She was then advised that she could sing three songs . . . and finally, "Then I'm told that I'm canceled and [that] this is Roulette Records' night. . . ." Her face tight and unsmiling, a trace of gin on her lips, Esther went off: "Well, I won't be short-stopped. You all know that I ain't no newcomer to this business. I've been out here for twenty-eight years and, motherfuckers, I will not be stopped like this. Just gimme a rhythm section—that's all I want—a piano player to play E-flat on the blues, no horns, just a rhythm section."

After an awkward moment or two of silence, musicians slowly began to respond as a stunned audience cheered. Esther launched into churnin,' no-shit blues, opening with the words "You must be crazy, baby," clearly directing the comment at the embarrassed NATRA organizers. Much to the amazement of those who didn't know she had the skill, she sat down at the piano to play some chords that would have done most Sunday-morning-holy-roller-in-the-spirit-get-down-with-the-get-down church organists proud. Some particularly stupid NATRA lackey asked if Esther was close to ending her impromptu set. Big, big mistake! She stopped for a moment, glowered, drew all 5'4" of herself up to the mike, and made it clear. "No, I ain't finished yet!" Those of us who were close enough to the stage could have sworn we heard the word "motherfucker" finish that statement. Esther, who evolved from child star, to junkie, to 1960s hit-maker, to recovered addict, to jazz diva, to disco queen, to blues mama, finished a cutting version of the bawdy "Long John Blues," picked up her award, said a curt "Thank you, NATRA," headed offstage, . . . and out of the building!" The next day she invited me to her room for a chat. "Sit down, child!" Esther smiled, informing me that she was searching frantically for tampons. "I turned it out last night, didn't I?" she beamed. "'NATRA motherfuckers, tryin' to mess with me! Shit!" Asking me to leave the room for a moment—tampons duly found—Esther then asked me to go with her to the hotel's kitchen. She told the staff that she wanted to make some fried chicken, Southern style.The next thing we knew, Esther Phillips—the sanctified, stomped-down, blues girl singer, who could put the fear of God into grown men with a mere glance—was cooking up enough chicken for almost the entire crew attending NATRA."

I saw Esther again a few months later at the Village Gate in New York. She was doing material from a new Kudu album, *Capricorn Princess*, which would in fact be her last for the label. She was in good voice and good humor, even when the mike she was using broke in half. She smiled, put it back together, and kept on going, once again delivering a stellar performance, something her growing audiences had come to expect. the highlights included tunes from the new record such as "Boy, I Really Tied One on Last Night," a Janis Ian song; "Candy," a Big Maybelle hit of the 1950s; and "I Haven't Got Anything Better to Do," a plaintive ballad that explored the melancholy aftermath of a relationship that has ended. Like so many of her other songs, it had a wring of personal testimony to it that gave a clue to Esther's own dealings with matters of the heart.

But Esther's attention was on other matters when she joined Mercury Records in 1977. It was a big money deal, probably the best one she'd ever nabbed in her career. She would act as executive producer for the albums she made for Mercury through Esto Productions, her own company, and she had the final say about songs, musicians, and producers. She chose to work with longtime friend and musical associate Pee Wee Ellis, and front cover of the first LP, *You've Come a Long Way, Baby*, depicted a smiling Esther standing next to a fancy Rolls Royce; the back cover including a photograph of her that was obviously taken during her formative years! I remember stopping by the studio when she was recording just to say hello, and she was in good spirits and upbeat about her new situation, and was busy chatting with Ellis (a former James Brown sideman) about what she wanted to do for the record. The album itself was probably the finest of the four albums she recorded for the company, mixing some nice blues tunes like "You've Been a Good Ole Wagon" with Van Morrison's "Into the Mystic" and Dinah Washington's "Somewhere Along the Way."

But album sales weren't great, and nothing much happened with the follow-up, *All About Esther*, even though it included some fine material like "Pie in the Sky," "Native New Yorker," and the biting "Ms.," which in many ways described Esther herself. In an attempt to revive her fortunes, she cut an album of mostly dance-oriented music, called *Here's Esther . . . Are You Ready*, in the hope that music buyers would embrace it the way they had her disco work at Kudu. But times had changed, and there was something forced about the whole thing. It must have been 1980 or 1981 when I visited Esther at her Los Angeles pad. She lived in an apartment building smack dab in the middle of Hollywood on Sunset Boulevard at the site of what is now the Mondrian Hotel. She was in a good frame of mind, looking out for songs for her next album, and was her usual earthy self, liberally throwing "motherfuckers" into her conversation, left, right, and center. I didn't overstay my welcome: I remember Esther asked me to help her find a tape of some songs she'd temporarily misplaced; once we found the tape, I went on my way when some more of her friends stopped by.

Esther's last album for Mercury, *Good Black Is Hard to Crack*, was released in 1981, but again there was little public response. Meanwhile, she'd finally fulfilled a dream by buying a home in the Mount Olympus section of the Hollywood Hills, and she'd married. Over the years, we'd never talked much about her personal life, and since she didn't bring it up, I didn't either. We'd established a good, warm, and friendly relationship, and I saw no reason to intrude in areas that seemed off-limits. I'd heard the rumors about her relationship with manager Jack Hooke; I also knew he was a married man and had been told that he simply idolized her. But Esther wanted more. As longtime friend Doris Troy told me, ". . . The thing about Esther was she wanted to be just an everyday person, settle down with a man, have some kids. . . ."

In her autobiography, her good friend Etta James reveals that Esther confessed to carrying a torch for R&B singer Latimore but married C.B. Atkins, a man who had previously been wed to the late jazz great Sarah Vaughan. The relationship didn't go well: Atkins ended up spending much of the money Esther had amassed during her good years and then split. When we last talked in 1983, she explained, "I wanted to settle down, get a house, and do all that kind of stuff. . . . I did everything I could to make it work, I cooked, I cleaned. . . ." But it wasn't to be, and although she was without a major record deal, Esther kept herself busy by doing dates in Europe and playing small jazz clubs. She talked with me about writing a book about her life. She was in a reflective mood, which might have accounted for a call she made to Didier Deutsch, her old friend from CTI. He mentions in his notes for the Sony music collection *The Best of Esther Phillips* that she'd phoned him out of the blue "to reminisce with someone who had been close to her during that time (with CTI).... I could sense that she was trying to say something. . . ." Those years at CTI were among the best in my life. At the time, I didn't realize it, but I did some of my best work with Creed (Taylor)."

The last time I saw Esther perform, it was obvious that her health had deteriorated. She seemed tired and worn, and I suspected that she was drinking again. Although she hadn't done hard drugs, it was obvious that she still liked her alcohol; I'd heard on the street that Esther was the kind of woman who had a tendency to befriend people who didn't always have her best interests at heart.

In Esther's final year, things seemed to be looking up for the woman who reportedly was Aretha Franklin's inspiration for "Sister From Texas," a song she wrote and recorded in 1972. Esther made a one-off single for a label called Winning, entitled "Turn Me Out," and Jack Hooke secured her last album deal with Muse Records. In the studios, she worked with arranger Dave Matthews, who had been one of the key players during her Kudu years. The album contained covers of songs ranging from the Shirelles' "Mama Said" to "Going in Circles," a song first popularized by the Friends of Distinction and, later, Isaac Hayes.

Ironically, "A Way to Say Goodbye," the last song on the album, which was eventually released in 1986, became the title track. Esther's final curtain call came on August 7, 1984, just a few months after she finished working on the record. She'd been admitted to a Washington, DC, hospital in the spring with a liver complaint, but the problem seemed to have been resolved and Esther was back to work. In fact, she was performing at the Vine Street Bar & Grill in Hollywood, which, thanks to owner Ron Bernstein, had become a regular spot for her just weeks before she was admitted to Harbor-UCLA Medical Center.

The official cause of death was liver and kidney failure, compounded by problems with her heart and lungs. Although Esther was fading fast, she had enough lucidity to spot her old pal Etta James singing at the Olympic Games in Los Angeles during the last few months of her hospitalization. "That's my friend," she told one of her nurses. When she finally died, Esther Mae Jones, age forty-eight, weighed less than ninety pounds. Years of struggle, heartbreak, addiction, and abuse had taken their toll. At a packed ceremony that Johnny Otis (who was now a minister) presided over at the Angelus Funeral Home, singer Linda Hopkins sang "How Great Thou Art," keyboardist Plas Johnson played "Release Me," and mourners cried their eyes out. Esther was laid to rest at Lincoln Memorial Park in Compton, and her body was removed to Forest Lawn Memorial Park in Hollywood Hills.

Altantic Records' chairman Ahmet Ertegun had a few final thoughts to share when the label issued its 1986 retrospective: ". . . I remember what is for me a historic evening when Otis Redding, Phil Spector, and I went to hear Esther in a small club. Otis got up and sang duets with her, and after the last show was over, the four of us stayed up all night together. She was one of my favorite singers of all time. I treasure the time I spent with her and the delightful experience of producing records with her. She is very much missed." And Jack Hooke, who had been with her through all the ups and downs of twenty years or more, commented, ". . . she had so much soul! Even when she was sick she could put over a song. I don't expect to hear anyone like her again." And, personally, I don't expect to meet anyone like her again: Esther was one of a kind, and I can still see that broad grin and that sly smile. I can hear that sharp wit. And no one I knew could say the word "motherfucker" quite like she did. Like Ertegun and all the others who were touched by her life, I miss her greatly.

just one look...

Chapter 5

Doris Troy performing
Credit: Michael Ochs
Archives/Venice, CA

Doris Troy's eyes became moist, and she tried to hold back the tears as she listened, incredulous, to the voice at the other end of the transatlantic call. "For real? Really, darlin'?" Doris was sitting in the neat living room in her London flat. I'd just handed her the telephone, and Suzan Jenkins, who was then executive director of the Rhythm & Blues Foundation, was informing the originator of the timeless classic "Just One Look" that she'd been selected to receive a Pioneer Award for her services to R&B. It didn't hurt that the award was accompanied by a check for $15,000, prompting the tears of joy and disbelief. It was way past due. Incredibly, Doris, who was lovingly nicknamed "Mama Soul" by her many British fans, had created an entire career out of her one U.S. hit. Her ability to survive against all odds earned her a place on the Foundation's honor roll—and in this book.

While likely the least well-known of the soulful divas covered here, Doris Troy's unstoppable faith and courage, along with a heart as large as her musical talent, made her a prime candidate. That she'd also been one of the first people to encourage me in my own journalistic pursuits was an added factor. But Doris's presence among super divas like Aretha, Diana, Dionne, Patti, and Gladys is justified since she represents all the workaday R&B stars of the 1960s who never received mass recognition but who continue to share their talent. She is quite simply a real soul survivor, and the only diva who can claim to have played the part of her own mother in a successful musical (*Mama I Want to Sing*) based on her own life story.

Remarkable, indeed, is that while many of the R&B hit-makers of 1963 have long since vanished, Doris has never given up, and through some lean and tough times she has persevered—and flourished. And as Doris has flourished, so has "Just One Look." In 1998 the song was used once again in a television commercial (for Direct TV), and on an almost annual basis the tune ends up in a film or jingle somewhere in the world. "You know, baby, when I recorded that song in that little basement studio in New York, I asked God to keep that song alive forever. And you know, He answers prayers! Cause something's happened with 'Just One

Look' every year since," Doris beams. "You know God is a good God!"

Beyond just the warm, distinctive, and soulful vocal style that has endeared her to music lovers most especially in Europe where she has always maintained her popularity as a live performer regardless of recording output, there are an upbeat personality, kindness, generosity, and happy-go-lucky disposition that have helped Doris get through countless music business ripoffs, personal heartaches, and health challenges. To those lucky enough to get to know her, she is a salt-of-the-earth kind of woman, funny, witty, and always "down-home." While she knows how to don a glamorous gown and her Diana Ross-styled wig—or, in her own words "fluff up!"—Doris never puts on airs and graces. Her unwillingness to be pretentious and her very basic "realness" might not have won her any favors among music-business high rollers who like their divas to be ultra-grand, but these qualities have won her many friends the world over.

In all the years since I met Doris (as a good friend to Enid Buckland-Evers, her first British fan-club secretary back in 1965), I've never seen her lose it. Sure, sometimes when she is upset, she is a little pissy. And more than a few times, I've heard her curse about some situation or other, usually in reference to some music-biz madness. But Doris doesn't get truly angry, get nasty, or be the proverbial bitch that most divas are expected to be.

Is Doris the one diva in this book that is in line for sainthood? I doubt it! Back in her day, she would laugh and joke with me about "poppin' her fingers," a down-on-the-ground 1960s expression that referred to matters of the flesh. Of course, there were a few guys whose hearts were no doubt bruised when Doris couldn't handle what she might have considered the confines or restrictions of a conventional relationship. She often had little get-togethers at her London apartment during the 1970s when she was recording for the Beatles' Apple label, but I never saw Doris drunk or messed up, only high-spirited, the life of the party, always ready with a big smile.

She was born Doris Higginsen in the Bronx, New York, to a minister (originally from Barbados) and raised in a pretty strict household. "My daddy had his own chapel in New York, and on Sundays you could go in there for the whole day if you wanted. You could pray and sing all day long; they even served soul food and refreshments in there," she told British R&B expert Dave Godin during a 1970 interview for *Blues & Soul* magazine. Although she never got to hear secular music at home, Doris didn't live that far from the famed Apollo Theater in Harlem, and she remembered sneaking into the popular venue in her mid-teens. "I guess

I was around sixteen, and I decided that I should go out and get me a job," she revealed in a 1974 chat we had. "Well, being a preacher's daughter, I was supposed to keep away from popular music. [But] the Apollo theater was just round the corner. . . . I knew I wasn't supposed to go in there but one day, I applied for a job there as an usherette. I lied about my age and I got it, and honey, I knew I just wanted to get up there onstage. I saw so many famous people, Dinah Washington, Pearl Bailey who was the first one I saw . . . and Sarah Vaughan, Etta James. It was a gas! Well, I got together with some girlfriends, and we formed a trio [The Halos]. Next thing, we got to appear just down the road [from the Apollo], and everyone dropped in to see us. . . ."

The job at the Apollo was big fun, Doris told Godin: "It was real enough. I had the uniform and a flashlight and everything. . . . I started to spend my off-duty hours in this restaurant in New York where out-of-work artists and composers hung out. . . ." The music bug had bitten Doris, and although her mother came by the Apollo and told her that she had to quit working there, Doris knew what she wanted. Hanging out with Vaughan, who she would occasionally sew gowns for, and Washington, who Doris considered "the greatest!", was the inspiration. After the Halos didn't pan out, Doris tried her hand at songwriting. She wrote "How About That" and in her own words, ". . . I just took it along to this publisher, signed a paper, and got a $100 advance! The next thing I knew was that [singer] Dee Clark had recorded it on Vee-Jay, and it was on the charts! . . . And it taught me that determination gets you a long way in show business."

Using "Payne," her grandmother's name, for her showbiz activities, Doris also recorded her first single, "I Want to Be Loved" for Everest Records. The record came out in 1960 and quickly disappeared, but Doris was just getting the hang of the New York music scene. It was an exciting time for pop and R&B performers in the Big Apple: independent labels like Scepter/Wand and Atlantic were making strides, and Tin Pan Alley, an area consisting of a few blocks in midtown Manhattan, was the place to be for aspiring artists and songwriters.

Doris made one more one-off single, "Dream Talk," as part of a duo known as Jay & Dee for the tiny Arliss label, but it went nowhere. She quickly found that one of the easiest ways to be in the mix and make some money was singing background vocals on New York sessions. She recalled in 1974, "I worked as a backup session vocalist . . . and . . . Dionne and Dee Dee Warwick came across from Jersey—they were still in school, I think—and [at first] they didn't want to do anything outside of gospel, but I managed to persuade them. . . ."

Doris, Dionne, and Dee Dee did many of the sessions at Atlantic Records for Solomon Burke and the Drifters all the way through to December, 1963, months after both Doris and Dionne had had their own chart hits. An entry log in the Atlantic Records' sessions reports showed the three D's on the Drifters' recording session at which writer Burt Bacharach "discovered" Dionne. Over the years, after she'd achieved international stardom, Dionne never forgot Doris and those early days. And during one of Dionne's visits to the U.K., she came by the Troy apartment in London. Doris had invited me along to hang out, and I was in awe when Dionne walked in the room. She'd been my first R&B love, and although I'd gone to the airport to meet her as a doting fan, I'd never been in a more intimate setting with her. I distinctly remember being nervous, but in her usual cheery way Doris made me feel like a part of the proceedings.

Doris, Dionne, and a few other friends, including then Apple labelmate Billy Preston, had decided to head down to a West End club. Although I was quite prepared to head home, Doris insisted that I tag along. I felt a tad more comfortable with Dionne and made some idle chat, but my awe for my idol was still apparent. Not knowing who I was or what I was doing there, Dionne was polite but a little distant. Doris wanted to make sure I was included: "C'mon, chile," she said with a grin, "come on and hang with us! You know, Dionne, David here is one of the best R&B writers. He knows his stuff. He can tell you who recorded what and when and where and all of that. You know how these British kids are all into R&B . . . well, he knows every record we ever made, girl!"

Years later, after Dionne and I got to know each other, she would always refer to Doris in the fondest way, and on more than one occasion she invited her longtime buddy down to her shows when she was performing in Las Vegas, which had become Doris's home in the 1980s. Doris noted that she was particularly moved during one performance: "Miss Dionne had me seated right in front, and when she was getting ready to sing her hit, "That's What Friends Are For," she introduced me, had me stand up, and told everybody about how we all started out together. Now that's what I call a friend!" Doris smiled.

"Those were real groovy days," Doris told writer Godin in 1970, referring to her session work on the New York music scene. Always street-smart and looking for new ways to move her career forward, Doris was buoyed by the success of the Dee Clark record that had made it into the R&B Top 10 in 1960. In between session work, she focused her energy and attention on writing more songs. The song that changed her life was cut just after Doris had finished a recording date with popular R&B crooner

Chuck Jackson for a song entitled "Tell Him I'm Not Home." Jackson, a hit-maker thanks to songs like "Any Day Now" and "I Wake Up Crying," had already asked her to tour with him as part of his live revue. As it turned out, the timing would prove perfect.

"You wanna know about 'Just One Look'? Well, baby, that was a demo!" Doris laughed when we got together in the spring of 1974 just after she'd finished recording a one-off album for a British label, B&C Records. Working in New York in a basement studio at 1650 Broadway, one of the main music-industry hubs in the city at the time, Doris and her friend Gregory Carroll had come up with the song. The demo of the nifty little tune with the ska-like beat was cut on a small three-track machine, with a quartet of well-known session musicians: Horace Ott on piano, Napoleon 'Snags' Allen on guitar, Barney Richmond on bass, and Bruno Carr on drums. The wonders of then-"modern" technology meant that Doris was able to sing her own background parts, double-tracking herself in what was considered a unique way at the time.

Knowing that she was heading out on a national tour with Jackson, Doris took her demo to Juggy Murray, the head of Sue Records, a label that was hot with Ike & Tina Turner. "He just sat on the tape," Doris recalled in a 1994 interview for the release of *Just One Look: The Best of Doris Troy* on CD, "so I took it over to Jerry Wexler at Atlantic Records, and they flipped out! Next thing I know, they put it out in the form we recorded it, as a demo!"

Naming herself after the historical Greek beauty Helen of Troy, Doris hit the road with Jackson while Atlantic released the single in each market they played. "The record took off so damn fast that it sold like crazy, and it was really lucky for me to be touring at the same time since Atlantic was able to arrange all sorts of promotional stints and interviews to tie in with the local radio stations I was visiting," Doris stated in 1970. Starting out as a featured singer with Jackson, Doris soon got her own spot on the national tour as "Just One Look" began to take off. "I remember we had (the R&B duo) Don Gardner & Dee Dee Ford on the show, too, and I ended up having the closing spot on the first half of the show. It was really something...."

The down side of Atlantic's rush-release of the single was the way the credits read on "Just One Look." The demo she'd made was supposedly "produced" by Award Music Productions with "supervision by Artie Ripp," who was working in the mailroom at 1650 Broadway at the time! Like so many other R&B stars of the day, Doris found herself caught up in music-biz madness, and her Atlantic contract would ultimately be the source of much contention and irritation since the parties listed had in reality nothing to do with the original recordings Doris made for the label. Not unusual in an industry where hype often succeeds over real talent, Ripp made a name for himself off his association with "Just One Look"; over time he ended up working at several major labels, even reuniting with Doris for a hot minute in 1977 when he made a brief deal for her with New York-based Midland Records.

As "Just One Look" spiraled up the charts, Atlantic waited patiently for Doris to return from her tour with Jackson to cut her first album. "The follow-up ("What'cha Gonna Do About It") was also a demo I cut in (that) little ole' basement studio at 1650 (Broadway). I added a few tracks at the Atlantic studios, but most of it was just me and the trio!" Doris revealed in 1974. The Atlantic Records' logs show that Doris recorded most of *Just One Look and Other Memorable Selections* on July 29, 1963. The album was a neat mixture of Troy-Carroll originals like "Someone Ain't Right," "Lazy Days," and the gospel-inspired "Draw Me Closer" alongside jazz'n'pop standards like "Stormy Weather," "Trust in Me," and "Somewhere Along the Way."

It was a good showcase for Doris's warm vocal style: she was never a great soul belter in the tradition of divas like Aretha Franklin and Patti LaBelle nor a blues stylist like her good friend Esther Phillips, but there was a plaintive, simple originality about her approach that made her voice eminently easy to listen to. The audiences at the Apollo theater agreed: the very venue where she'd first started as an usherette was now welcoming her back as a star. Along with Otis Redding, Rufus Thomas, the Coasters, and Ben E. King, Doris was captured on tape before an excited audience on Saturday night, November 16, 1963. The results could be heard on *Apollo Saturday Night*, a 1964 album that gave R&B lovers the world over an idea how Harlem's best could respond to their favorite performers. The rousing reception Doris got as a "hometown girl made good" no doubt warmed her heart.

For whatever reason, Atlantic didn't get behind the records they released on Doris in the ensuing year that she remained with the label. After the album session, Doris did some more dates that produced singles like the lilting "Please Little Angel" (co-written with then-up-and-coming writers Nick Ashford and Valerie Simpson) and the frantic "Hurry" (later re-recorded for her 1970 Apple album). What those twelve months did provide for her was a foundation for touring both at home and, for the first time in 1965, in Britain where "Just One Look" had been a hit for the Hollies and "Whatcha Gonna Do About It" had been a Top 10 single for the Small Faces. Both songs had also done well for Doris in the West Indies, and she got a chance to perform there a few times in the 1960s, establishing a name for herself among Caribbean audiences that would endure for decades.

"After the records started happening for me at Atlantic, I did a lot of 'package' shows," Doris recalled in 1974. "Back in those days you'd have, say, six to eight performers. One of the biggest featured James Brown, Ruby & the Romantics, Marvin Gaye. . . . We used to tour all over, including the deep South. I remember one of the first experiences I had down there. I went into a restaurant, and this waitress turns to me and says, 'We don't serve no niggers in here.' Being a New York girl, where it really didn't happen quite like that, I said, 'But, honey, I can't see no niggers here!' But believe me, it was really bad in some of those places. They had revolving stages—one side white, one side black. But thank God, things have changed."

On her first visit to the U.K., Doris was blown away by the adoration of British fans who knew everything she'd ever recorded. It was fashionable among the small inner circle of committed R&B fans to form fan clubs for different black American artists. Doris was no exception. Enid Buckland-Evers had started a fan club for "The Troy," as the singer was known affectionately. Enid took a few fans out to the airport complete with a "Welcome to Britain" banner to let Doris know how much her music was appreciated. The reception she got left an indelible impression on her, and she began a love affair with the country that lasted well into the 1990s when she returned to London for a couple of years. ". . . You go on stage, and you can hear people say things like 'There's Doris' or 'That's the Troy' and . . . it makes me feel good," Doris told Dave Godin in 1970.

A standout appearance on the popular television show "Ready, Steady, Go!" (on the same day that another diva, the "good doctor" Nina Simone, was making her British television debut, too) was a highlight of her 1965 British trip. The kind of respect and appreciation that she and other R&B stars received in Britain was different from what she was used to. At home Doris was just another soul singer who was mostly seen as only as good as her last hit record. She was so enamored with the response of fans, the press, and the British music biz, that—complete with her hip and highly memorable blonde wig—she'd headed down to a British studio to record a couple of songs while still with Atlantic. She might well have used some of the local musicians who backed her on her first British gigs, and the lineup included one Reginald Dwight, who later became none other than Elton John.

After leaving Atlantic Doris looked for a new recording home: she briefly journeyed down to Philadelphia to record a one-off single with fledgling local producer/writers Kenneth Gamble and Leon Huff, who years later were the "architects" of the "Philly Sound." The song was "I'll Do Anything (He Wants Me to Do)," and it became a classic among lovers of "Northern soul," a name applied to a particular kind of uptempo R&B track that kept young Brits on the dance floor in the late 1960s and throughout the 1970s. Doris remembered, some nine years after recording the song, "It was originally intended for (future Mrs. Gamble) Dee Dee Sharp, but the track was recorded in the wrong key for her so I put my voice on it. I changed a few words around 'cause I didn't like the way they were! Funny that record's been out three times now, and I hear people still want it!"

The song came out in the U.S. on Cameo Records in 1965 and was reissued on the New York label Calla in 1966 but had little impact. Doris, ever the trooper, wasn't fazed. She cut another single, "Face Up to the Truth," for Capitol Records and just kept on trucking, which was characteristic of her personality. Long before I heard the female group the Honeycone use the phrase for one of its big hits, Doris would tell me, in her best New York streetwise manner, "Baby, just remember, one monkey don't stop no show! Don't ever let anybody tell you you *can't* do anything! Cause you're one of God's children, and He ain't gonna let nothing stop your from going after your dreams!"

As I got to know Doris over the years, I was always inspired by her testimony. She would encourage everyone she met to move forward with their goals, and she used her own life as an example of what could be done with a little faith. In 1998 when ill health stopped her from going to Japan—which had become almost a home away from home, a country where she could perform a couple of times a year and always earn what she termed "top dollar, baby, top dollar!"—Doris refused to let the circumstances get to her. As always "Just One Look" had come through: it was being used in not one but two new commercials. Sometimes it was necessary to prod Doris just a little to make sure she got paid, but she assured me that she was going to make the call to the guy who was responsible for collecting her royalties. "Yeah, child, I think it will be a nice 'taste,'" Doris said. "And right on time, you know it!"

Right on time, back in 1969, was a move to Britain. Without any record success in the States, Doris looked at her options and realized that the loyalty she was receiving from British fans meant that she could likely get some steady work in the U.K. and in the rest of Europe, either doing background work, gigging, or recording. Her upbeat personality, quick smile, and the sharp and savvy "cash money" way of dealing with the music industry (something she'd obviously learned the hard way in New York) made her an instant fixture on the music scene in London.

On her first visit in 1965, Doris wound up in the studio with New York pal Madeline Bell (who had relocated to Britain after performing in a black gospel play a few years earlier) singing behind British star Dusty Springfield on "In the Middle of Nowhere." Doris's voice could be heard loud and clear on what would be one of Dusty's biggest U.K. hits. When she returned in 1969, it didn't take long for the word to spread.

"I got a call from Madeline inviting me down to a recording session that Billy Preston was doing for (The Beatles') Apple (label) and George Harrison was producing (the song) "That's the Way God Planned It." Billy and I agreed that we'd write some songs together for his Apple album," Doris explained in a 1992 interview for *Blues & Soul* in conjunction with the reissue of her own Apple album, on CD for the first time. "And that's when George asked me about my own availability to record. As it turned out, I wasn't signed to *anyone*. . . ." Within a matter of days, "we had three agreements: one for me as an artist, one as a writer, and one as a producer," Doris recalled.

With her own office at Apple's posh Savile Row location in the heart of London's West End, "Mama Soul" was in her element. One of her first Apple projects was to write music for "Timothy's Travels," an animated cartoon, but her focus was on making on her own album. The all-star cast that was in attendance for the sessions was mind-blowing: in addition to Harrison and Preston, Beatle Ringo Starr, Peter Frampton, Eric Clapton, Stephen Stills, and Leon Russell were all involved at different stages of the album's recording, which took place over several months. The sessions, Doris noted, "were a lot of fun—really spontaneous. George produced (the first single) "Ain't That Cute," and he pretty much let me produce everything else myself. People would come by. . . . I'd sit at the piano, and we'd bounce around some ideas. . . . We just jammed!"

A true rarity that could fetch up to $250 in Japan before it was reissued in 1992, the self-titled album was even more of a personal showcase for Doris than her first Atlantic album had been. "Ain't That Cute," written with Harrison, was a bitingly honest tale about the hangers-on, groupies, and wanna-bes who would befriend stars. Doris had penned "You Give Me Joy Joy Joy," a rousing gospel workout, with Harrison, Starr, and Stills. And "So Far" was a poignant ballad that Doris had written with bassist Klaus Voorman. For good measure, she threw in a languid, bluesy reading of the 1930s jazz standard "Exactly Like You." On the CD reissue, EMI Records added Doris's version of "All That I've Got," a song she'd written with Preston; a fun cover of the Beatles' "Get Back"; and Doris's take on "Vaya Con Dios," one of the songs she'd sung background on with the Warwick sisters behind the Drifters back in 1963.

Even though Doris later described the making of the album "one of the most creative times in my life," all the work she and others did on the record failed to translate into sales. Four years later, she noted, "People ask me what went wrong at Apple, and I think part of the problem may have been that George Harrison was trying to experiment with soul. Look at Billy (Preston). He had to go back to the States to get a hit, and now he's had two million sellers ("Will It Go Round In Circles" and "Space Race")."

The relative lack of success of the album and the two Apple singles didn't stop Doris. She stayed in London, working with the cream of the British rock world, singing behind all manner of folks from the Rolling Stones and Led Zeppelin, to the Moody Blues and Pink Floyd. In fact, her vocal step-out on Floyd's multimillion selling "Dark Side of the Moon" helped bring her to the attention of rock enthusiasts everywhere.

But it was the British soul brigade that continued to support Doris when she would gig. In December, 1971, now free of her contractual commitments to Apple, Doris recorded an album at the Rainbow theater in North London. The LP, *The Rainbow Testament*, leaned heavily on Doris's gospel background. She'd created her own backing group aptly tagged "The Gospel Truth," and the show consisted of "This Little Light of Mine," "Steal Away," and "To My Father's House," as well as R&B favorites like "I Wanna Testify" and "The Nitty Gritty," which fit nicely into the spiritual overtone of the evening's performance.

I was on hand for the show, and although the attendance was less than Doris or the assembled crowd (which included R&B star Rufus Thomas) might have liked, the energy level was constantly high. In my *Blues & Soul* review of the show the following month, I stated, "Not only did Doris prove that rock gospel is a reality but that her recognition as one of the leading ladies in the soul world is long overdue. . . ."

I was a little biased: by the time I went to the show, I'd become firm friends with Doris. Through our mutual friend Dave Godin, I'd met up with Doris, and we maintained contact. I'd been fooling around at home with my little tape recorder, putting down my own a capella versions of personal favorite soul songs like Sam Cooke's "A Change Is Gonna Come," and I wanted Doris's opinion of my chances of having a musical career. She was, as always, encouraging: "Yeah, baby, you got soul! Child, you can sing! All right now. . . that's a soulful feeling, child!" Such encouragement meant the world to me after the endless hours I'd spent singing along with my diva favorites, Aretha, Dionne, Nina, Esther, and, of course, Doris.

As much as Doris felt like I had something to offer, all of her friends didn't share her opinion. Not too many nights later, my sister Sylvia and I were over at Doris's flat near Baker Street. She had a whole bunch of folks around, including Billy Preston, her friend Gloria Howerd, and Madeline Bell. Everyone was having a good time, laughing, joking, smiling. Doris was playing a Nancy Wilson album, and I was "moved" to sing along with "Can't Take My Eyes Off You." I'd learned a little about bending and stretching notes, and I knew I sounded pretty good. But Bell was having none of it: "Tryin' to sound black, huh? Well, don't forget we got the real thing up in here!" she snapped at me. I was stunned, embarrassed, and uncomfortable . . . and Doris, who was ever the peacemaker, came to my rescue. "Girl, you don't have to go there," she berated Madeline. "The child is tryin' his best, and I think he sounds pretty good. . . . Now ain't nothin' wrong with a little encouragement, and you know, soul ain't got no color!" Madeline glared at me and wandered off to the kitchen while Doris comforted me. "Don't pay her no mind, child. She's on some kinda trip right now," she assured me.

After that experience, it was hard to write anything but praise about Doris because she'd shown that the care I'd seen her give others was genuine. Sure, she got upset when her business wasn't "straight," and one of the downsides of being a trusting kind of woman had meant that she'd constantly been ripped off by shrewd operators on both sides of the Atlantic. She was angry that people tried to take advantage of her in the treacherous world of contracts, lawyers, and managers, and these experiences left their mark.

But back in London in 1972, Doris was in no mood for giving up or giving in. Even though *The Rainbow Testament* had disappeared from the record racks soon after Polydor Records released it, Doris was pushing on. Over the course of one weekend, she appeared in no less than three major television shows. Along with Salena Jones and Esther Marrow, two other U.S. vocalists, she was featured on the BBC's "Wild & Winsome Women" show, recorded live at a nightclub in the north of England. She had the show all to herself on "Sounds For Saturday," following Thelma Houston and Roberta Flack, who had also been included in the series weeks before. Finally, Doris appeared on a Sunday evening religious program, singing "Oh Happy Day" and "My Sweet Lord." On all three shows, she was in top form, expressive, joyful, and ever the showstopper. All those years in her father's church and watching the stars of the 1950s at the Apollo were paying off as she shared her heart and bared her musical soul.

Doris was enjoying herself, making friends, making a decent living in Britain, packing audiences into Ronnie Scott's popular club in Soho, winning rave reviews from the press in the early part of 1974, and taking occasional trips to perform in Europe to work with stars like Johnny Hallyday and to appear on television shows in France and Switzerland. But when Doris and I got together in March, it was obvious that she was beginning to feel a little confined. She'd performed at a lot of major venues in the U.K. and had been seen on television regularly but without the benefit of a big hit record, not many new opportunities were available.

Sitting in the West Hampstead flat where I'd met Dionne Warwick months earlier, I was talking with Doris about *Stretchin' Out*, a new album she'd just finished for B&C Records. She'd worked on the record with reggae producer and recording artist Dandy Livingstone. "Yeah, baby, it's a different thing for me to get into," she agreed. "I figured that everyone, Marvin Gaye, Al Green, all those people were mellowing down so it was time for me to show everyone that I could do it, too. Everyone's seen me get down ... get into the gospel thing, you know, stomp around and all, but I want people to know that I can do other things!"

Doris had hooked up with Livingstone after singing backup on hits by reggae hit-makers Jimmy Cliff and John Holt. She explained: "... Thing is, I've always had a great deal for reggae, and I was determined that, in this case, I'd be able to do things my way. You know, baby, I been ripped off so many times that I just had to get this album together my way...." With a cover shot of a beaming Doris relaxing on a white sofa against a leopard backdrop, the record was an interesting mix of styles: the title track was really funky, and "In My Father's House" was a gospel treat. The reggae musicians supplied a nice backdrop for many of the songs, and Doris sounded mellow on tracks like her reworking of the Doobie Brothers' "Listen to the Music."

Following the fate of her Apple and Polydor albums, Doris was optimistically cautious about *Stretchin' Out*. And it was obvious from our conversation that she was hatching a game plan of her own. "I think the problem with the other product was that it wasn't aimed at any particular market, and not much promotion was put behind some of the things I've done here.... We'll just wait and see how the public reacts and from what they like, we can decide which direction to go in the future.... But I must get to Los Angeles—everyone tells me that's really where it's at these days. The thing is I've never worked in Los Angeles or Las Vegas. I've worked most everywhere else in the States, but the country is so big that there are always places you've never been. That's why I wanna get back there...."

Doris Troy in a
publicity shot for
"Mama, I Want to Sing"

Her mind made up, Doris headed back home where her younger sister Vy Higgensen, always encouraged by her older sibling, had started to make a real name for herself on New York radio. With her honey-textured tones, she'd become one of the star "voices" on WBLS, the most popular black music station of the day. And by 1976, she'd started her own weekly magazine, called *Unique New York*. By the time I'd moved to New York myself in February, 1975, Doris was living in Los Angeles, and her presence there was enough of a motive for me to fly out in August of that year.

I ended up staying with Doris at her apartment in the San Fernando Valley, and I could tell that she was having a tough time. In England, she was a big fish in a small bowl; in L.A., she was one of the many artists who had enjoyed some success without reaching superstar status. Doris was hoping for a deal and looking for work, and the only saving grace associated with being in California seemed to be the sunshine. She tried to put on a brave face, but I could tell that Doris was hurting. She was moody and easily irritated, and she seemed to be surrounded by so-called friends who had never enjoyed anything like the kind of acclaim she'd received in Britain, and who oozed jealousy and envy. Doris seemed to know it, too, but she didn't have a way out of the hole she felt she was in. She had her pride, so she'd try and talk about how things were going to be better any day. Nevertheless, it was obvious that her career had hit a roadblock. Although she might have played out all her options in Britain, L.A. was not the answer—a city filled with game-playing, flaky people in search of elusive fame and fortune.

I myself was ready to get out of New York, and with Doris on hand as one of my few buddies—along with Pat Arnold, a former Ikette who had made her home in London in the 1960s and had become a close friend—I decided to move out to L.A. Strangely, once I got there with my then-roommate Percy, I didn't see as much of Doris as I'd expected. We were both having our share of personal dramas, and Doris could tell what I was going through when I asked her if Percy, a talented but often lazy musician, could do some leadsheets for her to earn some money. Doris knew bullshit when she heard it, and after one session with Percy she told me, straight out, "He ain't bad. He can play the keyboards a little but, child, he's full of it! He took way too long to do one leadsheet, so I can't do nothin' to help him. And, David, you better watch out 'cause I don't think he's good for you. . . . Are you guys . . . poppin' fingers?" Doris asked without a blink. I assured her that we weren't, that we were just roommates, but she still wanted to let me know that her bullshit meter was going off! "Well, child, you know Mama don't wanna get in your business, but all I know is you better watch your step 'cause that child is lazy, I'm gonna tell you now!"

Doris wasn't too far off track, and I dealt with the situation the best I could—by eventually returning to New York by myself. Meanwhile, Doris was still struggling. She'd run back into Artie Ripp, the famed mailroom clerk who had mysteriously gotten his name on "Just One Look." Ripp, no longer with any major labels, was trying to jumpstart his own career as a producer. A New York sharpshooter, Ripp convinced Doris that he could get her a deal and in spite of some misgivings, she agreed to do some recording at a local studio in the Valley.

Ripp assured her that he could get a deal, but when it came time to give her some money while he was looking for a deal for Doris, he was less than cooperative. I remember sitting in her apartment while she talked with him on the telephone: "Man, I gotta have some money! Don't give me that shit. . . . I need some money today. I got bills to pay, man. This is some 'Mickey Mouse' stuff right here. . . ." Naturally, the conversation was appropriately spiced with a few choice expletives. But given the survival pressures Doris was experiencing, her reaction was understandable.

I knew that Doris, like other R&B stars of the 1950s and 1960s, had been used to dealing with industry "games" before, but I'd never seen close up what she'd been through. In the golden age of 1960s soul, much was promised yet little was delivered. Most young, up-and-coming black performers had little or no legal representation, and a contract with a piece of money upfront (or in some cases, a Cadillac or a mink) was like winning the lottery. Sleazy record men thrived on the naivete of young artists whose desire to record and perform often outweighed any consideration of fame or fortune.

Fortunately, Doris had learned from her days working in Tin Pan Alley as a background singer that there was money to be made but, like others, she, too, fell prey to the double-speak that wisecracking industry types could lay on an unsuspecting artist. She told me that one time she'd lost her cool with a New York record man, threatening to break his office apart if she didn't get paid. And like her good friend Esther Phillips (who operated with an even sharper tongue and attitude), she made it known that she meant business! However, it was obvious that getting mad, getting angry, and resorting to threats ran counter to Doris's innate nature. She would always try to see the best in everyone until they crossed her, and, understandably, she thought Ripp was trying to cheat her when he talked about getting her a deal but not giving her some money to tide her over.

Even though I was skeptical, Ripp actually did come through: in the August, 1976, issue of *Blues & Soul*, I was happy to report, "The ever-personable Doris Troy called the *B&S* office recently to tell us that she's back in the studios, recording her first album for Midland International Records. . . . The lady reports that she's working with Barry White's rhythm section, no less, and that a good deal of the material she's doing will be originals—disco sides, pretty ballads, everything!' Doris's initial single for the RCA-distributed label should be out by the end of July, and the album will probably see a September release. Meanwhile, Ms. Troy is working on details of a national tour. . . ."

Much to my amazement—given what I thought about Ripp's prior record with Doris—Midland actually did release a first single on Doris before the end of 1976. I remember hooking back up with her in New York, and actually going with her to the company's offices in Manhattan. She introduced me as her "publicist," and we talked with Bob Reno, the label's owner and president about ways we could ensure Doris would get a fair crack of the whip promotion-wise. "Whatcha think, baby?" she asked after our meeting with the cordial executive. "Well, Doris, I think it's gonna be all right," I replied. "They seem to be on the case, and they have good distribution through RCA, so I think it could work out fine." Midland had released a great version of the Eagles' "Lyin' Eyes" as Doris's debut record for the label; it got some good reviews and a little airplay without storming the charts. Ripp had promised Doris that it would be a full album deal, so she'd recorded some additional material. Her new LP was to be called *Another Look*.

After the first single failed to register, Midland put out "Can't Hold On," a chunky slice of driving disco produced by Philadelphia hit-maker John Davis, a respected songwriter and arranger who had racked up a few hits with his own Monster Orchestra. Doris traveled to Philadelphia to work with him, and I rode the train with Dee Dee Warwick, who was doing backgrounds with Doris for the date. I ended up sleeping on the sofa in the two-bedroom hotel suite where Doris and Dee Dee were staying. As I recall, there was a little tension between the two, and Doris seemed anxious, concerned that she would be ready for the all-important session the next day. It didn't go as well as she'd hoped. There were lots of stops and starts, and at some point I headed off to do some other interviews for *Blues & Soul* in Philadelphia.

"Can't Hold On," co-written by keyboard player Kenny Moore, one of Doris's longtime friends, should have been the segue into a first album for Midland, but it wasn't to be. The label—home to disco stars Carol Douglas and Silver Convention, as well as a twenty-two-year-old, pre-

Saturday Night Fever' John Travolta--was going through changes. Toward the end of its distribution deal with RCA, Midland became Midsong, and as the label left the RCA system, Doris's second release got lost in the shuffle. Once again without a recording home, Doris moved back to New York, and I ran into her and her sister Vy at a screening for *Shining Star*, a film starring Earth, Wind & Fire in which Doris had made a brief appearance. She seemed upbeat, looking at working with Vy on some new projects, including what she termed "a serious venture into acting!"

That would be a few years off. Doris spent a couple of years in New York, and we had occasion to hang out together. In fact, with my longtime buddy John Simmons (then musical director with Stephanie Mills), we went into a local New York studio to record some tracks. John and I had written a dance tune, "You Got Me Baby" for Doris, and we suggested a remake of the old Tommy Edwards song "It's All in the Game," believing it would work, too.

In the studio, Doris was the epitome of professionalism. She did take after take, never complaining and giving her all. The results were right in keeping with the music of the day. To complete the sessions, I worked with some other musicians on a track for the O'Jays' song "Let Me Make Love to You," which featured a special rap between Doris and sister Vy. As strong as my connections in the music business were, people still perceived me as a journalist, and although Doris had plenty of faith in what I could do, it was tough getting people in the industry to accept me as a producer and songwriter. We tried several different avenues both in the United States and in Britain but to no avail. Doris's stellar performance on those late 1970s tracks remain unreleased.

Hanging out with Doris also meant dealing with her role as my music-industry godmother. And like all good mothers, Doris could be protective if she thought "her child" was up to no good. One time, I was visiting New York after moving to Los Angeles, and Doris had kindly offered me a sofa to sleep on. I was hanging out with some of my friends, including my good buddy Eric Brogdon, whom I'd originally met when he was working at Vy Higgensen's *Unique New York* magazine. Well, as can often happen in the Big Apple, I got waylaid! I didn't make it back to Doris's place until way past midnight. She was waiting up. With a huge grin, she opened the door: "Been out poppin' your fingers, child? Uh huh. Well, just as long as you are being safe, that's all that matters. . . ."

As the 1970s became the 1980s, Doris decided to venture west and follow her dream of living in Las Vegas. It didn't take long for the word to spread. A couple of years earlier, she'd signed with comedian Redd

Foxx's management company, so she'd already set up some connections for herself when she got a call from a Vegas regular, entertainer Lola Falana. She had in fact made a living for herself performing on "the Strip": having Doris as a backup vocalist was a big plus, and she always introduced Doris as the originator of "Just One Look," which had been turned into a Top 50 pop hit in 1979 by pop star Linda Ronstadt just five years after Canada's Anne Murray had also recorded it. Indeed, well into the 1990s, the song was continually used in commercials for everything from Mazda and Hyundai automobiles, to Clorox bleach and Pepsi-Cola; it was even featured in Cher's 1991 movie *Mermaids*.

Feeling the need to stretch her wings musically, Doris left Falana and around 1983 began performing at different hotels in Las Vegas with her own show. In between gigs, she would often head out to the local flea markets to sell love pillows she'd made or inspirational books she'd bought. Never going on the kind of star trip that some of her peers felt compelled to take, Doris always loved interacting with everyday people. Years later she set up her own "Mama's Gift Shop" in a room in the home she bought in Las Vegas in the mid-1980s, inviting friends and fellow churchgoers to come in and buy books or trinkets as gifts.

Doris was getting ready to embark on a whole season at one of the key Las Vegas hotels when she got a call from her sister Vy. A couple of years earlier, Vy had previewed a show she'd written based on Doris's life, entitled *Mama I Want to Sing*. I remember going to one of the earliest incarnations of the show, and I reviewed it in the January, 1981, issue of *Blues & Soul*: "The basic story line traces Doris' childhood in New York, her participation in her father's church choir, her spell as an usherette at the Apollo and her eventual debut on the stage of that famed venue. The play has some superb acting, some excellent music and some incredible singing and once it hits Broadway, it's going to be one of the year's biggest hits! Combining energy and excitement together, it's a rousing tribute to the foundation of much of today's black music."

Doris was elated that her life was to be immortalized through a musical, but neither she, sister Vy nor Vy's partner Ken Wydro had any idea that the play would become the highest-grossing off-Broadway show in history. Over time, the show would not only be performed at Madison Square Garden's Paramount theater in New York with gospel great Shirley Caesar in the cast, but would also travel to London where Chaka Khan and then Deniece Williams would have key roles. The original cast took the show to Japan, and it became almost an annual pilgrimage for a road company to perform there, as well as in Germany, Italy, Greece, Switzerland, and Egypt. The impact of *Mama* led to *I Want to Sing II* and another spinoff, *Let the Music Play!* Over the years, a number of young recording artists got their start in the New York cast of the original play, including Tony Terry, Desiree Coleman, and D'Atra Hicks.

Vy's call to Doris contained a simple request that would result in a whole decade of work for her older sister: "I was knocked out and I just felt like I couldn't walk away from something like that," she recalled in a 1992 interview. "And once I started getting into the script, I knew I had to be a part of it." In 1984, Doris joined the cast in the role of her own mother: "It's been such a miracle to have my own mother watch as I've played her onstage. Truly, being a part of the show has been unbelievable!"

Aside from giving Doris a chance to express her musical and comedic skills night after night, her appearance in *Mama* and its various spinoffs, the show revived interest in her own recordings. In 1992, EMI reissued her Apple CD, and two years later, I was proud to produce a compilation of her work for Atlantic and Cameo/Calla for "Soul Classics," a series I started at Ichiban Records. As a result of touring with *Mama I Want to Sing*, she also got to do gigs in Japan and Turkey, and when the company finally made it to London in 1995, Doris decided to return to the country that had been her home back in the 1970s.

"Doris, you know, people love you in Britain," I reassured her as she expressed some concerns about whether she would be able to sustain herself by relocating to London. Using her stint in the London run of *Mama I Want to Sing* as a springboard, Doris quickly found a growing demand for her services. She performed at the Jazz Café, at 100 Club, at benefits, on national television, and on "Soul Weekenders" for diehard fans. Everywhere she went, Doris was greeted with excitement and enthusiasm. Over the years, she'd lost none of the drive and passion that drew people to her, and when I went to London in October, 1995, I was thrilled to see her as the first live artist to perform at the ritzy Mezzo restaurant.

During my visit I got to hand Doris the telephone so Suzan Jenkins could proudly tell her that she'd won that Pioneer Award from the Rhythm & Blues Foundation. As it turned out, Doris would be performing in Japan just prior to the event in Los Angeles on February 29, so the timing was perfect. That evening at the Hollywood Palladium, Doris was every inch the star. Foundation trustee Bonnie Raitt was enthralled at finally meeting Doris, and board member Ruth Brown, a longtime friend and fellow Las Vegas resident, was overjoyed at seeing Doris finally get her due. I wiped away more than a tear or two when Doris took the stage to perform "Just One Look," with Patti Austin, Mavis Staples, and Darlene Love providing the vocal backing. Doris beamed, and the audience gave her a much-deserved standing ovation. The press coverage of the event was wonderful, and aside from reuniting her with folks she hadn't seen in ages, such as Betty Everett, Jerry Butler, and Eddie Floyd, it gave Doris a real boost in terms of her media profile.

In fact, some nine months later, Doris flew back to Los Angeles for a one-off gig as part of an oldies show at the Greek theater, her first time ever performing publicly in the city. She was greeted with a standing ovation: for years, music lovers had wanted to see the original "Just One Look" girl in person—and here she was, live and as always, with a big smile on her face. Doris returned to London after the gig, and it looked as if she would be able to maintain a career in the U.K., with occasional visits to Japan and brief runs in different versions of *Mama* in the U.S. and abroad, but her health wasn't as good as it had been.

As it turned out, Doris discovered, quite by accident, that she'd been inhaling noxious fumes during her residency at one of the London flats she'd rented. The level of poison in the atmosphere was dangerous, and she wasn't lying when she said, "I could have died, child!" She made what seemed like a reluctant return to the States, but it wasn't long before Japan was calling once again. And in December, 1997, Doris headlined a series of gigs, using members of a London choir to produce a special gospel show. Japanese audiences, familiar with her from *Mama I Want to Sing*, always called Doris "Mama." In addition to the gospel shows, "Mama" did some nightclub work, performing the kind of blues and jazz material that had been the basis for some of her London gigs.

Even though Doris's style of pop-flavored R&B had been the launching pad for her career and she'd shown a penchant for working jazz numbers into her show—no doubt inspired by her early exposure to Dinah Washington and Sarah Vaughan at the Apollo—it was gospel music that was her foundation. Time and again, praising the Lord would be the one enduring element for Doris in her work life. So it was no surprise that in the 1980s, she herself became an ordained minister. Not that she needed a license to spread the good word: like all true soul survivors, throughout her life Doris has always been there to uplift friends and family with an expression of love, a heartfelt moment of kindness. Back in 1970, she told buddy Dave Godin, "... all the while I'm regarded as Mother Soul, I'm gonna make sure my children get this message. It's a bit of a cliché . . . but like (The Beatles') record says, 'All You Need Is Love.' It's that simple."

And love was what I felt when I visited Doris in the fall of 1998. She'd returned to New York, back to the family-owned building where she'd spent most of her childhood. She was in great spirits when I headed up to Harlem to play a couple of (the popular card game) Uno with her. I discovered my lifelong friend, the Reverend Doris "Just One Look" Troy was a serious Uno player! Like we always did, we had big fun. And it was a joy to see Doris, surrounded by family and friends, a soul survivor whose life-affirming endurance and courage make her truly one of a kind! Amen!

NA
OSS

he Diana!"

Diana Ross reaching out
to her audience in 1991
Credit: George De Sota, London
Features International USA

It is hard to say when exactly it became popular to bash Diana Ross. Popular, primarily among segments of the African-American community, although by no means restricted to it. When I first arrived in the U.S. in 1975, I was shocked to hear how some people would trash her music and her persona, and how in certain instances the mere mention of her name would elicit all manner of nasty epithets. Generally speaking, I would hear her referred to as a "bitch." It amazed me that none of the people who talked about her with such vitriol, including some other performers, had ever met or spoken with her at any time. Such is the power of gossip, rumor, and the fixed public persona or image that a diva can acquire.

I was prompted to reexamine the American public perception of Diana Ross when I was invited to conduct an interview with her in person for a special tribute to her in *Billboard* magazine in 1993. Before we sat down face to face at a production office she was using in West Los Angeles, I analyzed the commonly held notions about her and their possible roots. Yes, it was true, she'd been an ambitious member of the Supremes, unquestionably the most popular female group in pop history. Yes, she and Berry Gordy had both admitted that they'd had a relationship and that his position as the founder of Motown Records hadn't exactly hurt Diana's career. Yes, it was true that Florence Ballard had been asked to leave the Supremes and that Diana's opinion was presumably sought on the subject. Yes, her solo career had been launched with much flare and fanfare while the Supremes never quite recovered their consistent hit-making ability. And yes, she'd married not one but two white men.

Oh, and yes, Diana's music, both as a Supreme and as a solo artist, had "crossed over" and she did appeal to—gasp—white as well as black audiences. Many black people thought that she'd sold out by marrying white men, by making pop rather than hardcore R&B records, and by sleeping with the boss, in itself a reflection of a conniving, competitive, cutthroat bitch who wouldn't let anything or anyone stand in her way. Diana Ross, folks said, had lost her "blackness," and regardless of the whys and wherefores, she should never have left the Supremes. After all it had been the first black female group to really make it, and Diana's exit was seen, people said, as a betrayal: she'd become successful with two other girls, and now she was leaving them behind. Years later, former Supreme Mary Wilson told her version of the group's story in her book *Dreamgirls*, and she didn't exactly paint a flattering picture of her former partner.

In other words, Diana Ross personified a myth. And in the same way that other powerful women have often been vilified for their desire to succeed, she was someone to be scorned, disliked, and diminished. Once again I was amazed that at least on this side of the water, she elicited such strong reactions from most black men and women I spoke to. The power of myth is such that it is ordinarily used as the basis for how someone is perceived forever. Even when I would talk to Motown executives—supposedly in place to help sell Diana's records—before doing the 1993 interview with her, they would roll their eyes, grunt, or try to add weight to the notion that she was the ultimate in difficult divas. Lost in all the rush to judgement about her was the fact that she'd been a pioneer, that she'd made some great music, and that she was the role model, consciously or unconsciously, for a whole generation of young black women who regarded her success as an inspiration to move forward in their own musical or acting careers.

I'd spoken with Diana Ross a few days before we sat down together for our interview. Mindful of all that I'd heard and knowing that we'd met only briefly at different times in her career, I politely called her "Miss Ross." She immediately responded, "It's fine, just call me Diana!" she said. One myth down, several more to go. After Diana had welcomed me at the door and I was seated in her office, I found her to be intense, interesting, and very intelligent. And then it began to fall into place: part of the reputation she's saddled with might have just a little to do with the fact that she is smart and like most good divas, she knows what she wants. Now, in a white male-dominated entertainment industry, these qualities aren't good. Black women are generally "supposed' to be difficult but also passive, a little "country," and invariably dependent on managers who are either husbands, brothers, sons, or lovers. Speaking up for themselves only adds to the myth about how difficult they really are. Diana Ross obviously isn't a "dumb broad," and it is easy to see how her ability to focus would intimidate powerful men and make enemies out of fellow performers. Another myth gone.

It is common knowledge that the story of Diana Ross's rise to fame reads like some kind of storybook fable. Basically, Diana joined a local Detroit group, the Primettes (which consisted of friends Florence Ballard, Mary Wilson, and Barbara Martin) in 1960 at the tender age of sixteen, replacing original member Betty Travis. Through Diana's neighbor William "Smokey" Robinson, the group auditioned for Motown founder Berry Gordy Jr., and while he liked their sound and look, he wanted them to finish school before signing them to his fledgling musical empire. In the liner notes for her 1993 *Forever, Diana* boxed set, Diana recalls, ". . . that summer, before we got our contracts, when I needed a job to make some extra money, I asked Berry if I could work for him. He actually hired me as a secretary, probably because I was cute and persistent, but I really wasn't a secretary. All I remember doing was clearing off his desk several times a day, awed by the important looking papers that he handled and so wishing to have my name on some of them. . . ."

As the Primettes, the quartet signed with Lupine Records, another local label, and made a couple of singles that were released only after they became successful over at Motown. A year later, in 1961, in the presence of their parents, the rechristened Supremes signed their first contract with Motown Records. In 1962 Barbara Martin left the group, and it would take six releases before the Supremes finally achieved any measure of success: "When the Lovelight Starts Shining Through His Eyes" became a Top 30 hit in October, 1963. Teamed with producer/writers Eddie Holland, Brian Holland, and Lamont Dozier and with Gordy—in Ross's own words—"at times my surrogate father, at other times, my controller and slave driver," the Supremes flourished.

Those were indeed heady times, as Diana mentioned in our 1993 face-to-face interview: "Mostly I remember that the time started to pass really quickly. Once we got that first record, when the records were Top 10, everything started to soar. The business started to grow, it was moving so very fast." Between 1964 and 1967 when Florence left (to be replaced by Cindy Birdsong, formerly with Patti LaBelle & the Bluebelles), the group had thirteen Top 10 pop and R&B hits, ten of which topped the charts. Five of their first ten albums made it to the nation's Top 10 LP listings; in Britain and other parts of Europe, the Supremes quickly became the top-selling American act at a time when groups like the Beatles and the Rolling Stones were spearheading a musical revolution of their own.

Diana, in her 1994 liner notes, states: "In mid-1967, Berry officially changed the name of our group to 'Diana Ross and the Supremes.' This was not my idea. It came from Berry. He discussed it in detail with Mary and me. It seemed inevitable. He explained to us that it would also be easier to demand more salary if we were a lead singer and a group. Instead of pressure lifting, it only increased. Something had to give." Inevitably, it was Diana's departure from the group—but not before it had racked up another dozen hits, including duets with the Temptations and tunes with a social message (like "Love Child" and "I'm Livin' in Shame"). Years before the split, Gordy had been instrumental in creating an audience base outside of the teenage and young record buyers who were lapping up each new Supremes single. Concept albums like *Sing Country & Western* and *Sing Rodgers & Hart* were directed at an older, middle-class, white audience, and when the Supremes appeared at the prestigious Copacabana nightclub in New York, the group was setting a precedent.

With Gordy prodding the Supremes toward an audience that he considered more affluent (and thus more likely to buy albums rather than singles), it is right here that the idea of Diana Ross selling out might well have its root. Black audiences liked their heroes, soul brothers and sisters who had made it without compromising. And the word in the "hood" was that the Supremes had gone white, pandering to the whims of the ritz-and-glitz crowd. Certainly, directing them toward the supper club, to the Vegas brigade, would take the pressure off consistently making hit records. Gordy wasn't alone in his strategy: a few other black performers of the day who had crossover success, such as Dionne Warwick and Sam Cooke, had also reached across racial barriers. Warwick had even been able to create an audience among Europe's upper classes, specifically in London and Paris, before Ross and the Supremes first crossed the Atlantic in 1965.

For some reason, other black artists weren't accused of the same kind of sellout. It was perhaps indicative of what the Supremes had achieved that Diana Ross's much-heralded departure from the group didn't occur at the Detroit Fox or the Apollo but at the Frontier Hotel in Las Vegas on January 14, 1970—one day shy of the date Mary, Florence, and Diana had signed with Motown nine years earlier. Making her exit at the Vegas hotel simply gave credence to the notion that from, a career perspective, Diana Ross was only interested in a career geared toward pop—read "white"—audiences.

The scuttlebutt about Diana hadn't been helped by Florence's reported "forced" departure from the Supremes and the growing rumors that Diana and Berry, who was still married, were having an affair. In their respective 1990s autobiographies—Diana's *Secrets of a Sparrow* (Villard Books, 1993) and Berry's *Berry Gordy: To Be Loved* (Warner Books, 1994)—both Diana and Berry admitted that her first daughter, Rhonda, was the result of their union. Then, a year into her solo career, Diana married Robert Silberstein, whose professional name was Bob Ellis. He served as personal manager both to Rufus and Chaka Khan and to Billy Preston. He was also white, which supplied more "evidence" for the idea that

Diana was abandoning her roots—a ridiculous notion given the increasing number of interracial marriages occurring in the 1970s.

Whatever the undercurrent might have been among the members of the black community, Diana Ross was moving on with her life and career. For her all-important, self-titled first solo album, she'd been paired with Nick Ashford and Valerie Simpson. These two talented producer/writers had come to Motown after penning hits like "Let's Go Get Stoned" for Ray Charles and had achieved considerable success in their work with Motown sweethearts Marvin Gaye and Tammi Terrell. In my 1993 interview with Diana, portions of which were used in *Blues & Soul*, she reflected on how she was feeling about the union: "Berry called them in. . . . They, in turn, started planning the album. . . . I wasn't checked in with, like 'which songs do you want to have?' and all that kind of thing. They just put together the songs, and we went in and did the album. . . . I just loved working with the two of them. . . ."

The album contained two major hits; both "Reach Out and Touch (Somebody's Hand)" and "Ain't No Mountain High Enough" went on to become virtual anthems for the singer. With Diana pictured waif-like on the cover, the LP was a vocal triumph for her. When she was a member of the Supremes, her voice often sounded pretty and cute. But Ashford & Simpson provided tracks that required Diana to sing with a certain kind of passion and emotion.

Diana sang with a kind of abandon, especially on *Surrender*, her 1971 release: "A lot of things had happened to me by then. And I'm sure that I was probably reflecting that. I had gotten married by then, and I was really going through major changes in my life," Diana stated in 1993. "You know, there are peak points in your life where you're having a real learning experience and a real change. A lot of things were happening in the early '70s and I think, in a sense, it was frightening . . . leaving the girls . . . but there was a freedom, a freeing of myself. . . . It's just like I was beginning to feel happier, you know. . . . I also felt like I could sing. I was beginning to trust myself more as a singer. I was getting much more confidence, and I think that may have shown through, too. That [also] has a lot to do with working with people that trust you and love you. It's amazing, and I've said this a hundred times in my career: if people believe in you, you can move mountains. . . ."

Twenty-three years after she'd originally stepped out on her own, it was somewhat surprising to hear Diana Ross, the icon, the strong, independent woman who had climbed many a mountain in her career, admitting that when she left the Supremes, she had some fears about how her solo career would go: ". . . I had spent ten years building a name, you know, an image . . . and we had become successful. . . . But it was a change that just had to happen. I couldn't have stayed where I was. . . . The fear was, you know, *Will I be okay? Will my records be hits?* People had done some of the same things, and they weren't successful. Mary Wells had left Motown and went to other companies and tried, and nothing had materialized. The first year maybe it comes out all right, then after you wonder if it's going to keep going. I think the same thing [happened] with Florence Ballard. When she left, she was going to get married and have children and then she went to other record companies. When you make a decision to split, you need to take responsibility that what happens you've caused and you've created. I think at that time, I was mature enough to know that . . . it might not work. I did know that I had a lot of courage, and I was just beginning to build my self-esteem. I mean, who knows . . . (The Supremes) could have gone on to be a success, and I could have maybe had a couple of records out for a while and then it didn't work . . . and then how long will record companies stick with you. . . ."

Of course, Diana didn't have that worry as her solo career kicked into gear. Admittedly, her record sales weren't exactly in the stratosphere, although *Ain't No Mountain High Enough* had topped both the pop and R&B charts in late 1970. A second album, *Everything Is Everything*, did just about okay; one track, the ballad "I'm Still Waiting," had been a major hit in the U.K. but didn't make much impact when it was released in the U.S. *Diana!*, her third LP, was essentially the soundtrack to an ABC-TV special of the same name that starred Motown's hottest teen act, the Jackson 5, along with comedian Bill Cosby. The show gave Diana a chance to display her acting skills when she did skits in which she appeared as Charlie Chaplin, Harpo Marx, and W.C. Fields, and won rave reviews when it was aired on both sides of the Atlantic.

As a solo performer, Diana had started out with quite a bang: her September, 1970, debut in Las Vegas reportedly cost some $100,000 to stage. And before packed audiences, she opened her first run of shows by saying, "Good evening, ladies and gentlemen. Welcome to the 'let's-see-if-Diana-Ross-can-make-it-alone' show!" In person, audiences loved the mix of music and comedy, as well as the numerous costume changes that became a standard element of every Ross performance. As 1971 came to a close, her attention shifted to the silver screen. With Gordy as the film's producer and Diana's professional mentor, she began production on *Lady Sings the Blues*, an adaptation of the late Billie Holiday's life story.

In April, 1973, Diana and I had our first in-person encounter in London on the eve of the British premiere of the film when we conducted an interview for *Blues & Soul* magazine. She confessed that she'd met with considerable criticism for taking on the role of the legendary jazz singer, particularly in the black community: "People really felt that Billie and I were worlds apart, and there is a general feeling that my own life has been easy throughout. But, after all, it's only what everyone reads. I'm not saying that the problems that Billie faced are the same as any that I've had, but I can relate to problems and tragedies also. . . . To begin with, there was such a total 'no' about the whole idea of me playing Billie, especially since there were so many others in line for the part. . . . I was so upset by it all that one day I phoned Berry and asked if were too late to stop before we'd actually started."

Whatever criticism there might have been about the notion of a glamorous star like Diana Ross playing the tragic role of Billie Holiday, the film was a success, earning her an Oscar nomination and giving her a No. 1 best-selling album in the form of the two-LP soundtrack. In the afterglow of Diana's first major venture as an actress, she admitted, "Somehow I feel [a little] lost between 'Baby Love' and 'Lady Sings the Blues.' I'm not sure which direction my career will take now. I do know that whatever happens, I intend to spend a good deal of my time with my family. I've been traveling and working for twelve years now, and I want to make sure that my two children (Rhonda and Tracy) grow up properly. I know that as children of a mixed marriage, they're going to face a lot of problems, and I want to help them as much as possible."

Six months later Diana was back in Britain for her first European shows, and we met up once again at a press conference. The ballad "Touch Me in the Morning" had already become a No. 1 pop hit in the U.S., and the album of the same name was firmly planted in the Top 10. This was the first time that Diana had tried her hand at producing, choosing John Lennon's "Imagine," as well as a medley of Marvin Gaye's "Save the Children" and Oscar Brown Jr.'s "Brown Baby" to showcase her skills. As she commented in a 1973 *Blues & Soul* article that resulted from our interview, "I've learned to work the board and I'm beginning to find out what producing is all about. . . ."

Much to my surprise, Diana expressed some concern that her solo recording career hadn't progressed as much as she might have liked. "Well, I wasn't too happy about the way some of the records weren't as big as we'd hoped—things like *Surrender*. Of course, you don't expect everything to be a smash, but I wasn't satisfied with the *Everything Is Everything* album. . . . When I do an album, I like it to be good all the way through—I don't want no 'throw outs'!"

Diana dispelled a few of those famous myths during our chat. She was full of praise for fellow Motown recording artist thelma Houston, noting "it's really only a question of the right song for thelma, and I know she's got to make it. We've spent quite a lot of time together since she joined Motown, and I'm sure it won't be long now before she's a really big star." Then Diana dropped a mini-bombshell with another revelation. As I wrote back then, "she spends time with her 'competitors' whenever possible. "I see Aretha, Roberta (Flack), you know. In fact, I was talking with Roberta only the other day about hairstyles, fashions, and her forthcoming film on Bessie Smith. Sure, I look on all girls as competition— you know, it's good for you; it gives you something to fight for!"

Diana was back on the charts as 1973 came to a close with an album of duets she'd recorded with Motown's leading man, Marvin Gaye. In my interview with her twenty years later, she didn't mince words in describing the experience: "Marvin was such a mysterious person . . . loving, very sensitive for a man. We did the first couple of things together, and then I wouldn't record with him in the studio. . . . I found it hard to work with him in the studio so we started singing separately. I'll tell you why: because he used to smoke grass, and I didn't want to be in there. At the time, I was pregnant. . . . I remember distinctly saying, 'If you want to do this, do it outside.'"

Whatever problems Diana and Marvin might have encountered in the studio, the result of their collaboration was commercially successful. The album became a Top 30 best-seller and produced two Top 20 pop and R&B hits, "You're a Special Part of Me" and "My Mistake (Was to Love You)." Intent on restoring Diana's supremacy as a hit-maker, Motown released her third album in twelve months as 1973 came to a close. *Last Time I Saw Him* was a bit of a hodgepodge, and the cutesy title track brought Diana to a total of four hit singles (including the February release "Good Morning Heartache" from *Lady Sings the Blues*) in the space of one year. It was just as well that Motown had released so much material on Diana in 1973. More than two years would pass before the label would have a new studio recording to release; one live LP, recorded at Caesar's Palace in Las Vegas, was issued in the summer of 1974. Not long afterward, Diana was honored at New York's Radio City Music Hall when some of the top names in jazz, including Charlie Mingus, Art Blakey, Max Roach, and Clark Terry, performed a special tribute to her work in "Lady Sings the Blues."

In between studio albums, Diana gave birth to a third daughter, Chudney, and completed her second film, *Mahogany*, which had begun production in November, 1974. In a *Blues & Soul* Hall of Fame article in 1980, writer Sharon Davis described the film as "based around the fashion world . . . and Diana played Tracy Chambers, an ambitious young secretary who became a high fashion model. . . . It was a Berry Gordy film for Paramount and involved a filming schedule that was divided between Chicago and Rome. Diana not only headlined the film but designed [all] the clothes she wore. . . ." Davis quoted Diana as saying, "In high school, I studied fashion design and costume illustration, but the only opportunity I ever had in this direction was in my own personal wear with the Supremes. When the opportunity to do *Mahogany* came up and I took the script home, I realized it was about a fashion designer; I wanted to design the clothes but Berry wasn't too keen on the idea. But he trusts me and knows that if I take on a responsibility, I'll do it to the best of my ability."

Gordy needn't have worried: Diana delivered not only some great gowns but a strong performance that reaffirmed her skills as a burgeoning actress. *Mahogany* was a box-office hit after its release in 1975, and life in the Ross world appeared to be going well. But underneath the surface, Diana was dealing with some personal challenges. Just a few weeks before an interview she did with Bob Killbourn for Britain's *Blues & Soul* in March, 1976, Diana had attended the funeral of Florence Ballard, her former partner in the Supremes who had died of cardiac arrest. "I was, and still am, deeply shocked. I had spoken with Florence a week or two before, and all seemed well with her. Although she still had personal problems, she appeared to be making headway and was philosophical about her (past) life." Diana and Motown had set up a trust fund for Florence's three children, and according to Killbourn, "It was apparent that Ms. Ross was [still] emotionally upset [so] the matter was no longer pursued."

Diana was in a candid mood when she talked with Killbourn at *Blues & Soul*, talking about her work with "est," then a very popular and somewhat controversial two-weekend seminar designed to cause a transformation to occur in whatever areas of life the participants chose to work on. She'd been told about est by Suzanne de Passe, a high-level Motown executive who had worked with her on "Lady Sings the Blues" and had been closely involved with the development of the Jackson 5. The est principles would turn out to be a major motivating force for change in Diana's life and a common discussion point for the two of us many years later. Back in 1976, she told Killbourn, "I had reached a crisis in my life. . . . The everyday joy of life had diminished. . . . Simple problems became major dilemmas. . . . Things in general were at a pretty low ebb. Both my private and professional life suffered. After being introduced to est and getting over the initial reluctance of 'opening up' in front of total strangers, I discovered the sharing of problems with others who had similar difficulties helped me considerably, and I was able to get things into perspective and treat them accordingly."

One of the immediate outcomes was Diana's divorce from Bob Silberstein just four months after the interview appeared in *Blues & Soul*. On the career front, Diana was looking at new challenges. She'd told Killbourn that although she'd focused on making movies, she'd lost none of her enthusiasm for music: "While it is true to say that I am continually seeking out new challenges and other creative outlets, music is and always will be a motivating force for me. As a means of expression, music is a priority. . . . I love to sing!" A new self-titled Motown album gave her the chance to do just that, jumping up the charts thanks to the irresistible "Love Hangover," a dance-club smash that topped the pop and R&B charts in the summer of 1976. It was Diana's first No. 1 pop hit since 1975's "Theme from *Mahogany* (Do You Know Where You're Going to?)."

In my 1993 interview with Diana for *Billboard*, she mentioned her 1976 smash: "I remember Suzanne de Passe bringing me "Love Hangover," and she had to make me believe in the song because it wasn't exactly a song. . . . I mean, it was a lot of improvising; it was all 'feel.' . . . It was like the beginning of the disco, kinda dance things. . . . She played it to me in my kitchen, and I kept saying, 'Yeah, but. . . .'" Then I went in the studio and did it in one take. . . . It was all ad-lib, every little thing. . . ."

Weeks before "Love Hangover" began its climb up the international charts, Diana had mounted her second European trip. "An Evening with Diana Ross" ran for more than an hour-and-a-half, and featured mime dancers, background singers, an eight-member rhythm section, and a 35-piece orchestra. Diana had worked on the show with famed director Joe Layton, and when it finally hit the Palace on Broadway in the summer of 1976, it was a resounding success, featuring Supremes classics, tributes to Billie Holiday and Josephine Baker, and current hits. Extended to a total of three weeks, the concert broke all box-office records at the prestigious venue. Diana subsequently took the show to the Ahmanson theater in Los Angeles, where it was recorded for a live 1977 release.

Diana's next challenge was a return to movie-making. But rather than providing the much-anticipated hat trick, Diana's third film didn't achieve the kind of critical acclaim or box-office success her first two films had. Based on the Broadway version of the original *The Wizard of Oz*, the much-touted screen version of *The Wiz*—complete with an all-star cast that included Diana, Michael Jackson, and Lena Horne—didn't receive universal raves. Part of the problem stemmed from the idea that Diana was playing the role of Dorothy, which Stephanie Mills had been doing so triumphantly for several years on Broadway. The film, with a score by Quincy Jones, would have been the perfect vehicle for taking Mills to a new level of recognition. Instead, Diana's portrayal of a young girl from Kansas had an element of disbelief about it, and the legion of Ross detractors had a field day. Finally, Diana appeared to have taken a misstep, and all the people who had been waiting to tear her down publicly used *The Wiz* as their opportunity. Admittedly the film had flaws, and those who had seen the Broadway production felt the film left something to be desired.

Recovery came in the form of a new album that provided instant restoration to critics and foes alike. Diana returned to the team that had helped launch her solo career, Nick Ashford and Valerie Simpson. Now married, parents, and a successful recording-and- performing duo in their own right, they were the perfect choice for resurrecting Diana's musical career. A couple of albums, *Baby It's Me* and *Ross*, had done only fair business, while *The Boss*, an aptly titled album of Ashford & Simpson originals, was an out-and-out smash. It was Diana's first gold LP and was recorded in Manhattan, where the single mother of three now made her home. Reflecting on the album in 1993, Diana mentioned, "[Listening back], I started to notice how good Nick and Valerie's songs were for me. . . . I was listening to 'The Boss,' and it still sounds really good. I remember when I used to do the high part at the end of that song, and everybody thought that wasn't me, that [it] was probably somebody else!" The record was done, Diana recalled, "as a complete album. . . . It was not 'go and record' and do different songs and put them in the can. . . . I selected the songs and [at that time], I was taking a little more responsibility as an artist. I was fighting a lot to have a voice. . . ."

Aside from appealing to pop and R&B audiences, almost the whole album was adored by Diana's many gay fans the world over. Tracks like "No One Else Gets the Prize," "I Ain't Been Licked," and the sizzling title cut were standard fare every Saturday night at the Paradise Garage in Manhattan and, likewise, at every other gay (and for that matter, straight) disco from London to Los Angeles.

While Motown had been focusing on other superstar artists like Stevie Wonder and Marvin Gaye and turning others like Rick James and the Commodores into major sales winners throughout the mid- to late 1970s, it seemed that the company was finally giving Diana's recording career the attention it warranted. Ironically, just as she became one of the company's hottest hit-makers, she was beginning to think about moving on to new pastures.

Diana's last few years with Motown were in fact most successful purely from a sales standpoint. Hot on the heels of *The Boss*, Diana teamed up with Nile Rodgers and Bernard Edwards, two New Yorkers who had masterminded a run of hits with their own group, Chic, and with female quartet Sister Sledge. Working with the duo, Diana said in 1993, "was a really good experience because by the time I had moved to New York, and I had put my kids in school there. I had also gone through the things you go through in your life. I remember finishing 'The Wiz,' and I think people start making changes in their lives when they feel dissatisfied . . . and I was really making changes in my life right at that time. That's when I met Nile and Bernard, and we were talking about this up at my apartment. Then they went away and wrote about all the things I was saying. I felt like I was 'coming out,' and my life was 'upside down.' I think about the only song on that album probably was *not* an identification with me was 'My Old Piano.'"

With catchy lyrics and infectious rhythms, *diana* became the first of her two platinum albums; the singles "Upside Down" (a gold record and a No. 1 pop and R&B smash) and "I'm Coming Out" were unqualified hits. But the project had a few post-recording problems. Apparently, when Diana and senior Motown executives first listened to the finished masters, they weren't happy with what they heard. Without making any further requests of producers Rodgers and Edwards, Diana and Motown engineer Russ Terrana remixed it. Publicly, the Chic producers expressed their displeasure, noting that the final album bore little or no relation to the tapes they'd turned in to Motown. During a visit to London in the fall of 1980, Diana explained to British writer Graham Betts in a *Blues & Soul*, interview, "When I listened to the tapes, they sounded pretty much like Chic or Sister Sledge. In fact they were a bit too much 'disco.' . . . You have to remember that both Nile and Bernard have only been in the industry for two or three years. . . . In remixing the album, I felt that I [was] able to put a little of *Diana Ross* into the product. In many cases, all I've done is take out some of the musical interludes. As to whether or not I'll be working with Nile and Bernard again, well, I hope so because I enjoyed working with them. . . ."

The upswing in Diana's recording career came at a time when she seemed to be having fun personally. On the subject of a romantic hookup with Cher's former beau Gene Simmons of the glam rock group Kiss, Diana was surprisingly forthcoming: ". . . Let me say that I'm interested in many forms of music, and I enjoyed Kiss when I saw them live for the first time. As you know, Gene has a 'hard' image onstage,

Diana Ross after
receiving *Cue* magazine's
twelfth annual Entertainer of
the Year Award in January, 1973
Credit: Archive Photos

what with spitting blood and such. Offstage, Gene couldn't be more different. He's really quite gentle." Diana also addressed rumors that she and Cher were no longer speaking, noting, ". . . That's rubbish! In fact, it was Cher who first introduced me to Gene, and just recently Gene and I had dinner with Cher and her current boyfriend."

Diana ended 1980 triumphantly with "It's My Turn," the title song for a film of the same name. The tune's lyrics seemed to sum up her own state of mind since 1981 was very much a year of change. Diana's initial twenty-year association with Motown came to an end (although she reappeared on the label's roster in 1989 after Berry Gordy had sold the company to MCA Records and Boston Ventures and a small number of other investors including Diana herself). She ended her link with the company that had launched her first as a member of the most popular female group in recording history and then as an international superstar on an up note: the theme from a film of the same name, "Endless Love," a duet with Lionel Richie, then the lead singer of the Commodores, became a platinum-selling pop and R&B chart topper and aside from receiving multiple Grammy nominations, it was also nominated for "Best Song of the Year" at the Academy Awards.

The pair sang the song at the ceremony in 1982, by which time Richie had launched a successful solo career. Although "Endless Love" didn't win an Oscar, the duo turned in a stellar performance; it is worth noting that both on the record and during the Oscar show, Diana was exhibiting a new power in her voice, a strength and confidence that had seeped into both *The Boss* and *diana* albums.

By mid-May the negotiations were complete, and Diana Ross became an RCA recording artist, at least in the U.S. and Canada, signing a reported $15 million-plus deal that would last for eight years. In a shrewd business move, she negotiated a separate contract for the world outside North America, signing with EMI in London, a decision that would definitely have an impact on the success she maintained in Europe throughout the 1980s and early 1990s. In 1993 she talked about the move to RCA, revealing that her departure from Motown was not easy: ". . . It was tremendously hard. . . . I had moved to New York . . . and I was beginning to grow up, take responsibility for my own life, take a step out. . . . It was important for me to stand on my own two feet. . . . Things were different. . . . Motown was no longer in Detroit. . . . The people [at Motown] trying to give you directions were not the people from the beginning. . . . People were telling me what to do, and I didn't know who they were. Berry was always very busy. . . . The Motown family relationship was really gone. . . ."

The RCA years weren't necessarily as consistently hit-filled as Diana's last few years at Motown had been, but they did offer her an opportunity to stretch creatively. "This was the first time I started to get so involved. . . . I just wanted to put my feelings on paper more. I didn't do a lot. . . . The first [song] I did was "Work That Body." When I made this move [to RCA] . . . it was just like there was a relationship with the musicians, I got to know the people who did the arrangements, . . . and I was there in the mixing. . . . I spent time at the mastering session. . . ." It was also a time for Diana to step up to the plate as owner of a number of her own companies: "In 1980, I went into business. I created my own management company. . . . I had my own offices, secretaries, the whole setup. I started having a few people that were my team, I started employing people . . . I started my own little Motown. . . .When you start setting up your own company, then you know you've grown up!"

RCA was thrilled at having such a major name on the roster and threw a big party for Diana just before the release of her first product for the label. We briefly spoke at this function, and I whispered in her ear that we had something in common since I'd also participated in the work of Werner Erhard and est. She smiled, and we talked about some of the programs we'd both done before it was time for one of the hundreds of other guests to greet her.

Why Do Fools Fall in Love, Diana's debut album for RCA, was a triumph for her since she'd produced it herself; she chose the title track, a remake of the 1956 Frankie Lymon & the Teenagers hit, because she said it was always one of her favorite songs as a preteen growing up in Detroit. Her skills as the creative controller of her own destiny were validated when the LP went platinum and the single made it to the R&B and pop Top 10 charts. Two other hits emerged from the album, the catchy "Mirror, Mirror" and her own "Work That Body," the latter rising into Britain's Top 10.

In Europe, Diana could do no wrong. Appearing at Britain's Wembley Arena in June, 1982, she wowed the packed stadium with a show that was a complete crowd pleaser even though she expressed her displeasure with the sound crew by kicking a monitor offstage and stopping the band four times while adjustments were made to the sound quality. Her public display of irritation endeared her to her fans, who understood that she wanted to give her best; the press, meanwhile, had a field day and even *Blues & Soul* wasn't above having a little fun with her with the headline, "Diana Throws a Wembley Wobbler!"

Leaving Britain, Diana headed off to other parts of Europe before returning to the U.S. for a triumphant show at the enormous

Meadowlands Stadium in New Jersey with special guests Miles Davis and Frankie Beverly & Maze. A second RCA album, 1982's gold LP *Silk Electric*, got off to a strong start thanks to the single "Muscles," written and produced by Michael Jackson, who had acknowledged Diana's role as a mentor and inspiration. The song would be Diana's last Top 10 record in almost two years. The 1983 *Ross* album did moderately well, but one of the more significant events of the year for the Manhattan-based entertainer was her appearance on Motown's famed twenty-fifth-anniversary celebration. Controversy reared its head once more when Diana invited Berry Gordy to the stage at the climax of the show, with Mary Wilson alleging that Diana had pushed her out of the way, grabbing the mike to bring Gordy up to receive his due acclaim. In 1993 Diana made no secret of how important Gordy was to her: "I guess you can tell that I admire him greatly. I really, really do. There were . . . difficult times . . . and I always think . . . that when people are difficult, you think they're difficult but they're *teaching* you in a sense. . . . In your life, I think there's somebody that pushes you forward regardless of whether they were driving you batty or not!"

Two months later, Diana set some new records by performing free before almost one million people in New York's Central Park, with a goal of raising enough money from sales of merchandise, such as posters and T-shirts, to create a children's playground in the park. That first night, July 21, Mother Nature had some other plans: the sky opened up, sending down sheets of rain. But Diana kept going until she literally had to be pulled offstage! Fortunately, the second night of the show, which was called "For One and For All," was rain-free. In the liner notes for her *Forever* box set, she states, "The performance was a big success. We all left there in the sunshine, feeling very happy and complete."

In 1984 *Swept Away*, which was Diana's fourth RCA set, went gold, spearheaded by a Lionel Richie-penned-and-produced poignant tribute to Marvin Gaye, who had been murdered by his father eight months earlier. This would be her last gold album for RCA, and although "Chain Reaction," a single written by the Bee Gees and taken from her 1985 *Eaten Alive* LP would be a huge No. 1 British pop hit, Diana's relationship with RCA had come to an end with *Red Hot Rhythm and Blues* in 1987. The release of that last album also prompted an ABC-TV special of the same name, which included Etta James as a special guest. The R&B, blues, and jazz stylist had apparently been a major influence on Diana as a young girl: ". . . I used to watch her, and I used to try and sing like her when I was little," she revealed in our 1993 chat. "I must have been twelve or thirteen, and I'd stand in front of the mirror singing [her hit] "At Last.'"

The television show received some nice ratings, but the album had little impact. Diana looked back on her six years with the company in our 1993 *Blues & Soul* article: "My contract was up and they had changed manpower there. Now [new] people had come in, and the truth is, they didn't value me; I really felt like they were into this new, young crop of artists, whoever was coming up at the time. I remember thinking, 'I need to be somewhere where people are happy to have me.' And the records hadn't been hits at the end of those years and, again, it's about making money. . . ."

While Diana was in the midst of leaving RCA, she'd met and married Norwegian shipping magnate Arne Naess. The couple were wed in Switzerland in February, 1986, and longtime Motown pal Stevie Wonder sang at the wedding. After Diana gave birth to their first son, Ross Arne, in October, 1987, and to another son, Evan Olav, ten months later, she took time off from recording and performing to enjoy married life.

1987 was also the year that *Dreamgirls*, Mary Wilson's autobiography, was published. Responding to comments about it, Diana told a television interviewer (according to a 1987 issue of *Blues & Soul*), "Mary is entitled to have her say. But if that's how she really saw things, then it's totally different from how I saw it. . . . [Now] I find it really hard to be close. But I really don't bear ill will. . . ." In *Secrets of a Sparrow*, Diana's 1993 memoir, she includes a few more comments about the autobiography. The bottom line was that Wilson's comments had hurt, and clearly the relationship would never be the same.

Looking ahead as 1988 approached, Diana was considering her options in terms of her next move as a recording artist: "MCA was interested in me. . . . Somewhere around that time, Berry sold the company [Motown] to MCA, ... and I didn't know that. I had already made a deal with MCA when they approached me and said, '. . . we'd like you to be on Motown.' I had a lot of thoughts about it, so I said, 'If I come back to the company, I would like to come back in the capacity of being more than just an artist. I would like to try to be the keeper of the flame, to keep Motown the way it was in the early days, to be nurturing to the artists, to try to give them the wisdom that I had learned over these years about business, about the road.' And that really is what [Motown president] Jheryl (Busby) wanted—to make Motown like it was with new, young artists. I wanted to be there to nurture it, to be involved in that, so I went back basically because I just didn't want to let Motown disappear. I'm not saying it would have [if I hadn't gone back], but I just thought maybe I could keep it the way it once was without it becoming the big kinda factory situation. . . ."

Diana's intentions might have all been good, but it soon became evident that her second tenure with Motown would be fraught with challenges and disappointments. Her first album for the newly restructured label was 1989's *Workin' Overtime*, an obvious attempt to take Diana into the next decade, complete with a new image—ripped jeans, leather jacket and all—and some hip tracks, produced by Nile Rodgers. The results were less than stellar. Asked how it was to be back with Motown, Diana spoke candidly during our 1993 meeting: ". . . It's been very much a grind. I stayed off work for about a year. . . . I was having my babies, and during that time I spent a lot of time watching BET (Black Entertainment Television) on television, the kids doing the hip-hop and so on, . . . and, you know, I'm a risk-taker. So I decided to do *Workin' Overtime* because I don't really wanna do just what's expected. . . . I did that album, and I like it very much. It did not do that well, and I think it could have done well if it had been promoted better. Even with Motown's name, it was still like a brand-new company, a baby company, and a lot of things had to be worked out. Some business things seemed to interfere with getting the material out there. . . . I was caught in a little bit of that. But when you start a business, I think it takes almost seven years [to get going]. . . ."

Diana's prediction wasn't quite fulfilled: nine years into her contract and three more albums later, she has yet to achieve the kind of success with Motown that her new pact with the label promised. *The Force Behind the Power*, a 1991 release, held much promise, and in the wake of an R&B Top 5 hit earlier in the year with new-jack swing singer Al B. Sure! (on the track "No Matter What You Do"), there was every reason to think that Diana might have achieved more success. As it turned out, the album—which boasted a title track written by Stevie Wonder along with a version of his classic "Blame It on the Sun," as well as some other new songs, including "When You Tell Me You Love Me," which became a Top 5 British pop hit at the end of 1991, would do only moderately well. In a 1992 interview with Sharon Davis for *Blues & Soul*, Diana talked about the loyalty of her British audiences. ". . . I haven't left the hearts and minds of a lot of Europeans but sometimes at home, people say, 'When are you going to have a new record out?' And I say, 'Huh? I have one out right now. . . .' I've said this often, there's a loyalty here that I don't experience anywhere else. . . ."

While EMI, still Diana's recording affiliation outside North America, was giving her additional hits, Motown in the U.S. was struggling to deliver. In 1993 the label released *Stolen Moments*, a live album of jazz and blues standards recorded in December, 1992, at the Ritz theater in New York. In the fall of 1993, the company put out *Forever, Diana*, a four-disc retrospective that she'd compiled to celebrate thirty years of Top 30 hits. The project included five new songs, plus one tune from her *Stolen Moments* album that had been released only outside the U.S. The accompanying booklet includes notes from Diana, and the entire set was the focus of a major campaign that also included the publication of her memoirs by Villard Books. 1993 was also the year that Diana began work on a made-for-television movie, "Out of Darkness," which was produced by her own Anaid Productions company and shown on ABC-TV. In arguably her best performance as an actress, Diana portrayed Paulie Cooper, a paranoid schizophrenic; her work was superb. The story was told with compassion but a number of scenes were disturbingly real, and Diana's acting was so strong that she made the character completely believable.

After finishing the project, Diana focused on recording a new album for Motown. The company had been through a number of changes when Diana's last album for the label was released in 1995. In 1993 MCA and Boston Ventures had sold the company to PolyGram. Two years later, president Jheryl Busby was replaced by Uptown Records founder Andre Harrell just as Diana's *Take Me Higher* album was issued. Once again, the record had been carefully made, using the services of established hit-makers like Narada Michael Walden and Nick Martinelli alongside singer/songwriter Brenda Russell and young hip-hop producers Jon-John and the Boom Brothers. A revival of Gloria Gaynor's "I Will Survive," complete with a video with special guest RuPaul, should have been a sizable hit, but once again Motown seemed unable to take Diana Ross back up the charts in the U.S.

While other divas from the 1960s, such as Dionne Warwick, Gladys Knight, and Roberta Flack, have faced the challenge of producing hits in the 1990s, Diana Ross hasn't been helped by the myths that still exist surrounding her public persona and image. In Europe and other parts of the globe, she remains a constant attraction as a performing and recording artist. In the U.S., however, while she continues to perform, her records are all but ignored by the mass music-buying public even though she has worked with contemporary producers and writers.

While preparing to write this chapter, I decided to check in with a few people I know to try and discover the root of the myths surrounding Diana Ross. It was true that some individuals had observed her at close range and were quick to validate the idea that she was indeed an unholy bitch who was difficult, temperamental, aloof, and unfriendly. I knew from my observations of every diva in this book that there were times when each could have been accused of the same thing.

I considered the source when listening to these unflattering remarks and thought about my own brief but notable experiences with Diana. I could tell, particularly from our lengthy 1993 interview session, that she was very focused. She admitted that the kind of perfectionism that seemed to drive her career came from an early age: ". . . I don't know where this came from, but I have always had this thing about professionalism, about time and all of that stuff. I've always been like that, and I've always been about keeping my word. . . ." She agreed that the drive she'd always had, starting out as a child, could be a problem for some people: "I think that I wear people out—I'm sure I do; I wear them out! Sometimes, you know, I have to calm myself down because I know other people work at different tempos than I do. . . ."

When asked, a few folks said that the source of their negative perception of Ross began when her name appeared out front when she was still with the Supremes. "It was like the group was ours, as black people. We were proud of them, of what they had done as a team, and now here was Diana stepping out. We thought, 'Wow, why is she breaking this team up?' and 'Who does she think she is?' and we were pissed off about it. Then, when she went solo, it was like she had deserted them completely. . . ."

Validating my notion about the apparent dislike that some black people felt for Diana Ross, another source noted that it was the fact that her records were too pop, that she was perceived as an artist who did not want to be thought of as a black or R&B singer. In a 1987 article in *Blues & Soul*, writer Sharon Davis reported: "She . . . says that Motown's success was due to Berry Gordy having a vision of what he wanted and his determination to push black artists into the position held by whites. Unlike other companies of the time, who chased and promoted white acts who could sing like blacks, Gordy wanted to find black acts who had a commercial 'white' sound. 'I don't know if he really sat down and said, 'this is what I'm going to try and do' but most of the performers [at Motown] had such commercial sounding voices, you'd never know if they were black or white. What was coming through was a spirit in the music. Berry pulled the best out of everyone there. . . ."

Diana's marriage to two white men seemed irrelevant to those I asked, as did her relationship with Gordy, which for years had been only a rumor. What seemed important was the idea that she would do whatever it took to make it, that she was so ambitious that she would walk over anyone who stood in her way. I turned to Dionne Warwick, another diva, to try to get some perspective on what it was about Diana Ross that upset people in a way that no one else did. Dispelling another myth, Dionne said that the image that had been created for Diana was in fact Gordy's doing. "She and I have been friends for a long time, and I can tell you that the whole idea of Diana Ross as this untouchable, inaccessible star was something Berry Gordy created. When she first started out, Diane (her real name) had to follow every step Berry gave her to follow. And that was in everything, from who she could be seen with, how she conducted herself, everything. She was a 'product' of Motown from the beginning. Of course, there had to be something there to work with, and Diane is certainly very talented. But the whole thing of her as this aloof star, this unreachable diva, that was all part of the image that Gordy created for her. . . ."

Dionne shared how she and Diana had often giggled about the supposed rivalry that existed between them. Dionne also revealed that while they hadn't been "hanging-out" buddies, as she was with Gladys Knight and Patti LaBelle, "Diane's been to my house a few times, we've been at parties together, and so on. In fact, we flew on the Concorde to London [in 1998], and we sat and talked about the things we both want to accomplish. She and I both want to have our own record companies and like I want to find and groom the next Dionne, she wants to do the same thing with new recording artists. . . ."

Dionne and I both agreed that Diana Ross had done some incredible things in her career (though strangely enough she'd never received a Grammy Award), and even her detractors had to agree that she deserved praise and respect for what she has accomplished as a black pioneer. Perhaps being a woman who is driven to accomplish, can be tough for some people to handle, and yes, there are going to be times when such people will be difficult or hard to work with, but that notion cuts across all racial, economic, and social lines.

As I left Diana's office in 1993, I had to smile. An assistant had asked her what she wanted for lunch. Ross-bashers might have expected her to say caviar and champagne. But those who thought Diana, the skinny girl from Detroit's Brewster projects, had lost any of her "blackness," might have been surprised at the answer. "Can you get something from Roscoe's?" she asked, sweeping back her trademark hair, referring to a famous L.A. soul-food restaurant. "You know, the one on La Brea. I'd like some smothered chicken with lots of gravy and some waffles. . . ." I grinned. She might hang out with kings, queens (both real and unreal), dukes, duchesses, presidents, and prime ministers, but Diana Ross is still a true Detroit diva!

GLA

KNIC

th

nitty

DYS

GHT

he real

gritty

"I get my natural high just singing!" Gladys Knight said with a big grin. She was sitting in her room at a plush hotel that was a little way down the street from fashionable Knightsbridge, home to Harrod's, London's famous store. It had been a long day for Gladys and the Pips, brother Merald (nicknamed "Bubba") and cousins Edward and William. The publicist had made it clear: either I wait patiently for Gladys to return from a quick shopping trip and have dinner with her, or we don't do any interview. As if I could say no! I don't remember all the details of our meeting, such as what she was wearing or what we had to eat, but I do remember that Gladys came across with the kind of genuine, down-to-earth manner that has made her one of the more basic divas. No pretense, no airs and graces—just a down-home good woman who was happy to talk about her life and career.

Gladys balked only when I mentioned Aretha Franklin and inquired whether people had compared the two since Aretha had had her commercial breakthrough in 1967 and Gladys and the Pips had started a run of Motown hits at the same time. I was comfortable enough in her presence to speculate that many of Aretha's songs seemed to be based on her own experiences, especially in her relationships with men. "Well, that's Aretha," Gladys said, the only time she got just a little bit frosty during the two hours we spent together. "The songs I sing may not necessarily come from situations I've experienced, so I used my vivid imagination. And, no, I don't consider we're similar vocally. . . ." And that, to paraphrase one of Gladys & the Pips' fifty-odd hits, was the end of that road!

Or maybe not. Twenty-six years after my first face-to-face interview with Gladys, I'm sitting in the ballroom of the Sheraton Hotel in Manhattan and Gladys is reuniting with the Pips while the entire group is honored with a Lifetime Achievement Award from the Rhythm & Blues Foundation. This is a trip down memory lane for most of those in attendance as Gladys and the Pips deliver hit after hit, from "Letter Full of Tears," to the inevitable "Midnight Train to Georgia." Stevie Wonder gives the group its much-deserved award, and he and Gladys tell a funny story. "I remember when we were on the road and Stevie would keep messing around with this song," Gladys smiles. "He kept telling us he was writing it for us...." She breaks into the melody of "Until You Come Back to Me (That's What I'm Gonna Do)," and Stevie laughs. "I wonder what happened to that song, Gladys!" Stevie quips. "Aretha Franklin!" Gladys roars. Everyone is chuckling, especially since they know that Gladys makes it plain in *Between Each Line of Pain and Glory,* her 1997 autobiography, that she has had her share of problems in dealing with Aretha.

In her book Gladys alleges that Aretha snubbed her at a Grammy event years before, as well as that, although the two have occasionally spoken, there has always been some distance between them as a result of Aretha's coolness toward her. Some weeks after the publication of Gladys's autobiography, Aretha sends a photograph of the two of them sitting together to *Jet* magazine, wondering how much closer they could be. The diva saga continues.

In reality, through twenty-seven years with the Pips and another ten as a solo artist, Gladys has clearly established her own legacy, and comparisons with other female singers seem pointless. It hadn't been easy, especially after she finally ventured out on her own in 1988. Even though Gladys had an instantly recognizable vocal tone and style, the public perception was that she was part of a musical institution. In the same way that Patti LaBelle had stepped out from the group Labelle ten years before, Gladys wasn't sure how the record-buying public would respond. And while her solo performances have won rave reviews and she has managed to establish her own identity as a super diva, her record sales haven't necessarily matched her general popularity. In a 1994 interview for *Blues & Soul* at the San Fernando Valley home she shared with now-ex-husband Les Brown, Gladys told me that she'd made *Just for You,* her last album for MCA, "for my fans, the folks who aren't sixteen anymore, who crave the kind of music I'm known for."

That kind of music has its roots way back in the earliest recordings of the family group known as the Pips. Like so many other soulful divas, Gladys first sang in public in church, specifically the Mount Moriah Baptist Church in Atlanta. But unlike any of her contemporaries, she won first prize on "The Ted Mack Amateur Hour," the popular 1950s national television show, at the age of eight, captivating audiences in 1952 with her rendition of Nat 'King' Cole's "Too Young" and walking home with a check for $2,000. That same year, she and brother Merald were singing together at his birthday party when their sister Brenda and young cousins Eleanor and William Guest joined the action. James "Pip" Woods, another older cousin, thought the quintet had potential and began working with the Pips, as they became known. Gladys was just ten when the family group started performing at the Royal Peacock, a popular music spot in Atlanta. Just two years later, in 1956, the Pips were on the road with Sam Cooke and Jackie Wilson, two of the hottest hit-makers of the day.

By 1958 Brenda and Eleanor had left and were replaced by two other cousins, Edward Patten and Langston George, who would stay with the group until 1962. The Pips' first record was made for the national Brunswick label, which was also Jackie Wilson's new recording home. "Whistle My Love" didn't exactly run up the charts but three years later, Gladys, by now a teen bride, & the Pips had a hit. In fact, in 1961 the group had two hits with the same song! As Gladys details in her autobiography, club owner Clifford "Fats" Hunter had recorded the group singing "Every Beat of My Heart," a Johnny Otis song, at his club in 1960, and without their permission had put it out on his own HunTom label. Sensing that it could well be a national hit, he sold the master to Vee-Jay Records, which promptly issued it under the name "Pips" in May, 1961.

Word had spread about the record and about the exciting sound that Gladys Knight & the Pips had created, tight harmonies behind Gladys's earthy, gospel-trained, deep blue tones. Marshall Sehorn, a New Orleans character and talent scout had mentioned the group to Bobby Robinson, a Harlem-based record man who had started his own group of labels, Fire, Fury, and Enjoy. The company had some national success with Wilbert Harrison's "Kansas City" in 1959, and once Robinson heard what had happened with the first unauthorized version of "Every Beat of My Heart," he took the group into the studio to recut the song.

Robinson released the new recording of the song on his Fury label under the name "Gladys Knight & the Pips" to compete with the Vee-Jay version. The two companies started battling it out to see whose record would make it nationally. Ultimately, the Vee-Jay version (for which the group didn't get paid) ended up at the top of the R&B charts and in the nation's pop Top 10.

Fury issued a second single, a version of "Guess Who," a song that had been a hit for R&B star Jesse Belvin two years earlier, but it failed to make the grade. Finally, Gladys and the Pips found themselves with a Top 10 R&B and Top 20 pop single for which they could expect to get paid: "Letter Full of Tears" was released toward the end of 1961 and spent five months on the charts. It looked like the group had arrived. But Gladys's attention was on other matters. She'd married James Newman, a local Atlanta saxophone player, and given birth to her first son, James Jr., in 1962. She stayed off the road for a year, during which daughter Kenya was born, while the Pips soldiered on alone, releasing just one single, "Darling," which made some noise in the South. Newman had courted Gladys even though, as she recalled in a 1983 interview with Sharon Davis for *Blues & Soul*, "I felt somewhat sheltered because I was on the road so early.... [The Pips] in a sense raised me. We spent so much time on the road, and after I got to be a teenager, I wondered if something was wrong with me because there weren't any guys approaching me. I found out later that they felt threatened by Bubba, Edward and William."

Those early years were no walk in the sun for either Gladys or the Pips: traveling up and down the country, encountering blatant racism in the South, working three and four shows a night, and sometimes wondering if they were going to get paid. Somehow, Gladys was also trying to raise her two children and keep her marriage together. Yet, through all the struggle, she and the Pips had been building a stellar reputation for their stage shows. In addition to their clear harmonies, the Pips—a trio with the departure of Langston George in 1962—were doing some nifty footwork behind Gladys, whose powerhouse singing would slay audiences night after night. The group members' energy endeared them to the crowds, who would flock to see them at various theaters on the chitlin' circuit. Unlike other acts that were dependent on current hits to get work, the group found itself getting consistent bookings on national tours during the mid-1960s.

A hit record or two didn't hurt, and in 1964, after leaving the Fire-Fury setup with a final release, "What Shall I Do," the group signed with Maxx Records, an independent label created by veteran record man Larry Maxwell. Working with up-and-coming songwriter and producing Van McCoy, Gladys & the Pips cut some of their most soulful work. The lead-off single was McCoy's "Giving Up," which would become a "deep-soul" classic, particularly for R&B connoisseurs who were blown away by the sheer emotion that Gladys expressed in her gut-wrenching delivery of the song. Some eight years later renowned singer/songwriter Donny Hathaway would put his personal stamp on the song, but up until that point, the ballad belonged exclusively to Gladys and the group.

"Giving Up" wasn't a major hit in the U.S., edging its way into the R&B Top 40, but it became a cult classic in the U.K. When Maxx issued an entire album in the States, I can remember how soul fanatics like myself went nuts trying to get a copy. Because it was on a small label and wasn't exactly a big seller, it wasn't as easy to find as albums by other

1960s artists who were popular with R&B aficionados, like Maxine Brown, Irma Thomas, and Barbara Lynn. I'll never forget trudging down to a tiny basement store just off Leicester Square in London's West End week after week, my little pocket money in hand, hoping that one day I could get a copy of the LP with the green-bordered sleeve. The day finally dawned, and it was like Christmas in July! I loved tunes like "Lovers Always Forgive," another McCoy gem; the strangely constructed "Maybe Maybe Baby," and the lyrically deep "Either Way I Lose," which the good Dr. Nina Simone recorded a few years later.

In all, Maxx released five singles for the group before going belly up and filing for bankruptcy. According to Gladys's autobiography, Motown's Berry Gordy asked label owner Maxwell to work for the company; Gordy also asked Gladys and the Pips if they wanted to join him at the Detroit-based label. He knew a good thing when he heard or—in the case of Gladys and the Pips—saw one. After having the group perform with some of his own budding stars on the famed Motortown Revue, he offered them a contract. The word on the street was very positive about the kind of performances that Gladys and the Pips could and would deliver. They'd also benefited from working with choreographer Cholly Atkins and vocal coach Maurice King long before Gordy hired both men to work with his growing roster of artists at Motown.

The decision to make the move to Motown was by no means unanimous. In fact, Gladys herself was the holdout. She feared that once they were at the burgeoning company, the group's individuality would be lost and they would never be in the first division of acts that Gordy himself had "created" or discovered, such as the Supremes, the Miracles, and Martha & the Vandellas. The group, which made major decisions democratically, voted three-to-one to join the label, and in 1966 Gladys Knight & the Pips officially became recording artists on Motown's Soul Records subsidiary; they even moved their home base from Atlanta to Detroit. That move alone should have served as something of a warning sign: all the biggest hit-makers, the "A" list of artists at Gordy's "Hitsville" were on the main Motown, Tamla, and Gordy labels. Soul Records, in existence since 1964, featured artists like Shorty Long, Jimmy Ruffin, and Junior Walker, but none of the really big heavy-hitters. And at least a year would pass before Gladys and the Pips would have the full weight of Motown's promotion machinery behind them.

In fact, neither of the group's first two singles for Motown made any kind of chart impact in the U.S. But British music buyers responded favorably to the second release, "Take Me in Your Arms and Love Me," co-written by Barrett Strong, the man behind the early Motown hit "Money," and produced by Norman Whitfield, who would play a key role in the group's development at the Detroit hit factory. The single made the Top 30 In the U.K. Ironically five years later, Motown reissued "Just Walk in My Shoes," the group's very first single; it also became a British hit record.

For dedicated British soul fans, the sight of Gladys Knight & the Pips on the U.K. charts was astonishing. A year after the record's release, the group crossed the Atlantic for the first time and performed at a small theater on London's Shaftesbury Avenue. The review in *Blues & Soul* at the time says it all: "On stage they were too much. The dance routines were so slick that it became no surprise why so many performers call Gladys Knight & the Pips the best group in the union. . . ." This engagement marked the beginning of a love affair between the group and British audiences that would last into the 1970s and early 1980s.

Back at home, it was a different story. Gladys and the Pips were waiting for their first Motown break. It finally came in the summer of 1967 when the mellow ballad "Everybody Needs Love," another Whitfield production, made the R&B Top 10. However, it was the exciting, energy-packed follow-up that gave the group its national breakthrough. "I Heard It Through the Grapevine," with Gladys' torrid, edgy lead vocal and the Pips' inimitable harmonies, took the group to the top of the R&B charts and became its first legitimate pop hit when the song finally made it to No. 2 on the Hot 100. This achievement prompted the release of the group's first Motown album, which was named after its first hit for the label. Unlike subsequent LPs the group made for the company, *I Heard It Through the Grapevine* contained almost all original material.

The success of "Grapevine" was slightly dampened by Motown's decision to release Marvin Gaye's slower, darker recording of the song in 1968. During my first face-to-face chat with Gladys in 1972, she revealed a little-known fact: the track used for Gaye's version of the song had been intended for a song called "Restless," which Gladys and the Pips were going to do as a follow-up to their version of "I Heard It Through the Grapevine." As it was, Marvin's even more successful reading of the song stole some of the group's thunder: it would be another three years before Gladys Knight & the Pips would have another chart topper. In between times, they had some significant hits, all produced by Norman Whitfield; "The End of Our Road," "It Should Have Been Me," a cover of Shirley Ellis's 1963 hit "The Nitty Gritty," "Friendship Train," and "You Need Love Like I Do (Don't You)" were all Top 10 R&B hits with varying degrees of pop success.

The albums were so-so musically and did only marginally well from a sales standpoint. *Silk'n'Soul*, a 1969 set, was entirely made up of cover tunes, from the Temptations' "I Wish It Would Rain," to Dionne Warwick's "(Theme From) *The Valley of the Dolls*." Like its predecessor, *Feelin' Bluesy*, the album did relatively poorly. It took a change in producer to reverse the group's fortunes, and for a while it seemed as if Gladys's initial fears about being lost in the Motown machine had merit.

The change came in 1970 when the group began working with Clay McMurray, a new Motown producer. The song was "If I Were Your Woman," a gutsy tale of a strong and confident woman declaring her love for what we can assume is a married man. With Gladys's passionate reading, the record couldn't fail. In fact, it made it to the top of the R&B charts and became a Top 10 pop hit in the process. And in the same truth-telling vein, "I Don't Want to Do Wrong," the story of a woman who has been trying to stay faithful but is rapidly losing the fight—co-written by, among others, Gladys, her brother Bubba, and her cousin William—climbed up the charts in 1971 and helped to give the group its first best-selling album for Motown, four years after it joined the label. "We recorded "I Don't Want to Do Wrong" back in 1969, but no one really considered it worthy of release," Gladys revealed in our 1972 meeting. "Somehow, they just put it on the . . . album, and it took off from there. It came as quite a shock to everyone!"

Completing a trio of similar tunes was "Make Me the Woman You Go Home to," a logical follow-up to "If I Were Your Woman," which was the first single released from *Standing Ovation*, the group's sixth Motown album. It also made the R&B Top 10. But it was the next single that returned the group to the British charts. "Help Me Make It Through the Night," a song penned by country/pop singer Kris Kristofferson, with a poignant monologue written by Gladys, became a Top 20 U.K. hit toward the end of 1972. The group had been performing the song in concert when playing certain venues, as Gladys explained, "There are a lot of standards—pretty songs—that we were never able to include in our act until we started playing places like Vegas and the Copa. They're songs we'd always wanted to do but never had the opportunity."

Even playing in upscale settings, Gladys Knight & the Pips had lost none of its skills as one of the most potent live acts in the business. ". . . We've always put a lot of hard work into the act and spend a lot of time selecting what goes into it each night. It's very important how we line up the songs . . . and we usually get the 'feel' of the place when we get there. . . ." Performing at the famous London Palladium on November 5, 1972, Gladys and the group were magical, as I reported in a rave review in *Blues & Soul* magazine later that month: "If you've ever thrilled to the spine-tingling yet velvet tones of Miss Knight . . . or to the outstandingly tight harmonies of the Pips, then you haven't heard a thing until you witness the glorious group in action. . . . Gladys Knight is the embodiment of what soul is all about: she oozes emotion with every move, every step, . . . [and] everyone who left the Palladium that night was filled with the sense of having seen and heard something wonderful, an experience of a lifetime. They'd just witnessed an act with class, dignity, guts, talent, artistry, dynamism and one helluva lot of soul!"

No doubt, the group's ability to give a first-class performance carried weight when it came time to find a new recording home. In tandem with its manager Sid Seidenberg, who also represented B.B. King, the group had opted for Buddah Records, a New York-based label founded by record executive Neil Bogart, which had scored some success with a variety of acts, including Melanie, Lou Christie, the Five Stairsteps, and the 1910 Fruitgum Company. Equally as important from the group's standpoint, Buddah was distributing both Curtis Mayfield's Curtom label and record man Clarence Avant's Sussex Records, whose roster included hit-making singer/songwriter Bill Withers. As a result, the company knew its way around both the pop and R&B markets. All that was missing from the main Buddah label was a major crossover act. Gladys Knight & the Pips fit the bill to a tee.

"Our contract [with Motown] expires on March 23," Gladys reported in a 1972 interview with *Blues & Soul* editor John Abbey, "and we are expecting to record around the first of the month [for Buddah]. Naturally, we are working on the material already and I honestly feel that at this stage we have some good songs. . . . We are really looking forward to the move to Buddah. . . . It is important that for the first time, somebody will truly be interested in Gladys Knight & the Pips." Ironically, the week that the group was ending its six-year stint with Motown, it was enjoying what in retrospect would be one of its three biggest hits with the company.

Released at the end of December, 1972, "Neither One of Us (Wants to Be the First to Say Goodbye)" was a beautiful ballad penned by Jim Weatherly, who would play a key role in the group's future at Buddah, and produced by Joe Porter. "We actually recorded it about ten months ago in Los Angeles," Gladys revealed. ". . . It is a chance for us to go back to what we were doing years back. . . . But you know, we really had to fight to get it released, and now it looks like it will be our best seller ever." With its self-descriptive title, the lyrical theme of the song was one that had universal appeal, and within a few months the single was perched at the top of the R&B charts and at No. 2 on the Hot 100. The album of the same name was a mixture of songs Gladys and the Pips had recorded with both producer Porter and Johnny Bristol, and it became the group's one and only Top 10 LP.

The record's success was a real validation for the group members, a sign that they were more than capable of making some superb music that could also sell. All that had been lacking at Motown was the kind of priority that had been reserved for the company's home-grown Detroit superstars, who tended to get better material and a great deal more promotion and exposure. The kind of treatment accorded the group was reflected in the way Motown executives basically ignored Gladys and the Pips' pleas for them to check out a young family group from Gary, Indiana, that they'd heard in 1969. It took the additional interest of Bobby Taylor, another Motown artist (and producer), for the Jackson Five to finally get the audition with Berry Gordy Jr. that would result in the Jacksons signing with Motown. To add insult to injury, no one ever mentioned that Gladys and the Pips had made the first attempt to bring a group that would become one of company's hottest acts to the label; instead, Diana Ross was credited with discovering the Jacksons in the hype and hoopla that surrounded their arrival at Motown in late 1969.

But Motown's loss was Buddah's gain, even though about six weeks before the group's first Buddah single was issued, Gladys and the Pips were riding high with the perky follow-up to "Neither One of Us," a tongue-in-cheek "Daddy Could Swear, I Declare," co-written by Gladys, Bubba, and producer Johnny Bristol. Since the group had begun its sessions for Buddah, it was already feeling the difference between its new recording home and its previous affiliation. The group co-produced "Where Peaceful Waters Flow," its very first single (also written by Weatherly), with Tony Camillo. In its first post-Motown interview with *Blues & Soul*, Gladys was happy to report, ". . . It's the first time we've produced our own sessions ... well, the first time we've been given the credit! That's just one of the freedoms we're looking forward to at Buddah. . . ."

Rather than detailing complaints about the quartet's tenure with Motown, Gladys was typically philosophical, expressing herself honestly without feeling the need to place blame. Her ability to be diplomatic in interviews was something I noted during the years that she and I would talk. She wasn't one to point a finger in blame, and there has always been a kind of down-home warmth and realness in how she responded to questions. She was being generous when she commented on the group's Motown stint: ". . . they opened some doors for us. . . . They helped us get into the Copa, for example, and a lot of the big supper clubs. Once we were in there, of course, it was down to us and happily we succeeded—but they surely opened those doors."

As it turned out, the group's association with Motown ultimately ended on a sour note. Two years after leaving, Gladys & the Pips sued the company for $1 million in damages. According to Sharon Davis in her 1990 *Blues & Soul* profile, "the group demanded ownership of their compositions recorded while signed to the company plus royalties for four albums issued after their recording contract had expired. They also sought to prevent Motown from releasing further product which would inevitably clash with their Buddah recordings." Motown had in fact issued three albums' worth of never-before-issued material, 1973's *All I Need Is Time*, 1974's *Knight Time*, and 1975's "A Little Knight Music," to cash in on the incredible success that Gladys and the Pips were having at Buddah.

Gladys had no idea what lay ahead for the group during what would be its six-year run with Buddah when she speculated about her own future with *Blues & Soul* editor John Abbey in the spring of 1973: "I guess the guys can go on indefinitely, but me, I'm a mother and I have my family to think of, and I do feel that they are missing me and that they are needing me. Myself, I figure that about four years [from now] will be the time to start thinking about slowing up. We work on the road about 330 days a year, and even the month that we're not working shows, we're working on something—a new act or a new album. It's been that way for seven years or more now, and we do really need to slow it on down a little. But we'll never retire—it's in our blood, I guess. . . ."

Thoughts of slowing down were far from the minds of Gladys, Bubba, William, and Edward once their first Buddah album took off. *Imagination*, their first gold LP, contained no fewer than four back-to-back hits. Just a couple of months after "Where Peaceful Waters Flow" was beginning to fall down the charts, what would become the familiar sound of the Pips emulating the sound of a train's whistle could be heard all over the country. The song "Midnight Train to Georgia" virtually became the group's timeless anthem, as well as a gold single, a pop and R&B chart topper, and a Grammy winner.

The origins of the song, which was penned by Jim Weatherly, remain a matter of some controversy. It is an undeniable and undisputed fact that Cissy Houston, the former lead singer with the soulful vocal group the Sweet Inspirations and mother of Whitney, had recorded the song for Janus Records in 1972, and the label had released it in March, 1973, five months before Gladys and the Pips were jumping up the charts with it.

In the August, 1974, issue of *Blues & Soul*, Cissy Houston stated, ". . . the song was originally called "Midnight Plane to Houston" and it really didn't sound right to me—especially with me having the name of Houston. So I sat down with my producer (Sonny Limbo) and we came up with the idea of changing it to "Midnight Train to Georgia." We called over to [songwriter] Jim Weatherly's publisher's office and got permission to change the words and off we went. . . . I don't know about my having on influence on the way Gladys sings it but I remember shortly after Gladys's record started selling big, she did a radio interview and she said what a great version I had done of the song and how at the time she recorded it, she really didn't know what she could add to the song."

In her 1997 autobiography, Gladys seems to suffer from amnesia! In that account, she explains how she and the Pips were working with writer Weatherly and changed the words from "Midnight Plane to Houston" because she hated flying, preferred trains, and had never been to Houston. Maybe only songwriter Weatherly knows the real story of how the song title changed. (I hope that one day I can get Cissy and Gladys in the same room to do an interview, and I'll find out the real deal!)

Regardless of the song's origins, "Midnight Train" took Gladys and the Pips to a new level of national recognition. The quirky "I've Got to Use My Imagination" followed "Midnight Train" up the charts, and "Best Thing That Ever Happened to Me," now considered a Gladys Knight & the Pips classic, was a third gold single. Buddah Records celebrated a first great nine months with Gladys and the Pips by throwing a gala affair at the fancy Waldorf-Astoria Hotel in New York City. Several stars of the day, including Dionne Warwick, Melba Moore, and Paul Simon, attended the event. Three months later, the group was back on the charts with the soundtrack for the movie *Claudine*, which starred Diahann Carroll and James Earl Jones. The film was a big hit with black audiences, and "On and On," the first single released from the album, became the group's fourth consecutive gold record.

The creative marriage between Mayfield and Gladys and the Pips seemed like a perfect union, and the soundtrack—which became yet another gold album—contained some of the best music the group made at Buddah. "The Makings of You," a song Mayfield himself had recorded for his own first solo LP, was beautiful and remains high on my list of all-time favorite recordings, and "Hold On," with its gospel feel, was given a gloriously blues-y workout by Gladys and her guys.

Eight months later, Buddah released a third LP. *I Feel a Song* spawned another three hits: the title track, "Love Finds Its Own Way"; a live version of "The Way We Were," which had been a major smash for Barbra

Streisand earlier in 1974; and "Try to Remember," from the musical *The Fantasticks*. All three singles went into the R&B Top 10 but had only variable results on the pop charts. The bottom line was that Gladys and the Pips were still bestsellers for Buddah, and once again the group earned a gold album. An interesting side note: twenty-one years after they were recorded, the tapes for an entire live album, which included "The Way We Were"—were uncovered by BMG as part of a Buddah reissue program. *The Lost Live Album* is a fine example of what audiences could expect when they went to see the group in action.

A year later, in 1975, came *2nd Anniversary*, an album title that refers to the group's second year with Buddah. Once again two hits came tumbling out of the collection, "Money" and the poignant ballad "Part Time Love." This was also the year that Gladys got a divorce from Jimmy, her first husband, and met and subsequently married Barry Hankerson, the president of a youth-services program in Detroit. The marriage lasted only about two years, and in addition to the birth of son Shanga in 1976, the union would also result in Hankerson's involvement with Gladys's career. He wrote the script and performed in the film *Pipe Dreams*, with Gladys in the lead role as the wife of a pilot living in Alaska. Essentially, it was the story of a couple trying to keep a marriage together, and, in retrospect, fiction became fact when the Hankersons' marriage dissolved in 1977. In a 1983 interview with *Blues & Soul*, Gladys shared her feelings: "I accept pain because it's part of life and I've had my share. I've been through two marriages. The only thing is that mine has to be publicized, whereas the average person can go to court and not be subjected to things being public, airing their dirty laundry in public, so to speak."

While Gladys does talk about her marriage to Hankerson in her book, the reasons why the two split are unclear. And like many other divas, Gladys hasn't felt the need to disclose more than the bare minimum about why the relationship didn't work out. That is her prerogative.

But Gladys felt somewhat confessional in a 1983 interview with John Abbey for *Blues & Soul*. Talking about her ex-husband six years after their split, she said, "I actually don't feel bitter about it anymore. I learned a great deal and there were times when I was very, very upset at what happened. . . . I actually learned a lot about myself that I didn't know before. I certainly found out a lot of things in life that I don't want for myself! I think I was a little naive when I got married. But I learned . . . believe me, I learned!" Gladys also revealed publicly that brother Bubba and cousins Ed and William hadn't been too thrilled about her marriage to Barry Hankerson: "I respected their opinions but you have to live your own life and I've always been the kind of person who has to see and do things for myself. . . . [But] I wouldn't change a thing about my life—even the mistakes! . . . In my case, God has blessed me—I have been rewarded immensely. God gave me this voice and with it, the ability to take care of my children and my family. . . . Believe me, I am truly blessed and I know it!"

In a lengthy interview with Sharon Davis for *Blues & Soul* in the fall of 1978, Gladys discussed her life offstage without divulging the problems she was encountering in her marriage at the time. Talking about her children Jimmy and Kenya, she noted, "I don't get to spend as much time with them as I'd like to. My mother has been keeping my two eldest over the years, but now she's moved to Las Vegas I'll see more of her and them. . . ."

Gladys also explained about her approach to being a public figure: "I see a lot of female entertainers and they really have a certain philosophy about being in the business. They won't be seen without makeup and they're at all the parties. I don't do a lot of partying. If I have to go to the store and buy my groceries, then I go and I'm not made-up. I might be wearing dungarees or jeans and [a] T-shirt. . . . I'm a very casual person, I don't like a lot of fuss and the style of my clothes is usually very simple. I don't like a lot of feathers and furs, and when I'm at home, I like to be comfortable. . . . But there's one thing I must confess, I'm a shoe freak! I've got quite a few more shoes than I do anything else. And so has my mother. Between the two of us, we have closets of shoes. A hundred or more pairs. . . ."

At home, just like Aretha Franklin, another Detroit resident, Gladys revealed that she could often be found in the kitchen: "I love it, just love it. It's like therapy for me because the way my life is set up, I'm always dealing with the public as far as my business is concerned and when I'm home I'm busy catching up as far as the kids and family are concerned that I get very little time alone. So cooking fills that gap and I get most of my thinking done in kitchen. . . ."

Gladys had had a lot to think about during the year before her chat with Davis in London. That *Pipe Dreams* didn't become a box-office success as a film or as a soundtrack album with the exception of the single "So Sad the Song," which would be the last Gladys Knight & the Pips record to make the Top 50 for another three years, was likely a source of much concern. While Gladys was dealing with personal challenges, the whole group was in turmoil. In 1977 Buddah released the album *Still Together*, reuniting the group with songwriter/producer Van McCoy. But this effort did only moderately well, especially in comparison with its previous albums for the label. The LP's title might have been an affirmation because as 1978 began, suddenly new albums from the Pips on Casablanca and Gladys on Buddah were released!

The word was that after the relative failure of *Pipe Dreams*, the group had finally decided to split up. And amidst all manner of legal complications, Gladys tried to explain what was happening during a telephone interview with *Blues & Soul* in 1979: "It's been rough! I think this is the worst period we, as a group, have ever endured during our entire career. . . . We've always maintained a stable image and mutually feel it essential to dispel the rumors that we are no longer together—that I'm going my way and they're going theirs. I've worked too hard and too long with this thing to chuck it all now. . . ."

Gladys went on to explain the thinking behind the making of separate albums: "The guys had never really had the opportunity to develop themselves as I have, which naturally has been a constant source of frustration for us all. We hoped to secure an identity—record-wise—for the Pips, plus there were some things that I personally wanted to do outside of the group and this seemed the ideal way to implement both proposals."

In reality, Gladys had made a self-titled solo album for Buddah in 1978 following the commercially disastrous Gladys Knight & the Pips LP *The One and Only*. Buddah had basically gone out of business, and main executives Neil Bogart and Cecil Holmes had moved over to Casablanca. The Pips had recorded two albums for Casablanca, *At Last* and *Callin'*, but neither had made any real impact. Meanwhile, Gladys had signed a deal with Columbia Records, which proudly released a first self-titled LP on her in 1979. Like the Pips' albums, it died, with just one single, "Am I Too Late," making a weak showing on the R&B charts in late March.

In the middle of professional problems and lawsuits, Gladys also began to indulge in a vice that she would later admit in her 1997 book had become an addiction. According to her own account, gambling became her way to ease the pressures of two failed marriages and, no doubt, the concern she was feeling for her own future and the future of the Pips. Her confessions about addictive gambling habits came as a shock to people like me who had no idea that away from the spotlight, Gladys, the open-hearted, natural woman, was dealing with a truckload of personal challenges. She never let this show during interviews, always coming across as confident and assured without ever being arrogant or egotistical. I was always struck by the genuine warmth that Gladys seemed to extend to those around her; that she was in her own private hell was something that only those closest to her knew.

By December, 1979, Gladys felt like talking on the record about some of the problems she and the Pips had endured during the previous two years. "I started smoking again about two years ago," she told Bob Killbourn at *Blues & Soul* during a visit to London. "That period was a very traumatic one for me, what with my divorce and all the legal hassles with Buddah plus the rumors concerning my relationship. . . . I could cope with all that, but when my son [Shanga] became involved—that was my breaking point. My ex-husband literally snatched my son away from me and for a time, I didn't even know where he was. That was when I felt the need for some sort of crutch, and smoking is merely a crutch to lean on to help alleviate the pressures when they get too great. I have never had to cope with so much disruption. It seemed that everything happened at once—both professionally and personally. Trying to sort out the problems was a thing I don't particularly want to have to endure ever again. But it was also a lesson from which I learned many things. . . ."

Gladys had a respite as a new decade began. Finally, lawsuits resolved, Gladys and the Pips settled into a five-year relationship with Columbia Records. It was an up-and-down affair: two of the four albums the group recorded for the label did well; the other two had poor sales. Things looked promising with *About Love*, the first LP, which was produced by old Motown buddies Nick Ashford and Valerie Simpson, who had worked with the group back in 1969. The first single, the upbeat "Landlord," became a Top 5 R&B and Top 50 pop hit. But while the musical union between the husband-and-wife team and the veteran family group—back together after two years away from the studio— was sound, the public response to tunes like "Taste of Bitter Love" and "Bourgie, Bourgie" was lukewarm.

A second album with the Ashford/Simpson duo didn't remedy matters: 1981's *Touch* also had some strong musical moments—notably the fiery "I Will Fight"—but again, reaction was tepid. Gladys and brother Bubba had already made some plans to expand, which they shared in a 1981 *Blues & Soul* interview: ". . . I am now producing a solo album on Bubba," Gladys reported. "I feel very excited about working with Bubba because . . . I tend to sing most of the leads for the group. And that is restricting to the guys. . . . There are some tunes that I know I couldn't sing as well and as much as I may talk about 'getting down' and 'boogie-ing,' I know I can't do it! Bubba's album will fill that gap. . . . I may help out a little on the backgrounds for the album but I really want to make it 100% of Bubba. It's been a lot of fun working with him. . . . It's funny being on the other side of the board, too. Now it's my turn to try and extract the best from the vocalist—and I'm enjoying it!"

The relationship between Gladys and her brother was clearly growing stronger both on- and offstage. At the end of 1982, Britain's Sharon Davis had been chatting with Gladys, once again for *Blues & Soul* magazine, and she added more weight to the comments Gladys had made a year earlier: "Gladys Knight and her brother Bubba are actually recording an album together. What the other guys are doing isn't clear. However, a nine-track gospel album is or has been recorded by the brother and sister. . . . As well as working together . . . Gladys and Bubba live in the same building complex. . . . Gladys's second marriage has ended in divorce, and Bubba's, too. . . . Because she and Bubba are in the same situation, it has brought them closer together emotionally. . . . Professionally, the two have formed various companies. . . . KDK Corporation is a production company and it is under this banner that Bubba and Gladys are recording the gospel album, together with a solo set on Bubba. . . ."

The fate of both the gospel album and Bubba's solo set was never revealed: brother and sister returned their focus to group activities by 1983, when the pair co-produced several tracks on the album *Visions* with talented songwriter and producer Sam Dees. The approach worked: "Save the Overtime (for Me)," the first single co-written by Gladys, Bubba, and Dees, among others, and co-produced by the team, sailed to the top of the R&B charts in the summer of 1983. The trio also produced "Hero," a stirring ballad that Lou Rawls had recorded earlier in the year as "Wind Beneath My Wings" and that Bette Midler would revive in 1989 as a No. 1 hit.

Visions became the group's one gold album for Columbia and included a minor R&B hit, "When You're Far Away," written by a pair of musicians who had been working as members of hit-maker Prince's band, the Time. James "Jimmy Jam" Harris and Terry Lewis had one of their first chart singles with the song. Some eleven years later, the superstar producers who had given Janet Jackson and a host of other artists a truckload of hit records, teamed back up with a solo Gladys for *Good Woman*, her second MCA album.

The next few years would prove to be no piece of cake for the group. *Life*, its last album for Columbia, did poorly. Gladys commented on the Columbia tenure in our first interview in many years in 1987: "I loved [our last album], but I had my doubts because I didn't feel that Columbia was really behind it. You must have a team effort whenever you put a product out there. Although our first album for Columbia went gold, we didn't feel that the company really got behind what we were doing."

Gladys had also begun to step out on her own by doing several television projects. Uniting with Dionne Warwick and Patti LaBelle, two other divas, she'd produced "Sisters in the Name of Love." In addition, Gladys had been seen in television guest spots on "The Jeffersons" and "Benson." She also did a season with comedian Flip Wilson on the situation comedy "Charlie and Co." Gladys also appeared on Dionne's chart-topping single "That's What Friends Are For," along with Stevie Wonder and Elton John. Another turn of events in her life: her son Jimmy Newman started working as her personal manager.

Even though Gladys Knight & the Pips had signed a recording contract with MCA in 1985, the group didn't complete its first album until 1987, partly because Gladys had been so involved with her acting work. Although the quartet had been on the road in the summer of 1987 to do a series of one-nighters, traveling by bus as they had in the 1960s, something didn't seem quite right when I interviewed Gladys and the Pips on the eve of the release of what would be *All Our Love*, their one and only MCA album.

I noticed during the interview session that Gladys seemed irritated, which was unusual. It was also odd that I talked to William and Ed in one room and then to Bubba and Gladys in another. She seemed to correct comments that Bubba was making, and all in all it was a strange meeting that had none of the usual warmth that I'd always associated with the group. The quotes I got out of the session were mostly standard artist quotes about their upcoming LP, which as it turned out would be a gold record. The album spawned the hits "Love Overboard," which went on to earn the group its third Grammy, and "Lovin' on Next to Nothin'." I remember seeing a show the group did in Los Angeles shortly after the release of the album, and I was struck by the slowness of the Pips' movements. The usual nifty steps were just not quite as nifty as they used to be. And after the relative strangeness of that 1987 interview, I was hardly shocked when I heard that Gladys had finally stepped out on her own in 1989.

Gladys's very first official Pip-less record was *License to Kill*, the theme from the James Bond movie of the same name. It wasn't exactly an overnight success, and another two years would pass before a record bearing her name would be released. When *Good Woman* finally hit the streets, it was an interesting mixture. There was a powerhouse duet featuring diva sisters Patti and Dionne on the song "Superwoman," which had been a hit for Karyn White in 1988; "Men," one of the six tunes Gladys co-wrote for the project and her first Top 5 R&B hit single; the hiphop-flavored "Give Me a Chance," a duet with David Peaston; and

"Mr. Love," a standout ballad that Gladys had to battle with MCA to keep on the album.

A few other aspects of the album were also quite interesting. For starters, the cover photograph wasn't exactly what fans might have expected. Rather than a smiling Gladys, she looked stone-faced, without a trace of a grin. This image was, to say the least, different. And when she and I conducted a lengthy telephone interview for *Blues & Soul* around the time of the album's release, I didn't have the guts to ask Gladys about the concept behind the cover photograph! I did, however, find the nerve to ask her about two of the main credits on the album: her ex-husband Barry Hankerson was listed as executive producer along with Gladys, and with son and manager Jimmy, as a management consultant.

Talking on the telephone from her new home in the San Fernando Valley, Gladys ventured, ". . . Jimmy was a big catalyst in bringing us back together to work together. I think it's important for people to know that things can work out positively. . . . Barry and I have both grown a good deal over the years, and we've found that we have a lot to offer each other, particularly when it comes to dealing with this business. We have a very special relationship and working with Jimmy and Barry, we've created a great team. Sure, we went through some things over the years but working together has given us a chance to rectify some of those things. [It] has definitely been a positive thing for all of us."

Diehard fans might be equally interested in knowing why Gladys and the Pips had decided to call it a day. She didn't have too much to say in our interview for *Blues & Soul* other than to comment, "Basically, we all had other things we wanted and needed to do. Every time we got ready to do something personal, we'd put Gladys & the Pips first. Whatever it took to keep that mechanism going, we did it. Individual ventures we tried never really happened or got done properly, and we all felt that, career-wise, we needed to grow. We'd won all the awards, we'd gotten gold . . . records, we'd played every place, we'd toured and done just about everything a group could do. I wanted time to work on some other areas like acting. . . ." Bubba, she said, was attending college and "taking music lessons because he's always wanted to be able to read music and [he's] also getting his real estate license," while cousins William and Ed "are busy taking care of a business they began several years ago that they've never really had time to deal with."

Gladys noted that when she recorded solo albums for Buddah and Columbia in the 1970s, she received "hate mail from fans who thought I was getting too big for my boots and that I was becoming a 'star'!" She never promoted those albums with live solo performances, but once it became clear that Gladys Knight & the Pips was no longer a touring entity, she started doing shows alone in 1988, performing in small cities and at private parties. ". . . There was a whole psychological thing to deal with. In fact, the very first night I ever performed onstage without the Pips, I couldn't control my hands, let alone my voice," Gladys said.

Gladys's very first all-out solo project did well without breaking any records. A performance of "Superwoman" on "The Oprah Winfrey Show" with Patti and Dionne certainly helped, and a national tour with David Peaston drew justifiable rave reviews: I remember vividly seeing Gladys at the Universal Amphitheater, and she was even more energized and dynamic than she'd been with the Pips. It was as if something had opened up, and she suddenly seemed more free vocally. She also generated greater communication with the audience, expressing even more of the "woman next door" persona that I'd come to know through our interview sessions together.

It was obvious from her comments that Gladys was having her fair share of challenges in dealing with MCA. "I've been with fourteen record companies over the years, and the one thing I can say is that basically, they're the same! To tell you the very honest truth," she stated, "The Pips and I signed with MCA because of [executive] Jheryl Busby (formerly head of MCA's black-music division). He actually 'recruited' us to be with the company when we were between labels and to be honest, I was real upset when he left the label [to go to Motown] and I was ready to leave, too. . . ." One of the problems Gladys was having with MCA in the aftermath of the release of her first solo album for the label centered around the lack of pop airplay and sales. "I do get upset . . . because I have more than [just] black fans. I still seem to have a battle getting my music across, and my attitude with the record company is, 'Put it out there and let the people decide.' . . . I feel like I've been fighting this particular battle so long it's not funny. . . . I must say that with all the pop hits we had as Gladys Knight & the Pips, it's upsetting to still have to deal with this. Fortunately, during the Seventies, we were with one record company (Buddah) who had the vision even if they had no money. That was a company that allowed us to be free creatively, which is why we were able to have such major hits. . . ."

In our interview, Gladys made no references to anything that might have been happening in her private life, but her comments about the song "Men" are worth noting. Working with producer Attala Zane Giles one night in the studio, Gladys recalled, ". . . We were sitting around talking about relationships. Then we got on the subject of fidelity and the more we talked, the more I got riled up! I gave him the female side of things, and I told him how sick we women were of hearing all the same excuses from men . . . he suggested I go write a lyric about it. . . ."

Interestingly, the very next time I got together with Gladys was at a house she shared with then-fiancé Les Brown, a successful motivational speaker who had been steadily rising in popularity over the years in part through his own national television show. The occasion was the release of *Just for You*, her second MCA album. Les had opened the door to the tastefully decorated home nestled on a side street in Chatsworth in the San Fernando Valley, just thirty minutes or so from Hollywood. He was pleasant and conversational while I waited for Gladys, and when she emerged, she seemed happy, content, and eager to talk. Naturally, most of our chat for *Blues & Soul* was about the new record. Gladys said that she'd named the album *Just for You* as a direct message to her loyal fans. "I didn't want it to be like past projects where there might have been some pressure of trying to compete musically with what's happening today. I've got to be me. . . ."

To ensure that the record would receive appropriate attention, Gladys had enlisted the services of top producers, including Kenny "Babyface" Edmonds and Jimmy Jam and Terry Lewis, the team of writers-turned-producers who had supplied her and the Pips with a hit back in 1984. One of the high points on the album was a great medley of two 1970s classics, "If You Don't Know Me by Now" and "Love Don't Love Nobody," bound together with a raw, impassioned version of "End of the Road," the multi-million-selling No. 1 hit that had given Motown group Boyz II Men international mass recognition. In an opening rap Gladys explained how she missed some of the great music of the 1970s but how hearing the Boyz II Men song had renewed her faith that great material was also being written in the 1990s. As it turned out, the eleven-minute medley, recorded before an invited audience at a New York studio, was one of the chief selling points for the album and when Gladys performed it in concert, she blew the roof off every time.

An updated version of Curtis Mayfield's "Choice of Colors" is worthy of mention, as is "Guilty," a song Gladys and producer Attala Zane Giles had written and that she used in "Miss Lily," a short-lived play that she'd starred in several months earlier. A couple of lyric lines summed up the challenges that Gladys and other soulful divas faced: "There are two strikes against me when I come up to bat: one strike for being female and one strike for being black." As liberal and tolerant as the music business is supposed to be, the fact was that when dealing with the industry, black female artists were automatically branded as difficult or temperamental even before they opened their mouths. It was as if the combination "black" and "female" spelled "bitch" for more than a few male executives, black and white.

As Gladys and I were winding down our conversation, she did talk a little about Les Brown, the new man in her life. "We became friends first, and when we first met I was not looking for a relationship . . . when I first met Les, I thought he wasn't my type! But once our relationship started developing, it scared both of us. I mean, we had to both look at the fact that we spend time on the road and the question was whether we could handle that. . . ." The relationship had blossomed into romance, and at the time we met, Gladys and Les were engaged. She ended our conversation with a laugh, "I know a lot of ladies out there see him, and they say he's fine. I've never been jealous before but . . . !"

"Come on up, Mr. and Mrs. Les Brown—Gladys Knight and Les Brown!" As the mistress of ceremonies, Aretha Franklin was bringing the couple onstage at the Rhythm & Blues Foundation Pioneer Awards on February 27, 1997, at the Hilton Hotel in New York. After a couple of words the pair left the stage, and Aretha, in rare form, witty, funny, and relaxed, quipped, 'Hey, Gladys girl, where'd you find *him*? I want to find a man like that myself!"

One year later, as Gladys Knight, Merald Knight, William Guest, and a wheelchair-bound Ed Patten (who had apparently had a stroke) were accepting their much-deserved Lifetime Achievement Award, Les Brown was nowhere to be found. Gladys and Les, who had married in August, 1995, had split up, and Gladys had a few words to say about the breakup in her book, prompting a public response from Les.

As 1998 draws to a close, having faced the ups and downs of three marriages, Gladys Knight is focused on music, the one constant in her life. She has released *Many Different Roads*, a gospel album on Many Roads Records, while her children prosper. Jimmy is still very active as her manager, Shanga is looking to a career as a restaurateur, and Kenya is the owner of a couple of very successful bakeries in Las Vegas—where you can get some cakes that will blow your mind, as I discovered on a visit to the city in October, 1997! As Gladys celebrates fifty years of singing in public, she seems strong, confident, and, as always, a down-home, good woman from Atlanta, quick with a smile and some good old-fashioned motherly wit and wisdom, as well as that honey-textured voice. She is a soulful diva if ever there was one!

AKA AN

backbone...
ugh the fire

Chaka Khan performing at
an outdoor concert
Credit: Michael Ochs Archives/
Venice, CA

Most people hear the name Chaka Khan and think "hair," "lips," and "Is she 'high'?" Well, the hair is still out there and the lips will always be there, but anyone who has been following Chaka Khan's illustrious career will know that the drug reference is a remnant of the time when she went "to hell and back in a limousine!" Chaka first used that line when she and I did one of the many interviews we've conducted since 1974, when she was the twenty-one-year-old lead singer with the legendary band Rufus.

The "drug thing" can get mighty tired. And while I can think of two occasions—one during a live performance in 1976, the other when I was doing an interview with Rufus in 1979—when Chaka was under the influence of something, and the rest of the time she has been more than just lucid. She has been forthcoming, painfully honest, street smart—a take-no-shit woman who knows far more than she lets on.

Chaka can also be very funny. I was getting ready to walk into a conference room at Warner Brothers, her recording home for almost eighteen years, and the publicist who had arranged our umpteenth interview for *Blues & Soul* began to introduce me. "I know Mr. Thing!" Chaka boomed, grinning from ear to ear. I then turned every shade of crimson while Chaka just smiled. "Sit down, honey!" she beckoned, and like old pals, we talked about life, love, and the pursuit of hit records.

Chaka has been a fixture on the music scene for close to thirty years, has influenced a whole generation of singers (everyone from Mary J. Blige to Miki Howard, from Faith Evans to Sandra St. Victor, from Erykah Badu to Vesta), and has amassed a wealth of hits both with Rufus (from 1973 to 1983 or thereabouts) and as a solo artist. Nevertheless, Chaka is seldom lumped together with other soulful divas like Aretha, Patti, and Gladys. This might well be a generational thing: it is easy to forget that in 1998 Chaka turned forty-five, younger than all the other women covered in this book with the exception of Anita Baker who is just four years her junior, and the young divas, Janet Jackson, Whitney Houston, and Toni Braxton. That said, Chaka's contribution to music has been no less valid, and if anything, she has never been fully accorded the kind of respect and props she deserves for what she has done.

I was guilty of not fully comprehending Chaka's impact on music for many years myself. Sure, I loved many of her records with Rufus. And while I could never single out an entire solo album that I considered musically even, I found more than a few Chaka slow jams and groove tunes to make me happy. But when people talked about the divas who had been most influential, I would immediately mention Aretha without considering how Chaka's powerhouse vocal style might have affected a truckload of female vocalists born in the late 1960s and early 1970s.

My perception of Chaka Khan and her place in the annals of contemporary music changed one night around 1993 or 1994 when I saw her at the Strand nightclub just outside Los Angeles. I had a great seat right up front, and when Chaka hit the stage, mike in hand, she started singing at the top of her more-than-extensive vocal range with such ease that I had to suppress a gasp! I couldn't ever remember hearing any other singer start a song there so effortlessly. I called every one of the many diehard Chaka Khan fans I know and confessed that I finally understood why they considered her the true queen of soul, R&B, jazz, or whatever music form she might be turning her hand to on any given day!

For what seemed like the first time, I also knew why Chaka, through the ups and downs of a mostly flamboyant life lived in the limelight, had been able to establish a strong bedrock of loyal fans for more than twenty years. It had everything to do with vocal power, strength, and an innate ability for lyrical interpretation. She wasn't just the wild, sexually aggressive rocker who kicked her leg in the air as she strutted across the stage declaring, "I'm a Backbone" or the full-maned siren who belted out "I'm Every Woman" when Whitney Houston was fresh out of puberty. Chaka was the jazz singer who could take "My Funny Valentine" and stop the yelling mob at a "Soul Train Music Awards" show and give them cause to pause. She was also the soulful balladeer who was able to breathe new life into the Burt Bacharach-Hal David classic "Alfie" with a worldliness born from a wealth of experiences, good, bad, and ugly. "Sure, I've lived a lot of my life on the edge, and there's always a danger of falling off," she told me in a 1992 *Blues & Soul* interview. "The question is, if you fall off, do you have what it takes to get back on? I've lost my grip several times. . . . What kept me coming back was my children. That's what kept me going more than anything. . . . The sense of duty to them . . . [that] and my love for music."

Born Yvette Marie Stevens, Chaka Khan's natural interest in music stemmed from listening to a whole range of styles and sounds during her early years growing up on the South Side of Chicago. Asked about her interest in the blues, an inherent part of the Windy City's music scene, Chaka told *Blues & Soul* editor John Abbey in 1975, "I was raised more on [the opera] *Madame Butterfly* . . . I have to admit it, I don't really care for the blues—it brings me down and depresses me. . . ." She was more likely to be listening to Billie Holiday's *Lady in Satin*, an album owned by her grandmother that would be a constant favorite in the Stevens household, doubtless the source of Chaka's ever-present interest in jazz. Even though her vocal style later suggested it, Chaka's roots weren't in the gospel music that was so much a part of the roots of most black female singers.

You might have to wait for Chaka's autobiography for clarity about how she first got into music as more than just a household interest. According to Kevin Murphy, one of the original members of Rufus, in a 1975 *Blues & Soul* interview, ". . . she had been around singing with little local groups around Chicago since she was fourteen. One group that she was with—The Crystalettes—had even recorded. . . ." The *All Music Guide*, an online bio on Chaka Khan by Jason Ankeny, fills in some other blanks, noting that while Yvette was still in high school, she joined the Afro-Arts theater, a group that supposedly toured with the late Mary Wells. After leaving high school in 1969, Yvette joined a dance-oriented band named Lyfe. Yvette became Chaka Khan around the same time, adopting her new first name after working with the Black Panthers—according to the *All Music Guide*—and Khan, after her first marriage to a gentleman of East Indian origin. Chaka "is appropriate to me," she explained in our first face-to-face interview (for *Blues & Soul* magazine] in 1975. "In one particular African dialect, it symbolizes fire, war, heat—the color red. . . ."

Chaka left Lyfe for the Babysitters, a vocal group that had sung behind popular Chicago soul man Baby Huey. Curtis Mayfield signed Huey and the Babysitters to his Curtom label in 1969. A little-known fact: Mayfield sued Chaka for breach of contract after she started enjoying success with Rufus, and although she was a little miffed—as she confided in 1975—the matter was eventually resolved.

Chaka's induction into the group Rufus came around 1972. The band had been formed out of the remnants of American Breed, a pop aggregation that had hit the charts in 1969 with "Bend Me, Shape Me." the nucleus of that group went through various incarnations. It was initially known as Smoke, featuring vocalist Paulette McWilliams, who would later go on to make some solo records and tour throughout the 1980s with Luther Vandross; then as Ask Rufus, named after a column that appeared in a local Chicago newspaper; and finally, in 1971, simply as Rufus. And because she was friends with McWilliams, Chaka would often hit the road with the group, and when the original lead singer finally quit, it was natural for Chaka to take her place in the band.

Through Kevin Murphy, the band hooked up with ABC Records producer Bob Monaco, who had worked with American Breed in the late 1960s. Monaco arranged for the group—Chaka, Murphy, Ron Stockert, Al Ciner, Dennis Belfield, and Andre Fischer—to record three songs that would form the basis for its first self-titled ABC album, which was released in 1973. A debut single, "Slip'n'Slide," was released but did nothing sales-wise. It was left to New Orleans producer/songwriter Allen Toussaint's "Whoever's Thrilling You (Is Killing Me)" to make the first of what would be the group's twenty-five chart impressions over ten years.

Significantly, the first LP included songs penned by Ashford & Simpson, who would give Chaka her first solo hit six years later, and by Stevie Wonder, who would be responsible for the group's first Top 10 single just one year later. Between the recording of Rufus's first and second albums, the group began working with manager Bob Ellis, whose client roster included Billy Preston and who was married to Diana Ross at the time. "He saw something in us when we almost couldn't see it in ourselves," Kevin Murphy said in his 1975 *Blues & Soul* interview. "He first saw us do a set at the Whiskey-A-Go-Go in Los Angeles, and he said he had to close his eyes because we were so bad visually—but he heard something in our music which he felt could be worked on, and he's been there behind us ever since. . . ."

With a ground swell of growing interest, Rufus began touring sporadically. As an interracial band, the members were breaking new ground, and by the time ABC released *Rags to Rufus,* its second album, in June, 1974, the band was enjoying a major smash with the now-classic "Tell Me Something Good." This song was written especially for the group by Stevie Wonder, with whom they toured later that same year. Apparently, he'd heard the group's version of his song "Maybe Your Baby" and was so impressed that he wanted to meet them. An impromptu writing session was the result and between them, Chaka and Wonder created the basis for the sexually charged "Tell Me Something Good," which would go on to become the group's first gold single.

Hitting the road with Wonder and later the Crusaders, Rufus went through some personnel changes, and new members Tony Maiden and Bobby Watson would become the nucleus of the hitmaking team, along with Chaka, Murphy, and Fischer. They were joined in 1977 by David 'Hawk' Wolinski. With a distinctive brand of funk, R&B, and rock, Rufus was creating a name for itself, distinguished from other soul and pop bands by Chaka's soaring, searing vocals and wild onstage persona.

With the release of the R&B chart topper *You Got the Love* in the fall of 1974 and the gold LP *Rufusized* a few months later, the group became known as "Rufus Featuring Chaka Khan." It was obvious that her kick-ass, high-energy onstage presence was helping to bring the group even more notoriety. In an age when most female vocalists were still being demure and polite, Chaka was breaking down the walls, expressing herself with the kind of power usually associated with rock singers. With skimpy outfits made from feathers, a bare midriff, and a trademark mane of hair, she was one of a kind. The only other black female who had exhibited the same kind of funk'n'fury onstage was Tina Turner. When I had my first chance to sit down with Chaka toward the end of 1975, I asked her about any comparisons between her and the original bold soul sister. "I don't feel that I'm competing with anyone else because I'm doing my own thing, . . ." she replied without a blink.

Earlier in the year, Chaka had talked extensively with *Blues & Soul* editor John Abbey when Rufus had flown into London for a whistle-stop trip that involved an appearance on the renowned "Top of the Pops" show and a performance as special guests of Elton John at Wembley Stadium. Other group members had been quick to emphasize that Rufus wasn't simply another R&B or funk band, and Kevin Murphy told John Abbey, "We don't like to be pigeon-holed. Sure, we play funk but we're not a typical R&B group. That would imply a restriction and we have no restrictions. . . ."

Chaka began to elaborate on where she wanted to go with music, and for the first time publicly she mentioned a desire that would prove to be a constant theme all the way past her years with Rufus and into her solo career: "I guess that my own personal ambition for myself is to get deeper into jazz—whether it be with the group or without. The type of jazz that people like Phoebe Snow are into right now," she told John Abbey. "They are singing about the truth and it doesn't have to revolve around the man-woman love thing. I'd like to get to the point where I don't have to think about being commercial. To me, music should not be restricted to the 'I love you, you love me' business. Rufus hasn't reached the point yet where we can say exactly what we want to say. . . . We want to become a little more daring as we grow more popular until we reach a stage where we can one day say exactly what we are thinking! . . . I admit it, I'd love to be able to make a record that offended people and then get away with it. Maybe I shouldn't say 'offend' because I don't mean to be offensive—I'd like to tear away the mask from a lot of people. Don't you feel that so many people live their life with a mask covering their real feelings? I'd love to wake them up so that they can see themselves for what they really are. . . ."

My first in-person meeting with Chaka was held at manager Bob Ellis's office on Sunset Boulevard when I was living in Los Angeles toward the end of 1975. I remember it well because I'd expected to meet the wild, outrageous, fiery performer I'd seen on the few Rufus shows I'd attended. Instead, I came face-to-face with a reflective, intelligent, thoughtful young woman who took her time to respond to my questions. While she wanted to talk about Rufus, the group's new album—its fourth, simply entitled *Rufus Featuring Chaka Khan* and its continuing success, she was also interested in revealing more about herself. She had given birth to a daughter, Milini ("an Indian name for fragile") in 1974 and "that was like the icing on the cake for me. . . . I worked right up until the last two weeks of my pregnancy. It made me sing stronger, I guess because I had that extra bit of life inside me. It's important now for me that my baby be happy, so I've got to be happy, too. Which is what I'm working for: the financial security that will bring me that happiness. Plus I want to have another two children, and I'm working now so that I can reach that point in the future where I can pace myself out and have the time for myself that I need and that my children need. Sure, I like privacy and I'm basically a homebody. And the pace can be grueling. But you deal with it by giving people just enough and never too much. . . . "

What emerged from the interview was a portrait of a woman who was proud of her individuality but just a tad concerned about an overtly sexual image that seemed to be emerging, aided by stuff like the artwork on the group's fourth album cover. It depicted two sensual lips with drops of sweat—or some other liquid substance—dripping from them. The back cover showed Chaka, wide-legged, sitting on a sofa shaped like the lips. "Well, to be honest I'm not overkeen on it myself," she stated. "I was concerned what my mother would think but she didn't seem to mind. She asked me if they were trying to put me over as a sex bomb. Well, I guess what's happening is that the whole thing is being accentuated. Basically, I'm a wild-natured-type of person and on stage . . . I really work hard and give over that image. The album sleeve is how people picture me, I imagine."

Chaka was committed to using music to bring about change: "It's very important for me to put over through my music some of the ideas that I feel should be expressed. There is so much wrong that . . . I do want to see change. . . . I was very active in school in politics, you know, but I was very unhappy . . . about the things I saw around me. . . . The secret is to get into a position where maybe I might want to stop singing and go into another career where I can do something about the things that need changing. . . . "

On a personal level, Chaka said that she had "been through a lot of changes myself—learning to deal with situations, keeping control." With the suddenness of the fame that Chaka and other members of Rufus had experienced—making three gold albums in less than eighteen months and enjoying an overwhelming degree of national popularity in just two years—she admitted that there were new pressures. "About once every two months, I'll go off on everyone, and I have to cry at least six times a month because it's necessary for me to get all those things out of my system. You know, there are a lot of things in this business that you don't like to have to deal with but find that you have to anyway. I don't get too involved in the heavy business side, but I do know how to count my money and read a contract." Working night after night and traveling the country with four men had its own share of stress and strain, but Chaka was reassuring when she asserted, "It's like an average family. We have our ups and downs, and after spending several months out on the road together, we're bound to get tired of looking at each other. But we always iron out our differences."

The interview session was really cool, but three months later, I was sitting at the Forum in Inglewood on my birthday, preparing to watch Rufus and Chaka blow the roof off what I expected would be a dynamite show. Instead, the audience and I were treated to a less-than-satisfactory performance: Chaka was clearly in "outer space," and every time she would attempt to begin singing, she would literally knock over the microphone stand! Another group member would pick it up, and within a minute or two, Chaka had knocked it over once more. She was incoherent on some of the tunes, storming through songs and barely communicating with the audience. It was as if we weren't there. And while other band members tried to compensate with their sterling musicianship, Chaka was the center of attention—and the audience wasn't happy. This was my first clue that she just might not be handling life and success at the top quite as easily as she'd made out in our interview, and that she just might have resorted to different methods to deal with the pressures of the music business.

Those pressures were mounting as the group's fame spread. Many of the tunes on the group's second, third, and fourth albums had become favorites among a wide-ranging audience, black, white, and brown, who cherished the group's fresh fusion of rock and soul. Lyrically, the band was offering up some real gems: original tunes penned by various members of the group, including "Smokin' Room," the poignant "Please Pardon Me (You Remind Me of a Friend)," the righteously funky "Once You Get Started," the gorgeous "Sweet Thing," and Chaka's personal theme tune, "I'm a Woman (I'm a Backbone)." Several other people contributed songs to Rufus's albums, and material like Gavin Christopher's "Fool's Paradise," Ashford & Simpson's "Ain't Nothin' But a Maybe," Bobby Womack's "Stop on By," and the Bee Gees' "Jive Talkin,'" was truly Rufus-ized.

With the release of *Ask Rufus*, the group reached a new level of recognition on an international basis. Rufus headed to Britain to perform at the Queen's Jubilee with the Doobie Brothers and Joni Mitchell in June. The new album went platinum and yielded no less than three Top 20 singles: "At Midnight,"a driving groove tune; followed by "Hollywood," a telling commentary on the trials and tribulations of making it in that city; and "Everlasting Love," a gentle, mid-tempo tune that became an instant favorite among the growing legion of Rufus fans. Of particular interest to the group's hardcore followers was "Egyptian Song," a tune penned by Chaka with keyboardist David 'Hawk' Wolinski that referred to Chaka's long-held interest in reincarnation and things Egyptian. Many years later, she and I would talk about the song at length because it was a personal favorite and because I'd made a tape of it, which I played among ancient ruins during my own trip to Egypt in 1984.

Whether or not Chaka had lived in Egypt in another life, she was dealing with some tough issues in the United States in 1977. A huge image of her dwarfing the other members of Rufus was the featured art for *Ask Rufus*, while the back cover was a photograph of Chaka alone. Asked about going solo, she was adamant in telling John Abbey in the spring of 1977, "That's a continual rumor. . . . For me to quit, it would be like cutting off my right arm or leg or something. We have something that is very rare in this business—we have a family combination and I'm not about to ruin any of it."

Right. Although Chaka's comment was all well and good as a public statement, the reality was something else. The group completed one more album together in 1977: *Street Player*, released in early 1978, went gold but its success was limited. By the end of 1978, she was telling me, "I can't say I'm with them, and I can't say I've left! I will be recording at least another album with Rufus in 1979 but I won't be going out on the road with them—that's definite. Now as to whether I'll do any more than one album with them remains to be seen. From here on in, I do know I'll be recording solo albums, and I will be out touring by myself."

The decision to make a solo album for Tattoo Records (at the time affiliated with Warner Brothers) was, she said, "No problem. It was a natural progression for all of us, and I can hardly say it was unexpected. I just decided that this was the year I'd do the album, and I did it!" Chaka was excited about her prospects, noting, "the whole idea of doing a solo album came from a need for further self-expression. . . ."

Called *Chaka*, the LP was produced, as would be much of her subsequent solo work—by Arif Mardin, long known for his sterling work with Aretha Franklin and Bette Midler at Atlantic. The album was critically acclaimed, included the R&B chart topper and Top 30 pop hit "I'm Every Woman," which was written for Chaka by Ashford & Simpson and recorded in New York with a bevy of great musicians, including Richard Tee, Steve Gadd, Phil Upchurch, Anthony Jackson, Steve Ferrone, and the Brecker Brothers. The album also contained "Some Love," a song penned by Chaka and brother Mark Stevens, a talented musician in his own right. Just as Chaka had hoped, Warner Brothers got behind the project, which achieved gold status.

Chaka had signed with the label because "they simply made me an offer I couldn't refuse," and she was ready to do whatever it took to kick off her solo career, which meant hitting the road for the first time, alone. "I feel absolutely gung-ho," she beamed. "I'm really looking forward to it because I think I'll be able to do so much more now. . . . I'm not worried about being accepted—that's something that's never really bothered me, to be honest." And in a bold statement of confidence, she declared, "I don't think about the competition because I don't feel I have any! I'm my own person, and as long as I can come through with good music, that's what's important." there was also no plan to change her image, although the new music on her first solo project had none of the inherent funk and rock "feel" of her work with Rufus. "No, I won't be suddenly appearing in long evening gowns!" she grinned. "Sure, the media has painted a particular image of me but," she asked me, "how do *you* know it's an image?" I had to confess that I didn't know whether that aggressive, passionate bundle of energy that I'd seen onstage was the real Chaka, but I suspected it was no act—that behind the more subdued woman I was speaking with lurked a gutsy, earthy Chi-town sister who didn't suffer fools gladly.

Chaka began her selected solo dates at New York's Avery Fisher Hall before a star-studded crowd that included producer Mardin, Roberta Flack, Luther Vandross, James Mtume, and members of Chic, but I have little recall of the show. I do remember a solo Chaka a year or so later in Los Angeles during which she seemed a little lost, and while she was vocally proficient, there was little charisma between Chaka and the audience. A few more years would pass before Chaka became entirely comfortable as a solo performer—and it only happened after another stint with Rufus.

While Chaka had been off making her first solo LP, so had members of the band. Their effort, entitled *Numbers*, met with only a lukewarm response, and when it came time for Rufus to do a new album under their contract with MCA (who had purchased ABC Records), Chaka was contractually required to return. She headed back into the studio with her old bandmates shortly after giving birth to a son, Damien, in March, 1979, the one child she bore during her marriage to Richard Holland. The group needed both a hit and someone to oversee the project who could ensure that everything went well. Quincy Jones, fresh from his major triumph producing *Off the Wall*, Michael Jackson's first solo album for Epic, was the perfect candidate. Jones had worked with Chaka in 1977 when she sang lead vocals on "Stuff Like That," the R&B chart-topping title of Quincy's 1978 album.

In conjunction with the release of "Do You Love What You Feel," which would go on to become one of the group's biggest hits from the gold LP *Masterjam*, I conducted the strangest interview I was ever to do with Chaka and the band. We met at a hotel in Manhattan, and initially it was just me, Kevin Murphy, Tony Maiden, Bobby Watson, and David Wolinski. Sometime in the middle of the interview session, Chaka stumbled in and acted *very* strange. She kept pacing back and forth, staring out of the window, and literally speaking over band members as I asked questions. It was obvious from the expression on the faces of Murphy and Wolinski in particular that all wasn't well in the camp.

When I suggested that the group might have lost some momentum with the 1978 *Street Player* album, Chaka got defensive and shot back a "No way!" "Maybe you know something we don't," she countered, "but as far as we can tell, the public hasn't deserted us!" When I wondered whether working with hitmaker Quincy Jones had been a calculated move that was designed to return Rufus to the chart stakes, members of the group stated, "It wasn't a preconceived attempt at being commercial—sure, we went to get a hit but we didn't go in to change what we're all about. . . . Although it's become rare for people to say it, we're about playing the music and enjoying it and about music as an art." Before anyone could continue, Chaka had returned from a prolonged stint at the window and interjected vehemently, "I think art is pure, and I think that it's been raped and whored because of greed and selfishness—people no longer respect music as an art form the way they should. And that, to me, is a real sin."

There was an awkward silence as I regrouped before starting on my next question. Maybe a comment or two about touring, which the band hadn't done for over a year. . . . Chaka volunteered an immediate response, noting that her own solo stint on the road "was kinda trying—there was definitely a lack of groove! Tony (Maiden) came out just to oversee it all but it was hard." The group had some plans to go to Europe and then do some domestic dates, but no one could offer any concrete information as to when that would happen. And just watching the vibe between Chaka and the members of the band, I suspected that a tour would be a while away from being a reality.

As I left the less-than-comfortable interview session, I knew that Chaka was going to do another solo album and that the band Rufus would be doing one, too. Even though everyone seemed genuinely excited about the prospects for *Masterjam*, the strained atmosphere that clearly existed between Chaka and her bandmates left me doubting that they would be doing anything else anytime soon. In fact, putting aside any differences that might have existed, Rufus and Chaka did embark on a successful nationwide tour with the Brothers Johnson after the album's release.

It was obvious that Chaka's involvement with *Masterjam* had been the fulfillment of a mandatory obligation and that her attention had been focused on other areas of her life, such as raising her two young children. She'd confessed in our one-on-one interview in late 1978 that she intended to slow the pace: "Sure, it's been pretty exhausting, working consistently on the road. . . . Now I won't be doing quite so much road work because I want to spend more time with my family at the farm I just bought nearly Malibu. . . ." She told *Blues & Soul* editor John Abbey a few months later that she liked being home: " . . . I stay in the house a lot. I'm not one for going to parties—I don't enjoy them. You see, the social life that most people lead does not appeal to me. . . . Though I am reserved, I do enjoy having visitors—but people I *want* to see. I love entertaining but that is why I live where I live . . . it's a ranch and I choose to live there to be away from the city." She demanded her privacy and made it clear that she drew a clear line between work and home: " . . . that image and how I am on stage is all I owe my fans. I don't owe them my private and personal life. . . ."

Home life might mean "[taking] in a movie—my husband is a movie freak! And so we do a lot of that—just good flicks with good actors. And I read an awful lot; I'm always with a book." Chaka said that music had always been an obvious career choice although she'd made one attempt at a nine-to-five gig: "At the beginning of my career, I was working clubs at night and a regular job during the day, and I couldn't handle it. Unless it had been something like a school teacher or a job that is colorful and creative. . . ."

Making a statement that she would subsequently contradict several times, Chaka declared in early 1979 that Los Angeles felt like home. "Visually it satisfies me, and one's surroundings have a lot to do with one's state of mind," she said. "I am by nature a moody person, and if I were living in Chicago right now, I'd be on the verge of suicide! [You see] I'm very affected by my surroundings—people, places, things, smells—everything! I'm highly sensitive to what's happening around me."

By early 1980, Chaka had changed her mind about L.A. "I think that I would like to move away from Los Angeles," she told John Abbey. "Because, although it is very convenient because of my job, I don't like living there. I'd prefer London. Or Paris, New Orleans, Canada—or even New York. And I will be moving—very, very soon!"

During this interview Chaka was talking to Abbey for *Blues & Soul* in conjunction with the release of her second, Arif Mardin-produced solo album, *Naughty*, which contained the hit single, "Clouds" (another Ashford & Simpson composition). At the time of her conversation with Abbey, Chaka was in a somewhat reflective mood. ". . . Chaka Khan is just a singer—a good one, maybe! But just a singer and I know what *I* am! I don't agree with 'stars' being put on pedestals by people. I will always remember something my father told me and that is that everyone sits on the toilet! If you always remember that, you can't go far wrong. . . ."

The period between the release of *Naughty* in June, 1980, and the end of 1981 when MCA put out *Camouflage*, another Rufus and Chaka album, provided plenty of challenges for everyone concerned. Chaka's third LP, *What'cha Gonna Do For Me*, hit the streets, and the title track became an R&B chart topper, helping the album to go gold. The Brazilian-flavored "I Know You, I Live You" was a standout, and her desire to pursue a more jazz-oriented musical course was finally given some weight with the inclusion of "And the Melody Lingers On (Night in Tunisia)," a vocal reworking of a Dizzy Gillespie classic that quickly became a cherished favorite among Chaka's loyal fans. She was carving a real base for herself as a solo artist, but she was obligated to deliver another album with Rufus and neither MCA nor the band would allow her to renege on that obligation.

The recording of *Camouflage* had taken place with a lot of stress, tension, and strain. Tony Maiden confessed that all had not gone well in a June, 1982, *Blues & Soul* interview: ". . . We were undergoing internal problems at the time we were recording . . . and that is never a good way to be. A lot of things could have been a lot better . . . when you are recording everyone has to be in complete harmony for it to come off properly. Like the old Rufus albums. We were like one happy family and it reflected in our music. . . . We found ourselves forcing a lot of things to happen when we were recording this album. It's hard to put your problems aside and simply concentrate on recording, especially when it involves personal relationships and people you care about. A lot of the time, Chaka wasn't even there for this album and that has never been the way before."

In the same *Blues & Soul* interview, Maiden referred to comments Chaka had made to the media about what she considered a final split from the group. "It was definitely blown out of all proportion. . . . You know, all groups go through their traumas and breakups because different people want to do different things. . . . But in the case of our breakup, I don't think there's any lasting ill will. . . . And we are about to hit the road for what may well be the final tour [together]. Chaka and I have been like sister and brother for years and we have a family type close relationship. We'll always stay close and in touch. . . . Like everybody else, Chaka has her little ways and she takes a little time to understand and then some patience. I think I know her and understand her—but not *everybody* does."

For her part, Chaka was temporarily silent on the subject of her feelings about the group, which had finally left MCA in 1982 and was now signed to Warner Brothers. A final resolution for the back-and-forth status of Chaka's role with Rufus emerged when Warner Brothers A&R executive and producer Russ Titleman persuaded everyone involved to cut a final live album. With the proviso that there would also be four new studio recordings, Chaka, Maiden, Murphy, Wolinski, Watson, and drummer John Robinson performed at the Savoy, a hot spot in New York City, over three consecutive nights in February, 1982.

Culled from the shows were the thirteen sides that really captured the energy and excitement that had made Rufus and Chaka undeniably one of the hottest bands of the 1970s. It was more than a memorable occasion: in essence, it was the end of an era. Whatever eventual personality or creative differences had dogged their final years together, Chaka and the band had reunited for one last triumphant show, a reminder of the magic that that they'd created together over the previous decade.

Almost a year would pass before the four studio recordings would be completed, thereby delaying the release of the album. Chaka's busy 1982 schedule might well have been a major factor in the holdup. She was finishing a fourth LP for Warner Brothers. Released at the end of the year, *Chaka Khan* merely grazed the Top 60 album charts even though it included a Top 10 R&B revival of Michael Jackson's "Got to Be There."

In a twist of fate, though, the album did earn Chaka her first two Grammy Awards as a solo artist (for "Best R&B Female Performance" and for "Best Vocal Arrangement" for the track "Be Bop Medley").

Focusing away from the charts and hit records, Chaka finally got her wish to record her first jazz album, *Echoes of an Era*. This live recording had an all-star cast that included Lenny White, Stanley Clarke, and Chick Corea. Released in 1982 on Elektra, the LP gave some indication of what Chaka might be capable of when she turned her hand to standards like "I Loves You Porgy," "Them There Eyes," and "I Hear Music" but it was far from being her best vocal performance. In a 1989 interview Chaka and I did, she agreed that it was the one album she'd recorded that she didn't like. "I just wasn't prepared to do a whole jazz album at the time. . . ." she admitted.

Chaka was in fine form, however, for the four final studio recordings that would complete *Stompin' at the Savoy*, her fitting finale with Rufus. "Ain't Nobody," a funky Hawk Wolinski composition, became a runaway hit after its release in the summer of 1983, the group's biggest pop hit in eight years and first No. 1 R&B smash in five years—and an international hit to boot. The other standout was Chaka's beautiful reading of the jazz standard "Don't Go to Strangers," which featured the legendary Joe Sample on piano. All in all *Stompin' at the Savoy* seemed to give everyone what they wanted.

Or maybe not. During a pretty tough, no-nonsense interview that appeared in *Blues & Soul* in November, 1983, just two months after the double album's release, Chaka was blunt about Rufus. And even though she acknowledged that having a major hit was nothing to sneeze at, she was edgy and irritated about all the apparent fuss being made over the final Rufus album. "The public seems reluctant to separate me from the group—it's as if they really want us to stick together," she said at the start of what seemed like a lengthy tirade. "Right now . . . Rufus is nonexistent as a group. My problem is that I always need a challenge and, to be truthful, it was no longer a challenge for me. We were doing the same old tricks all the time and I felt as if I was stuck in a rut and that I wasn't growing. If you really listen to "Ain't Nobody," that could just as easily have been a Chaka Khan solo record, anyway. I don't want to make it sound like an ego thing because I don't feel that way at all. But I want to get acceptance for myself. Having a No. 1 record is beautiful and I'm really happy about it, but I feel that I've done some great things on my own and never really got the credit . . . and that upsets me at times. Maybe I'm difficult to promote or market or something but I have never understood why more promotion wasn't done behind my solo records.

A very young,
exuberant Chaka Khan
Credit: Michael Ochs
Archives/Venice, CA

But I guess I'll just keep on working at it until it comes out right."

Even though Chaka laughingly suggested that she might consider doing another album with Rufus "if the money were right!" it was quite obvious that a whole lot of water had passed under the bridge in the relationships between Chaka and specific members of the group. She no longer felt compelled to maintain any silence about the problems she felt she'd encountered.

Turning her attention away from the issues that might have dogged her situation with Rufus in the past, Chaka was looking at the next step in her relationship with Warner Brothers. It was clear from the statements she was making that she was less than satisfied with what she considered a lack of promotion for her solo music, and now she was dealing with what appeared to be creative constraints. Even though "Don't Go to Strangers" from the *Stompin' at the Savoy* LP with Rufus had been universally acclaimed as one of Chaka's best performances in reviews of the album, her record label was looking to Chaka to deliver hit records. " . . . I've already been told by Warner Brothers that there are to be *no* jazz tunes on the next album. *None!*" she told John Abbey. "To me, that's an infringement on my artistic freedom and I don't like that. However, I have to acknowledge that the company stuck by me through some pretty remarkable circumstances so I'll go along with them for a while. But . . . I can't see the day ever coming when I get the chance to record a jazz album for them."

Chaka's prediction would turn out to be accurate. Even though she did some jazz-oriented shows around 1995 and even began finally working on what would have been a jazz record for Warner that same year, she'd left the label by 1998, and, even with some material already completed, the proposed project was abandoned.

Concerns for exactly what would constitute her fifth LP for Warner Brothers were uppermost in Chaka's mind as 1984 began. We talked briefly on the telephone during the spring of that year, and she didn't seem happy. Apparently, the powers that be in Burbank, the label's headquarters, had in effect told Chaka and producer Mardin that if they didn't deliver the goods with the new album, she might end up without a record deal. When we talked about the music she'd already done, Chaka was less than enthused. "There are some things on there I like . . . but I'm not wildly enthusiastic about it," she proffered rather coolly. Subsequently, she'd warmed to the project but explained a few months later, " . . . my record company had [always] left my producer [Arif Mardin] and I alone when it came time to working in the studio. We'd 'Michelangelo-d' ourselves out—just coming up with stuff that we liked, like the jazz stuff we did—and not thinking too much about the kids that wanted some music to dance to. Well, the company said, 'It's time to come up an album that's real commercial' and I haven't had a big hit in a while, so we agreed."

Ironically, the album *I Feel for You* would end up being Chaka's most successful project for Warner Brothers, her one and only platinum set, yielding her lone Top 5 pop hit and a Grammy to boot. With no less than eight producers working on the set, the record's success had a great deal to do with the title track, a tune penned by Prince for his self-titled 1979 best-selling album. Producer Arif Mardin had cleverly inserted a rap by Grandmaster Melle Mel and a sample from Stevie Wonder's 1963 hit "Fingertips"; the result was an out-and-out smash, although Chaka's initial reaction to the changes Mardin made to the track was one of shock: "I was EMBARRASSED!" she confessed in *Blues & Soul* magazine in December, 1984, referring to the famous "Chaka Khan, Chaka Khan, let me rock you Chaka Khan" refrain crafted by rapper Mel. "I first heard it, I said, 'Oh my God!' and I turned to Arif and asked him how he could do that to me! [Now] I just have fun with it when we perform. . . ."

The album included some other notable moments: Burt Bacharach and then wife Carole Bayer Sager had submitted the soulful "Stronger Than Before" while hit-making writer/producer David Foster offered the heartfelt ballad "Through the Fire." Mic Murphy and David Frank, members of funk'n'soul duo the System delivered the groove with "This Is My Night," French keyboard player Philippe Saisse provided "La Flamme" and "Chinatown," and Michael Sembello had co-written the standout "Eye to Eye." It was, track for track, Chaka's most obviously commercial album.

Chaka was definitely in the mood to talk about *I Feel for You*—and a whole lot more when we got together for what would be one of our most memorable conversations in November, 1984. I wasn't prepared for her frankness or for the range of topics we talked about. I'd learned many years ago that unless artists wanted to share personal information, it was best to focus on music-related matters. Prying into people's private lives was best left to others; my mission was to be a channel for artists to talk about their art. But Chaka wanted to *talk*.

I arrived at the plush Belage Hotel in West Hollywood, fresh from listening to her new album *I Feel for You* on my personal stereo. The catchy "Chaka Khan" hook was fresh in my brain as I entered the hotel suite where the lady herself was sitting, a familiar mass of red hair atop a smiling face, dressed neatly in black, sipping white wine, and looking particularly radiant. I was immediately struck by a certain calmness that seemed to emanate from a woman who could, I knew, be testy, impatient, and abrupt. I flashed for a moment on that last interview with Rufus, five years earlier, when she'd obviously been under the influence of some substance and was apparently feeling no pain. The pretty woman in front of me had changed, and I wasn't sure what had happened.

Chaka was ready to testify: "I think life's divided into two parts: one where you get to really learn what [it's] all about and the other part where you get to live it, choosing what you want. I just got tired of being kicked around, learning about life and believe me, I've lived it!" And then, the phrase she would end up uttering for many years: 'Like to hell and back in a limousine." She elaborated: ". . . about two-and-a-half years ago [in 1981], I decided it was time to make some changes, to eliminate things from my life which weren't helping me any." Chaka made some oblique references, but my instincts were telling me that whatever she'd decided to eliminate had something to do with her erratic behavior at our last meeting in 1979.

Chaka added that a change of scenery had also made a big difference in her demeanor and attitude: "In 1982, I moved from Los Angeles to New York City and . . . I love it. I'm happier there than I've been in ten years. I think it's because with all the activity that's going on in the city, I'm stimulated. It's like a good kick in the behind . . . and I need that. I found Los Angeles just too convalescent, too 'Cinderella-like.'" Manhattan had some other attractions for Chaka, who had split from husband Richard a few years earlier: she was now living with a school teacher [Albee] and living what she laughingly called "almost a 'normal' life! I get up around 7 A.M. and get the kids [Milini, 10, and Damien, 5] ready, make them some breakfast. The housekeeper takes Damien to school, and Albee takes Milini to her school and after they're on their way, I go back to bed 'til 2 P.M. Anyway, after the kids get home, we just hang out together for a few hours until it's time to eat and they have to go to bed. . . ."

The effects of living such an "ordinary" life even caused Chaka to fantasize about leaving the music business behind, "going on welfare, maybe working at a department store, something like that" until she remembered that "I *have* to sing. It's like a neurosis—you have to be a little crazy to want to do all this stuff! Why do I do it? Deep down, 'cause I love people. There are times when I don't want to be around them, and there's a certain reclusiveness that comes out. . . . But if you love people, you can't go off and live in an ivory tower—even though I know there are some stars who've done that successfully. . . ."

Even though Chaka was enjoying the trappings of a day-to-day existence, it was obvious that she was happy that her solo career was taking her to a new level. She confessed, "I've learned a lot during the years since I went out on my own. . . . I had to be self-sufficient, and I had to stand back and take stock. There was a certain nakedness which I've had to deal with. . . . But I don't regret anything that's happened since I ventured out on my own. . . ." She wasn't, she ventured "a household name yet" but she wasn't entirely sure she wanted *super* stardom: " . . . I don't know if I'll ever have that super mass appeal because I think I'm more of a cult artiste. [And] that's a lot of responsibility, and I know I'd have to forfeit something if I did reach that level of success. And I'm not sure I'd want that."

Chaka had had a new taste of how audiences were reacting to her when she headlined at Radio City Music Hall in October of that year, packing the place with some 6,000 people: "Those folks went crazy! You couldn't get a ticket anywhere, and people were trying to get through the backstage to see the show—it was amazing. It was great [though] I've got to say I didn't think so at the time. . . . I felt kinda detached from the audience because that place is so big . . . but it seemed like the people had a good time."

Chaka admitted that, all things considered, she was having a good time with her career, but she'd been around the block enough times to know what she was dealing with. Show business was a risky business, and according to Chaka, "it's anchorless, it's crazy, and honey, if you don't say when you are going to stop working, they'll work you to d-e-a-t-h!"

What had been a most enjoyable interview session appeared in *Blues & Soul* in December with a curious—and ultimately erroneous—news story on how Chaka had signed some new deal with Warner Brothers that meant she would be doing albums with the group Rufus every year alongside her own solo projects. Right—not! Whatever "special deal" had been done, Chaka never cut another album with Rufus while at Warner Brothers, and the band itself remained relatively inactive through the 1980s.

Chaka was way too busy thinking about how to handle the expectations that she now had to face as a Grammy-winning, platinum-selling solo artist. Striking while the iron was truly hot, she'd spent most of 1985 touring, and she had time to reflect on the success of "I Feel for You." The universal impact of the song was evident to me when I was the lone guest at a hotel in the south of Egypt in December, 1984. All of a sudden, I heard "Chaka Khan, Chaka Khan, let me rock you, Chaka Khan!" and I almost choked! Blaring out from the hotel radio, in among the latest Egyptian hits, was Chaka Khan herself, being heard all across the Nile. I couldn't wait to tell her when we talked again in the spring of 1985. While *I Feel for You* had worked wonders for her, I was hardly surprised at her reaction to the album's success when we talked on the telephone that spring: "Of course, I'm very happy that this is my first platinum album. . . . "Through the Fire" is a great David Foster song which is doing well for me, too. . . . But I still want to have more say in what I'm recording, and that's what's going to be happening with the next LP. For the first time, I'm going to start producing myself. I'll be doing at least four cuts on the next album. You see, I did all the vocal production on previous albums, but I just never got credited for it. This time, I'll be consciously producing myself . . . like getting the credit for it."

While admitting in the *Blues & Soul* interview that she might have been through a slump in regard to her own songwriting, Chaka was in a new space. "I've experienced a creative rebirth," and her new songs, she promised, "[are] going to be very *personal*—emotional, almost like a session between me and my 'shrink' on record! I'm going to tell it like it is in these songs—so I'm sure people may find some of them controversial—we shall see!" Chaka said the previous twelve months had been tough: "This has been an extremely revealing year for me. Like a metamorphosis. It's been full of new responsibilities: I've been reevaluating my life in many ways. I've been willing to confront some of the problems that dogged me in the past . . . face up to them, deal with the influences that may have been a real damper on my moving forward. I think that spending more time with my two kids . . . has definitely affected the whole way I'm dealing with my life. It's almost like my kids are making me more aware of my responsibilities in life. I love them, so I don't mind at all."

Once again, I sensed that Chaka's comments about the "influences" that she claimed had dogged her in the past were veiled references to her drug use and to the kind of hangers-on that substance abuse inevitably brings. While her demeanor had obviously changed, a few more years would pass before she would make any public statement about those activities and before she would become even more focused on her career.

Meanwhile, the results of Chaka's work in the recording studio in 1985 received only lukewarm attention from Warner Brothers and, thus, the public. The 1986 LP *Destiny* was the beginning of what would ultimately be a downward spiral in her relationship with the company that had been Chaka's recording home since 1978. She went through several changes in personal management over her last decade with Warner

Brothers, and Arif Mardin was no longer the sole producer on the last three albums she cut for the label. There were changes, changes, changes, and rather than building on the success of *I Feel for You*, her recording career seemed in flux. When we spoke in the early part of 1989, Chaka admitted that she hadn't been as committed to her career as she was becoming: "I really had a fear of success, but I realized recently that I wanted to get past that. It's really time for me to shit or get off the pot when it comes to my career. After all, I'm not one of those singers who's dying to move on to the silver screen." What she *had* done in the few years following the success of *I Feel for You* was make some fine guest appearances on records by British pop stars like Steve Winwood, Phil Collins, and Eric Clapton, none of which exactly hurt her industry profile.

While Chaka was taking a hard look at her career progress, her private life was also going through upheavals. She'd dismissed Los Angeles as her place of residence back in 1982, but after her relationship (in New York) with Albee ended, Chaka was back in Los Angeles for a few years. That didn't last, and she was planning a move back to the Big Apple when we spoke in the early part of 1989. Although she was definitely more involved in the creative process for *C.K.*, the 1988 follow-up to *Destiny*, she could muster up only mild enthusiasm for the project. "It rates up there somewhere," she mused when I asked how she thought the new album compared to some of her previous work. She was particularly happy to have recorded "The End of a Love Affair" and "I'll Be Around," the two songs from the Billie Holiday LP *Lady in Satin*, which had been so much a part of her upbringing. She felt good about the participants on her latest work, including Brenda Russell, Stevie Wonder, Prince, Bobby McFerrin, and Miles Davis, with whom she felt a particular affinity. "Seriously, I've been talking to Miles . . . about doing something like a whole record together but before I really get more into jazz, I want to get more under my belt, metaphorically speaking."

The one out-and-out positive statement to emerge from that 1989 interview was that Chaka had completed a six-week European tour, which she'd loved. She'd always enjoyed visiting Europe, but she had a new sense of admiration for the place and its people; within a very short time, her appreciation for things European would take on an even greater significance. As it was, in 1989 she waxed lyrical about her recent trip: " . . . I loved the sense of history, the shopping, the 'piazzas de something'! [And] the guys? Well, they're still a little macho—I got lots of invitations and bouquets of flowers from the guys at the shows, but that kind of attention is always good for a woman's stuff!" she laughed.

Chaka had encountered the same kind of admiration in Japan, and she giggled as she shared how she'd met one Japanese man "who wanted my underwear—I think he wanted to create a whole line of "Chaka Khan edible panties" or something. It sure is interesting some of the ways I'm thought of by the public!"

Even though Chaka was not the "wild woman" she'd been with Rufus, it was tough for the general public to accept that she'd mellowed out, particularly since she still wore a massive mane of red hair that alone contributed to the notion that she was this "hot mama." She seemed calmer and more focused, but fortunately in the process, she'd lost none of her vocal prowess. As the 1990s began, Chaka was sounding better than ever. Quincy Jones had teamed her up with the legendary Ray Charles for a chart-topping, Grammy-winning cover of the Brothers Johnson's hit "I'll Be Good to You" from his *Back on the Block* album in 1989. She was also featured on the song "The Places You Find Love" from the same LP. Chaka was still a viable recording artist and in a smart move, Warner Brothers created *Life Is a Dance/The Remix Project*, bringing all of Chaka's most danceable hits—obvious candidates like "I'm Every Woman," "I Know You, I Live You," "Clouds," and "I Feel for You"—together in one collection. The album did well but when it came to taking her new music to the next level of mainstream recognition, the label seemed bereft of innovative ideas.

Chaka's frustration with Warner Brothers might have contributed to her decision to move to London, which she did by the time her next interview appeared in *Blues & Soul*. When writer Jeff Lorez sat down at Chaka's apartment in fashionable Chelsea to find out the whys and wherefores, Chaka was as brutally honest as ever! "Life in the States was really going to the dogs," she told a fascinated Lorez. "It was really getting me down. I mean the basic principles that apply to everyday life were really jacked up, whether it be the money scene, the gun laws, the drug scene, the educational systems. It's like morals have gone out of the window." That was Chaka's viewpoint on life in general at the time. More specifically, she was ready to do some L.A.-bashing: "Nothing there grows—it's all artificial . . . [and] the air is so fucked up in L.A. . . . When you're coming in to land on a plane, it's like descending into a cesspool of brown shit! You can't even see the city from the sky!"

Chaka's decision to move to Europe had a great deal to do with her children: "My kids are coming over here . . . and then I want to put them in school in Hamburg [Germany]." She admitted, "It's really a strain bringing up kids . . . [though] I'm really happy with the way they're turning out. Sure, we have problems and fights but then that's all part of being a family. [But] they're not 'star' babies or little brats or anything like that. . . ." Her choice of Hamburg as a location for her children's ongoing education had just a little to do with her love interest at the time. "I met him some years ago," she told Lorez. "He's really the type of man I'm attracted to . . . [I like] wise people who have some real depth of character. [To me] the best and deepest type of friendships . . . don't run smoothly . . . The best type of friendship is one where there's real honesty . . . The type of relationship that breathes in and out!"

When Chaka turned her attention to musical matters, the U.S. record industry didn't escape the "Wrath of Khan," as Lorez tagged the article: "Money is the major sidetrack in this industry. Art dies for money and to overcome its hold, you really have to have some kind of inner strength." Chaka conceded that she'd met a few folks on the music scene that she genuinely liked. In addition to expressing her admiration for Miles Davis—" . . . he's brutally honest . . . he's the most honest motherfucker I've met and I love him for it!"—she considered Prince "a dream to work with. . . . People have different ideas about him because he's not accessible. He just doesn't want to get misinterpreted." Prophetically, some eight years later, Chaka would find herself collaborating with the Artist Formerly Known as Prince and making her first record away from Warner Brothers for his label.

Back in 1990, Chaka was still cherishing her dream of making a jazz album at Warner, she told Lorez. "I do plan to age gracefully into jazz and in fact . . . I'm in the process of putting a jazz band together with Herbie Hancock and we're going to do some dates in Holland, just covering the standards. . . ." She had little to say about what her next recording project might be: in fact another two years would pass before there was a new LP from Chaka. When *The Woman I Am* finally hit the streets in 1992, it did little to stem the tide of poor promotion and exposure that had adversely affected her last few efforts.

All the elements seemed to be in place: Chaka was the executive producer "in charge of production" (according to the credits), she'd contributed to six of the album's thirteen tracks, she'd worked with strong producers like Marcus Miller and Wayne Brathwaite, and she'd even recorded some of the music in Germany, her new adopted homeland. She was finally exercising the creative control she'd long sought. Chaka was understandably optimistic when we got together in the early part of 1992 just before the album's release, but she admitted that taking on the multiple responsibilities for the album had been a daunting task. When I asked her how she felt about wearing so many hats at one time, she was her usual candid self. "Honestly? *Petrified!* I knew this was a proving ground for me, that I had to deliver. It's really paid off. Sure, it's a lot of work and responsibility but I could never go back to doing records the way I used to."

Her fans, Chaka told me in our umpteenth *Blues & Soul* interview, would discover through the songs on *The Woman I Am* that she was "a bit of a romantic. It's something I've always tried to deny. People have always related to me as hardcore and wild but I suspected that underneath all of that was some marshmallow! I just never surrendered to it until now, to the more vulnerable side of me. . . . " This new softness and calmness permeated not only the music but also Chaka's manner when we met. Although she was still upbeat, funny, and very down-to-earth, I detected a freedom from the stress or tension that sometimes seemed to be bubbling just below the surface in previous conversations. I wasn't far off the mark: "I've been in Europe for the past three years. . . . Going to Europe helped me so much to get away from the scene I was on, to really get some distance and some perspective on what was happening in my life. Certainly, as you get older, you begin to assess what you have around you, who loves you and who's been there for you through the years. You start to see what your life is all about—and that's what I've done. . . . That my family and the people close to me love me, that means something to me. [Industry recognition] really makes no difference . . . it's nice but it's not what keeps me going."

When I mentioned the influence she had on so many others, Chaka reluctantly accepted the compliment. "Everyone tells me they 'hear' me in other singers. From time to time, I hear my licks in other people's vocals . . . it's a great thing . . . and I take it as the highest compliment but I'm not here for that . . . I'm here to get my musical rocks off! . . . The music I do is my expression and, even if I can't make anyone else happy, I have to please myself. If I please others in the process, that's truly great and I hope to continue to do that."

Hope sprang eternal because, once again, Warner Brothers failed to bring the album home. Although the LP generated only moderate sales, Chaka didn't stand still. It was obvious that her relationship with Warner Brothers was deteriorating; the continual changes at the label hadn't helped, and Chaka's frustration was growing. She diverted her attention from the stalemate that seemed to exist in her dealings with the company by encouraging her daughter, Milini, who was in a new group of her own called Pretty in Pink that had recorded an album for Motown. Keeping her name out there, Chaka started making several key guest appearances. She could be found "guesting" on albums by Lionel Hampton, Quincy Jones, Fourplay, Steve Winwood, Bruce Hornsby, and rapper Guru. She made a major impact with her moving interpretation of "My Funny Valentine" on the multimillion selling soundtrack of *Waiting to Exhale*. She could also be heard on the soundtrack of the successful film *Set If Off*. She co-hosted "The Soul Train Music Awards," could be seen with far more regularity on television, and made a memorable appearance at the Grammy Awards in New York in 1997.

True to form, Chaka wasn't letting the politics of her relationship with Warner Brothers get in the way of her career—or her life. My sister and I ran into her at Heathrow Airport in October, 1995, and Chaka was in good spirits, a little tired physically, but conversational nonetheless. She was on her way back to the United States to record some new material, and the same sense of focus I'd detected during our last few interviews was there. And earlier in the year I'd seen her perform during a mini-tour of major cities that focused on her jazz stylings. While some people in the crowd wanted to hear "Ain't Nobody" and "Tell Me Something Good," Chaka's readings of everything from "I Loves You, Porgy" to "Alfie" resonated with soulful feeling.

I encountered a feisty Chaka Khan at the Newsroom, a trendy vegetarian eaterie in West Hollywood, when we sat down for a 1996 interview for *Blues & Soul*. By now, twenty-two years after our first conversation, we shared the kind of familiarity that made for fun and frankness. I was aware that Chaka was at the end of her rope with Warner Brothers, but since one of the company's reps was eating with us, her comments were tactful. She left lunch to do some promotional work at a local L.A. radio station in light of the release of *Epiphany*, a collection of hits that also included five new songs. The first single was "Never Miss the Water," a funkier-than-funk groove she'd worked on with hip musician, poet, and rapper Me'Shell NdegeOcello. Because Chaka was conscious of the Warner Brothers rep's presence, we agreed to complete our conversation a few days later on the telephone. But the bottom line was that Chaka was looking for a new place to express her creativity as a recording artist. Rumor had it that Clive Davis, the head of Arista, had made her a big money offer after the success of the *Waiting to Exhale* soundtrack. Chaka grinned, "Well, I've had lots of offers! But I'm with Warner's . . . because I still have a contract with them. . . ."

Chaka had in fact completed an entire album with producer David Gamson and had finally started on her much-anticipated jazz project with the German arranger/producer Peter Herbaltzheimer. Reading between the lines, the Warner executives hadn't been too thrilled about releasing either project and suggested a "Greatest Hits" package, a move Chaka initially resisted: " . . . when people started pointing out to me that this was my twenty-fifth anniversary of when I started singing professionally, I said okay to doing a 'Best Of' collection. . . ." the one thing that was apparent both during lunch and when we spoke on the telephone was a new attitude that Chaka had adopted about her career. She explained, " . . . I've decided to do it in a big way. What I mean is take my career to another level and to do it for real, to make it happen. . . ."

Chaka's sister Tammy McCrary was now managing her, and she was, in her own words, "ready to get paid!" She spelled it out: "I was never really interested in dealing with all the business stuff. You know, I've always loved to sing . . . and when it came to finances, I just didn't pay much attention. Now it's all about balance: Tammy . . . is really good at demanding that I get paid for what I'm worth. You see, all the managers I've had have told me, 'Hey, we know how great you are and we can get top dollar for you . . . blah, blah, blah,' and then they take their share of the money, and I didn't see it. Now Tammy's collecting my paycheck . . . and she's really good at it! . . . It's taken a few years . . . but as far as I'm concerned, nepotism is the way! I got sick of strangers ripping me off, and it's a situation now where I trust . . . and know she has my best interests at heart and the expertise to do what needs to be done. "

During 1996 Chaka had also ventured off into a new area. She'd played the award-winning role of Carrie in the London debut of the off-Broadway musical *Mama, I Want to Sing*, the successful play based on the life of Doris Troy, who appeared in the show with her. "I wanted the opportunity to sing gospel," Chaka said, "and I got to do that with the play, but I have no more desire to act on stage than I did before the show. I found it tough doing the same thing night after night . . .so I don't think I'll be doing anything like that again!"

As we concluded our chat, Chaka revealed that she was still maintaining a residence in London ("I can go about my business, and people don't bother me") and that she was starting work on her autobiography with longtime friend and associate Pepsi Charles. As Chaka explained: "I'm gonna be telling the truth about my life up until now. But preparing it has been tough. It's been like going through major therapy sessions! It's been cleansing but at times painful going back over my life. . . ."

Ah, but I mused to myself, what a life it is! One filled with triumphs, letdowns, sex, drugs, and rock 'n' roll, rip-offs, standing ovations, accolades, groupies, and ass-kissers. Even if she isn't in the same generation as some of the other soulful divas, Chaka Khan is right there with them in terms of life experience and the ability to express all that she has witnessed powerfully through her music. Fortunately 1998 was the year that Chaka's self-expression hit a new height: she set up her own label (Earth Song Entertainment) and worked with the Artist (Formerly Known as Prince) on a spectacular new album entitled *Come 2 My House*. Filled with funky tunes and soulful ballads, the record was a reminder to one and all that Chaka had lost none of her power and energy, that if anything, she sounded better than ever! At a photo shoot just before the album was released, I got a chance to tell her that one song in particular, "Don't Talk 2 Strangers," had become like an affirmation for me, evoking a range of emotions every time I played it. Ain't nobody like Chaka—and as far as I'm concerned, she just gets better with time!

LITTLE BELLE
Chapter 9
soul sister!

Patti LaBelle probably doesn't remember saying it, but she was in her usual truth-telling mode in the spring of 1980 (in one of the many interviews she and I've done for *Blues & Soul* over the past twenty-five years): "It's time to really kick ass! I can't let people walk over me anymore. . . . I've given all I can give; now it's up to everyone else to run with [the music] and make it work, invest in me, realize the potential that's there."

A few more years would pass before that potential began to be fulfilled and before Patti LaBelle became a household name, which she did by the late 1980s. But by the time she made that statement on the eve of the release of her fourth (and last) solo album for Epic Records, Patricia Edwards had been singing professionally for twenty-one years through various incarnations from the 1960s almost doo-wop-like-Bluebelles to the glamorous, rock'n'soul pioneering style of the 1970s trio Labelle. When Patti finally emerged as a superstar in her own right, as a diva known for her earthy funkiness and high-octane vocal range, she was drawing from a rich musical history. Her body of work encompassed everything from the nineteenth-century Irish air "Danny Boy" to the overtly sexual, get-you-in-the-gut style of former partner Nona Hendryx's "You Turn Me On." Along the way, Patti acquired a new attitude, a new nose, and a certain sophistication, as well as lost a number of family members to cancer and close friends to AIDS. But, one-on-one, she never stopped being an in-your-face down-home Philly girlfriend.

At a London restaurant in January, 1975, Patti was with Nona and Sarah Dash, her two Labelle sisters, and Vicki Wickham, the miracle-working manager. Wickham, who was also the former producer of Britain's 1960s favorite television show, "Ready, Steady, Go!," had transformed this sometime-hit girl group into pioneering soulful, space children. "You seem kinda suppressed," an unsmiling Nona said without a blink. We'd met only once before in New York, when a few months earlier I was on my first visit to the United States. Nona continued, "Like, repressed or something. . . ." I wasn't sure how to respond because as a fledgling journalist, I wasn't used to having my interview subjects "analyze" my personality. Patti softened the blow just a little. "You need to lighten up, honey. You know, let loose. Let go, release yourself," she chirped. Sarah was eating, listening, and saying nothing. I was embarrassed and got out only a meek "okay." A few weeks later at my official leaving-the-United-Kingdom party, I figure they would be proud of me all in silver with a feather in my bushy, Afro-styled hair in tribute to the impact Labelle was having on me then.

A few days later, Labelle performed for the first time at London's Lyceum, giving British audiences a chance to hear "Lady Marmalade," the group's soon-to-be gold record and first and only pop and R&B chart topper. Patti wanted someone to come up and dance with the group. She spied me in the wings and decided that she was going to force me to lighten up! As she literally pulled me onstage, I protested wildly and summoned up every piece of rhythm I could muster; I was soon dancing in the light with Patti, all decked out in futuristic gear, and freeing myself to be myself. As if I had a choice!

Patricia Holt, born May, 1944, in West Philadelphia, probably wasn't always as forthright and pushy. You get no clues as to where she got her outrageous onstage manner and beyond-the-roof vocal pyrotechnics by checking her early musical influences. She has maintained in various interviews over the years that she used to listen to the jazz stylings of Gloria Lynne and Nina Simone, among others; you can only assume that Simone's dramatic approach to even the most trite tune likely affected Patti a little more than the staid but pretty style of vocalist Lynne. It doesn't take a genius to figure out that singing praises in the Beulah Baptist Church choir on the city's south side where Patti was raised, was more likely an outlet for her burgeoning musical expression. "I was a homely little girl," Patti told British writer Sharon Davis in 1986 for a *Blues & Soul* magazine article, "with red hair that changed color as I grew older. I was so shy my mother offered me money to go and play with the other kids! . . . I wouldn't go—I used to stay in our house and sing in front of the mirror. . . ." Patti's repertoire, she said, included standards like "My Funny Valentine" and "The Party's Over."

Fueled by the enthusiastic response Patti got singing in church, she formed a teen group, the Ordettes, with school friend Cynthia "Cindy" Birdsong. In 1961 the two girls united with Wynona "Nona" Hendryx and Sarah Dash, who sang in a rival group, the Del-Capris—and the Blue-Belles were born. After recording a few sides for a small local label, the quartet teamed up with Philly producer Bobby Martin in 1962 to record "I Sold My Heart to the Junkman," and although when it was released under the Blue-Belles' name, the final recording featured another group, the Starlets.

All of a sudden, the Blue-Belles were in demand for a hit they didn't officially record. The situation was rectified a year later when the group changed its name to Patti LaBelle (French for "the beautiful") & the Blue

Belles and scored its first legitimate Top 20 R&B hit and Top 40 pop hit on the Newtown label with "Down the Aisle (Wedding Song)," one of the six singles the group recorded from 1962 to 1964. That same year (1963), the quartet switched to Parkway Records, where they would score two strange hits: a version of "You'll Never Walk Alone" from the Rodgers & Hammerstein musical *Carousel* and "Danny Boy," the aforementioned nineteenth-century song that was based on the traditional Irish tune "Londonderry Air." As would be the case on subsequent recordings, Patti turned in soaring lead vocals that bordered on the histrionic. Almost from the start, audiences loved Patti's dramatic performances; with Nona, Sarah, and Cindy offering gospel-infused harmonies in back of her, Patti pushed the vocal envelope.

In Patti's 1986 interview in *Blues & Soul*, she explained that the group was doing "five shows a day, seven days a week," and if they cleared one thousand dollars a week, they considered themselves successful. This was in the early 1960s when black girl groups were in vogue: the Ronettes, the Chiffons, and the Shirelles had all been constant hitmakers, and the musical climate was good for members of female trios and quartets in their tight-fitting gowns, high heels, and bouffant wigs.

The Blue Belles were busy blowing other groups off the stage with their vocal power, performing on the chitlin' circuit and appearing at theaters like the Apollo in New York, the Fox in Detroit, the Howard in Washington, DC, and the Regal in Chicago. The group's raw energy in front of its fast-growing audience was captured on tape when Atlantic Records cut one of the R&B package shows that crisscrossed the country: called "Saturday Night at the Uptown" after the Philadelphia theater where the recording was made one hot night in July, 1964, the bill was filled with favorites, including the hometown girls Patti LaBelle & the Blue Belles.The Drifters headlined, preceded by the Vibrations, and other artists on the bill included Barbara ("You'll Lose a Good Thing") Lynn; up-and-coming Wilson Pickett; another female group, Patti & the Emblems; and the Carltons. One listen to the final album, and there is no question about who stole the show that night!

Six months later, Patti LaBelle & the Blue Belles were featured once again on a live recording of popular New York deejay Murray the K's "Holiday Show," issued through Atlantic. Cut on December 30, 1964, at the famous Brooklyn Fox theater, the record of the hit-filled bill featured Patti and the group, the Shangri-Las, Ben E. King, the Drifters, the Shirelles, Chuck Jackson, and twenty-four-year-old Dionne Warwick. The group's performances captured on tape, indicative of its growing reputation as one of the hottest live acts in the R&B world, must have convinced the people at Atlantic Records that signing the quartet might prove to be a smart move.

The group's first recording date for Atlantic was in October, 1965, and it was a scorcher. Two of the tunes, "Patti's Prayer" and "All or Nothing" were over-the-top soul gems. I can remember seeing Patti and the Blue Belles perform the latter tune, the debut single for the label, on, of all things, a British children's television show when they came to the United Kingdom for the first time in late 1965. I'd never seen anyone sing the way Patti did that evening, and I remember putting my homework aside to watch, mesmerized as the group brought me to the edge with the most emotional performance I'd ever seen up until that point.

Unfortunately, the record did nothing on either side of the water, chart-wise. At the same session, the quartet had also recorded "Groovy Kind of Love," a song that local British group the Mindbenders "stole" and turned into a British and American hit in 1966, which Phil Collins revived as a pop chart topper in 1988. While no other song Patti and the Blue Belles recorded during their three years with Atlantic suffered the same fate, the basic flavor of their tenure with the label was the same: some great material was buried, poorly promoted, or quickly forgotten.

Pandering to the notion that maybe the group could do well with a burgeoning supper-club audience if it recorded some jazz and pop standards, Atlantic executives arranged a December, 1965, session at which Patti and her soulful cohorts cut eight songs, ranging from Barbra Streisand's "People" to Al Hibbler's "Unchained Melody." Atlantic was employing the same strategy with Esther Phillips and Barbara Lewis, two of its other female artists, but the effect sales-wise was minimal.

This isn't to say that Patti didn't put her all into the session. And while it spawned nary a hit, the very last song cut that December night in Atlantic's Broadway studio would remain with her for more than thirty-three years. The group's reading of "Over the Rainbow" was electrifying, and it was no surprise that it became the title cut for the quartet's debut Atlantic album. "I remember that we all picked the songs, but I wouldn't record anything that I didn't love," Patti stated in a 1996 interview for the MCA "Greatest Hits" collection, " . . . and 'Over the Rainbow' was one of those songs I always loved from the time I heard Judy Garland sing it in *The Wizard of Oz*. It has such a beautiful melody and that line, 'If birds can fly, why can't I?'—that's always been *my* line because I have often thought of myself that way, as a bird who could fly. . . . "

Little did Patti or the rest of the group know that the song would become virtually an anthem for her, and certainly, after she began her solo career in 1977, "Over the Rainbow" was a song audiences eagerly awaited night after night, wherever she appeared. As she revealed during the 1996 interview, "It didn't happen right away but gradually, over time, we began including it in our show and [now] it's one of those things where if I don't do the song in every performance, I'd probably get lynched!"

But back in 1966 "Over the Rainbow" was simply the title of an album that didn't exactly live up to its name in terms of how it affected the group's career. Hoping for better results, Patti and the Blue Belles went back into the studios a few more times in 1966. Finally, "I'm Still Waiting," a beautiful ballad penned by Curtis Mayfield, still the leader of the Impressions, brought the quartet back onto the R&B charts for the first time in two years. Three months later a version of "Take Me for a Little While," previously recorded in 1965 by both New York singer Evie Sands and Chicago soul sister Jackie Ross, finally made the charts for the first time, courtesy of Patti and her friends.

1967 wasn't an easy year for Patti and the group. "It all came as such a shock," Patti noted in a 1970 interview during a visit to the tiny offices of *Blues & Soul* in London's West End. "We just arrived at a show one night and Cindy wasn't there. That's how quickly it happened. We were very hurt at the time though it probably was the best thing. Cindy really wanted to go places; she was very ambitious and wasn't really satisfied with the progress we were making. . . ." Unbeknownst to the group, Cindy had been approached to join the Supremes when original member Florence Ballard was unceremoniously requested to leave the hitmaking Motown trio.

Now a trio themselves, Patti, Nona, and Sarah soldiered on, but as 1967 turned into 1968, there was just one reigning diva at Atlantic—and her name was Aretha. Jerry Wexler, the same man who had signed Patti LaBelle & the Blue Belles to the label, had also signed Aretha Franklin in 1966. By the spring of 1968 Aretha had racked up no fewer than six consecutive R&B and pop hits, and she doubled that number in 1968 alone. So it would hardly be surprising if Patti and the group were feeling a little ignored. In his autobiography, *The Rhythm & The Blues*, Wexler confesses, "We didn't find her [Patti] the right material and even worse, [we] made the ghastly mistake of trying to turn her Bluebelles into the Supremes."

The group spent its remaining year or so with Atlantic floundering. Although successive recording sessions resulted in some good material, they also produced a bunch of failed singles. Enter Vicki Wickham who had presented the group members on "Ready, Steady, Go!" when they were in the U.K. in 1966 to promote the single "Patti's Prayer." A Brit with a vision, Wickham took over the group's management, and in the book *She Bop* she is quoted as telling the trio, "If we're going to do this, it's a new day. . . . You can't wear those nice little frilly frocks and wigs, we've got to rethink it. You've got to make a statement, you're women, there's a lot to be said."

Wickham took the trio to London to regroup. "I fought the whole time with Vicki. . . . We fought about the songs we were singing, we fought about the name change [to Labelle]," Patti stated in the liner notes for *Something Silver*, a Warner Brothers' 1997 reissue. "Me and her—just like [boxers] Joe Frazier and Muhammad Ali." Group member Sarah put it bluntly in an nterview with *Blues & Soul's* John Abbey when they came to Britain in 1970, ostensibly to sign with the small, independent Fly Records label: " . . . to be honest, we're all a little bored with having nothing to do while we're here. It's the longest layoff we've ever had and we're getting depressed about not playing any dates while we're here..." Patti's boredom had a more personal root. She'd married then-school principal Armstead Edwards in 1969: ". . . we've never been apart for so long and I'm missing him. Still, he's coming over to spend the last few days with us before we go back home," she stated with a sigh.

Several months later, battles fought, won, and lost, Patti joined Nona Hendryx and Sarah Dash on the stage of New York's Town Hall for the unveiling of the group Labelle. Signed to Warner Brothers in 1971, with a self-titled album produced by Wickham and British music man Kit Lambert (known for his work with the Who, among other groups), the trio was ready for the world. But was the world ready for Labelle? Sarah told *Blues & Soul* writer Alan Elsey in 1975, "We were on a show with [British blues and rock singer] Long John Baldry, we closed the show I think. . . . There's a lot of mixed opinions about the show, 'cause we didn't really know where we were going. Pat was in a dress or something and Nona and I were all in black and they hadn't see any girls outside of us wearing gowns. The music was so hard and different from what we had been doing that some of our friends said, 'I don't know if we like it' and some said, 'it was o.k.' . . . [some] just couldn't understand songs like "Morning Much Better" [a song about early-morning sex], you know, [like] 'what is this?' . . . it was so LOUD but it was good. . . ."

During our 1996 interview regarding the liner notes for MCA"s *Greatest Hits* package, Patti was unsure how people would react: "I was thinking the fans wouldn't appreciate us for changing. . . . I was a scaredy cat." She was right in one sense: it would take four more years of hard work for the general public to catch up, and even then the love affair was relatively brief. From 1971 to 1975 when "Lady Marmalade" became an international smash and, essentially, Labelle's only major across-the-board hit, manager Wickham plotted and planned, and Labelle underwent more change.

After two critically acclaimed but commercial failures for Warner Brothers (a second album, *Moon Shadow*, gave Nona more exposure as a thoughtful, insightful lyricist), the group headed to RCA in 1973 for the one-off *Pressure Cookin'* album. Even with a helping hand from none other than Stevie Wonder—who wrote one song and performed on another, billed under an alias simply as "Friend"—the LP didn't register on a mass scale although at this stage in the group's development, it had built a strong, loyal following, mostly on the East Coast of the U.S., particularly among black and Hispanic gay men. A 1971 collaboration with popular singer/songwriter Laura Nyro on her best-selling *Gonna Take a Miracle* LP, a collection of mostly classic R&B hits that were among Nyro's personal favorites, on which the trio sang background vocals, helped heighten awareness among Nyro's own hip, cross-cultural audience.

By the time *Pressure Cookin'* was released, the trio was decked out in silver "spacesuits," breastplates, feathers, and what one commentator called "outrageous drag." Long gone were the sequins of the Bluebelles' days: thanks to the avant-garde approach of designer Larry LaGaspi, Labelle looked like no other female group! The cult following was growing, thanks to highly original material like Nona's "Can I Speak to You Before You Go to Hollywood" and covers of show-stoppers like Gil Scott-Heron's "The Revolution Will Not Be Televised."

The one missing piece was a record company that could take Labelle over the edge. But in 1974 when the group signed with Epic Records it finally seemed to have found a label that understood its potential. To achieve the commercial breakthrough everyone was seeking, the label dispatched the group to New Orleans to work with Allen Toussaint, a writer/producer who was known for his work with such local acts as Lee Dorsey, Irma Thomas, and Ernie K-Doe, and who was a recording artist in his own right. On paper the pairing did look a little strange, but miraculously the combination worked—although not without some tension. "We got quite agitated to start off with because everyone works at such a slow pace down there," Patti stated when we got together for the first time at Vicki Wickham's apartment in Manhattan in November, 1974. "But once we realized that Allen was just taking time to work everything out—the man is just so clever, we knew it would be all right. And we all agree that this is our best album—it should have been the first one!"

231

To celebrate the release of *Nightbirds*, named after one of a number of tracks Nona had written for the album, the group became the first pop act in history to appear at the prestigious Metropolitan Opera House at Lincoln Center in October, 1974. Then-correspondent and photographer for *Blues & Soul* Kwame Brathwaite reported, " . . . It was truly a spectacle and the overflowing standing room only crowd had a 'gay' time to say the least. . . . There were plenty of space children in the audience, universal lovers . . . [And] the group's entrance was not to be believed . . . the build up climaxed with Patti floating down from the stage. . . . ."

A full-scale production, way-out costumes, strong new material, and, above all, the three soulful voices of Patti, Nona, and Sarah made the evening a smashing success. And the word was out: Labelle had really arrived. I'll never forget that the very day I arrived in New York for the first time ever, Gary, my former London roommate, who had moved to Brooklyn, took me back to his apartment and told me to take a shower and get dressed for a house party later that Saturday night. The crowd at the party was mostly black and gay, and was having a good time until "What Can I Do For You?," one of the standout tracks from *Nightbirds*, came on. The place erupted! Everybody, including me, was on the floor, boogeying, hollering, screaming, and, for those who knew the words, singing along. Labelle was the darling of the proud-to-be-black-and-gay crowd, and the group can do no wrong in its eyes.

Thanks to "Lady Marmalade," a cute ditty about a New Orleans hooker and her invitation to an unsuspecting john, the enthusiasm for the group spilled over to mainstream audiences, although not without some controversy. The original French lyrical line, "Voulez-vous coucher avec moi ce soir?" means just what it says: "Would you like to sleep with me tonight?" The line's direct approach offended some people, and Labelle was forced to amend "coucher" to "danser" on some national television shows.

Based on the way everything was going, the Labelle story should have ended well. But there were pressures and when the group's next two albums, 1975's *Phoenix* and 1976's *Chameleon*—as good as they were musically—failed to live up to expectations sales-wise, Labelle became history. It was almost as if "Isn't It a Shame," the group's very last charted single and a tale of a final breakup ostensibly between two lovers, was also a public statement about how three people who "laughed together, loved together sometimes end up far apart."

Even to this day, although people who were around at the height of the Labelle era have accepted Patti's emergence as a superdiva, they still mourn the group's demise. As I listened to much of the material the group recorded as I wrote this chapter, it was hard not to get a lump in the throat or a tear in the eye. The blending of voices and the sheer soulfulness of the group dynamic made Labelle one of a kind, a vocal team the likes of which has never been heard of or seen again.

But strange as it might seem, Patti makes little reference to the split other than to say how tough it was initially to go solo, even in her 1996 autobiography *Don't Block the Blessings*. In October, 1977, during our first interview after the group broke up, Patti had just one comment: "We'd gone as far as we could with the framework." She said a little more to John Abbey during a *Blues & Soul* interview in 1979: " . . . I doubt if we could ever go back together again because we reached the stage where we could go no further. I think we broke up at just the right time because if we had gone on, we may well have reached the point where none of us could have gone on at all. . . ."

Patti did, however, mention some of the possible conflicts when discussing producer David Rubinson, who had worked on the *Chameleon* album and ended up producing her solo debut. "I chose David [to work with me] because when we were working on the *Chameleon* album, I felt we were beginning to sing some of the things I wanted to sing. You see, he'd wanted us to record "Isn't It a Shame" and I agreed—because it was the kind of thing that I felt like I wanted to do. But we had problems because [manager] Vicki Wickham really didn't want us to do the song. Well, I didn't fight for it but David did. . . ." Nona offered no further comment when she and I spoke a few weeks earlier in conjunction with the release of her first solo album, leaving people to wonder what had really happened among the trio members. Patti did concede in a 1996 interview for the MCA *Greatest Hits* collection that the final two albums the group recorded were "classics that have the best singing we ever did as a group together. It was time for us to part as singing partners while remaining friends." The industry rumor mill suggested that if there was any conflict, it was between Patti and Nona, specifically around the predominance of Nona's material that the group was recording. But because no one has ever made a public comment to that effect, exactly what led to the seemingly abrupt end to a fifteen-year association remains mere speculation.

In 1996 Patti admitted, "I was afraid of being blamed for the group's breakup," and was concerned because "[I] didn't know how people would respond to me as an artist out on my own." Nevertheless she was initially eager to talk about the challenges of being by herself for the first time in her professional career. "I always had Nona and Sarah to fall back on. I mean, they were there if I needed a shoulder to cry on. Well, when we weren't together anymore, I had no choice—I had to start depending on ME, on Patti," she said in our *Blues & Soul* interview. "I've found that because of that alone, I've grown a lot, become a better, stronger woman. I'm more adventurous now, I'll take chances. You know, I was always very punkish but now I'm maturing. Sure, I'm still crazy—that will never change! But I'd have to say that one of the positive things to emerge from the whole split was my developing into a stronger person." I remember being a little taken aback by Patti's comments about how she'd felt about herself apparently for a long time: "Since the split happened, I've been a far more positive person. You know, I used to be really negative about myself. No, honestly, I did! I didn't have confidence in myself, I didn't think I was a strong leader. I was always afraid of falling on my face. . . ."

It was hard to imagine that Patti LaBelle, the outspoken, up-front, silver-clad, vocal dynamo could possibly have been suffering from low self-esteem, especially after seeing her very first public performance as a solo artist. I'd been fortunate enough to witness it firsthand when CBS Records flew a select group of music journalists to London for its international convention in the summer of 1977. At a swanky hotel on Park Lane, we dined, got up to all manner of stuff, and enjoyed the parade of talent that performed each night. Thursday evening was reserved for Patti's debut. David Rubinson, known for his work with the Pointer Sisters, had produced the Philly diva's all-important debut album for Epic, and he was on hand to conduct a forty-piece orchestra. The backbone of what would become Patti's regular rhythm section—under the direction of James "Budd" Ellison, who had been with the group Labelle for a while and who would remain with Patti through thick and thin—was on hand along with members of the Waters family, renowned for their tight, soulful background harmonies.

Patti was in a word, spectacular. She might have had a case of nerves, as she reports in her autobiography, but no one watching her performance that night would have guessed. As I reported in *Blues & Soul* a month or so later, "The lady wailed, sung notes reaching up to the heavens, cajoled, joked and gave her all!" Patti concentrated on tunes from her eponymous new album, including the pop/R&B evergreen "Since I Don't Have You"; the upbeat "Joy to Have Your Love," the first single and a Top 40 R&B hit; and "You Are My Friend," a highly personal song that would become a staple in the LaBelle repertoire for many, many years.

In the months that followed, Patti set out on her first tour as a solo performer. All the fans that she'd amassed during the years with Labelle seemed to show up for appearances at such venues as Philadelphia's Academy of Music and New York's Avery Fisher Hall. The only challenge Patti seemed to be facing going into her second album was that Epic executives, champions of the group Labelle at the outset, seemed unable to jump-start Patti's recording career. Her records did reasonably well, but none of the meager eight singles the company pulled from four consecutive albums between 1977 and 1980 hit the R&B Top 20—and the pop charts weren't even a consideration. The albums fared all right but rather than enjoying an increase in sales with each successive LP, from 1978's *Tasty*, through 1979's *It's Alright With Me*, to 1980's *Released*, the sales seemed to drop or level off quickly.

Patti was still giving amazing performances, hits or no hits, and it could be said that her tenacity in continuously offering spellbinding shows night after night was ultimately responsible for the hardcore audience she'd created by the time she finally had her breakthrough as a solo hitmaker in the mid-1980s. That kind of work ethic is still very much a part of her approach to performing: she acknowledges that her audience pays the rent and that when they shell out their hard-earned money to see her, they want to be entertained and to see a show. This is her aim-to-please way of relating to performing that has her shows filled to capacity on a consistent basis, as well as the reason why she is still considered one of the most exciting artists to see in concert.

This was the exact kind of approach that Patti took when she shared the stage with Al Green at Radio City Music Hall in New York in 1978. And although the Reverend Green was the headliner, there was no question about who came out the winner. "The question that practically everyone left asking was simply who deserved to be the headliner," I noted in a *Blues & Soul* magazine report. "Quite honestly, Patti LaBelle gave one of the most energetic and soulful performances we've seen her do ever . . . whereas Mr. Green . . . gave a performance which left many wondering if he hasn't lost all the spark and magic that once singled out his shows as among the best you could hope to see."

Patti herself commented on the bill in a 1978 interview she and I did in Philadelphia: " . . . it was basically his audience—I didn't go out there to steal them, just to let them see and hear me." She was upbeat when we spoke, laughing about the sales potential for *Tasty*, her then-new album. "I've got the gold spray paint ready!" she joked, hoping to be able to use it on a copy of the LP to signify its gold status. We were in one of the more exclusive hotels in Philly since Patti had just moved into a new house that wasn't quite ready for the prying eyes of visiting journalists. Two albums in, she seemed quite happy about the direction her career was taking: "I feel very happy and very grateful for everything. . . . You see, when the group first split up, I went through a lot of mental changes. I really didn't think people would accept me. I didn't quite know what would happen. But one thing I did conclude. That was . . . if my career ended, I still had my family . . . and that's important to me. Some people put all the emphasis on their career—they're in love with that alone. But having a contented 'other' life—my husband, my son, my dog, the new house—that's really important to me. Because when I thought about which one I could be without—I realized that it was my career, not my home life. And that helps put it all in perspective."

At the time, I had no idea what challenges Patti might be facing in her life away from the limelight. Like so many other divas, she wanted to focus on her music, with only occasional references to matters of a personal nature. Patti didn't want to necessarily share the hurts and disappointments, so I was really shocked when, years later, I read her autobiography and found out about the health problems she was facing with her family. I was surprised that she opened up as much as she did during our 1978 interview: " . . . People thought I was too passive and maybe took me for granted, thought I was a joke because I didn't always speak up. . . . Maybe at times in the past, I was just a pushover—people could really tell me what to do but I've learned that if you stand up for what you want to do, you get a lot more respect from everyone. . . . I'm the kind of person that you can always come to and you'll always get love, you'll always get warmth. But I've been learning, especially recently, that you can't put your trust in everyone that comes along. I've had to deal with particular situations that have really hurt me. So now I'm being careful. . . ." She didn't elaborate.

Patti might have been facing all kinds of personal issues at the time and no doubt, it didn't help that the album she was hoping would take her to a new level of recognition didn't fare too well. Despite standout tracks like "Little Girls," which Patti sang with that strange kind of "other" voice that she would use from time to time on certain songs to create emphasis, or the dance-flavored "Teach Me Tonight," complete with Spanish subtitle ("Me Gusta Tu Baile"), the LP *Tasty* did only moderately well. Undaunted, Patti hit the road for a four-month tour with comedian Richard Pryor, which undoubtedly exposed her to a wider audience than usual since Pryor was enjoying an immense degree of popularity at the time. It was a tough time for Patti personally: during the tour, her mother passed away, and she noted that Pryor had been there for her "to help me through."

While touring, Patti had completed *It's Alright With Me*, her third Epic album. For this project, she worked with producer/songwriter Skip Scarborough, who had supplied the Emotions and Earth, Wind & Fire with several hit songs, including "Don't Ask My Neighbors" and "Can't Hide Love." The result was a strong record. But once again, Epic seemed unable to get the album or the couple of singles that were released from it off the ground.

At a little café in Philadelphia in the spring of 1980, Patti and I talked about some of her frustrations. I remember that although she was obviously feeling irritated about the way her career seemed to be going, she was relaxed and in good spirits. Over the many years of doing interviews together, we'd gotten to know each other without being bosom buddies. Her greeting was always warm, and the conversation was always spiced with Patti's well-known terms of endearment: a "sugar" here, a "honey" there, and an occasional "boyfriend." She might have been feeling good, but she wasn't about to mince words in this particular *Blues & Soul* interview: "I thought that as I went into the eighties, I'd be turning down [television] specials, movies, picking up Grammys and so on. I figured more would be happening for me."

Patti was speaking out on the eve of her fourth album's entry into the marketplace. In hindsight, it was appropriately entitled *Released*, and that is exactly what Patti would be in regard her contract with Epic Records! But at the time we talked, she still had high hopes for the album, a reunion with producer Allen Toussaint from the *Nightbirds* days. The album's release almost seemed incidental as Patti let fly: "Truly, if they ever decide they want me at the Grammys, *just to show up*, I'll be there! I already know what gown I want to wear and I'm prepared to pay for my air ticket to go . . . I'm qualified, I didn't come here unequipped. The problem seems to be that people (in the industry) just don't know what to do with me. I think we need a definite game plan because when I see people like Donna Summer having t.v. specials and Gloria Gaynor picking up Grammys, I know their careers involved a definite plan."

Patti had her own thoughts on why her solo career might have stalled. "I think it probably has a lot to do with my own vulnerability. People in this business have always seen me as easygoing, good ol' Pat . . . I can't let people walk over me anymore—I have to let them know that I'm at the source of whatever happens to me. Maybe, in the past, I've conceded just one too many times and although people didn't necessarily have harmful intention, they did take advantage. I have to let everyone see that this is a diamond not a rhinestone and that it's a valuable and buffable diamond—one that can be polished even beyond what it is now. I guess it does have to do with what you project but I really want people to see what I'm really all about. I'm a total . . . and capable person. I'm just amazed that after fifteen years, people involved can't see what they have to work with."

Patti was on a roll: "I used to think it was ego to believe that you were good. Fortunately, I got over that, I realize now that there's nothing wrong with being confident. It's about knowing what you are and as far as I'm concerned, I'm great! I'm a decent performer and I don't think I've been given the credit and that might be because I've been putting myself at the effect of other people. I'm determined not to let that happen, the same way I'm determined to have that recognition that comes from your peers through things like awards. I almost feel like I deserve an award for endurance!"

Whatever feelings Patti was expressing were the result of events that had unfolded the previous year: "I spent eight months without work—partly due to the way the industry was and the fact that concerts generally weren't doing great business but also because some of my fellow artists wouldn't let me open for them. I figured they cancelled because they were scared. I've encountered that before but it makes me very mad. In some of those cases where it happened last year, the performers were headlining after being hot with one or two hits and obviously, their level of professionalism was pretty low. In fact, I refer to them as 'rats' which is 'star' backwards. It wasn't so much a financial thing for me as the fact that I really dig the energy from the people. Not having a hit record at the time, I couldn't necessarily go out and headline everywhere myself particularly since disco had definitely influenced the way concert attendances were happening—that coupled with the general economic situation. So I was thoroughly mad that some of my so-called colleagues felt so insecure that they wouldn't let me work with them. Too many people find themselves out there after one hit record and they are just totally unprepared."

Patti added that she'd been talking to Phyllis Hyman and Chaka Khan about putting together an all-female show "just to show everyone that there's no ego with every single entertainer. It's not about being better, they do what they do, I do what I do and it's different. To think any other way is jive, tacky and dumb!" Patti might have been venting just a little about what she'd been through, but she was also looking ahead with a positive attitude: "I intend for 1980 to be the year when people get the message that I'm not playing. I'm here and I intend to stay here and I want people—from the record company, the industry, right through to the public—to see what Patti LaBelle is all about. It may be true that in the past some of my music may not have been considered very commercial but it's always been what I felt and if it means I have to wait for people to accept that, then I will wait. I can't change expressing myself . . . and this [new] album is saying my spirit has been 'released.' I'm no longer chained in to any situation that's not working for me. And I feel good about that, I feel good about me and I feel that it's time to get mine!"

That should have happened when Patti left Epic and signed with Philadelphia International Records (PIR), the label producers Kenny Gamble and Leon Huff created. The company, ironically distributed by CBS, had already achieved much success with such artists as the O'Jays, Harold Melvin & the Bluenotes, Lou Rawls, and Teddy Pendergrass, yet its success rate with female artists on the roster—Jean Carn and Dee Dee Sharp, wife of Kenny Gamble—had been weak in comparison. Patti should have been the one female artist to break the mold and have major hits. But it would take four years and her departure from the label for her to finally have the breakthrough she'd been waiting for.

During our 1996 interview Patti recalled, "Kenny Gamble and I grew up together in Philly and we knew it was just a matter of time before we would do something together. Working with the company was like being with a family of people I knew and loved. . . ." In a strange turn of events Patti ended up recording enough material for a total of three albums for the label, but only 1981's *The Spirit's in It* was actually released while she was still signed to the company. PIR had been going through its own set of changes with CBS, and although Patti had spent a good deal of time in the studio with various producers, including Gamble and Huff and songwriter/artist Dexter Wansel—and had even cut some live material at Washington, DC's Constitution Hall—her recorded output was minimal.

During the time Patti's recording career seemed to be in limbo, I remember seeing her perform at the Paradise Garage in New York. Since getting off the ground in the mid-1970s, the cavernous club had justifiably earned a reputation as a black-and-gay mecca, even though it attracted its fair share of women, straight and gay, and heterosexual men who just wanted to dance to the best music in the city. When Patti stepped on stage for one of the club's famous Saturday-night shows, the place was jampacked with adoring fans. She "preached" just a little about not having a record deal but still having the kind of loyal audience she was performing for that night—and perform she did! Singing to a backing track, she was amazing: being sweaty, soulful, and the over-the-top-but-down-home diva had made her No. 1 among gay men from jump street. If memory serves me well, she sang her gut-wrenching version of "If You Don't Know Me by Now" that night and people were falling out—especially when she continued wailing a cappella long after the track was over!

Turning her attention away from recording for a while, Patti hit the road for almost two years with the gospel musical *Your Arm's Too Short to Box With God.* The show finally hit Broadway to rave reviews in September, 1982, starring Patti and the by-now Reverend Al Green. Patti also acted in her first movie, *A Soldier's Story,* which would also earn critical acclaim when it was released in 1984. She'd even opened up her own boutique, called "La Belle Amis," in the middle of Philadelphia; although it was relatively short.

It seemed that Patti had all but given up on having a hit record. In 1982 she'd recorded a special guest spot with fellow Philadelphia resident Grover Washington Jr. and "The Best Is Yet to Come" ironically became her first Top 20 R&B hit since the Labelle split in 1977; the song also earned Patti her first Grammy nomination. A few singles on the PIR label hadn't even charted, and then Kenny Gamble went back and listened to the tapes he had in the can on Patti: out popped "If Only You Knew," a gorgeous ballad co-written by Gamble with Wansel and his songwriting partner Cynthia Biggs.

By the spring of 1984, "If Only You Knew" had risen to the top of the R&B charts and had even made the pop Top 50. Patti was in shock, as she told *Blues & Soul* editor John Abbey: " . . . It's funny how things turned out—I had given up worrying about hit records. I don't even get *Billboard* or *Cashbox* [magazines] anymore. I wasn't looking to having to have a hit record for me to work. . . . I really only record so that I can go out and perform on stage for people. Only on stage can you get the real deal Patti LaBelle. . . ."

The belated success of "If Only You Knew" put Patti in an envious position: " . . . Since I am not signed to any record company [right now], it puts me in a unique situation, doesn't it?" she stated in her 1984 chat. Indeed it did. And in one of those weird and wonderful examples of serendipitous timing, Patti ended up with no fewer than three back-to-back Top 10 R&B hits in the space of just six months—all without having a record deal! In addition to having a follow-up PIR hit with "Love, Need and Want You" (also taken from *I'm in Love Again,* her first-ever gold LP as a soloist), she was featured as a duet partner with soul man Bobby Womack on "Love Has Finally Come at Last," a key track from his 1984 Beverly Glen album, *The Poet II.* The two had been fellow road warriors for years: "Bobby and I have talked about doing some things together for years and a few months ago, he called me and asked if I was still serious. I said I was and the next thing I knew I was in Los Angeles recording three songs with him. He was really easy to work with and we had a lot of fun. . . ."

Speaking on a personal note to *Blues & Soul* editor John Abbey, Patti mentioned cooking for her husband, Armstead (who had by this time taken over management of her career), and their three children (her son Zuri, born in 1973, and two adopted children, Stanley and Dodd) on the eve of what would be her first all-out national concert tour in three years. "I am blessed in that I have a husband and family who are very understanding. But when I'm home, I am just a housewife—and I enjoy it. I like cooking, cleaning house and just doing what any other housewife does for her family. And I get a great sense of satisfaction out of it. . . ."

For Patti, satisfaction also came in the form of a long-term deal with MCA Records. The label was undergoing a rejuvenation of its black-music department under the leadership of executive Jheryl Busby, who would later become the president of Motown Records. The teen group New Edition was doing exceptionally well for the West Coast-based company, and Ready For The World, another young group, was on the verge of having major pop and R&B hits. Busby had just signed Stephanie Mills with the promise of kicking her recording career back into gear, a promise that the label would fulfill a year after she joined its roster in 1985.

This was also the year that Patti LaBelle signed her name on the label's dotted line. She recalled during our 1996 interview, "Jheryl [Busby] was instrumental in bringing me to the company. The first thing [it] suggested was that I record a couple of songs for *Beverly Hills Cop*, the Eddie Murphy movie. . . ." This wasn't altogether a bad idea since the movie became one of the year's biggest box-office draws, and Patti, complete with a new nose—the result of plastic surgery she underwent after seeing the effect it had had on Stephanie Mills—and a zany new hairstyle, had not one but two Top 5 R&B hits. Symbolizing where she was at in her career, the upbeat, zesty "New Attitude" leapt up the pop, R&B, and dance charts, followed swiftly by "Stir It Up." Next, "On My Own," a beautiful Burt Bacharach/Carole Bayer Sager ballad about two people coming to the end of a love affair, provided Patti and duet partner Michael McDonald with an across-the-board chart topper in the spring of 1986. The single went gold, and Patti finally got her first platinum album with *The Winner in You*.

Finally, after years of waiting for her career to really take off, Patti had flown over the rainbow. She faced an incredible demand for her services as a recording artist, performer, and all-round entertainer: highlight followed highlight, and she was making high-profile appearances. Two in particular had people buzzing. In May, 1985, Patti was one of the many special guests on "Motown Returns to the Apollo," a television show taped at the famed theater in Harlem that had been such an important venue for Patti back in the days of the Blue Belles. During the finale Motown diva Diana Ross began singing "I Want to Know What Love Is," previously a hit for the rock group Foreigner. She actually asked other singers to join in and passed the microphone to Patti. ". . . It did look as if we were battling away there, but that's only because of the way the film was edited," Patti insisted in her 1986 *Blues & Soul* interview with British writer Sharon Davis. "It resulted in us fighting for the mike which didn't *happen*. Diana and I have always been friends and the scene wasn't as ugly as it later appeared. . . ."

Two months later, Patti was being accused of stealing the show once more, this time at a "Live Aid" benefit in Philadelphia. As Patti told British writer Sharon Davis: "If someone gives me the mike, I'm gonna open my big mouth and sing. Some artists treat the mike as an enemy. It is my friend. God gave me a talent and I think it's selfish not to share that talent. . . . I feel that if I don't share it, God will take it away from me. Sometimes I know I'm too loud but I have good lungs and in the 'Live Aid' situation, I didn't take over, I just sang the loudest."

What the general public didn't know until Patti's autobiography came out in 1986 was that she'd run into a similar issue with longtime friend Dionne Warwick when the two were working together with Gladys Knight on the 1986 television special "Sisters in the Name of Love." Patti also subsequently discussed this on shows she did to promote the book, such as "The Oprah Winfrey Show." She mentioned how Dionne had asked her to "tone down" her vocals on the show they were taping together, and expressed how upset she'd been at Dionne's comments. To add to the drama surrounding the incident, Gladys Knight reveals in her 1997 autobiography *Between Each Line of Pain and Glory* that she felt Patti shouldn't have made public what had happened when the trio was doing the show. Certainly, any tension between Dionne and Patti must have subsided when the pair got together with Gladys to record the Karyn White hit "Superwoman" for Gladys's 1991 LP *Good Woman*. But in the world of divas, you never know how it is all going to turn out.

Indeed, while Patti might have been compared on occasion to "The Queen of Soul" just by virtue of her powerhouse vocals, it was surprising to hear her mention Aretha's name when she and I did a 1994 interview for *Blues & Soul*. This was especially true because of the connection with how she perceived her career was progressing, six albums into her association with MCA. "I'm not taking what I have for granted but I do feel I should be on the level of say, Aretha Franklin. It could be me . . . maybe there's something I'm doing wrong that I'm not aware of," Patti told me.

It was strange to hear Patti even make the comparison. As the 1980s gave way to the 1990s, her public profile had been affected in a highly positive way by some major television appearances, including a special with Luther Vandross, a starring role in the sitcom "Up All Night," and knockout performances at the Essence Music Awards, at which Patti performed a tribute to Aretha with an incredible performance on "Ain't No Way," a Franklin classic.

In a once-in-a-lifetime event, Aretha and Patti shared the stage with Gladys Knight on the occasion of Oprah Winfrey's fortieth birthday. There was much diva-tude: reviewing the tape, I saw Aretha seated while everyone else gave Gladys a standing ovation, and later Aretha left the stage and went down into the audience to ask Oprah to mention that the song she'd just finished was on her then-latest Arista album, *Greatest Hits*. For a split second the camera caught the look that Gladys and Patti gave each other as Oprah duly complied—and if looks could kill, a coronation of a new Queen of Soul would have followed shortly thereafter! Whatever happened that day obviously affected Patti to the degree that she reported in a subsequent *Ebony* magazine article how upset she'd been over the treatment she'd received at the hands of one of her fellow female artists.

That Patti, unlike some other divas, should even feel in any way competitive came as a surprise to me when we talked in 1994 on the occasion of the release of her sixth MCA album, *Gems*. She was still turning it out on national tours before adoring fans, and although her record sales had been fine without being massive sellers, she'd racked up six Top 10 R&B hits from 1986 to 1992. Her 1991 album *Burnin'* had gone gold, and it had even contained a duet with Nona and Sarah. "When the three of us got back together, it was a lot of fun and it was just like the old times," she'd told me as 1991 came to a close. "We were fussin' and fightin' and it would be, 'Hussy, you sang the wrong note!' or Sarah would be complaining that the dust from the carpet was making her crack vocally . . . and then I'd be telling Nona and Sarah how to sing another line. . . . Yes, it was just like . . . we hadn't gone anywhere!"

With sold-out shows, television visibility, and some nice hits, Patti's career seemed to me to be in its ascendancy. But Patti had a different perception of it in 1994, days after celebrating her fiftieth birthday at a big Hollywood party hosted by MCA and attended by a number of stars, including friends Luther Vandross and Ashford & Simpson. "I'm nowhere near where I wanna be!" she said as we spoke on the telephone a few days after a triumphant performance at the Universal Amphitheater when she had the audience—as usual—begging for more after she had kicked off her shoes and rolled around on the stage, singing at the very top of her range in the process! "I'm not on that multi-platinum level . . . I mean, Toni Braxton is much further along than me in that regard. I'm nowhere near the level of Diana Ross or a Barbra Streisand. I feel like there's so much to conquer, and to be honest, I feel left out. . . ."

Patti did, however, seem elated that her then-new single "Right Kind of Lover" was getting airplay, telling me with a hearty laugh, "Now you know I don't have that many hits, baby boy!" but the more we talked, the more she became animated about what she felt was a lack of recognition for her longevity in the business. ". . . Being a household name is something I've always wanted but I don't feel as if the industry has absorbed me the way it has some other female artists. [Making it is] having an album that sells and sells and sells. Sells like a Whitney Houston record, I mean. I'll start out with a couple of million. So far, I've only had a baby taste of that when "The Winner In You" went platinum. . . ."

For the first time in the many years Patti and I'd known each other, she finally shared a little about the personal challenges she'd faced when she said, "Honestly, I'm very happy to have made it to this point. You see, I lost all three of my sisters to cancer when they were in their forties. They didn't make it to fifty so I feel like I'm celebrating for all of them." That sense of celebration would continue for the next few years, and I lost none of my respect for all the accomplishments Patti LaBelle had racked up in the thirty-six years she'd been recording. She still kicks butt as a performer, even though a show at the Hollywood Bowl in 1997 sparked plenty of controversy: she accused the venue of racism, and the facility said that she hadn't adhered to its rules of conduct. I was at the show and was surprised to see that Patti was reading the lyrics for the special numbers she was doing with the Hollywood Bowl orchestra. I was surprised only because I knew her for her professionalism. On the up side, however, the other songs she did perform with the orchestra showed a whole other side of her musical skill. For example, her rendition of Duke Ellington's "Come Sunday" was absolutely brilliant, prompting me to wonder why she hadn't done an album of more of that kind of material.

Patti's 1997 album *Flame* sounded a little more toned down than previous records, and while it didn't achieve the multi-platinum status

Patti might have liked, she was no longer feeling the same sense of dissatisfaction about her career that seemed evident a few years earlier. "You know, until about two months ago, I would complain all the time about what I didn't have, what I hadn't done," she said in a telephone conversation we had for *Blues & Soul* in the summer of 1997. " . . . I would see other singers achieve all this mega-success and wonder why I hadn't reached that level. But you know, I love what women like Celine [Dion], Mariah [Carey], and Whitney [Houston] do, and I figure that some day, the same number of people will catch up with me! But in all seriousness, I know I am very blessed. At fifty-three, I am still kicking butt, and so many people come to see me in concert whether or not I have a hit record. So I'm not going to feel slighted any more about what I don't have! I'm going to keep counting my blessings."

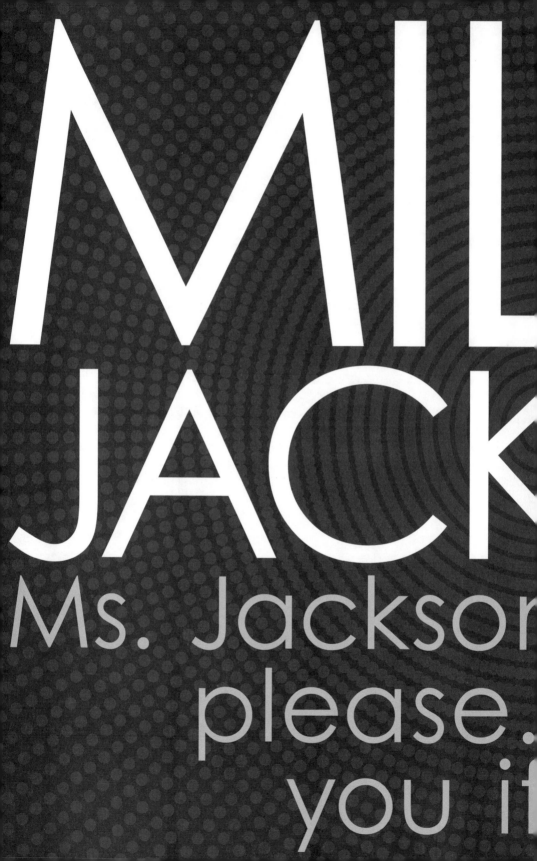

LIE

SON

h if you

and ****

...

you don't!

Y ou've read the chapters on Dionne, Aretha, Diana, Patti, and Gladys. If you are white and you love any of those divas, you might be wondering, "Who is Millie Jackson? Never heard of her." If you are African-American and over thirty, chances are you definitely know. If you are under thirty, you might have heard her name. And if you are under eighteen, just go ask your mother or father! Millie Jackson, the undisputed "Queen of Sex'n'Soul," has had forty hit singles and more than fifteen bestselling albums. She has also shocked, scared, and satisfied her loyal hardcore audience for nearly thirty years. Millie has been banned from the air, temporarily condemned by Reverend Jesse Jackson, offended symphony orchestras, and feuded with at least one of her Southern soul sisters. She is a deeply hilarious, highly comedic, salt-of-the-earth soul sister both on- and offstage. If you want to know who Millie Jackson is, for real, read on.

Shades of Gloria Gaynor: at first I was afraid, I was petrified. In November, 1974, I was in New York for the very first time, staying with my good friend Gary, who had moved to Brooklyn that summer. John Abbey, then editor of *Blues & Soul*, had suggested I call Millie Jackson during my visit to possibly do an in-person interview with her. Several months before, on the occasion of the release of *Caught Up*, her third album and ultimately her first gold LP, I'd spoken with the thoroughly magnificent Millie over the telephone. I guess I was feeling a little flushed from that first telephone interview since I ended the resultant article in the May, 1974, issue of *Blues & Soul* with the following statement: "All I can say is more power to Millie Jackson, a bold, outspoken, sassy but beautifully *bad* soul sister! She can come check me out anytime she wants!" I would have to consider eating those words on that cold, November day.

"Yes!" Millie snapped when she answered the telephone. "Can I speak to Miss Jackson, please?" I asked in my typically proper, reserved

English manner. "Who is it?" she yelled back. After I identified myself, Millie roared, "Yeah, child, I know John Abbey! You wanna do an interview? Well, you gotta come to my place in Brooklyn." When I told Millie that I was staying in that borough, too, she told me exactly how, via subway, to get to her place deep in the heart of what people called the ghetto back in the 1970s.

I attempted to follow Millie's instructions on how to get to her place by subway. "You get off at Washington and Clinton," she said in her famous raspy voice. I don't know what happened, but I found myself on the wrong side of the platform and was nowhere near Clinton or Washington! "Excuse me, Miss Jackson, I think I got on the wrong train," I ventured rather timidly. "Damn it! All right, you gotta get back on the train. . . ."

Thirty minutes later, my for-real Afro blowing in the chilly wind, I emerged from the right subway station, literally just outside the apartment building that Millie called home in 1974. Many years later, she would correct me when I said I'd met her at her place in the projects. "I didn't live in no projects!" she scolded me. Well, whatever the name of Millie's Brooklyn neighborhood was, I knew I was a stranger in a strange land as I walked toward the building. It was patently obvious from the stare I got when I asked a passerby if I had the right address that young, white men with bushy hair weren't exactly a dime a dozen in that part of the city.

Eventually, I found Millie's apartment on the twenty-something floor of the building. "Took you long enough!" she chastised me as I introduced myself again. As I'd noted in my first article on her, she was indeed bold, outspoken, and very sassy. "So how's that fuckin' John Abbey?" Millie exclaimed loudly. "You know, that magazine *Blues & Soul* did the first thing on me in Europe, and I know you guys love real R&B, don'tcha?" I told Millie how much R&B meant to me, how much I loved her first record *Child of God*, and how pleased I was to meet her in person. "Okay, okay," she countered with an almost shy grin. If I didn't know better, I would swear that big bad Millie Jackson was on the verge of blushing! "You wanna get some pizza?" she asked. "We got a great place just down the street, Joe's Pizza, and they make the best fuckin' pizza in Brooklyn!" We chowed down, and I thanked Millie, headed back to the subway, grinning and satisfied that I'd met one of the most real, down-to-earth women in the world of music.

Twenty-two years later, Millie was on the telephone with me, talking about a projected cable-television show and one skit that won't make the final cut. "I taped me singing the "Phuck U Symphony"—which has been part of my show for years—with the Denver Symphony Orchestra. It was so funny because we had all these white women playing the strings and these black guys doing the horns, and they saw the music but didn't know what it was! The women thought it was some classical shit— you know, the P. Huck U. symphony—until I started singing 'Fuck you, fuck you, fuck you.' You should have seen their faces!"

Millie hadn't changed through those two decades. She was still as earthy, funny, and outrageous as ever, and still a singing fool. As I thought about our first interview and the first time I'd heard her music, I mused that while she'd justifiably earned a reputation as the "Queen of Sex'n'Soul," people might have missed what a really great singer she was. Before she began shocking the world with four-letter words, rappin', cussin', and straight-ahead album titles like *Back to the S—t!* (a 1989 Jive album), Millie had made it obvious to people who loved soul music raw, tough, and honest that she was the real deal. Somewhere along the way, she'd established herself as the funniest woman in R&B, and folks forgot that she could sing her ass off. In 1988 she was busy promoting *The Tide Is Turning*, her second album for Jive. She explained the dilemma in a *Blues & Soul* interview she and I did: "The only problem I have now is that my old fans listen to my new stuff and they say, 'There's no dirt on the LP!' But they know they can come see me in person and I'm still gonna talk shit!"

Long, long before she ever uttered any four-letter word other than "love" on a public stage, Millie made a good impression at a talent show at a Harlem nightclub, singing her version of the Ben E. King hit "Don't Play That Song." In a 1978 interview with Rita Christian for *Blues & Soul*, Millie shared a little about her background: "My mother died when I was two. So I grew up mainly with my father except for a year-and-a-half when I lived with my grandparents. They were really the strict ones. . . . The funny thing was my grandmother loved me very much but she thought I was nuts. She really thought I was 'off.' Me and her youngest son, we just went against everything they tried to teach us. She called us the two bad apples. . . ." An only child, Millie quipped, "When I was born my father probably took one look at me and thought, 'I don't want another one like that!'"

Millie's early years were spent on a farm in Thompson, Georgia, but the discipline imposed by her grandparents proved too much, and Millie ran off to her father's home in Newark, New Jersey, at the age of fourteen. Two years later she was living with an aunt in Brooklyn and working regular nine-to-five gigs when she hooked up with a fashion photographer, who got her some work with black magazines like *Jive* and *Sepia*. "Back then, you didn't have too many black models," she told Randall Grass, author of the liner notes for a two-CD set that Rhino Records released on Millie in 1997. "And then, all of a sudden, black was beautiful and I wasn't black *enough!*"

Unlike many of the women who would later become her contemporaries, Millie wasn't actively pursuing a career in music when she sang that fateful night at the talent contest in Harlem. But once the music bug bit her in the mid-1960s, Millie could be found most weekends at local spots in Brooklyn, Long Island, and New Jersey, including Club Zanzibar in Hoboken, while working a regular job at a department store. Then, according to Grass, she toured with Sam Cooke's brother L.C. before going back to a nine-to-five job.

In 1969 Millie signed with a production company and had her first release on MGM Records, "A Little Bit of Something" backed with "My Heart Took a Lickin' But Kept on Tickin.'" The record did okay, but Millie went no further with the situation because, as she told Grass, she wouldn't sign a management contract with the production company: "I just never gave [control] up. When I read my first managerial contract, it said they had to place me with a booking agency—I already had one— and they were supposed to buy me pictures which cost me $80 a hundred, which we already had. I didn't see any sense in giving them 15 percent of my money!"

Millie was in no rush to sign a new deal. In her first of many interviews with *Blues & Soul* magazine in 1972, she told John Abbey that she was married to a Mr. Davis, who was the leader of her group, the Family Affair. "We really are a family affair because my two brothers-in-law are also in the group, on bass and guitar, with my husband on organ," Millie stated, noting that she worked only on weekends because, as Abbey wrote, "she plans to still concentrate on being a housewife until she really hits the top." In fact, Millie was already a mother, giving birth to a daughter, Keisha, in 1967.

The marriage didn't last, and in 1978 Millie said a few words on the subject to British writer Rita Christian in *Blues & Soul*, " . . . I've tried it . . . but [I'm] not trying it [now] and I might never try it again. . . . Marriage is a full-time job. It also takes a lot of consideration and understanding and I have neither. I mean, how many full-time jobs can you hold? I've got a full-time job singing. You just can't be married half-time."

Not too much longer after Millie talked to Abbey she did in fact become a full-time recording artist and performer. Millie had finished a song called "Child of God (It's Hard to Believe)," a no-nonsense ballad about double standards and hypocritical attitudes with co-writer Don

French. The demo ended up at Spring Records—a then-small independent label that Polydor distributed nationally—through Raeford Gerald, a friend of the label's then-only hitmaker Joe Simon. The song landed Millie her first Top 30 R&B hit as 1971 turned into 1972.

As would be the case throughout the career, even her first record was surrounded by controversy and was barred by some radio stations. The song's powerful storyline referred to a single woman who had a married man in her bed, to white men who preached equality by day and donned the infamous sheets members of the Klu Klux Klan wore at night, and to the hypocrisy that ran rife among holier-than-thou, church-going gossip mongers.

Playing it safe, Spring released three more singles from what would be Millie's first self-titled album in 1972: "Ask Me What You Want" and "My Man, A Sweet Man," both of which made it into the R&B Top 10—and "I Miss You Baby." The first two songs were uptempo, perky tunes that were miles away from "Child of God" and from the down-and-dirty material that would form the bulk of Millie's repertoire in the 1970s and 1980s.

On the plus side, Millie was gaining quite a reputation for her showmanship, touring with the "Steamroller Package," which brought together R&B stars of the day, including the O'Jays, the Chi-Lites, the Main Ingredient, the Detroit Emeralds, and the Moments, a group whose members would become good friends with Millie and share many a stage with her in later years. In addition to her own spot on the show, Millie was also the emcee—and you can only imagine that she performed the task with typical Jackson flair!

The record that would give Millie her national breakthrough was also featured heavily in the 1973 blaxploitation movie *Cleopatra Jones*, which starred actress Tamara Dobson. "Hurts So Good" was a stone-to-the-bone soul ballad, and it took Millie into the upper reaches of the R&B chart and became her biggest pop hit, making the Top 30. The song's success made it the natural choice as the title for Millie's second album, which featured "Hypocrisy," a funky, self-explanatory, no-holds-barred, Jackson-penned tune that focused primarily on male-female relationships, a subject on which she would become a musical expert. A heart-wrenching ballad written with famous New York disc jockey Gary Byrd entitled "I Cry" was another highlight of the album. This tune had its origins in a real-life experience: Millie had seen a man shot in cold blood outside a club in Brooklyn where she was performing. Like so much of the material she wrote, the song reflected Millie's willingness to share about the kind of situations that everyday people dealt with.

The *It Hurts So Good* album was important not only because it sold well, but also because it began a creative relationship that would last almost to the end of Millie's twelve-year association with Spring Records. She'd flown down to Muscle Shoals, Alabama, to work with producer Brad Shapiro on the song "Hurts So Good," and the musical marriage was perfect. The Alabama studio had spawned hits by such soul stalwarts as Percy Sledge, Etta James, Clarence Carter, and Wilson Pickett, with whom Shapiro had worked on the 1971 smash, "Don't Knock My Love."

Millie worked with Shapiro on many of the tracks on *I Got to Try It One More Time*, her third album, and it was as if the Georgia-born singer had found her natural creative home as a gritty storyteller making Southern-styled soul music that was deeply satisfying. "How Do You Feel the Morning After" got some chart action without coming close to the success of "Hurts So Good," but it set the stage for what was to follow. "It's the first time anyone's really tackled the 'love triangle' situation from the female's point of view," is how Millie described to me the concept behind what would become her bestselling album of all time in our first telephone interview in early 1974. *Caught Up* was the first of its kind, a record that made it plain: Millie was ready to tell it like it is, sparing no one in the process, but delivering the material with the natural humor that was clearly part and parcel of her real-life personality. One focal point of the album was "The Rap," a monologue that Millie had been incorporating as part of her version of "(If Loving You Is Wrong) I Don't Want to Be Right," Luther Ingram's classic 1972 tale of adultery. She talked about how it felt to be the other woman, someone who didn't have to clean her man's funky drawers (a job obviously left to his wife)!

Caught Up set the tone for many of the albums that would follow and definitively established Millie Jackson in a category of her own. Other female singers had made records about cheating, husband-stealing best friends, and women who tried to keep the home fires burning; these included Denise LaSalle, Betty Wright, and Ann Peebles. But Millie took the genre to a new level by doing a whole concept album, strung together with brief interludes, turning the LP into a musical story beginning to end.

Millie found herself achieving a new level of popularity, but not all of her female contemporaries were singing her praises. " . . . I had my *Caught Up* album out and here comes [the 1974 hit] 'Woman to Woman' and [the singer of the song] Shirley Brown developed some complex over this," she told me with great relish in a 1992 *Blues & Soul* interview we did. "Apparently she can't stand me! Well, we were working together somewhere and after she'd finished her set, she says, 'That nasty Millie Jackson is gonna be out here in a minute talking all that nasty stuff. Right now, she's sitting back there with her sneakers on. . . .' It turned out it was a time when I had broken my toe so I was wearing sneakers 'cause my foot hurt! Anyway, I got onstage and the audience asked me if I heard what Shirley said. 'I ain't thinkin' about what that whale said,' I told 'em! I explained to the audience about my toe and I said, 'Let's sweep this bitch's dress up off the stage' because she'd been wearing one of those long-assed dresses down to the ground! Anyway, that feud's been going on . . . and some promoters have been putting us on shows together. Now, she can sing but her attitude sucks! I have nothing to say to her. She went on some radio station talking about how I have to talk nasty and talk about other singers because I really can't sing . . . so I called up the station and said I felt it was only reasonable that I got a chance to respond. I went to the station and I said, 'Let's hear a very little of Shirley Brown,' put the record on and after one note, took it off! So that's what they got . . . *one fucking note of Shirley Brown!* [You see] everybody can't do what I do because what I do comes naturally. . . ."

What Millie did naturally became obvious after the release of *Caught Up*. As she explained to John Abbey during a chat for *Blues & Soul* in the late part of 1974, "In the past, I've done some pretty good records I guess but I've been really getting nowhere fast. . . . Everyone always says how they like the way I sing but. . . . So I wanted to stir them all up and give them something to sit up and take notice of. Even if they didn't like it, they would have to take notice of it, right?" *Caught Up* became Millie's bestselling record, a Top 30 gold album, and its success led to an obvious demand for a followup that was in much the same vein.

Millie gratefully obliged by offering *Still Caught Up*, which she said was a continuation of the storyline of the love triangle, described so potently on the preceding album. The biggest hit from *Still Caught Up* was "Leftovers," which was complete with a no-holds-barred confrontation between the singer, her man, and *his* wife. "It's where the wife comes back to the husband and she wants him back. Side two deals with the other side of the business, from the 'other woman's' side of things," Millie explained in a 1975 interview in *Blues & Soul*. To complete the concept, Millie had the other woman go insane—quite literally—on the final track, "I Still Love You." Millie began doing the song in concert after the album's release that summer, and for dramatic effect she would have two guys in white coats take her offstage screaming! Just for the hell of it, Millie also did the song, complete with the men in white coats, on the national "Merv Griffin Show"!

With her newly found success, Millie was pulling no punches, and her *Blues & Soul* interview with Abbey that summer was filled with straight talk. She coyly admitted, "I've experienced some of the things that happen during the albums," but she was far more forthright in her comments on the kind of audiences she was attracting with the *Caught Up* albums. "Not that many white folks involve themselves in Millie Jackson music. . . . Blacks buy my records and they are, in general, the lower class blacks. You could call me the 'Poor People's Queen' if you like because my ideas relate to that section of the people. Sure the upperclass folks are doing it [too] but no one knows about it. In fact, I'd say that there's more hanky-panky business going on in the wealthy classes than there is in the street. But it's all so discreet—hey, they can afford to hide it away, right?"

Millie's comments on the folks who did and did not buy her music were tame compared to her outrage at being pretty much ignored not only at the 1975 Grammy Awards but also at the annual awards ceremony sponsored by the popular magazine *Ebony*. Millie laid it out! "They nominated "If Loving You Is Wrong" for a Grammy Award," she told Abbey, "and I never expected to win. In fact, Aretha did and good luck to her. But recently in Los Angeles, they had the *Ebony* Awards—now that's a black magazine and a black tradition so we all felt that some sense of justice would prevail. Every black person in the business took the whole Grammy business with a smile but we all felt that the Ebony affair would straighten the records out. Now, to stress that I'm not put out because I didn't win—I wasn't even nominated . . . at least not in the same category as Aretha. Would you believe that they nominated me in the jazz section with Esther Phillips—of course, she won, she deserved to because I'm not a jazz artiste, right? Anyway, again Aretha won and I asked myself, 'what has Aretha—or even Diana Ross who came second—contributed during the last twelve months?' So what is it all—political bullshit! Aretha and Diana have white appeal and I was shocked that it even carried on down to *Ebony*. . . . "

Millie's earlier records hadn't given a hint as to the persona that had begun to emerge with the success of the two *Caught Up* records; however, the public was no longer in any doubt as to what to expect when they bought a Millie Jackson record or came to see her in person. ". . . I'm the same wherever you catch me—and you can take me or leave me!" she concluded in her *Blues & Soul* interview. "Okay, so I'm not as 'bad' as *Caught Up* would suggest but that's my general lifestyle and I don't care who knows it. There was a time when I used to go onstage and start off innocently singing lovely little ballads. But that isn't what the people want from me—why, they don't even start smiling till I drop my first 'shit' into the conversation! I have a reputation [now] for being outspoken so that's what I'm stuck with—I can't change it so it would be wrong for me to try. . . ."

As Randall Grass points out in his liner notes for the 1997 anthology, Millie's upfront approach also extended to her dealings with record-company executives. "I waited for the album [*Caught Up*] to come out so I could see my first production credit and then I saw the album credits. You talk about an irate bitch! Up till then, they had met 'Mildred'—now they met Millie! I cursed them out! I didn't know if they were going to tear up my contract or what. [Label executive] Roy Rifkind said, 'How many hats do you want to wear?' I said, 'Every fucking one that fits!' . . . But we had such a relationship at Spring [Records]—you could raise as much hell as you wanted and after the argument we'd go to lunch. The bigger the argument, the bigger the lunch!"

I remember running into Millie in the early months of 1975 at a party Spring Records held specifically to celebrate the success of *Caught Up*, and although Millie hadn't won any music-industry awards, she was happy to be the center of attention at the affair. She remembered me from my first visit back in 1974 and was aghast when I told her that I was now living in New York. "Can't stay away, huh?" she guffawed, following a hearty laugh with words to the effect that there was plenty to keep an Englishman *busy* in New York ! "Well, you know once you 'go black,' you ain't gonna wanna go back!" She was in great spirits when I introduced her to Bob Killbourn, the future editor of *Blues & Soul*, who was visiting from London. As I recall, Bob blushed as Millie bellowed, "And how the fuck are you?" Meeting Millie was clearly an experience for anyone willing to handle the heat!

Even though *Caught Up* and *Still Caught Up* had taken Millie to a new level, the proverbial heat was on regarding her career. Her first album of 1976, *Free and in Love*, was meant to finish the love-triangle concept she'd started with *Caught Up*. But the X-rated lyrics and the general subject matter of her records began to generate some negative response from such people as the Reverend Jesse Jackson. Millie explained the situation to Randall Grass: "We didn't intend to keep the story concept going forever. Jesse Jackson and others had gotten wind of me. They complained that I was unladylike and a bad influence. The record company figured [Jesse] Jackson had influence. And the deejays were complaining because songs labeled 'clean' played through to the dirty part if they didn't pay attention. . . ." When Millie and

I spoke in 1978, she recalled, "There's no justification for [Jesse Jackson] making . . . comments because, frankly, it's up to parents to make sure if they don't want to let their children hear particular records. . . . All I can say is that when I met the gentleman, I didn't get the impression that he was all that naïve about what the world is all about and what's happening today!"

Whether as a result of Reverend Jackson's comments or the negative publicity surrounding Millie at the time—partly as a result of a visit to South Africa that ran afoul of anti-apartheid groups that picketed some of her shows—the album *Free and in Love* did only mild business, yielding just two minimally successful singles. Instead of immediately returning to the outrageous flavor of the *Caught Up* series, Millie and Spring Records decided to play it safe by making a "clean" R&B LP. Released in the early months of 1977, *Lovingly Yours* got a tepid reaction, and Millie was less than happy. "I didn't really like the album," Millie stated in her comments for Randall Grass's liner notes. "That's why I didn't even put my picture on it: it didn't feel like me."

Millie knew the way to get back into the winner's circle: regardless of any controversy it might generate, the answer was to return to the musical and lyrical content that had endeared her to everyday black-music buyers. "I stay in tune with the public," Millie told me a few weeks after the release of *Feelin' Bitchy*, which would become her second gold album. "[And] that's how I know what they want. When I finish a show, I don't just go off into my dressing room and lock it. I rap with people—find out what they dig, what they don't like, what they want to hear. That's the only way to know if you're on target."

Feelin' Bitchy was right on target, and watching Millie perform songs from the album was a treat. Performing at New York's Radio City Music Hall with the O'Jays and the funk group Brick, Millie delivered high raunch! As I reported in a *Blues & Soul* review of the show, "She uses the cut "All the Way Lover" from her current album *Feelin' Bitchy* to literally lay it on everyone from the cheatin' husbands to the cheatin' wives, even giving mention of the gay contingent by warning the ladies in the audience that if they're not going to be more accommodating to their menfolk, they shouldn't be unduly surprised if the men in question turn to other men!"

The pairing of Millie and the O'Jays was in itself interesting. Millie had given birth to a son, Jerroll, toward the end of 1975. As Grass tactfully pointed out in his liner notes for the 1997 anthology, her newborn's middle name, Levert, "reflects his mom's admiration for O'Jays lead singer Eddie Levert." The music biz rumor mill suggested that the

258

"admiration" extended beyond platonic friendship . . . but Millie never said a word on the subject! In the late 1980s, she teamed up with Eddie and *his* son Gerald (a successful producer/songwriter/artist in his own right) to record songs for the album *The Tide Is Turning* and one of the songs, "Something You Can Feel," was inspired by Millie's onstage antics: ". . . I was doing something in my act where I used my little finger, talkin' 'bout, 'I can almost feel it!' Anyway, that inspired Gerald and the guys to come up with a song for me—something, they said that I could feel!"

Certainly, Millie's public attitude on the subject of love was typically caustic: "It's great if you have the time to deal with it!" she responded in our 1978 chat. And a couple of months later, she was pretty evasive when British writer Rita Christian asked if she was in love at the time. "I'm in love with many things," Millie answered cagily. Rita persisted: "Like what, for example?" "Well, I'm in love with life, with music. . . ." she shot back. "I meant, do you have someone special?" Rita pressed. "Listen, I love many people. . . . But if you mean have I got a man in my life at the moment—well, yes I have," Millie conceded, adding that she had a daughter of eleven and a son of sixteen months—I've been in love *recently*, huh? At least I've been *lovin'*. . . ."

Other changes in Millie's personal life also included a move to Teaneck, New Jersey. She was committed to spending more time at home with her children, specifically by working on weekends rather than during the week. Operating from an office on Broadway in midtown Manhattan, Millie was also busy expanding her business interests, initially by forming and producing a group she called Facts of Life, which ended up scoring two hits on the R&B charts in 1976.

Aided by her own soulful version of country singer Merle Haggard's "If You're Not in Love by Monday," Millie was also back on the charts in 1977. The track was a fine example of her interpretive skills as a first-class R&B vocalist. In many ways, she was a female counterpart to soul men like Bobby Womack, whose gritty, to-the-bone vocal style found an instant home with R&B crowds. It was no surprise that Millie chose a couple of Womack tunes for her repertoire, but it is interesting to note that, years later Womack became the darling of the white "I'm really into soul music" crowd, which considered it chic to show its appreciation for downhome R&B heroes, while Millie's name was never even mentioned in the same breath. Perhaps she just wasn't hip enough—although British superstar Elton John recognized Millie's foremost skills as a bold soul sister when he did a duet with her in 1985 on the single "Act of War."

Even as Millie was consolidating her black audience in the late 1970s, she wasn't mentioned in the same breath as other R&B divas: she didn't have the vocal range of an Aretha or a Patti LaBelle, the sophistication of a Dionne or a Diana, or the downhome warmth of a Gladys Knight, with whom she was occasionally compared vocally. In an early *Blues & Soul* interview she'd mentioned Gladys as one of her favorite vocalists. She joked about any comparisons made between her and the Atlanta-born singer in her comments to Randall Grass for his 1997 notes: "If I go to hell, Gladys Knight is responsible because I had to curse to get away from her!" In 1982, Millie told John Abbey for a *Blues & Soul* article, "When I started rapping, so did she, and since I always felt I sounded so much like her anyway, I started cursing. I knew she wouldn't follow that because she's a lady!"

While Millie wasn't being handed music-industry kudos, she soldiered on regardless. And, in fact, the album *Feelin' Bitchy* consolidated her preeminence as a bestselling artist. "It was a turning point for me," she told Grass years later. "I was feeling really bitchy! . . . This was my shot, I said, 'I'm going to do this album and see whether I'm going to be in this business or not. Either you like it [I told the record company] . . . or you can go to hell and buy out my contract! It was a hell of a chance to take. My contract was up!"

Millie had no reason to worry since tracks like the aforementioned "All the Way Lover," a song Southern R&B soul man Benny Latimore had originally written and recorded, were all about people's favorite subject! Millie's version of the tune unashamedly made a reference to the joys of oral sex when she rapped about about "partee-ing," which is distinct from "partying," and her loyal, hard-core audiences loved the song! In 1985, she told a British audience, in typical Jackson fashion, "I'm on a mission for black women. Girls, do your men 'partaaaay'? If they don't you gotta say Mister, no 'partaaay,' no pussaaay!'"

The hilarious rap Millie had created for the song included a dig at the women who loved to stay home and watch soap operas, gossip, and boast to their girlfriends about their mates' sexual performance. Indeed, if anyone ever wondered just why Millie Jackson had such a solid appeal among everyday black men and women, one listen to the *Feelin' Bitchy* album provided the answer. Millie was addressing the concerns of ordinary, hard-working people dealing with the ups and downs and the bumps and bruises of love and relationships. As the album was on its way up the charts, Britain's Rita Christian bravely asked Millie if her singing about sex was "a case of the ones who talk about it a lot are the ones who do very little?" With her trademark gutsy laugh, Millie was ready with a response: "What kind of question is that? You know, one gentleman

A pensive
Millie Jackson
Credit: Michael Ochs
Archives/Venice, CA

asked me something fairly similar earlier today, and I told him that once every ten days is enough!"

The pace in Millie's career began to accelerate at the end of the 1970s. In 1978, she followed *Feelin' Bitchy* with the gold LP *Get It Out'cha System*, at the same time launching a mini-musical based around the album, featuring the Moments, a ventriloquist called Starvin' Marvin ("a black guy with a white dummy!"), dancers, and background singers, complete with stage sets. Millie later confessed that the elaborate nature of the venture had been financially prohibitive: ". . . Although I lost money on it," she said in a 1979 interview with John Abbey, "I'm glad I did it. . . . It was new, it was a challenge and so to hell with the money! . . . That's why I have never had a manager—a good manager would have steered me away from that tour. I am a very spontaneous kind of person and nobody knows me like I know myself. Sure, a manager could get me some more money and better deals but I don't do things for money alone. . . ." She was, she admitted, a workaholic. "I hate to stay at home and not work. I don't mean I'm not happy at home but it's just that I love to work. . . ."

Millie was hard at it in 1979 with the release of no fewer than three albums: *A Moment's Pleasure*; *Royal Rappin's*, a duet album with Isaac Hayes; and the outrageous *Live and Uncensored* double set. The record with Hayes had come about almost by accident as Millie revealed when we hooked up in person the fall of 1979. I vividly recall sitting with a hyperactive Millie in her Manhattan office. She was fielding telephone calls, chatting about how hard it was to find a good secretary, and guffawing about the cover of a newly released album by a fellow female star! "What really happened was that I had wanted to record the Anne Murray tune 'You Needed Me,' and I'd tried it on my own and it just didn't work—it was horrible! It sounded like it would be right as a duet, so I called Isaac and just asked him about doing an album together," she said. Millie couldn't resist the temptation to have fun, and after the joint recording was all finished, she snuck back into the studio and changed one of the lines in a rap she'd done, making a hilarious, ribald comment about Isaac and his bald head, with an obvious double meaning thrown in for good measure!

For a sense of Millie's appeal, nothing compared to the *Live and Uncensored* album, which was recorded at the Roxy in Los Angeles. She chose the Hollywood nightclub rather than a hot nightspot in the 'hood because "the sound system there is good and George Benson did his there and it didn't do him any harm!" she told me in 1979 as I watched her try to conduct the interview in the midst of a continually ringing telephone! Depending on your viewpoint, one of the high—or low—points of the bestselling live double album was the infamous "Phuck U Symphony." The story goes that Millie had composed the side-splitting, neoclassical piece, which consists of constant repeating of the words "fuck you" during her visit to South Africa when she'd been given a list of words she could and couldn't use. "But," she told Randall Grass, "they left one word off the list. I guess they thought I'd never have the nerve to say it!"

One of the funnier aspects of her South African trip was the brief feud between Millie and popular British comic Max Bygraves, who was due to play at one of the same theaters the night after Millie's show. Millie's act apparently offended Bygraves so when he appeared, he brought a can of air freshener onstage with him when he did his own show. Word got back to Millie, who misconstrued Bygraves's action as a reference to her personal hygiene. The two were staying at the same hotel, and apparently the shit hit the fan when Millie's tour manager approached Bygraves about the incident! When Millie visited the U.K. some months later, Bygraves wasn't on the guest list for any of her shows.

Live and Uncensored made it clear that if Millie ever decided to abandon music for a career in comedy, she could easily have done it. Part of the problem was that her X-rated humor didn't make her a good candidate for mainstream television or the big screen. "It's not that I don't wanna do a movie or a TV thing—they just ain't asked me!" she said during our chat. "But maybe one day . . . maybe by the time I get to sixty, people will let me just get up and tell jokes instead of having to sing—maybe like [legendary black comedienne] Moms Mabley!" Although Millie isn't credited for it, she was in many ways a forerunner for the many young black female comics who now regularly use sex, love, and lust as central themes in their acts. Had Millie started her career twenty years later, she might well have become the darling of shows like "Def Comedy Jam."

After the live album with its many comedic moments, Millie's recording career seemed to lose some of its impetus. It could just have been the sheer volume of music she'd put out in the preceding years. Certainly, she'd become Spring Records' main moneymaker, outselling other acts on the label like Joe Simon, who had taken to wearing outlandish capes, wigs, and $500-a-pair earrings! Disco was in full swing, and although Millie had given a small nod to the burgeoning dance music trend with tunes like "Go Out and Get Some" and "Never Change Your Lovers in the Middle of the Night," she was no Donna Summer. Part of the problem might have been Millie's own desire to move away from being typecast for her raps. She knew that her audiences expected to hear them night after night, and she was concerned that her musical skills were being underplayed. "People expect me to be rappin.' I get tired of that," she explained to Randall Grass. ". . . In the beginning, I rapped because I didn't have much experience singing. I learned on the job. . ." As the 1980s began, Millie tried to move away from her own form of rapping, even stepping into another musical genre—albeit her own way—with 1981's "Just a Lil' Bit Country." But people wanted their Millie raw and raunchy. The 1980 album *For Men Only* was relatively "clean," but Millie still dealt with subjects like abuse in relationships, as in "This Is Where I Came in." A 1981 LP, *I Had to Say It*, was notable for the title cut, which was all about interracial couples. As Millie told John Abbey at *Blues & Soul* in 1982, "The actual idea for the song came about from me reading *Jet* [magazine]. . . . I saw O.J. Simpson with this white woman—and Arthur Ashe looked like he was with a white lady. And [actor] Richard Roundtree was getting engaged to this ravishing blonde. So it gave me this idea—someone has to speak out on the subject!"

While Millie hadn't had a Top 10 R&B hit in three or four years, she knew the way to restore her salability was to cut another album that focused on her mix of raunch'n'soul. 1982's *Live and Outrageous (Rated XXX)* was the answer, and as always, diehard Jackson fans lapped it up. Millie talked about her loyal fans in 1980, explaining to John Abbey, "My fans only have to worry about whether they spend this welfare check or the next when they buy my album. They are the lower income group and I will always stay true to them because they are the fans who have put me where I am today. The funny thing is that I am picking up a gay following now—the Patti LaBelle leftovers!" Two years later, she added, ". . . People feel they can relate to me and that I am involved with them and their thoughts and problems. They look at me differently. For example, if most people were to meet Diana Ross, they'd be quiet and shake in their boots, right? But when they meet me, they throw their arms around me and treat me like one of the family. . . ."

In the same interview, Millie acknowledged that she had two distinct sides to her personality. There was Millie the outrageous performer, and Mildred, who she noted, "is probably more happy when I'm down on the farm in Georgia. Away from the bright lights and happy just fishing." Few people got to see Mildred, and when Millie was talking to Randall Grass during the 1990s, she commented to him, "I'm a kind of loner, actually. When I'm home, it's crossword puzzles, television and the kids." She'd also led mostly a single life: "Marriage is not a priority for me. Why should I get married? I have all the benefits of marriage already. I have children,

I support myself and I have companionship. And I'm not madly in love with anyone. So why do it?" As Millie revealed to Rita Christian back in 1978, ". . . I'm romantic. I like to be wooed. Candlelight, seduction, the whole thing . . . the sweatin' part comes later on!" In a 1985 interview for *Blues & Soul*, Millie had a few words to say to my sister Sylvia on the subject of sex and, we can safely assume, the use of certain battery-powered aids: ". . . I simply take it with me. If I get the odd twenty minutes or so, I say, 'Let's do it!' I guess I'm exaggerating a little but I do try to get at least one night off every week in order to catch up on all those things we women have to take care of . . . you know what I mean?" Thoroughly modern Millie, indeed!

Touring on a package with B.B. King, Bobby "Blue" Bland, and the late Z.Z. Hill, Millie was expanding her audience somewhat. But it was her own tried and tested crowd—both in the U.S. and the U.K., where she'd consistently built a fan base—that kept her going when working at Spring Records began to get shaky. Her last couple of albums for the label, *Hard Times* and *E.S.P. (Extra Sexual Persuasion)* did moderately well but the company was on its way out. In 1988, she spilled the beans with great mirth in a *Blues & Soul* interview we did: "I was with them for 13 years, you know. When [distributors] PolyGram dropped the label, they couldn't pay me what they owed me on my contract—which was something like $425,000! They came to me and said, 'Can you work with us?' and I just kept saying, 'What do you mean?' Like, what the hell are you trying to tell me? Well, boy, I found out. They had enough money for me to do an album but no money to promote it and I didn't get anywhere near $425,000. The worst part is that just before all this happened, I put all my money, I mean every last nickel, into buying property. So here I am with no money and ten pieces of property and I had to sell somethin'! Now, you know, honey, you can't sell no piece of property in two minutes. [But] I had this trailer that I never used near a lake at my home in Georgia . . . [Well] a tornado had blown the trailer into the lake! I burst out laughing hysterically because it was insured—so I finally got me some money just when all the raggedy stuff was happening with Spring." Millie's tenure as a property owner had its funny side, too, as she revealed in her 1985 chat with my sister Sylvia on the eve of the release of her U.K. duet with Elton John: "[I] never quite realized the commitment required. I mean, when the tenants keep phoning to insist that you rush over and fix the plumbing, it's at that stage that you get to shouting. I may be able to handle many things but plumbing is not one of them!"

Finding a new recording home was one of the tasks Millie had to handle after Spring folded, and this took her a couple of years. She finally settled on Jive Records, originally a U.K.-based company owned by Clive Caulder, who was a South African record executive. By the time Millie signed with the label in 1985, Jive had experienced success on both sides of the Atlantic, specifically with singer Billy Ocean and guitarist/vocalist Jonathan Butler. "I was waiting for something interesting to come along," she said in a 1987 *Blues & Soul* article. "I never got so far as serious negotiations. Several companies were interested in me but to be honest, I wasn't interested in them! The New York office of Jive kept calling me. . . . At first, I wasn't interested. They must have made 50 or more calls and I'd keep putting them off. . . . Eventually, I was talked round into at least meeting up with Clive [Caulder]. . . . I was impressed that the company president had come down from New York to the [Newark] airport. If it had been an American company . . . then I wouldn't even have got to *meet* with the president. . . ."

As it turned out, the association with the label would prove less than satisfactory for either party. In all, Millie cut four albums for Jive and while they contained some pleasing musical moments, almost nothing equaled the spunk and fire of her previous work for Spring. The one exception was *Back to the Shit*, which depicted Millie on a toilet bowl, panties at her ankle, "taking a good one!" as she said in an interview we did around the time of the album's release in 1989. Recorded live, the album was hilarious and featured some vintage Millie Jackson, with in-between raps like the riotous "Getting to Know Me," in which she decries the problems of having women sit up front—"Do you know what it's like shaking my ass . . . and looking up and seeing some woman? . . . Last night, some women 'chose' me . . . but it ain't that kind of party!"—and having deejays play her records—"You won't be able to play a motherfuckin' thing off this record! The rap "Love Stinks," a segue from "Imitation of Love," the title track from Millie's first Jive LP, is just as funny, with Millie describing the problems of predictable lovers, female incontinence, and men's toilet habits before railing on women for their attempts to muffle their wind, appropriately entitled "Muffle That Fart"!

There were some stellar vocal performances, but Millie's raps were sidesplitting. "I'm Waiting Baby," which served as a lead-in to Millie's reading of the Shirelles' classic "Will You Love Me Tomorrow," described the predicament of a woman waiting for her man at "The Lovers Hotel." The lights stop flashing leaving a neon sign that says "Over Ho," which Millie concludes might be a message from him. The final piece, "Sho Nuff Danjus," ran the risk of offending more than a few people because Millie was initially addressing the new problems that people faced with the scourge of AIDS. But she made sure that she espoused the importance of safe sex.

Overall, the album was a throwback to Millie's X-rated, late 1970s material; however, Jive didn't know how to handle it as she explained in a 1992 interview we did: "The record company and I had some *differences*. I didn't want to be with the motherfuckers anymore! I did this nice clean album, *The Tide Is Turning*, and they didn't do shit with it. Then I did the live *Back to the Shit* album and there was a conflict between Jive and RCA/BMG who were distributing the label at the time. We were supposed to have posters of the album cover, with me on the toilet but RCA wanted some nice headshots . . . p-u-l-e-e-z-e! As it turned out, they didn't even make any posters, and the album got hardly any exposure at all. Anyway, they picked up the option on my contract even though I didn't want to stay."

Millie was experiencing a good deal of frustration. She'd attempted to stay away from getting involved with X-rated material through the albums *An Imitation of Love* and *The Tide Is Turning*, working with several young producers on each and singing hard on tunes like "Hot! Wild! Unrestricted Crazy Love!" and "Love Is a Dangerous Game," which were successful Top 10 R&B hits more through airplay than sales. *Back to the Shit* was supposed to help her regain her status as a bonafide chart maker, so when it failed to register, Millie was mad. She was looking at some of her contemporaries, who were enjoying renewed success at the time and couldn't figure out why she wasn't getting the same reaction to her records. "Look at Betty Wright and Gladys and the Pips—they must be doin' somethin' right," she said in our 1988 conversation. "But no one says too much about those of us who have been away from the charts for a while and then come back, unless we've been through some big drug thing or something. We don't get any awards for *staying clean* for twenty years—there are no medals for those who hang in here without goin' crazy!"

While Millie wasn't happy with her own recording career at the time, Millie was elated that daughter Keisha had stepped out and was experiencing her first taste of success. "We sound totally different," Millie said. "She has this nice, clear high voice and I have this lowdown deep style! But we sound great together." Back in 1978 when Keisha was just twelve years old, Millie had talked about her young daughter's musical ambitions with Rita Christian: "She has expressed the desire to be a singer. She's always singing and playing the piano and she loves the entertaining side of things. . . . She's heard me say on occasions that I don't want her to have a singing career—so now, when she's asked if she'd like to be a singer like her mom, she says, 'I don't think so.' But I think she'd really like to."

As it turned out, Keisha's chart run was relatively brief, spanning a couple of albums for Sony Music, and by 1993, she'd joined her mother for the highly successful musical that Millie had put together, entitled *Young Man, Older Woman.* The show had been inspired by the title track for what would be Millie's final album for Jive, released in 1991. The record had more of an even feel, and the subject matter was classic Millie, with tunes like the thought-provoking "Living With a Stranger," the self-explanatory "Are You Gonna Tell Your Woman (About Me)?" and the sexy "Are You Up on I?" She told a typically funny anecdote when explaining how *Young Man, Older Woman* came about when we spoke at length at the end of 1991: ". . . I was going to record a song with this guy who was driving my tour bus because he had a good voice. We were going to have him sing a song with me so the record company could hear him and I could get him a deal. Well, I was wondering what the fuck is the duet going to be, and one day I was watching Cher on television and I realized, everybody's doin' it, all these older broads going out with these young guys. Well, the driver went missing when it was time to do the duet! . . . We went ahead and cut it with [singer] Norwood, who has worked with me for a few years doing backgrounds."

Our conversation was particularly insightful because Millie shared about the public perception of her and how she'd begun to remedy the image of her as just an X-rated performer. "People really don't know me: I'm not someone you'll see hangin' out in a nightclub being sociable. The only thing people seem to know comes from what they hear and they hear a bunch of 'm-f's' on my records so they think I'm this black 'wonder' woman. I guess if I did a movie, people would expect it to be like 'Millie Does Minnesota.' It would be nice to do a comedy but I'm not going to pull off my clothes or any shit like that!," she said. The solution was "Ask Millie," a weekly radio program broadcast from a Dallas, Texas, station that included a special segment called "The Desperate Dallas Dating Game." Millie was in her element with the show: "What I love about doing the program is that people found out that I can talk for three hours without cussing so now people think, 'The bitch can't be totally stupid!' . . . We open up the phone lines so I can answer people's questions. . . . Some woman will call up and say, '*My old man won't give me none, what should I do?*' or . . . [Another woman] just walked in and found her husband in the bed with her sister. I told her to get out of the house!"

When Millie wasn't touring or heading down to Dallas for the radio show, she said she could be found at home in Georgia where she said, ". . . I've turned into a complete flower-bug. In fact, if you call my house, my answering machine says, 'We're not here right now, we're out beautifying America, we're in the garden' and that's not quite what people expect when they call Millie Jackson's house, you know!" Indeed, Millie's comment underlined the basic dilemma she'd been facing for years. Her outrageous, four-letter-laden records, and onstage antics had created a definite image and perception, and while that had unquestionably helped her establish a particular persona in the black community, Millie had felt confined and constricted by it for some years. She'd never been given a Grammy, barely ever invited onto an awards show and seldom asked to be a spokesperson for charitable causes, the exception being the National Coalition Against Domestic Violence, which she lent her support to in 1989. The image problem extended into her one-on-one dealings, particularly with people in the music industry. As I'd found out on countless occasions, Millie could be very, very funny, and she felt no reluctance to drop a "motherfucker" here or there in our conversations. But I also saw an intelligent, warm-hearted woman with the gift of worldly wisdom and insight, a woman who could sense injustice or stupidity and wasn't afraid to speak out.

Millie's level of frankness could have added to the overall absence of recognition for her contribution to the world of music and entertainment. The mostly white-run business didn't want its divas to be too real. As long as they could "s-a-n-g"—as black people would say—they were fine, but don't let them speak out too much about the systematic segregation that existed in the record industry. It didn't help that a lot of the highly paid black executives who could help give Millie the kind of props she deserved didn't want to be associated with a woman who had made her living from being essentially a working-class musical hero. While she never attempted to distance herself from her loyal audiences, she knew that she hadn't been given respect by the mainstream music industry and no doubt, on some level, I surmised it probably bothered her, especially after spending nearly thirty years in the business.

Still this didn't stop Millie from creating her own destiny. As the 1990s began, Millie made a wise move: she put together the musical *Young Man, Older Woman* and hit the road, initially for just a six-city tour. The response was so overwhelming that in 1994 Millie and company were hard at it again. ". . . Since last October, we've been kickin' ass!" Millie roared when we hooked up for a *Blues & Soul.* interview in Los Angeles in November, 1984, a day before the show made its debut at the Wiltern

Theater to a packed house. "It's hard work but the fun part is changing the script every night! Whenever I get bored, I change some shit to break the monotony and we do have fun." Douglas Knyght-Smith, one of the leads in the show, was the victim of Millie's boredom the night I saw the show. She literally grabbed him—and no prizes for guessing where! "Yeah, I like to be spontaneous. . . . We do a lot of ad-libbing [in the show]," she said.

The show contained plenty of double entendres throughout, and Millie's performance was brilliant. Unlike some of the popular black shows that had been doing the rounds for several years, *Young Man, Older Woman* was really strong musically, and it came as no surprise that it was booked through the summer of 1995. Finally free from her Jive contract, Millie had done a deal with Ichiban Records, ironically run by the same John Abbey who had conducted so many interviews with her for *Blues & Soul*, the magazine he'd created in the mid-1960s. Abbey agreed to release the cast album for *Young Man, Older Woman*, whose cover depicts Millie with a cast on her leg, provided she would also do a regular album for the Atlanta-based label.

The result was *Rock'n'Soul*, which reflected one of Millie's long-held desires: ". . . My whole thing was to do an album of rock-flavored tunes 'cause I like rock and roll. . . . I've always done a rock tune in my shows. . . . I always wanted to do this kind of album . . . [but] I put a little soul in there too because I knew it was something people would like. . . ." Unfortunately, the general consensus was that the 1994 record veered too much toward rock, and even though it boasted "Check in the Mail," a strong R&B tune that teamed her up with longtime friend Betty Wright and marked Millie's reunion with producer Brad Shapiro, with whom she' enjoyed all her major 1970s hits, the album wasn't as successful as Millie had hoped.

With *Young Man, Older Woman* finally completing its run in December, 1995, Millie headed back to the recording studios. *It's Over?!* was the result, and this time out she stayed away from rock, making a basically "clean," straight-up R&B album. Even though the album seemed to have the right mucial ingredients, Ichiban wasn't able to turn it into a bestseller, more a result of internal problems at the label rather than its musical content. The release of the record gave me a chance to talk with Millie again for a 1996 *Blues & Soul* article. And after talking about the usual stuff connected with new albums, she revealed just a tidbit of personal information when we were discussing the song "Don't Give Up on Me Now." She'd already indicated it was her favorite tune on the album but suddenly became untypically coy when I asked why.

"Okay," she finally relented, explaining the song's significance. "I met somebody when I was on the West Coast and we started seeing each other. But he told me, 'Hey, you live on the East Coast and I live on the West Coast so it's not going to work.' I saw him when I was getting ready to leave L.A. and I thought to myself, 'This is it, we're gonna be saying goodbye, it's over.' Well, we kept this lovely relationship going and I started writing this song because it didn't feel like he had given upon me . . . until he decided that he was right the first time, that it couldn't work with us living on two different coasts. So I figured, hey, if I must be brokenhearted, I deserve a good song out of it! At least, I could make some money out of the situation and record sales [might] almost make me forget I was miserable in the first place!"

That last comment really sums up who Millie Jackson is. Always a fighter, a downhome soul sister who has a kind of unspoken yet unstoppable drive to survive, no matter what the odds . . . and who can laugh at herself and at the absurdity of the world we live in. Hit records or no, Millie Jackson will always be one of my favorite divas because I can count on her to tell it like it is, straight from the hip, with humor, candor, and kindness.

A LIE
OLE

covered

As I watched Natalie Cole standing in front of a full orchestra, looking radiant in a beautiful white gown as the packed audience rose to its feet in 1991, I couldn't help but marvel at the her transformation. As she'd explained to *Blues & Soul* editor John Abbey in 1983, "Look, life is a big challenge and sometimes, we can move too fast and not be objective enough about what's happening to us. . . . This business is a killer. You can get so tired and weak and of course, that's when you're at your most vulnerable to negative things. . . ." He entitled the article "The Other Side of the Pain."

Few performers are able to withstand the pressures of fame, its loss, and their own subsequent private fall from grace. Natalie Cole's inner strength and fortitude have enabled her to conquer personal demons and emerge triumphant, a woman with a solid future as an international entertainer. Although her career began in 1975 with a flourish—a slew of hit records, million-selling albums, and Grammy Awards—she paid a heavy price. By 1983, hooked on drugs and divorced from her first husband after five years of marriage, she'd hit the skids. Concert bookings had ground to a halt, and record companies were staying as far away as they could. A self-imposed spell in rehabilitation began restoring Natalie's confidence, but it took her groundbreaking tribute to her famous father, 1991's award-winning *Unforgettable* album, to bring her all the way back.

Natalie was born in 1950 in Los Angeles, the daughter of the legendary Nat "King" Cole, an entertainer who had managed, to some degree, to defy the inbred segregation that pervaded show business throughout the 1940s and 1950s. Cole had crossed over and gained wide acceptance among white audiences, selling millions of records over a twenty-year period and, in the process, helping Capitol Records become an established entity in the music business.

Natalie had been forced to deal with the limelight from an early age. Eager tourists who found the Cole residence in the fashionable Hancock Park section of Los Angeles often peered into windows and snapped pictures, giving young Natalie and her sisters and brothers little chance at privacy. She also had to deal with issues other than the fame of her velvet-voiced father. In the wake of her across-the-board success with

Unforgettable in 1991, Natalie spoke with more than a little candor about those years, telling an eager reporter from *Jet* magazine how her mother, Maria Cole, didn't take too kindly to her daughter's attempts at fraternizing with members of her own race. "When I got friendly with the (black) people who worked for us, my mother was appalled," she said, adding that members of her mother's family felt that Nat "King" Cole "was too black for them. . . ."

Attempts at sheltering a teenage Natalie from other black kids might have fostered a certain sense of rebellion in her. Three years after her father's death in 1966, Natalie was studying child psychology at the University of Massachusetts and she felt she'd been living life "in a bubble." She became immersed in campus political activities, joining the first student strike in protest of the Vietnam conflict and learning about the work of the militant Black Panthers.

Initially, Natalie consciously avoided what might have been an obvious career in music, and her mother's fears of what a life in show business could mean weighed strongly in keeping Natalie away from the spotlight. But in her senior year at college, she did some singing with a local rock'n'roll band and was bitten by the music bug. "I had never really considered singing as a career despite the fact that my father had been so famous because everyone, including him, had always told me not to do it 'unless you really know how.' And I had worked in a sense not to get into it," she told me in our first interview over the telephone in 1975 just weeks before the release of her Capitol debut album. "Then in my senior year, I did some singing during the summer break. . . ."

After graduating with a B.A. in 1972, Natalie tried her hand at singing professionally; she was even willing to play dates where she was occasionally billed simply as "Nat 'King' Cole's daughter." She'd been developing her own sound but audiences expected her to sound just like her famous parent. "Yes, having Nat as my father helped inasmuch as some of his style, his vocal phrasing and so on was bound to rub off on me," she stated in 1975. "But then at the same time, it has been a problem in that some people expect me to sound just like him—and of course, I don't! My main influences from way back were jazz people like Sarah Vaughan, Ella Fitzgerald and of course, Nancy Wilson. And then Aretha came into my life when I was about 10! And although I've had no gospel influence per se, I guess I got that through Aretha."

After hooking up with manager Kevin Hunter in 1973, Natalie began to consider a recording career seriously. Just one year later, she'd hooked up with Chuck Jackson and Marvin Yancy, two Chicago-based songwriter/producers who had had some success as members of an R&B

group called the Independents. "They heard me at a club called Mr. Kelly's in Chicago, and neither party was sure who was rehearsing for who!" she confided in our telephone chat in 1975. "[Now] everyone says it sounds as if I wrote the songs [on the album] myself, but that's just how close those two fabulous guys have come to capturing how I feel. . . ." The musical marriage was instant, and although Natalie and her newly found partners didn't make an obvious choice to sign with the label that had been so instrumental to her father's success, it turned out to be Capitol Records (through executive Larkin Arnold) that most eagerly wanted to sign her.

I remember when I first heard Natalie's about-to-be-released Capitol debut. I'd gotten to know Matt Parsons, the head of R&B promotion in Capitol's New York office, and his secretary Janet Williams (who later went to work for Natalie for a brief spell) within a few months of arriving in New York from London to work as a correspondent for Britain's *Blues & Soul*. When Matt and Janet asked me to come up to Capitol's Sixth Avenue offices, I had no idea what to expect. After all, this was Nat "King" Cole's daughter.

A longtime lover of the kind of emotion-filled, soulful music associated with divas like Aretha Franklin and Patti LaBelle, I needed to hear only a few bars of "Inseparable" to get hooked and to know that Natalie had the kind of R&B chops on the album of the same name that I was raving about it in *Blues & Soul*: "She's funky, bluesy, soulful, soft, tough and very talented," I wrote. "Don't say we didn't warn you—just get ready for a lady that's gonna give every other female singer a run for their money." Songs like "I Can't Say No" and "You" (later recorded by Aretha) won me over; Natalie's vocal intensity made her an immediate favorite.

Indeed, *Inseparable* went on to become a gold album, propelled by the hits "This Will Be," which became one of Natalie's two Top 5 singles during her six-year stay at Capitol, and the title track. Both were R&B chart toppers. The LP also earned Natalie her first two Grammy Awards for "Best New Artist" and "Best R&B Vocal Performance, Female."

During this first conversation, Natalie confessed that she was just a tad nervous since mine was actually the very first full-out interview she'd done in preparation for the release of *Inseparable*. The first single, "This Will Be," was beginning to make some noise, and she'd started to adjust to what would turn out to be a whole new life. "Am I ready for it all?" she asked. "Well, if not, I'd better get ready!"

I got to see Natalie perform in person for the first time in September of that year. With a big Afro, the slender singer wore out the audience at a show hosted by Capitol at Buddy's Place in midtown Manhattan.

"Looking more than cute, with an unbelievable amount of energy and creative power, Natalie ran the gamut with such items as [the Beatles'] "Come Together" and "I've Got the Music in Me,". . . . as well as a surprisingly good "Up on the Roof" and a tribute to her father . . . in the form of "L-O-V-E." Ms. Cole's vocal abilities and range are stunning: yes, there are touches of Aretha in there, no one would deny. But Natalie does have her own thing . . . her opening night had a certain magic to it which will remain memorable to all those present. Watching the birth of a star," I wrote, "is always an exciting event!"

Only months later, Natalie was out in Los Angeles performing at the Coconut Grove: "Natalie hollered, danced, got down (really down, to the floor, mike in hand, to let out some really soulful singin'!)," I wrote in a *Blues & Soul* review in March, 1976. "Although her background is not in the church, Natalie took everyone there with her gospel-sounding style, and she not only sounded fine, but looked slim and trim and together too!" Aretha Franklin's name had consistently popped up in reviews of Natalie's first album and her first few shows, and she addressed the comments in an interview with John Abbey for *Blues & Soul* as "Inseparable" was rapidly becoming one of the year's bestsellers. "Hmmm, that's the first time anyone has said that. . . . There are times when I listen back to my own work and I have to agree with what you say. . . I have been more impressed by Chaka Khan but I would never dream of trying to sound like Chaka or Aretha or anyone. . . ."

By the spring of 1976, regardless of comparisons with the reigning Queen of Soul, Natalie was proudly watching her second album, simply entitled *Natalie*, go gold. And the hits kept coming. Producers Jackson and Yancy had come up with a musical formula that worked, and "Sophisticated Lady"—Natalie's third No. 1 R&B hit, which earned her a third Grammy Award—was followed by "Mr. Melody." While celebrating her second taste of chart success, Natalie also had her attention on matters of the heart, sharing that she was going to marry Kevin Nance, her musical director, in August, 1976. "We met in New York last June," she revealed in a 1976 *Blues & Soul* article. "I went to a private party . . . and Kevin's . . . was the resident band. . . . At the time, I was looking for a band [myself] and a girlfriend of mine had recommended that I see the band. . . . Needless to say, I took them on!" As it turned out, the marriage never happened, and Natalie confessed in 1978 that she had in fact wed Reverend Marvin Yancy, her producer, in June, 1976, only making the information public six months later.

At this point in time, Natalie's life seemed to be on the upswing. In addition to her new marriage, her records were selling. And she'd even conquered Broadway, with a nine-concert stint at the Winter Garden Theater, a feat only previously achieved by the likes of Diana Ross and soul man Al Green. The reviews were glowing. " . . . Ms. Cole (who) looked stunning in rust-colored cape and silver-and-black gown . . . nothing too gaudy or flashy, something just right," I observed in my report to *Blues & Soul* in early 1977. Gone was the big Afro that she'd worn during her first few years as a recording artist. Natalie had a smart hairstyle, but she'd lost none of her 'soul' in the process. ". . . Ms. Cole shines bright and clear, proving that soul is no longer limited to chitlin' circuits or concert halls," I added. A star-studded, post-concert-party brought out some of New York's finest and a bevy of R&B stars like Stephanie Mills and the late Ronnie Dyson.

Just a few months after the Broadway triumph, Natalie achieved her first platinum album with the release of *Unpredictable*; more hits like "I've Got Love on My Mind" and "Party Lights" followed. One of the tracks on the album, "I'm Catching Hell," would become a strong favorite among Natalie's solid audience, an emotional testimony to the ups and downs of relationships, an arena that would prove clearly challenging to the singer as her own marriage to Yancy went through changes.

Musically, Natalie had been pretty adamant that she wouldn't do anything that even closely resembled disco music, which was literally taking over the charts as the decade was coming to a close. As she told John Abbey at the beginning of 1978, " . . . I'm a little paranoid about the whole [disco] thing. Before I made it, I used to play dance hall gigs and I hated singing while people danced to my music and I used to pray for the day when I could play concerts and people would actually listen to my singing. And without wishing to appear rude to some of the disco artists, it doesn't take a great singer to make it in the disco stakes. . . ." Ironically, "Party Lights" from the *Unpredictable* album was a hit on the R&B charts and garnered some dance music play, as did "Stand By," the first single from Natalie's 1979 gold album *I Love You So*.

No matter what music Natalie was tackling, from the mellow, quiet storm gem "La Costa" to straight-ahead pop/R&B ditties like "Our Love," she could do no wrong. Still, even with three solid bestselling albums behind her, people continued to compare her to Aretha. Even I had to admit from the very first time I listened to Natalie's music, I could hear some of Aretha's influence on her although I knew that much of the gospel-flavored sound in her music might have been more the result of producer Marvin Yancy's musical background in the church. Natalie seemed to get increasingly irritated at the mention of Aretha's name, noting that Chaka Khan of Rufus was a singer she really liked (later she became a close friend and running buddy of Natalie's. " . . . I'm the first to admit that I owe a lot to Aretha—after all, she is one of the greats and I still idolize her today," Natalie stated in her *Blues & Soul* interview in early 1978. "But the media created a lot of that and I hope that they will now at least admit that this new album [*Thankful*] is me and only me!"

The media-concocted rivalry was easily fostered because Aretha was experiencing her first chart dip in more than a decade. While she'd been a top earner for Atlantic Records, that company had been purchased by Warner Communications and the musical direction had noticeably shifted from R&B to rock. Even longtime executive and Franklin producer Jerry Wexler was no longer a key player, and while Natalie Cole was topping the R&B charts, as well as making a dent on the pop listings, Aretha was struggling with relatively lacklustre performances on mostly less-than-inspiring material. At the Grammy Awards in 1976, Natalie's arrival on the scene gave industry gossips more to work with. For the first time in nine years, Aretha Franklin didn't win "Best R&B Performance, Female." That honor went to Natalie for the song "This Will Be."

Natalie had no reason to dwell on any rivalry. After her marriage to Reverend Marvin Yancy, she'd given birth to a son, Robbie, in October, 1977, and two months later, Natalie's fourth album began its chart course. *Thankful* became her second consecutive platinum LP and spawned the hits "Our Love," another gold single, and "Annie Mae." That Natalie was still very much a hot commodity on the music scene was without question. Everything in Natalie's life seemed to be moving in the right direction.

In a February, 1978, interview, Natalie said that working with her husband wasn't "a conflict" since the couple was able to separate their personal and professional lives when it came time to enter the recording studios. I can remember one of my first encounters with Natalie and Marvin when I was on a rare visit to Chicago for a "Super Soul" concert in the Windy City in 1977. Natalie had invited me to go with her to her husband's Sunday service, held at a relatively small storefront church where the Reverend Yancy, a stocky, charismatic man, delivered his dynamic message.

That Natalie was the pastor's wife was apparent by the way the church elders and the congregation treated her. Everyone knew that she was also Natalie Cole, international superstar. But on this summer Sunday, she was just one of the congregation, swept up like everyone else in Yancy's testifying fervor. She swayed, punctuating his remarks with an "Amen" here and there, and finally broke into song with all the passion of a would-be gospel diva. That is when everyone knew that she wasn't just another regular churchgoer. It was thrilling to watch as Natalie became caught up, oblivious to her surroundings, singing praises and giving thanks. I felt honored to be there, personally moved and stirred by the proceedings myself.

It seemed that nothing could stop Natalie from continuing her upward climb. In 1978, she had her own television special, with guests Johnny Mathis; Earth, Wind & Fire; and singer/songwriter Stephen Bishop. American Music Awards and hit records were now a given for Natalie. Capitol wisely decided to release a two-record set of Natalie's energetic show, and "Natalie . . . Live!," which included a fiery version of the Beatles' classic, "Lucy in the Sky With Diamonds," became her fourth gold album. *I Love You So*, her sixth LP, was a turning point, but it yielded just one hit, the uptempo track "Stand By," and was her last bestseller for Capitol. By the middle of 1979, Natalie racked up an impressive total of four gold and two platinum albums; by the end of the year, she recorded an entire album with labelmate Peabo Bryson.

When that album was released, I began to suspect that all wasn't as it seemed in the Cole camp. Janet Williams, who had worked at Capitol before Natalie had hired her as a secretary and relocated her to Los Angeles, confided in me that her parting from Natalie had been less than amicable, suggesting that some of the people around the star had less than her best interests at heart. When I talked to Peabo, who I'd known for the couple of years he'd been with Capitol, he made it known that the recording sessions with Natalie hadn't gone as smoothly as the press releases indicated.

Natalie herself was also less than enthused about the project with Peabo, and it didn't take a mind reader to guess that egos had clashed. A certain sense of frustration seeped through the interview Natalie and I did for *Blues & Soul* in conjunction with the release of the duet album. "People have this idea of me being a sophisticated lady, which is cool because it is a part of me. But it's not the whole thing! That means that I'm never allowed to be in jeans because it doesn't correspond with the public image and I resent that!" She was feeling somewhat constricted by the incredible success she'd enjoyed over five hectic, fast-paced years, and the wear was showing in her private life: "It's like my marriage: yes, Marvin and I separated because we let certain things slide. But we're back together and we're not going to let that happen again. . . . I think a lot of bullshit's been said about keeping your name out there whether it's good news or bad news and that just ain't true! I'm a firm believer in a couple of clichés like 'Ignorance is bliss,' 'What you don't know won't hurt you,' 'Silence is golden' and 'No news is good news'!"

Natalie was dealing with the price of fame and the media's consuming interest in her activities both on- and offstage, and she didn't like it. Later revelations of some of the personal issues she was dealing with at the time, such as her drug use, which was known only to industry insiders, might have made her more sensitive to the press coverage: "People think you've got to be plastered all over the media all the time and it just ain't so. If the media would only emphasize the positive and good things about people in the public eye, I think it would make things a lot healthier instead of dwelling on the negative or bad things when they go down. There's enough good things happening with people that they could just deal with that and it would be just fine!"

I sensed that Natalie was irritated—in fact, almost angry—as she spoke about her issues with the media. But I was unaware of what might have been happening in her private life that she wanted to keep behind closed doors. I remembered some of the comments that her former secretary, Janet Williams, had made about the people who hung out with Natalie and how she'd certainly witnessed some outbursts from her then-employer. But I'd attributed that to the usual diva-tude that seemed to be an inevitable byproduct of phenomenal success experienced in a relatively short period of time.

I'd always enjoyed talking with Natalie. We'd bonded probably because she always remembered that our first *Blues & Soul* interview had been the first major one-on-one she'd had with a music journalist before the release of *Inseparable*. Whenever we'd run into each other, we always exchanged a warm greeting, and there was a genuine sense of appreciation. But I had no idea that Natalie was having such a tough time both on- and offstage at the turn of the decade.

But I knew something was very wrong when I saw her backstage at an Angela Bofill show at the Roxy in Los Angeles in 1982. Other celebrities were milling around, including Dionne Warwick and Phyllis Hyman. I hardly recognized Natalie. She looked as thin as a rail; disheveled and completely out of it, she was also obviously on some kind of substance. "Why didn't you call me when you came out here?' she yelled at me, as everyone in the dressing room turned and glared. I proffered some lame excuse and quickly left, devastated by what I'd seen. This wasn't the bright, warm, and energetic woman I'd gotten to know over the previous seven years. She seemed like a former shadow of herself, and the expressions of pity and disgust on the faces of others gathered in Angela's dressing room spoke volumes about Natalie's condition.

The truth about Natalie's drug problems became public in 1982. She

spoke candidly with John Abbey of *Blues & Soul* as 1983 ended. " . . . I learned a lot during that crisis. My family and my real friends stuck with me—and my fans still cared. But I did learn that most people really don't give a damn what happens to you personally—and that was disappointing to me. How to avoid it happening again in the future? Well . . . I think the main thing is keep oneself on top and be good to yourself. Be No. 1 to yourself and yet don't be selfish about it. You need to allow yourself time and space to avoid pressure whenever you can. . . . I'd been through a lot of pain before I realized how real this business is—despite what some people tell themselves. . . . If I've learned one thing from it all, it's that I'm not as trusting of people as I was before."

The preceding three years had been tough on the singer in many ways. *Don't Look Back* and *Happy Love*, Natalie's last two albums for Capitol, had been relative failures. Also by the beginning of 1982, she'd parted company with the label—and with her husband, Marvin Yancy. In a 1983 interview with Mark Webster for *Blues & Soul*, Natalie said nothing about her split from Yancy but had a few choice words about the end of her tenure with the company: "The image that Capitol Records had created wasn't really me at all. I wanted to be a little raunchy, a little *funky*, but the whole Capitol concept—the albums, the concerts, the image—wouldn't allow me to do so. . . . So, the only real opportunity left open to me was to get a fresh start with a new record company and a new sound."

Natalie had moved to Epic Records, and she continued with some comments on Yancy and production partner Jackson, too. "Chuck and Marvin were getting into that same old rut as I had and so, for my last Capitol album, I changed the production team. . . ." Once she was with Epic, she'd reunited with the team for one album, *I'm Ready*, and worked with bassist Stanley Clarke on several tracks. But none of the magic that had given the trio such a long run of hits seemed to be there. The album stayed on the charts for all of three weeks, and even though Natalie had claimed that her drug days were over, she was using again. Knowing that she needed help, she finally checked into a drug and alcohol rehabilitation center and emerged six months later in May, 1984.

Natalie and I finally came face to face once again in late summer, 1985. The occasion was Natalie's return to recording. After going on a two-year hiatus, she'd made a new album for Modern Records, which was entitled *Dangerous*, and she was ready to get back into the limelight again, to talk honestly and openly about what had happened to her. The article was entitled "Dicing With Death," and I was taken aback by Natalie's candor. In our first face-to-face conversation, she told me about the hell she'd been living through away from the public spotlight. "I got my priorities screwed up. In this business, it's easy—particularly when you're successful—to forget who you are. You start believing that you're infallible, untouchable. I got to that point, and I surrounded myself with people who kept me thinking that way, people who were the 'yes' people, the hangers-on, so that the real people who could put you straight could never even get close."

I couldn't helped but be moved by Natalie's honesty. She explained that she'd reached her lowest point when she started canceling shows in 1982 and 1983. "I had to get right down there to the lowest point before I could see what had happened to me physically. Finally, I broke down, physically, mentally, and emotionally. It wasn't just the drugs and drinking—it was everything. I was no longer in control of my life."

Indeed, Natalie's drug addiction had affected every aspect of her life: "My relationship with my son Robbie bordered on negligence. Fortunately, I had a baby sitter to make sure he was taken care of. My finances were in total disarray, and, thankfully, my mother came in and took over my estate because, frankly, I wasn't equipped to deal with it. Even beyond all of that, I couldn't deal with myself any longer. I'd go to business meetings and I'd pitch a bitch. I became a monster—and no one really took any notice because they knew I was whacked-out. I'd lost people's respect and worse still, my own self-respect."

Natalie confided that after she started missing gigs, her family suggested a rehabilitation program. "I just couldn't go on stage. I had earaches, sore throat, my body just wasn't functioning," she said. But even after she entered the rehab program the first time in 1983, " . . . it was under pressure and I really wasn't committed to it—so it didn't work." She came out of the program thinking she could pick up where she left off; however, after she hooked up with personal manager Dan Cleary (whose clients at the time included the Commodores), Natalie found the encouragement and support she needed and headed to another rehab center in Minnesota. "[Dan] pointed out that I had to take some action because I was about ready to go right back to where I'd been before. The truth is that I was dying . . . in every way. . . ."

Natalie finally entered the Minnesota facility, but still with some trepidation, she said. "There were some sports people but no other entertainers, and the place was staffed by many former participants in the program. To begin with, I figured I'd go through it just like I had the last time . . . it was just thirty days after all. But something inside me woke up. I started finding out more about the disease aspect of drug and alcohol addiction, and I realized that the people running this program were committed to saving people's lives and mine needed to be saved. So I started getting antsy—I realized I wasn't ready to go out into the world again. They had this extended four-to-six month program, and by the end of my thirty days I was getting nervous that they wouldn't let me stay for the extended period because I knew I needed it." Natalie got her extension.

After Natalie left the center in 1984, she knew something had changed inside her. ". . . I was able to look in the mirror for the first time in many, many years and like what I saw. I felt more centered: there was like a serenity that I hadn't known for so long. I'd forgotten it was possible to live without the craziness." Understandably, she didn't know whether she could handle getting right back into the thick of the music business. "I didn't know if I wanted to deal with the pressures. I kept asking myself, 'Do I really want to be here?' After all, there had been a lot of changes in the business during these few years, and there was more competition. I knew that the only way I'd be able to really make it through—once I came out of the rehab program—was with people's support."

Some fellow entertainers strengthened Natalie's resolve to get back into the swing. She told me, "I ran into Smokey Robinson, Stevie Wonder, Lou Rawls, Patti LaBelle, and Thelma Houston, and every single one of them told me, 'Hey, it's so good to have you back,' and that made me feel really great. Naturally, it was important to have my colleagues accept me. . . . " But while some of her peers could empathize and understand what Natalie had been through, others in the music business were less understanding. As manager Cleary began talking with the record companies, he discovered that there was, hypocritically, some concern that Natalie hadn't fully recovered from her addiction. Given the widespread use of drugs behind the doors of some of the ivory towers of power in the industry, such attitudes didn't sit well with Natalie. "Quite a few of the executives had this attitude that I needed them more than they needed me, like 'take-it-or-leave it' and they wanted to offer me situations that weren't right for me . . . so I just walked."

Natalie's breakthrough came when Modern Records, a small company that Atlantic Records distributed, decided to give Natalie the green light. Buoyed by the success of "Dangerous," which was a catchy, uptempo, dance-flavored title track, the album (of the same name) did moderately well when released in the summer of 1985. More important, it restored Natalie's confidence and gave the public a chance to see her in action again. I remember a show at the Greek Theater in Los Angeles shortly after the album's release when she opened for Al Jarreau (if memory serves me well) and how impressive Natalie was. The energy and enthusiasm that had been so much a part of the performances in the earliest part of her career were back. Not only did she have energy but she sounded better than ever.

Still Natalie admitted to me that returning to the world she'd left behind was no easy task: "There were a lot of adjustments to make when I finally came back out into the world again. I couldn't face going back to my old house up in Benedict Canyon. It just had too many painful memories for me. Initially, I went to live with my aunt . . . I won't tell you that it's all been rosy. When Marvin, my ex-husband, died of a heart attack in March [1985], of course I reacted to it. Apart from whatever I may have felt, he was the father of my son and I knew I had to be there for Robbie. But I also knew I had to be strong and not even let that be an excuse for me to go get a drink or something. I'm proud to say I have stayed sober ever since the day I left the clinic."

Possibly for the first time in her career, Natalie felt really confident. Some of the ghosts that had been haunting her for years were gone. "I found that I lost all my insecurities about the comparisons people would always make about me and my father. That competitiveness is gone: I know I have a particular talent of my own, that there's something I do that no one else does like me," Natalie explained. I ended our interview knowing that I'd witnessed someone willing to bare her soul—something I'd rarely seen during my years as a music journalist.

Another two years would pass before Natalie experienced a true renaissance. This came in the form of a switch of record companies. Ironically, she returned in a sense to Capitol Records when she signed with EMI Records, the label's sister company, in 1987. By the end of that year, her recording career was back in high gear. Her album *Everlasting* shot back into the Top 50, and hit singles like "Jump Start (My Heart)," a version of Bruce Springsteen's "Pink Cadillac," and the ballad "I Live for Your Love"—the latter two—remnants from what would have been her second album for Modern Records if she'd stayed with that label—put Natalie fairly and squarely back in the public spotlight.

This time around, Natalie told me in August that year, she wasn't going to fall victim to the "record/tour/record/tour syndrome again. Don't forget I've been through that, and I know what it can do to people when you have a hit and lose control of your career. I want to get out there, generate lots of work, and then pace myself. I'm going to put money in some places that have nothing to do with music and watch it grow! Of course, there's nothing like doing a few months' worth of dates all at once! I'll be honest and tell you that having a hit album makes a big difference in the bank account!"

Sitting in EMI's Sunset Boulevard's offices with her nine-year-old son, Robbie (who clearly felt restless that day and had a hard time not interrupting his mother when she was talking), Natalie was able to reflect on some of the pitfalls that she felt had dogged her early years. "Maybe I'll put together the *Natalie Cole Guidebook* for new artists!" she quipped. "After all, I've been around long enough now to know the difference between stars that are born and stars that are made. I know how hard it can be just coming straight out of the box with a hit record. You become very vulnerable and open to a lot of criticism. You have to care about music and artistry, and most people in this business don't. I think young artists have to consider longevity: I know I certainly do, and I intend to be around for a long time!"

Natalie seemed so different from the woman I'd encountered years before when she was at the height of her drug addiction. This Natalie was alert, alive, excited about life, and unafraid to talk about the experiences that had led her down to what songwriter Laura Nyro once called a "stoney end." To paraphrase a song in Natalie's Capitol repertoire, she'd indeed caught hell but she was back: "I don't mind talking about it because it happened. But I think now that the only value is that I'm an example for people of someone who kicked something that was really damaging. Unfortunately, I'm not sure that people have learned yet. I'm not around that world of drugs anymore, but I know that people are still getting caught up in it. . . . I look where I am today and where I was a few years ago, and I feel very good about myself."

During this same interview session Natalie mentioned a pet project that was destined to alter her life definitively. She remarked that she planned to do a tribute album to her father: "I want to get on with that within the next two years. It may even be a double album cut with the Royal Philharmonic Orchestra—something very special." As it turned out, it took a change in record labels for Natalie to fulfill that dream. Eighteen months after *Everlasting* had put her back on the charts, Natalie was back in action with *Good to Be Back*, but EMI's staff wasn't able to take it to the same heights as its predecessor. The new album spawned just one hit single, "Miss You Like Crazy," which became a Top 10 pop smash in 1989. Nevertheless, Natalie's effectiveness as a chartmaker didn't seem to bear on her ability to draw audiences. "Just because I haven't had a hit record, it doesn't mean to say I haven't been working. That's the business for you," she told British writer Sharon Davis in a 1989 in *Blues & Soul* interview, conducted when she was in the U.K. for a promotional tour. "If they don't hear from you for a while, you must be lying in a dump somewhere. So, in that respect having a hit is important. . . ."

But live work seemed to be plentiful for Natalie, and her private life was taking a brand new turn. I got an invitation to her wedding to producer Andre Fischer (whom she'd met back in the mid-1970s when he'd been a member of Rufus), and I gratefully accepted. Natalie looked absolutely radiant that day, surrounded by family and friends (including Brenda Russell, with whom Andre had worked at the start of her career) at a church on Martin Luther King Boulevard in Los Angeles. Finally, it seemed Natalie had found personal happiness, and while her recording career was temporarily in limbo, she was doing just fine, performing regularly.

Shortly after the wedding, in late 1989, Natalie called me to ask if I could help her put together a choir to sing behind her at a Universal Amphitheater gig she was doing in Los Angeles opening for Smokey Robinson. She knew that I sang with a local choir at Unity Fellowship Church, and it took just one telephone call to my good friend Byron Motley to pull it all together. Initially, we worked with Natalie's musical director in rehearsals the day before we were to sing with her. We made it to the sound check at the huge auditorium, dressed in our church robes. I'll never forget the look on Natalie's face when she finally saw me getting ready to hit the stage for our first rehearsal together. "Wow!" she exclaimed, "Look at you! I can't believe it! Just think, we started out all those years ago with you interviewing me for *Blues & Soul*, and here we are sharing the stage!"

Less than two years later Natalie was again at the Amphitheater. Only this time, she was the headliner. After attempting to convince EMI that Natalie should do a tribute album to her father and failing, manager Dan Cleary approached the then-president of Elektra Entertainment Bob Krasnow, a man renowned for his primary commitment to artists and music-makers. Krasnow had had the foresight to sign Anita Baker to the label in 1986 and had been rewarded with a string of hit records with her.

It seems that Krasnow had also had conversations with Natalie and Cleary even prior to her signing with EMI in 1987, so he was open to what the manager had to say now that Natalie was actively looking for a new recording home. "The people (at EMI) were very lukewarm about me doing this record, and I couldn't get a real commitment from them . . .," Natalie shared with me at her Beverly Hills home one early-summer morning in 1991. It was my first visit to the house she shared with then-husband Andre, his children Kyle and Liz, and Natalie's fifteen-year-old son Robbie. At first Natalie and I sat in the living room, which was filled with gold records, awards, a grand piano, and a huge photograph of Nat "King" Cole, later adjourning to the pool where I talked with her as she exercised in preparation for swimming lessons she was about to undertake that morning.

Neither of us knew that Natalie was about to have the biggest record of her career—or that mainstream audiences would literally buy the CD by the truckload, amassing for Natalie a cool five million sales in the process. We couldn't have guessed that the album, filled with Natalie's exquisite interpretations of her father's music, would garner her the two most prestigious Grammy Awards any artist can receive, "Record of the Year" and "Album of the Year," at the ceremonies in February, 1992. We had no way of knowing that the specially created "duet" on the song "Unforgettable," uniting her voice with that of her late father via the wonders of modern technology, would be a career breakthrough for her. The song lead to more than a year's worth of concerts conducted entirely with complete orchestras and to a television special that would be repeated for more than three years after it was filmed.

Working with her then-husband and with producers David Foster and Tommy LiPuma, Natalie had crafted an album that took the music world by storm, reminding industry decision-makers that in the age of gangsta rap and heavy metal, an audience was still literally dying to hear good music and that people over the age of forty still bought records. "This is a project I've wanted to do for the past eight years," she told me as we relaxed in her spacious living room. "When I signed with Elektra, the head of the company told me he wanted this to be my first album for the label, and I was shocked, stunned. I'd already begun working on a regular album when I got the call to start working on this project. . . ."

Deciding what would end up on the record wasn't easy, Natalie said. "Basically, I sat around and made a list of songs my dad had done that I wanted to record. I talked with members of my family, with my manager, with my husband, and I realized I couldn't please everybody. . . ." The sessions for the milestone album weren't always easy for Natalie, she revealed. "It was a very intense experience for me and given the significance that my dad's music had for people, it was a humbling experience for me to be recording it. . . . [Then] we actually did a . . . session on February 15, the anniversary of my dad's passing, and I must say, it was kinda eerie. There were a lot of times when I could almost feel his presence in the studio with me, like he was talking to me. . . ."

In making *Unforgettable*, Natalie took a calculated risk. She'd built up a solid audience as a pop/R&B diva, and now she was taking what some considered a completely left turn. But she said she felt compelled to make a musical change during a show in 1990. ". . . I was shocked because I realized how much I hated [the song] "Pink Cadillac." Just for

290

a while, I thought, let me do some music that isn't so convoluted. That's why I really knew it was time to move away from what I had been doing if only for a short while. . . ."

Natalie had no idea that she would in fact be doing the music from *Unforgettable* for a good three years after its release. "When I decided to make this record, I really couldn't think too much about how people would react . . ." she said between breaths as she bobbed up and down in the pool. The interview wound down, but it was obvious she wanted people to like what she'd done.

When the public embraced *Unforgettable* so wholeheartedly, I felt an overwhelming sense of joy for Natalie. I'd seen her at her best and when she'd hit the skids, and I'd been present for her transformation, her rebirth. As I sat in the audience for her concert at the Universal Amphitheater in late 1991, my heart almost leapt out of my chest. A whole lot had happened in the sixteen years since we'd first met, and Natalie Cole, a true fighter and survivor, and an articulate, intelligent, and sensitive woman who had experienced life on the edge who was now in a whole new space, with a rejuvenated career and her life back.

Natalie's follow-up album to *Unforgettable*, entitled *Take a Look*, was released in 1993 and once again, Natalie revisited songs that she'd grown up listening to, an eclectic mix that included standards like "I Wish You Love," "I'm Beginning to See the Light," and "Cry Me a River." The public responded with less enthusiasm, and the album did moderately well without taking Natalie back to the exalted heights she'd achieved with her 1991 smash album. A third Elektra album, *Stardust*, released in 1996, was another attempt at reprising the success of *Unforgettable*. This album even included another "duet" with her father ("When I Fall in Love"), but once again, the public reaction was somewhat tepid.

On a personal level, Natalie and Andre divorced in 1996 amid rumors of domestic violence, abuse, and restraining orders, and while not much has been said publicly, Natalie has indicated that she'll talk about the relationship in her planned autobiography. As 1998 comes to a close, she is planning a new album and continues to perform both at home and abroad.

That Natalie is no longer regarded simply as an R&B hitmaker is obvious, although people who saw her at the House of Blues in Los Angeles in the summer of 1998 say she was as funky and soulful as ever. Her future seems secure. Like Ella, Sarah, and others in the jazz lineage, and indeed just like her father before her, Natalie Cole will continue to have a solid career as a performer, regardless of her status as a chartmaker.

PHY

HY

old f

I was in San Diego when I received the message from my then-new friend, Johnny Butler, who was calling from Washington, DC. The night before I'd been to see Dionne Warwick and Burt Bacharach in concert with my good buddy Byron, and on Saturday morning I was ready to head back to Los Angeles. Like all good Angelenos, I felt compelled to check my voice mail. Johnny had left a brief message for me to call him back urgently.

I was stunned when he told me the news. Phyllis Hyman, my old friend and New York neighbor, was gone. The details were initially sketchy but it seemed that she'd taken her own life. When I got back home, I spoke to Johnny again. And then it hit me: this was for real. The woman I'd interviewed at least half a dozen times, hung out with in New York, seen in concert more times than I could remember—the woman who made me laugh, sometimes made me mad, and always cheered my soul with her voice—had left. Gone. Not coming back. There would be no more hit records, no more tours, no more interviews. I felt the loss even more keenly than I had the day Esther Phillips had passed away; Esther's body had simply given out after years of emotional and physical abuse. Phyllis had reached the end of the line, unsatisfied, unfulfilled, her spirit broken. It would take a long time for me to fully comprehend what had happened and, three years after she'd left, I missed her laugh, her smile, her loudness, her brashness, and her music.

During the fifteen years we knew each other, we had more than a few "moments," but I never doubted Phyllis Hyman's artistry or musical skill. She could sing rings around most people, and she had an innate sense of rhythm and an awesome ability to interpret lyrics. Her vocal range was impressive, expansive. But as I found out in the last few interviews we did, Phyllis didn't think so. She was plagued by self-doubt and uncertainty, and the fact that her career hadn't skyrocketed the way she might have liked only added to the insecurity she felt. It had much to do with surviving as a black female in a white man's world: strong, black women like Phyllis often had to fight for the kind of support that was offered to their pop counterparts.

Not that all of Phyllis's problems came from the music business, far from it. Long before Phyllis ever even signed a recording contract, the seeds of doubt and insecurity had been sown by who knows what kind of circumstances. As I discovered with practically every diva—as with

295

every human being—certain events that take place during the formative years affect your entire development, growth, and self-expression. Phyllis was no different from anyone else in that regard. She seemed compelled to sing as a way of easing whatever inner pain she might have felt. Behind the bravado and the pushiness that occasionally bordered on the obnoxious, I suspected there was a little girl who just wanted to be accepted and loved for who she was. Not Phyllis the star, but Phyllis the woman, who needed to experience loving and being loved. An auditorium full of adoring fans couldn't solve the inner challenges; a bottle of booze or a joint couldn't do it any more than casual one-night stands could. And the more she became known—and her career was in an ascendant phase the last time we spoke in 1992—the harder it was for her to hide the private pain.

My very first encounter with Phyllis occurred in the early part of 1977 at the apartment she shared with then-husband-manager Larry Alexander on 55th Street in Manhattan, just one block over from my own New York home. By the time I met her, she'd already accomplished quite a bit in the couple of years she'd been in New York. Phyllis had arrived in Manhattan from Florida, where she'd established an enviable local reputation with her own band, the P/H Factor. Her love affair with music began early in her life. "I've been singing since I was a young girl," she told me in what would be the first of many face-to-face *Blues & Soul* interviews. "You know, singing in churches, in colleges. I'm from Pittsburgh and when I decided it was time to take my career seriously, I realized that there wasn't exactly a surplus of work in my hometown!"

Phyllis had been born in Philadelphia in July, 1950, the first of seven children; the family eventually moved to Pittsburgh. She revealed that one of her teachers had described her as "inherently musical." She was a devoted radio listener, and as Jeff Lorez recounted in his tribute to her in a 1995 issue of *Blues & Soul*, she credited James Brown as a major influence. "I learned storytelling from Nina Simone and The Last Poets and later on from Karen Carpenter. I also learned a lot about range from Minnie Riperton."

Phylllis's first singing experiences came in school, and she became a member of Pittsburgh's All-City Choir during her teens. She was the recipient of a music scholarship to a local business college, and after leaving, Phyllis, already a statuesque beauty, took a job as a secretary at a neighborhood legal-services company. ". . . I'd even worked selling ice cream at one time!" she told me in 1980. "The thing is that whatever I did, I always put everything into it—never did things halfway!" Innately, Phyllis knew that she was destined for a career in music. She joined a local group known as New Direction, singing Top 40 and R&B hits and hitting the road throughout the United States and the Caribbean. After the group broke up, Phyllis relocated to Miami and began singing with the group All the People. By 1975 she'd formed the P/H Factor and was wowing audiences—and her future husband, musician Larry Alexander—with her sense of style, soul, and a voice that had its own unique timbre and sound.

Handsome Jamaican-born Larry, brother of renowned jazz musician Monty Alexander, had mentioned his then-girlfriend to New Jersey-based producer George Kerr. In the liner notes for the 1998 Hip-O reissue *One on One*, Kerr told writer A. Scott Galloway how he flew down to Miami to hear Phyllis. Kerr, already established as a bona-fide producer thanks to 1960s hits with the O'Jays and soul songstress Linda Jones, persuaded Phyllis to sign with his production company. ". . . We decided it was time to make a move," Phyllis told me in 1977. "So we packed our things and moved to New York." Larry had taken over responsibilities as her manager although he was also busy with his own burgeoning career as a songwriter for funk bands B.T. Express and Brass Construction and as a member of the short-lived rock'n'reggae duo Tornader.

Arriving in New York in 1975, Phyllis was quickly ensconced in the studios for her first sessions with Kerr, who recorded some eight songs with her. He placed the first single he cut with Phyllis on the Private Stock label. "Leavin' the Good Life Behind" was a typical slice of mid-1970s disco that benefited from a mix by Tom Moulton, the then-king of New York mix engineers and producers. As disco had begun to take hold, more and more small companies were releasing product, and the single simply disappeared into thin air.

With all the hard work Phyllis had done as a live performer in Miami, she wasn't about to hang all her hopes for success on what was in essence another dance record. "It's destiny or karma or whatever you want to call it," she said during our 1977 chat, "but we started working straight away at Rust Brown's restaurant—doing originals, album cuts that no one knew! I guess we were there for about one-and-a-half months, and a whole lot of things came out of it." According to Scott Galloway in his *One on One* liner notes, it was renowned musician Onaje Allen Gumbs who first alerted drummer Norman Connors to Phyllis after she performed at the restaurant and mesmerized him: ". . . She had on something out of the roaring '20s, a beaded gown with a matching headdress that hung over her eyes. It was slammin'! . . . Then she opened her mouth. . . . That night, I became a Phyllis Hyman groupie."

Gumbs's reaction prompted him to call Connors, a Philadelphia drummer who had been making a name for himself with a series of jazz albums and was finally reaching a wider audience thanks to his 1975 album, *Saturday Night Special*, which included the song "Valentine Love," a hit duet featuring Detroit bassist and singer Michael Henderson and vocalist Jean Carn. Gumbs insisted that Connors come down to check out his new discovery, and Phyllis's vocal performance floored the drummer/producer. He wanted her to work with him on an upcoming LP for Buddah Records, specifically on a remake of the song "Betcha By Golly Wow," a tune the Philadelphia team of Thom Bell and Linda Creed penned, which had been a hit for the Stylistics in 1972. Gumbs did the arrangement for the haunting ballad, while sax man Gary Bartz (who happened to live in the same building as Phyllis in 1977) laid down a wonderful sax part, and Phyllis turned in a truly remarkable performance on one of the three songs she'd agreed to record with Connors.

Gumbs and Connors were just two of the people who had heard about Phyllis. She proudly told me that other admirers had included Ashford & Simpson, Al Jarreau, George Harrison, Lamont Dozier, George Benson, and Main Ingredient vocalist Cuba Gooding (father of the 1990s movie star). "It was just fantastic and so unexpected!" she enthused as we sat in the cozy living room of her one-bedroom apartment.

Inevitably, Phyllis's success at Rust Brown's led to a gig at the even more prestigious Mikell's, located just down the street. I remember when I first moved to New York, the same year Phyllis arrived there, I quickly found out that Mikell's, in particular, was the "in" place, especially for people in the black-music business. It was a hangout, a place for entertainers to rub shoulders with each other and hear some new music. It was also the perfect place for Phyllis to make even more impact in a city already overcrowded with great singers and musicians, as well as a whole bunch of wannabes. The buzz on Phyllis had gotten so strong that mainstream music-industry executives were making sure they checked out this dynamic new singer, who word had it was as adept with jazz standards as she was with R&B grooves and pop tunes. It hadn't escaped anyone's notice that Phyllis was also simply stunning looking!

"While we were there [at Mikell's], all the record companies came down—CBS, Atlantic, Warner's—everyone. But we didn't make any decisions on the spot," Phyllis said during our 1975 *Blues & Soul* interview, noting she still had a contract with George Kerr. Since the first single had vanished without a trace, ". . . when it came time to record again, the company let us choose the material so we did some of [my husband] Larry's tunes, including "Baby (I'm Gonna Love You)." The record was released [in 1976] around the end of April, and by August it was starting to break in a few markets," Phyllis recalled several months later.

The single had appeared on Kerr's own Desert Moon label and made some headway on the R&B charts. It was the release of "We Both Need Each Other," a duet between Phyllis and Michael Henderson from Norman Connors's *You Are My Starship* album, that really brought her name to the attention of both radio deejays and record buyers after its release in July, 1976. Phyllis took to the road with Henderson, Connors, and his band for several months, and by the time Buddah released "Betcha By Golly Wow" in January, 1977, the ground swell of interest in Phyllis had grown considerably.

When the single became a Top 30 R&B hit, Phyllis and Larry considered their options. She explained, "We decided to go with Buddah because we liked what we saw in terms of the promotion the company was doing with Norman. . . . So they bought my contract from Desert Moon and when we came off the road, we started working on the album." At the time, the label was still doing fine with artists like Gladys Knight & the Pips, Melba Moore, the Andrea True Connection, and, of course, Connors and Phyllis seemed like a promising addition.

Phyllis's debut album included tracks produced by Larry and musical partner Sandy Torano, noted producer/arranger Jerry Peters (known for his work with, among others, Earth, Wind & Fire), and Philadelphia dance music maestro John Davis. "It was [Buddah executive] Lewis Merenstein who suggested we use three sets of producers because we wanted to show as many different sides of me as possible," Phyllis reported. ". . . I was kinda nervous and excited at the same time because this was my first solo album and I wanted it to be good. It really turned out to be extensions of what Larry and I had been planning for four years and I learned a great deal from the whole experience. Everybody had the freedom they needed to be creative. . . . I wanted the album to project what I want to say to the public—and I think it does just that."

Indeed it did: the self-titled album didn't set the charts on fire, but it did attract the attention of discerning music buyers who heard the real magic in Phyllis's voice on songs like "Loving You—Losing You," a Thom Bell composition that became a Top 40 R&B hit; "No One Could Love You More," from the pen of Skip Scarborough of "Can't Hide Love" fame; "Deliver the Love," an Onaje Allen Gumbs collaboration; and "The Night Bird Gets the Love," which Phyllis said, "is a pretty unique example of racial harmony—it was written by a Muslim and a Jew!" *Phyllis Hyman* also contained a beautiful interpretation of "I Don't Want to Lose You," a song the Spinners had recorded for a 1975 album, and Phyllis's husband Larry's "Beautiful Man of Mine."

The record had already hit the streets by the time Phyllis and I did our first interview in 1977, so she'd already had a taste of the work involved in promoting a record. She found the experience stimulating rather than burdensome: "I've always subscribed to the belief that your public is the most important thing of all. Going to stores and so on has opened that up to me even more, what with so many records out there. You realize that when people pick up your album, it's really something—they have so much to choose from, that it's an honor. It just reinforces my belief that you can't take your public for granted."

Even though Phyllis had yet to experience any mass recognition when we spoke, she'd been around long enough to know about some of the potential pitfalls that came with being deeply entrenched in the music industry. I was impressed with her insight into what might lie ahead on the crazy pathway to success. Years later she would find herself dealing head-on with the self-same challenges that she was describing: "Entertainers are human beings . . . susceptible to everything that everyone has to deal with. I've always tried to just be myself, stay regular, because I can't deal with that whole ego thing. Plus, through the years, I've learned that there are other things happening in people's lives besides their careers. In other words," she confided, "it's dangerous to allow your whole life to revolve around that. You've got to be able to do other things besides singing, entertaining, whatever. To me, making records is a bonus, a blessing, and I'm truly grateful for that opportunity. And I'm realistic enough to know that nothing is guaranteed. . . . I want to put back into everything what I've taken out. And I really can't complain about the way the world is treating me right now—it's been good to me, and I want to continue to do very best for everyone." Our first conversation went so well in fact that, as neighbors, we agreed to stay in touch.

I'd shared with Phyllis and Larry, who had been present for the interview, that I'd been writing some songs myself and that I'd even done a demo. When I wondered if Phyllis and Larry would mind giving me their critique on what I'd done, they agreed to do it. When I stopped by a few weeks later, I sensed a little tension between the couple but Phyllis was gracious, so I presented my tape. Although Larry seemed to really get into it, Phyllis insisted on talking after hearing just a few bars. I assumed that she didn't care too much for what she'd heard. On the other hand, Larry was enthusiastic about what he'd heard and encouraged me to pursue my musical ambitions while continuing my career as a journalist.

I never found out what Phyllis thought of the music I'd done, but she

300

did show some neighborly support when I invited her to my rehearsal with a band I'd put together. Steve Hyman, my keyboard player, who bore the same last name as Phyllis, was a sho'nuff, get-down-with-the-spirit, sanctified gospel keyboard player. He was excited about meeting her, convinced that they must be related in some way or other, likely cousins. Phyllis didn't appreciate his familiarity, and it didn't help matters that I was in a foul mood with most of the musicians, spending most of the rehearsal cussing them out and being a diva myself! Phyllis, who left before the rehearsal was over, told me a few days later that she didn't think I'd acted very professionally. She also decided to read me! "I don't know about some of those guys you have hanging around you," she said, making what I figured was an oblique reference to her male namesake. "I think they're only around you because you're in the music business. I'm telling you, David, I know how these guys operate. Don't think they really like you, they're just trying to get ahead. . . . "

I wasn't happy with what she said. I felt that Phyllis had overstepped her bounds, that she and I didn't enjoy the level of friendship that warranted her comments. I wasn't privy to whoever Phyllis hung out with so I didn't feel she had any right to talk about my friends, even though I know her comments likely derived from a genuine concern for my welfare and well-being.

When Phyllis and I sat down for our next *Blues & Soul* interview in 1980, she'd been through a number of changes. Buddah had folded, and her contract had been taken over by Arista Records, which was distributing the label toward the end of its existence. Tracks she'd recorded that were intended for a second Buddah album were used for a first Arista LP, and label head Clive Davis wanted to take her in another direction. He wanted her to work with pop superstar Barry Manilow, who was hot off success with then-new Arista signing Dionne Warwick. Manilow had given Dionne her first platinum album and two Grammy Award-winning hits, "I'll Never Love This Way Again" and "Déjà Vu," and Davis thought the writer/producer, and hitmaker in his own right, could do the same for Phyllis. As it turned out the team did only one song together. "Somewhere in My Lifetime" became the title track for the LP and, surprisingly, a Top 20 R&B hit that didn't get a showing on the pop charts!

When Phyllis and I sat down together at the beginning of 1980, she pointed out that the record "did all right, but it was more of a turntable hit than a seller." Sensing that she might need to make a record that would appeal to a core R&B audience, Davis gave the green light for Phyllis to work with James Mtume and Reggie Lucas. The two former members of Miles Davis's band had enjoyed success as the songwriters on the Roberta Flack and Donny Hathaway smash, "The Closer I Get to You" and had also formed a futuristic funk'n'soul band known as Mtume. They'd also been working with a young Stephanie Mills, fresh out of her role as Dorothy in the Broadway hit musical *The Wiz* and ready for some chart action. Mtume and Lucas—who would later gain fame as the producer behind Madonna's earliest hits—had delivered a gold album for Mills and a crossover hit with "Whatcha Gonna Do With My Lovin'"; Arista president Davis and renowned executive Larkin Arnold, a new hire at Arista, were both hoping they could work some magic with Phyllis.

I'd befriended James and Reggie after we did an interview for *Blues & Soul* in 1978, and it wasn't unusual for me to stop by a session or two at Sigma Sound, just a few blocks from my midtown-Manhattan abode. At James's invitation, I came by when they were finishing a song with Phyllis, who was happy to see me. She was putting the finishing touches on "You Know How to Love Me," a danceable, funky groove that would end up being her second biggest hit for Arista. The relatively long, seven-minute-plus song called for Phyllis to sing and hold a note that extended over several bars. As was their usual practice as producers, James and Reggie kept insisting that Phyllis repeat the note until they were satisfied. After about four or five takes on the exact same musical passage, Phyllis was getting mad! "I'm not singing this fucking thing anymore!" she yelled through the recording booth. James tried to appease her: "C'mon, Phyllis, I know you got one more great one in there. . . ." "Fuck, man, I can't sing this shit anymore," she responded.

James pushed: "I promise, this will be the last one," and probably out of rage and frustration, Phyllis sang the hell out of the phrase. "That's it! I'm outta here," she shrieked. "If that ain't it, too fuckin' bad! You'll have to work with what you got!" she said with a menacing glare. "Phyllis, it's cool," James replied, trying to calm her down. "Come on and hear it!" We all listened, and it sounded incredible. But Phyllis had to have the last word: "Look, motherfucker, it's okay, but just as well you got that one on tape because I'm through. See ya later!" I don't know if she left right then and there because I was ready to head home, smiling to myself because I knew I'd heard what sounded like Phyllis's first big, big hit.

"You Know How to Love Me" was released in October, 1979, and spent seven months on the R&B charts, more time than any other Hyman hit record would. There wasn't much pop response, but the dance crowd loved it. Phyllis finally had a real breakthrough on black radio. Forgetting all the angst of the recording session that had produced her biggest hit, Phyllis was positively elated. "["You Know How to Love Me"] has come right on time—it's definitely given me more recognition and acceptance, and I'm not complaining about that," she told me when we did our 1980 interview. During the preceding months, Phyllis had toured with a variety of different artists, including Peabo Bryson, Gino Vanelli, and Grover Washington Jr., and at the time we spoke she was working with the O'Jays. The variety of audiences she'd performed before augured well for the future, but Phyllis was cognizant that she wasn't easily categorized: ". . . I do have a loyal R&B audience that I want to maintain because they've been the ones who have supported me all the way through . . . [although] it's nice to think that I can go across the board."

Phyllis said she really enjoyed uptempo tracks like "You Know How to Love Me" even though her audiences primarily enjoyed her on slower material. ". . . I find that people really react to my ballad material and see me as an interpreter. I'd like to be that one entertainer who can bridge the gap. . . . No one's ever really done that totally— be able to include a jazz-oriented tune along with pop . . . and funky material all in one package." Even aside from her own records, Phyllis's guest spots with jazz saxophonist Pharaoh Sanders on his Arista album *Love Will Find a Way* and on the soundtrack for the film *The Fish That Saved Pittsburgh* had received approval and acclaim. Her phrasing skills, her ability to evoke emotion, and her way with a lyric were earning her much praise among critics and fans alike.

Fortunately, "You Know How to Love Me" gave the Hyman career a real boost. But she admitted in our 1980 conversation that she hadn't made an all-out commitment to her recording career. It didn't help that she and Larry were splitting up, or that she was less than comfortable with the people at Arista who had in essence inherited her from Buddah. But she also knew that she could have done more to take her career to the next level: "I guess I haven't been centered enough about it. . . . I didn't get into the business till a little later in life than most people do, and I've always said that I kinda fell into it. Now I'm taking it very seriously, so I'm determined that it will work for me. All I wanted to do was just be a singer but I see now that it takes a whole lot more . . . it's a lot of hard work, planning, strategy, and so on. I think up to this point, I may not have put forth all the effort to make it happen totally because maybe I had a fear of getting too big and that's made me a little laid back. . . . I've determined that since I am in this business, I might as well work at it the same way I've worked at everything else I've done."

Over the years, I came to understand that Phyllis had a real fear of major success: she felt that gaining full mainstream exposure would also reveal that she wasn't as great as other people thought she was. A decade passed before I heard her utter words that suggested that she'd never fully accepted her own vocal skills, but back in 1980 she wasn't letting on. Rather, she was putting her best foot forward, making a more determined effort to attain greater visibility: ". . . I guess I've been guilty of underplaying all I could do for myself in my career. But that's going out the window now. I want people to see me for all the things I can do, and I want that to happen in such a way that I have a universal audience."

The opportunity to expand her career horizons came more quickly than Phyllis had expected. Up against singer Marilyn McCoo and singer/actress Leslie Uggams for the role of Etta in the hit Broadway musical *Sophisticated Ladies*, Phyllis won. The musical was based on the works of the legendary Duke Ellington and had opened to rave reviews in Philadelphia and Washington, DC, before opening on Broadway in February, 1981. The role was a major challenge for Phyllis, and in a conversation with *Blues & Soul* editor John Abbey, she said, "It all came at the right time. I wanted a break from the record industry and the whole concert business was in something of a slump anyway. I had just undergone a nationwide tour and truthfully, it hadn't resulted in any real record sales. . . . Naturally, I enjoy playing for the people and that in itself is a good reason to tour. But everything about the industry was in a slump so this was a tremendous opportunity for me to elevate my career."

After the initial excitement of opening night, Phyllis was having an increasingly tough time doing the show, which went on to earn her a Tony Award nomination. I remember catching up with her for lunch on one matinee day and she was frazzled, frantic, nervy, and a little irritated. She admitted that being on Broadway had become a real chore, that she couldn't wait either for the show to complete its run or for her contract to be up, whichever came first. I'd seen the show myself and thoroughly enjoyed it. I'd been captivated by her readings of such time-honored Ellington standards as "I Got It Bad and That Ain't Good" and "In a Sentimental Mood," and in spite of her own reservations about the toll the show was taking on her, Phyllis was in fine form vocally, and her performance was superb.

Even though Phyllis was having misgivings about the wear and tear of daily shows, she admitted that *Sophisticated Ladies* had provided a major career boost. As she told *Blues & Soul* editor John Abbey, ". . . I'm really very happy and grateful for the opportunity. I realize how lucky I am to be doing the role. At the time [the producers] were looking for anything but an unknown—and that's what I was in those [Broadway] circles. . . . We've been told that the show is one of the few Broadway musical successes this year so that's made us all feel good." By the time

Phyllis talked with Abbey again in 1983, she'd left the show, and she had a different perspective on what it had meant to her. In retrospect, Phyllis said, "It was simply the best experience I could ever have had. . . . I actually intended to only do the show for one year but I ended up doing it for two-and-a-half years. And the more I did it, the better I enjoyed it. Being an improvisational type singer, I was able to get more and more into the songs. . . . It all became so addictive and the longer I stayed, the more dedicated I became to the Ellington name."

Since Phyllis had been complaining so bitterly about the rigors of doing Broadway, I had to admit to some surprise when I read how Phyllis had eventually adjusted to the regimen of working six days a week on the same stage. ". . . The theater gets in your blood and I'd love to be able to do more in the future," she told John Abbey in the summer of 1983, adding that, aside from the exposure through key national television appearances on "The Tonight Show with Johnny Carson" and "The Mike Douglas Show," her stint on Broadway had provided some personal gains. As she explained, "It gave me tremendous confidence and I feel freer to take chances now than I did before. But the biggest benefit is that I learned discipline! I was never late for concerts or anything like that —but I would sometimes be a few minutes late for meetings and appointments. But in the theater, you can't be late at all. It simply doesn't exist! [Yes] during the time I was in the show, I gave it 100 percent of my loyalty and spent just about every waking hour on it. . . ."

Somehow, between shows, Phyllis had managed to squeeze in recording sessions for two albums during the course of the two years she spent in the musical. Her 1981 release, *Can't We Fall in Love Again*, reunited her with Norman Connors who produced the bulk of the album including the title track, a powerhouse duet with Michael Henderson that became Phyllis's first and only Top 10 R&B during the five years she was with Arista. Chuck Jackson, not the 1960s singer but the musical partner of Marvin Yancy, with whom he'd produced Natalie Cole's 1970s hits, was responsible for additional production work on several of the tracks with Connors as well as for producing a couple of tracks by himself. The results were a mixed bag. The album contained some brilliant moments, such as the emotionally powerful "Just Another Face in the Crowd"; the superb "The Love Too Good to Last," a Burt Bacharach-Carole Bayer Sager-Peter Allen tune that the Pointer Sisters had also recorded; Ashford & Simpson's perky "I Ain't Askin'"; and "The Sunshine in My Life," one of the last songs Phyllis had written with ex-husband Larry Alexander. However, tracks like "You Sure Look Good to Me"; "Don't Tell Me, Tell Her"; and a pretty dreadful, disco-driven, obvious rip-off of Michael Jackson's "Don't Stop Til You Get Enough" entitled "Tonight, You and Me" were pretty dire and seemed unworthy of Phyllis's commanding vocal style.

Arista hoped that pairing Phyllis with Philly music master Thom Bell might provide a better musical synthesis since she'd done so well interpreting such Bell-penned tunes as "Betcha By Golly Wow" and "Loving You—Losing You." She'd also worked with him on the soundtrack for the film *The Fish That Saved Pittsburgh*, and the combination looked like a musical winner. In fact, Phyllis did a fine job on tunes like the gritty "Your Move, My Heart," the melodic "Let Somebody Love You," and a wonderful Bell tune, "Just Me and You."

But in the true Arista tradition of wanting surefire hit singles, label executives had decided that Phyllis needed to work with drummer/artist-turned-producer Narada Michael Walden to come up with music that was more chart-friendly. Thus, the balance of what would be Phyllis's fourth Arista album was done with Walden: "Riding the Tiger," the first single, was another attempt to cast Phyllis as a dance diva; while it squeaked into the R&B Top 30, it was far from being her best work! The album contained some better moments, such as "Why Did You Turn Me On," but overall, the album, entitled *Goddess of Love*, had an uneven quality to it that was reflected in its mediocre chart performance.

Three more years would pass before Phyllis's name would grace the charts again. Fortunately, she kept busy. She'd expressed a strong desire to do commercials, telling John Abbey in a 1981 *Blues & Soul* interview, "I've done a lot of jingle work and I enjoy it so much more than the record business. . . . I'll tell you—if I could get the amount of work that Patti Austin gets in jingles, I'd *retire* from the record business! I'd just make albums for the sheer fun of it and for the people. . . . Everyone in the jingle business seems so happy and that's what is missing in the record industry." By 1983 Phyllis was jingling away! She could be heard on commercials for Burger King, Sasson Jeans, and Clairol hair products.

Phyllis's contract with Arista was finally over, but fortunately she'd built a strong enough audience base so she could perform on a consistent basis. She loved playing small, intimate nightclubs. Jazz joints were her favorite spots, she said. "Where there are only two or three hundred people and I can feel completely relaxed . . . above all else, where I can touch people! I can feed off of them! That's how I get off. In fact, I just played at the Blues Alley is Washington, DC, and I loved every minute of it. . . . You see, that's where I come from. The small clubs are my background and that makes me different from quite a lot of the recording artists these days. In a lot of cases, they come from the recording studio. But if it's pure satisfaction, let me play a dirty, smokey jazz joint any time!"

Phyllis also frequently appeared on shows with R&B favorites the Whispers; I remember seeing her name on a marquee with the group during a visit to Atlantic City. She also made a guest appearance on the group's 1984 LP, *So Good*, and while negotiating a new record deal, Phyllis could be heard on albums by a variety of artists, including Barry Manilow, McCoy Tyner, Joe Sample, and the Four Tops.

The idea of Phyllis singing on other artists' records while she was carefully choosing her next recording home was part of a calculated strategy that Glenda Gracia and Sydney Francis, two Philadelphia attorneys, came up with. They began to manage Phyllis after she left *Sophisticated Ladies*. Together the team seemed attuned to the special attention that their chief client required. (Eventually Gracia dealt with Phyllis herself when Francis moved to Florida.) Not that everything was easy: in the wake of Phyllis's breakup with Larry, she was emotionally raw—although she'd found a new love by the time she spoke to John Abbey in the summer of 1983. "I live, breathe, think and eat music but I am happy because my mate truly understands me. I feel relaxed with him because he's the first man I have ever known—*ever!*—who has no hang-ups about my job. . . . You see, all of the career success is fine but it doesn't mean an awful lot unless you've got someone to share it with. I don't hang out anymore and it's meant an end to all of my bad habits. Except for one—I still love eating!"

While Phyllis was making light of her addiction to food back in 1983, her weight would become a major issue that would dog her pretty much for the rest of her life. This was symptomatic of much deeper problems that were connected with self-esteem and self-love. In 1991 Phyllis was comfortable enough with me to talk openly about how she'd felt about herself for so long: "I haven't been happy for the past twenty-five years. I've been through a lot of therapy, and I discovered that I'd been playing the game of life, smiling on the outside. . . . "

Even though I'd known Phyllis for ten years when we got together in 1987 to talk about her new contract with Philadelphia International Records (PIR), the legendary super label that Philly hitmakers Kenny Gamble and Leon Huff owned, I had no idea that she'd been dealing with so many personal challenges. She was still "smiling on the outside" when we hooked up at her hotel after she'd finished taping "The Tonight Show with Johnny Carson." She was upbeat, seemingly happy, and, as ever, blunt and candid about matters related to her career. A few more years would pass before she would be as honest about the more private aspects of her life.

As it was, Phyllis really did have plenty to smile about as we talked for the *Blues & Soul* cover story. After signing with PIR, Phyllis had made what many would ultimately consider her best album. *Living All Alone* was a true masterpiece. The songs seemed tailor-made for her: the wistful, atmospheric title track that seemed to echo a personal sentiment Phyllis could relate to, body and soul; the beautiful "Old Friend," the album's first hit single, a meaningful song that was one of the last compositions penned by Linda Creed with longtime writing partner Thom Bell just before Creed succumbed to cancer; "You Just Don't Know," a brilliant cut that became a staple in the Hyman repertoire and a constant quiet storm radio favorite; and a pair of great tunes from Philly producer Nick Martinelli, "Ain't You Had Enough Love" and "Screamin' at the Moon." And for good measure, Phyllis co-produced a strong version of Bobby Caldwell's "What You Won't Do for Love" (a song that she frequently performed live) with Terry Burrus, a key member of her road band. Thom Bell was involved with production on four of the songs, two of which he did with Kenny Gamble, while Philly producer/arranger/musician/artist Dexter Wansel and PIR staff producer Reggie Griffin did one each.

All in all, Phyllis's return to the marketplace was triumphant, and she was happy about the whole thing. "First thing is, *I'm glad I waited!*" was her opening salvo on why she hadn't signed a new deal immediately after leaving Arista in 1983. "I definitely think this is the best album I've done since my very first one for Buddah because, like that first one, it reflects Phyllis Hyman—not what producers think I am or should be musically." She continued, "most of the records in between have been fragmented; they've had great moments but no consistency. I can be fully responsible for this one—this is definitely *my* record!"

The opportunity to work with PIR fulfilled yet another dream: ". . . I loved the idea of working with a black-owned record company. When you consider the millions of dollars that black artists generate and the pitifully small number of black-owned companies in the business, it seems to me that we owe it to the community to work with each other at every opportunity." I was initially surprised to hear Phyllis make this statement because I'd never thought too much about how she dealt with the issues that surrounded being an African American in the entertainment industry. By the time we finished our interview, it was clear that she had strong feelings about the importance of economic power for African Americans. "I'm going to be going out on a lecture tour of major black colleges throughout the States to talk about this whole business of black people getting into the music industry. It's very important to me that we support each other, and I don't think that happens nearly enough for my liking. We should hire black lawyers, black accountants, black business managers—and I plan to bring a list of them with me on this lecture tour so when people ask, 'What do I do to be famous?" or how to get into this business, I have people I can refer them to."

Four years later, I was thrilled to have Phyllis as a participant on an industry panel at the first gathering of the International Association of African-American Music (IAAAM). I was moderating the panel, which was open to the public. James Mtume, Gary Byrd, and Phyllis, among others, were discussing the importance of international exposure for African-American artists. Phyllis made some valid observations and comments on how she'd benefited from visiting Europe, cultivating a loyal following there even though initially it meant taking a cut in pay. Indeed, she'd performed for the first time in the U.K. in early 1987, and the reaction had been incredible. British audiences went nuts for her, as a *Blues & Soul* review noted, ". . . Phyllis made a dramatic spotlight entrance from within a darkened stage and immediately secured a rapport with the audience comprising largely longtime fans and sophisticates who have been waiting some years for the lady to visit these shores."

Phyllis might have visited Britain earlier in her career, but international exposure hadn't been a prime factor during her years with Arista Records. Our 1987 interview was an opportunity for Phyllis to express—passionately—how she felt about the five years she was with the label: "Firstly, I came to be with the label because of the takeover of Buddah back in 1977. So I didn't have much choice in the matter. Then, I'd say I was pretty much overlooked or ignored, and no one paid much attention to what I was doing. There were some nice records but I'd say 70 percent of the time, being with the company was a nightmare. . . . A lot of the Arista records weren't really me; they were other people's ideas of what I should do. . . ."

In the aftermath of her experience with Arista, Phyllis questioned whether she wanted to record at all: ". . . There was a six-month period where I figured I could do fine if I never made another record again. Fortunately, I've always been a hustler—I'm not one of those artists who sit back and wait for someone to do something for me. I get out there and make things happen. So I managed to work consistently for all the years in between deals and kept myself busy with doing commercials and endorsing cosmetics, activities like that." She'd started her own company, Command Performance Inc., and proudly stated, "My company is solvent, and I did that without a record deal! I think it's very important to be totally involved in my career and not leave the decisions up to others."

Phyllis had started to divide her time between New York and Philadelphia in 1984, primarily because of the relationship she'd mentioned in her 1983 conversation with John Abbey for *Blues & Soul*. She didn't say whether the relationship was still going on, but apparently spending more time in Philly had proven beneficial since her managers Glenda Gracia and Sydney Francis were there, as was PIR, her new recording home.

When I left the interview, I got the sense that Phyllis was happier than she'd been in a while. She finally felt she had the support she needed from a record company, and the public was responding well to her music. Even without a new release in three years, she'd taken advantage of a fan base that she'd built from her early records with Norman Connors. Like a few other 1970s female artists, including Angela Bofill, Randy Crawford, and Patti Austin, Phyllis had attracted an audience that liked jazz and R&B, and her stint in *Sophisticated Ladies* hadn't hurt. Although she'd never had any pop success, Phyllis had managed to earn a decent living and maintain herself, irrespective of the charts. And that was something she could justifiably be proud of.

Some time after the release of *Living All Alone*, I saw Phyllis in concert at the Greek Theater in Los Angeles. She was amazing. Her voice sounded as clear as a bell, ringing out through the air; it was truly spellbinding. I remember quite vividly how dry ice had created clouds of steam as Phyllis sang "Living All Alone," and the effect was unforgettable. She was in her element. Devoting one portion of the show to responding to audience requests, she obliged by singing snippets of everything the excited crowd yelled out to her. "Oops, I'm not sure I remember that one!" she joked, as someone asked for a little-known album cut. She tried it nonetheless, singing a cappella, enchanting the audience with the purity of her tone.

Backstage, after the show, however, it was a different story. I found her surrounded by a whole bunch of cronies, and I felt decidedly uncomfortable. I wanted to tell her how much I loved the show, and I tried to communicate that but Phyllis was abrupt and, I could tell, under the influence. She had a drink in her hand and was being loud and somewhat obnoxious. "Yeah, right!" she sneered as people told her how great the show had been. I made a hasty exit. It was hard reconciling the onstage performer who had been so magnificent with the brassy, impolite woman I encountered afterward.

Four years later, our paths crossed again. And it was quite an event when they did. Phyllis and I had seen each other at the IAAAM celebration and then a few months later in Los Angeles when she was performing at the Wiltern Theater and celebrating the release of her second PIR album, *The Prime of My Life*. The show itself had been interesting: Phyllis was on the bill with Will Downing, who had been a good friend of mine for many years. For whatever reason, Phyllis decided to parade around the auditorium while Will was singing. As always, she was wearing a large hat and with her towering physical presence, she was hardly invisible. Some members of the audience were obviously distracted from watching Will by the opportunity to say hello to the star of the show. After a few minutes, Phyllis and a small entourage headed outside. When she spotted me in the audience, she invited me to join her. I reluctantly got up, not wishing to appear rude, and went with Phyllis as she posed outside the theater's marquee while one of her buddies took a photograph! I hurriedly returned to my seat, embarrassed and a little puzzled by her behavior.

The situation didn't improve when it came time for Phyllis to hit the stage. She hadn't yet learned the songs on the new album, so, inexplicably, a member of her entourage brought out a music stand complete with sheet music every time she got ready to sing one of the new tunes! It would have made sense just to leave the music stand there. The constant back-and-forth was irritating, and the mere fact that Phyllis hadn't familiarized herself with the material made for a disjointed evening. After the show, Zoo Records, then the new distributor for PIR, hosted a brief press reception for Phyllis, and she was cordial if not altogether enthused about the whole event.

A few days later, I met with Phyllis for another interview. Because I knew her personally, we'd agreed to meet one evening at her West Hollywood hotel. After checking with Phyllis, I took along a friend who had written some songs for different recording artists, forgetting that back in 1977, she'd warned me about some of my "friends." Once we got to her room, we found Phyllis sprawled out on the bed, watching television. She asked if I minded if she watched the end of the program she'd gotten so engrossed in, and I asked if there was another television around so I could watch an episode of the program "Dynasty"! She sent me packing to her road manager's room. I'd been there only five minutes when the telephone rang. It was Phyllis. She was furious. Apparently, Peter had felt "comfortable" enough to get on the bed next to her and had started talking to her about his songs! "You better get down here fast so we can do this interview!" she fumed. Needless to say, the interview was uncomfortable for both of us, and to my horror, my friend occasionally interjected his thoughts, opinions, and comments.

The next morning I called Phyllis to apologize. She listened, but she was still annoyed. "David, don't ever bring anyone with you when we're doing anything," she said. "I mean, I couldn't believe that guy. He didn't even know me, and he acted like we were best buddies. I think from now on, it would be better for both of us if you come alone to anything we do from now on." I agreed, feeling embarrassed that I'd subjected her to such behavior.

Even though our conversation had taken place under less-than-desirable circumstances, it was very revealing. Phyllis was in a self-confessional mode and for the first time in our relationship, she wanted to talk about some of the problems she'd been facing away from the spotlight. "I probably had a reputation," she said. "My mouth could be very deadly, and I could curse you out and [I'd] feel okay about it. I didn't know any better. Now that all feels very ugly, and I've discovered I have a choice in how I deal with people. . . . I was a very insecure person, suffering from low self-esteem. I acted my way through my life, through my career. I guess things came to a head when I reached a really low point last year. That's why [the title track of the album] "Prime of My Life" says a whole lot to me: I feel like I've arrived. I'm more comfortable with me, with what I'm doing, with who I am."

The most shocking revelation for me was when Phyllis shared how she related to her own talent and ability as a singer. She revealed, "Up until five years ago, I didn't listen that much to myself. Now I've learned to appreciate my voice and my talent in a way that I didn't before. It's funny because people's descriptions of me didn't mean that much to me. When people would say they loved my voice, I'd wonder, 'Why are you moved?' Now I'm beginning to understand how people can be turned on by my singing. I'm starting to appreciate my talent, and I feel a whole lot less uptight. I'd say now I understand the spiritual, the emotional, and the physical aspects of my voice. I think people can sense that when they see me perform these days. I've been told that people can feel a lot more love and calm coming from me. . . ."

Phyllis revealed to me that she'd been through a "personal transformation—spiritually, emotionally, mentally, and musically. I'm really excited about getting on that stage and making people smile and making a dollar at the same time. I guess I never thought about how grateful I should be, how appreciative for all the people who've bought my records and come to see my shows. [Yes], I'm much more calm now, and I don't let things bother me the way they used to. . . . I don't take everything so personally, and I try not to get involved with some of the stuff that used to drive me crazy in this business because I don't want to 'go off.' These days, I let other people handle those things so I can concentrate on doing my best in music."

Whatever had happened in Phyllis's life, she'd clearly gone through some spiritual awakening. I would later learn in conversations with others that she'd been diagnosed as clinically depressed and she'd started treatment for her depression. I also knew that she'd been more than a little partial to alcohol. In fact, the final phrase in her list of thanks for the *Prime of My Life* was the saying "God grant me the serenity to accept the things I cannot change, the courage to change the things I can, and the wisdom to know the difference," commonly used in twelve-step programs that deal with alcoholism and other addictions.

The seeming change in Phyllis's attitude brought some immediate rewards. In the fall of 1991 "Don't Wanna Change the World," an uptempo groove track that included a brief rap became Phyllis' first and only No. 1 R&B hit. It was followed by two more Top 10 R&B singles, "Living in Confusion" and "When You Get Right Down to It." I didn't consider *Prime of My Life* to be one of her better efforts, but the album was well received commercially. I liked the honesty of the title track, and "Living in Confusion," the one song that Phyllis had co-written, reeked of authenticity. During our interview, Phyllis had even said, "[It's] a song about me! It's a song about someone who's not being honest with themselves." I admired her veracity, and when I digested all that we'd spoken about, I realized that Phyllis was far more complex than I'd ever imagined. In hindsight, after I looked back on the conversation and acknowledged to myself that divas, just like ordinary people, had many layers of "stuff" to deal with. And, most likely, the burden of dealing with some of those inner struggles was made even greater by her being a public figure.

Phyllis and I did one more interview together a few months after "Don't Wanna Change the World" had hit the top of the charts. Zoo Records had hired me to write what is known as a "canned feature," an article that can be mass-circulated to newspapers and magazines to reprint in the absence of a one-on-one interview with the artist in question. Although I didn't know it then, this would be the last time Phyllis and I would ever see each other.

The interview was scheduled for 10 A.M. at a meeting place a good thirty-plus minutes from my house. I realized at about 9:20 A.M. that I wasn't going to be on time. I called Phyllis, expecting her to be understanding. She snapped back at me, "Well, shit, get here as quickly as you can!" I was surprised at her reaction but figured she'd be cool by the time I got there. When I called from the lobby, she commanded, "Well, come up!" The tone in her voice was just as off as it had been when I'd spoken to her earlier. When I entered the room, I found Phyllis in her night attire, still in bed, glued to the television. "Hi!" she said coldly. "Look, I want to watch this program. Can we talk after it's finished?" By this stage in my own career, my level of patience with demanding divas had reached a low point. "Well, Phyllis, I guess . . . but I do have to be out of here in about an hour. I mean, I know I'm late, and I'm sorry . . . but. . . ." "All right, whatever," she shot back. I left her to watch the program for a few minutes, and she made idle chitchat, finally sitting up in the bed and deeming that it was time to talk, for real. "Okay, let's get on with it," she yawned.

As it turned out, the interview went fine. Phyllis expressed how happy she was to have finally gotten a real hit record, a No. 1 single, but she was concerned that she hadn't been able to successfully maintain a diet. That seemed to be her main preoccupation, and she didn't know how she was going to deal with it. "I know I'm a food junkie," she confessed, "but it's hard, man. I've been cleaning up a lot of things in my life, and it's just not easy giving up the food, you know. . . ."Afterward, Phyllis gave me a warm hug and a big smile, and we parted friends. If I remember well, we even reminisced a little about how long we'd known each other. It had been fifteen years, during which we'd both been through many peaks and valleys, personally and professionally, and I thought she was reaching a turning point in her career. Sure, she was still battling the weight problem, but overall she seemed happy.

I was wrong. But I had no way of knowing that when I read, with much amusement, an interview Phyllis did with Jeff Lorez for *Blues & Soul* in the spring of 1992. She was obviously in a rare mood that day and spent a good deal of time talking about love, relationships—and sex. "For years, I'd be depressed because my relationships were going wrong or because I didn't have a boyfriend. I thought I needed somebody to make me happy, but my problem was myself. I wasn't happy with myself, so how could I make a relationship work? . . . I'm a lot more confident than I was. . . . Now I realize I don't actually need a man in my life to make me happy. I actually had a one year celibacy mission!"

Lorez couldn't resist probing more, asking if she'd missed sex. She laughed, "Let's just say I didn't have any physical human contact for a year but the electricity bills were paid!" Lorez didn't quite comprehend, so Phyllis was her usual frank self: "[I used] a vibrator, Jeff! And you can print that . . . I don't care! I mean, masturbation is no big deal. Everybody does it! There's too much emphasis put on sex in a relationship and when that happens, they're not going to work out. You have to bring two whole people to the table—to that relationship—for it to work. That was always my problem. When I was younger, I was a lustful person, but emotionally, I needed to be stronger. I needed to believe in myself."

No one knows where that belief went on Friday, June 30, 1995. Phyllis had been due to perform at the famed Apollo Theater in Harlem with her good friends the Whispers. Two days after she committed suicide with an overdose of pills in her 56th Street apartment, a New York radio station opened its telephone lines. One of the callers was a friend who had known Phyllis for twenty years. He recounted how she'd confided in him that Friday, the day before her forty-fifth birthday, would be her last show. He initially thought she meant she was quitting the music business, but when he realized that she was contemplating her own death, he tried to dissuade her. Phyllis wasn't having it. "You choose to be here. I don't," she'd told him before angrily hanging up the telephone. He called her back to try and reason, but again Phyllis didn't want to hear what he had to say. He had resolved to bring some of her friends together at the Apollo to offer her what was obviously some much-needed support. It was too late.

For a myriad of reasons best known to herself, Phyllis couldn't stand the pain of living any longer. Perhaps she couldn't handle beginning to work through the deep issues and challenges she was facing in her personal journey. It was obvious that Phyllis had begun to work on those issues from the conversations we had a few years before. I knew from my own life experience that working on my inner self wasn't necessarily an easy task. I sensed that beneath Phyllis's bravado, the brash exterior was a supersensitive little girl who just wanted to know that she was all right just the way she was. It didn't matter how much others told her she was great—Phyllis needed to know that for herself. She also needed to know that, even without the superstardom, she was deeply appreciated, respected, and loved not only for her gift but also for who she was.

PIR released an album of material that was in various stages of completion late in 1995. It was called *I Refuse to Be Lonely.* I listened to it just once in order to write the bio that would accompany it. It took three years for me to put on the CD and revisit Phyllis Hyman's music, which I finally did with the Hip-O reissue of *One on One* and what I now consider to be her best album ever, a PIR release entitled *Forever With You.* Rather than dwell on the sadness of her departure from this life, I basked in the beauty of her voice, that wonderfully rich, totally distinctive sound, full, passionate—and so soulful. Just like my old friend, who remains forever with me in spirit.

ROB

FLA

quie

ERTA
CK
t fire

An Atlantic Records
publicity still of
Roberta Flack

Long before I ever met Roberta Flack, I'd heard the scuttlebutt. She was "difficult," "temperamental," and "moody"—all in all, a bitch. I even told her what I'd heard when we did our first interview for *Blues & Soul* in the spring of 1978 at her spacious West Side apartment in Manhattan. Fixing me some tea, she laughed when I shared with her what I'd been led to expect from conversations with other journalists. Over the years, Roberta and I would get to know each other and develop a certain closeness. I never saw the bitchiness. But I did discover that she was a woman of many moods. By 1994 when I wrote the liner notes for *Roberta* her last Atlantic album, I considered her probably one of only a couple of the divas covered in this book to be a friend, in the everyday sense of the word. But a strange and lengthy silence from that year to this left me in a state of wonder and surprise.

As I referenced in those 1994 liner notes, Roberta is one of those entertainers who is hardly ever mentioned in the same breath as high-profile women like Aretha, Patti, Gladys, Dionne, and Diana. Maybe the reason is that she has never had an outrageous persona. Or that her music is too pop-flavored. Or she is thought of as "too serious." This fact might or might not be by design: she and I've never had that conversation, nor have I seen anything in print that reveals how she views herself in relation to the other soulful legends. I do know that when she first read my notes, praising her accomplishments, her artistry, and her character, she had to turn away because the tears were flowing freely as she took in my comments. The seeming change in my relationship with her puzzles me. But then who knows what goes on in the hearts and minds of divas, let alone mere mortals.

Pre-diva, Roberta Flack's own mortal beginnings go back to Asheville, North Carolina, where she was born in February, 1939. A 1972 profile of Roberta in *Blues & Soul* outlined much of her early history. She came from a musical family in which her mother played the church organ and her father the piano in a style she called "very primitive Art Tatum." A younger brother also played the piano, and Roberta was naturally gifted with the ability to play by ear by the time she was four, an ability she shared with another North Carolinian with whom she would be compared at the outset of her career, the good Dr. Nina Simone.

The Flack family moved initially to Richmond, Virginia, and then to Arlington when Roberta was around five. In a 1997 bio, she noted the role the church had played in her musical development. According to the bio, "The local AME Zion Church gave everyone the opportunity to get out of the house but Roberta recalls, the music 'didn't have the raunchy, wide-open, free, spontaneous, full-of-life thing that you could hear at the Baptist church down the street.' Whenever she could, she'd sneak over there to hear such gospel luminaries as Mahalia Jackson and Sam Cooke with the Soul Stirrers."

By the age of nine, Roberta had started taking piano lessons, and listened to a wide range of popular music that included R&B, jazz, blues, and pop. When she and I spoke in 1994, she mentioned how she used to listen to her father's old 78 records, and how memories of that time had inspired her to record "I Don't Care Who Knows (Baby I'm Yours)," which Buddy and Ella Johnson first did in the 1940s, and Billy Eckstine's "Cottage for Sale," which was a hit in 1945, when Roberta could barely reach the piano.

Roberta developed a strong interest in classical music and in 1952, she won second-place honors with her performance of a Scarlatti sonata in a statewide contest for black students. Her musical aptitude was such that Roberta was offered, and naturally accepted, a scholarship to prestigious Howard University in Washington, DC, two years later. Within a year, according to the 1997 bio, "she was conducting her sorority's vocal quartet; was accompanying pop, jazz, and opera singers; had changed her major from piano to voice; and was assisting the school's choir conductor. To earn extra money, she also taught privately and [still living in Arlington], she played the organ at her parents' church. . . ."

Roberta switched her major to music education and became the first black student teacher at an all-white school near Chevy Chase, Maryland. By the time she graduated from Howard at the age of nineteen, she'd already directed a production of *Aida*, earning a standing ovation from the faculty after her final-exam recital. Although she began graduate studies in music, the sudden death of Roberta's father meant she had to leave school and return home to begin teaching to support herself.

Life was moving fast for the young Roberta, who was only a year or so out of her teens when she found herself in Farmville, North Carolina, a town she described as "very segregated, very backward," earning a mere $2,800 a year teaching students English and music. Her 1997 bio states, "The frustration of teaching basic grammar to high school students—some of whom were older than she—was nearly outweighed by the small triumphs of exposing music to the school's 1,300 students. When the year was over, Roberta returned to Washington where she held teaching posts at several junior high schools over the next four years." As she stated in 1997, "I found myself unable to teach music. How was I supposed to teach them to sing the national anthem when they couldn't read it?"

While ending her stint as a teacher, Roberta began focusing on her own musical career and landed a gig at the swanky Tivoli Club in Washington, DC, where she served as an accompanist for opera singers. During intermission she sang a wonderful mixture of music that included blues, jazz, folk, traditional spirituals, and pop standards and played on an old upright piano. Before she could blink, Roberta had been hired to perform at the 1520 Club.

According to the 1972 *Blues & Soul* article, Henry Jaffe, owner of Henry's Pub, which was located on Capitol Hill, gave Roberta a regular spot at Mr. Henry's Downstairs. Her 1997 bio states, "the upstairs was constructed especially for her, with its unforgettable church pew setting. People like Burt Bacharach, Al Hibbler, Carmen McRae, Eddie Harris, Woody Allen, Bill Cosby, Ramsey Lewis, and Johnny Mathis were in regular attendance. She would often share the stage and the piano stool with them, and even found herself playing with Liberace one night."

Entering the picture was keyboardist extraordinaire Les McCann. In the liner notes for her first of just fourteen albums she recorded for Atlantic Records over a period of twenty-five years, McCann recalled how he was playing in the summer of 1968, he arrived a day early with the specific intention of going to see the young woman he'd heard so much about. She was doing a benefit, and McCann managed to find a seat in the packed-to-capacity club. "It was a good thing that I found a seat before she took her place at the piano and sang her first note because my knees would never have made it standing," he stated in the notes for her 1969 debut album. "Her voice touched, tapped, trapped and kicked every emotion I've ever known. I laughed, cried and screamed for more. . . . When she sang a love song, I was in love, we all were in love. . . ." Roberta's ability to convey emotion with an almost understated passion and quiet but heartfelt subtlety would single her out as one of the most popular artists of the 1970s and early 1980s. And the combination of heat and calm, fire and tenderness would mark practically all of Roberta's recordings from 1969 on.

The next night, McCann, himself newly signed to Atlantic, was on the telephone to his producer at the label, Joel Dorn. When Les called him, he insisted that Dorn check Roberta out. Les and a friend, Victor Rykken, had taped a performance of Roberta's at Mr. Henry's that contained the jazz standard "All the Way." This tape convinced Dorn to investigate further. In 1991 that original recording was issued on a Les McCann collection, entitled *Les Is More*, released on the Night label through Virgin Records. Hearing twenty-nine-year-old Roberta in the setting where she'd honed her craft and first gained a measure of public recognition is incredible. Even back then in 1968, her voice had real power, her phrasing was right on time, and her piano playing was deliberate, never overpowering.

Dorn needed little convincing. Out of a repertoire of some 600 songs, Roberta selected forty-two to perform for the young Atlantic producer, a feat she accomplished in just three hours. The ink was barely dry when Roberta Flack was sitting at the piano at RCA's Manhattan studios, cutting no fewer than thirty-nine demos! The Atlantic Records logs show the amazing musical range she covered in a matter of hours, everything from Sam Cooke's "A Change Is Gonna Come," to Oscar Brown Jr.'s "Afro-Blue," and from Leonard Cohen's "Suzanne," to Burt Bacharach and Hal David's "A House Is Not a Home." She also performed Cole Porter's "Love for Sale," Marvin Gaye and Tammi Terrell's "Ain't No Mountain High Enough," and Gene McDaniels's "Compared to What," a tune that would be Les McCann's first charted single with jazz saxman Eddie Harris in the early months of 1970. Roberta's diversity was simply stunning.

After sifting through the songs, she and producer Dorn chose six of the tunes she'd performed during her demo session and added two more: an Ewan McColl song that literally would change the course of Roberta's career entitled "The First Time Ever I Saw Your Face," and the haunting "Ballad of the Sad Young Men," from a short-lived 1959 Broadway musical *The Nervous Set*, recorded by Johnny Mathis in 1963. This song dealt with the plight of gay men forced undercover long before it was more acceptable to openly declare their homosexuality. Roberta performed the song in concert in January, 1973, at London's Royal Albert Hall. It was unquestionably one of the most beautiful and poignant performances on an outstanding night, and one that stayed with me personally for many, many years.

Working with a trio that consisted of John "Bucky" Pizzarelli on guitar,

Ron Carter on bass, and Ray Lucas on drums, Roberta recorded the eight songs that composed her 1969 debut album, *First Take*, over three nights at Atlantic's studios in February of that year. The result was a wonderfully eclectic mix of material: the traditional spiritual "I Told Jesus," which Nina Simone had recorded some years earlier as "If He Changed My Name"; Leonard Cohen's "Hey, That's No Way to Say Goodbye"; the marvelous, evocative "Angelitos Negros"; and a pair of songs co-written with Donny Hathaway, a musical genius Roberta had met during her years at Howard University. "Tryin' Times," written with Leroy Hutson, one of Hathaway's former college roommates, was a brilliant commentary on a rapidly changing society caught up in social, civil, economic, political, and personal turmoil. Close to thirty years later in her 1997 bio, Roberta recalls the sessions as having "a very naive and beautiful approach. . . . I was comfortable with the music because I had worked on all these songs for all the years I had worked at Mr. Henry's."

It would take a while for the general public to catch up. *First Take* finally made its debut on the nation's charts some six months after its release in the June, 1969; a first single coupled "Compared to What" with "That's No Way to Say Goodbye." But Roberta was no easy sell as an instant chartmaker. Her music couldn't be easily reduced to a standard two-and-half-minute, radio-friendly 45 single—and besides, she wasn't an artist that could be easily categorized. She certainly wasn't straight-up R&B or hardcore soul, although she sang with plenty of soulful feeling. She wasn't a folk singer, although she was clearly at home with music made acoustically. She wasn't an ordinary pop singer by its most narrow definition, a commercial hitmaker. She wasn't a jazz performer, since her singing style didn't include the vocal gymnastics usually associated with performers of that genre, although the broad range of material she chose put her closest to the eclectic Nina Simone.

This was funny because Roberta said Nina had certainly been an influence on her during her club days in Washington, DC. When Roberta and I met in 1978, she told the story of how Nina had developed almost a phobia about her, threatening to blow up Atlantic Records after they signed Roberta to the label. Roberta had appeared on a British television special, and there was such a strong degree of Afro-centricity to her performance that, as a die-hard Simone follower (who had been running her fan club from 1965 to 1969), I was truly annoyed; I thought that Roberta was simply copying Nina's style, manner, and attitude.

Roberta herself mentioned Nina's name among those she was being compared to in the 1972 *Blues & Soul* article. The uncredited writer of the piece said, "She has . . . been labeled a jazz singer and a folk singer who is also at home in a rhythm and blues context." Roberta admitted, "I've been told I sound like Nina Simone, Nancy Wilson, Odetta, Barbra Streisand, Dionne Warwick, even Mahalia Jackson. If everybody said I sounded like one person, I'd worry. But when they say I sound like them all, I know I've got my own style." Even back then, when her recording career was in its relative infancy, Roberta didn't want was to be pigeon-holed. "I want to be a singer, not a black singer," she stated in 1972. "I *am* black. I grew up in a lower-middle-class black home. I think black is beautiful but there is so much gorgeous music in the world that has nothing to do with black."

But expressing black pride and dignity was a significant part of Roberta's persona. In April, 1971, *Blues & Soul* reporter Anita Fassman wrote about her performance during "Black Culture Week" at the University of Miami. Ironically, during Roberta's version of a Nina Simone composition she made a telling comment: "Telling it like it was during 'To Be Young, Gifted and Black,' Miss Flack reminisced about growing up in a section of Arlington, Virginia . . . where she wore Sears & Roebuck organdies, plastic (not patent) leather shoes and had her hair 'pressed' using 'half a jar of Royal Crown.' With a proud smile and Afro waving, adding, 'Times have changed, haven't they?' she sang, 'My great joy today is that I'm proud to say I'm young, gifted and black . . . and that's where it's at!'"

Where it was at for Roberta in late 1969 and early 1970 was the recording studio. Aside from a collaboration with buddy Les McCann for his Atlantic LP *Comment*, she was busy beginning work for what would be her second album. Appropriately entitled *Chapter Two*, the album was produced by Joel Dorn and the brilliant saxophonist King Curtis, a fellow Atlantic artist. Donny Hathaway was featured prominently on the album as an arranger and keyboard player, contributing the unforgettable "Gone Away," a song he'd written with Leroy Hutson and the legendary Curtis Mayfield.

Completed in April, 1970, and released four months later, *Chapter Two* included another heady musical mix, ranging from Bob Dylan's "Just Like a Woman," to Jim Webb's "Do What You Gotta Do." Buffy Saint-Marie's timeless "Until It's Time for You to Go" preceded a strident reading of "The Impossible Dream," but the true gems on the album were "Reverend Lee," a wry, biting piece about the battle between the temptations of the flesh and the salvation of the soul from the pen of the very talented Gene McDaniels; and "Business Goes on as Usual," a song about the effects of war that was particularly relevant as the U.S. became increasingly embroiled in the conflict in Vietnam.

It was evident that the executives at Atlantic were treating Roberta as a creative artist rather than as a guaranteed hitmaker. And true to the times—and long before the corporate thinking of the 1980s and 1990s rendered artist development a thing of the past—the company was willing to hang in there with her. The notion was that each album would build upon its predecessor, as key television appearances, concerts, and word-of-mouth could take an artist to a decent and acceptable sales level, without the pressure of a hit record.

Roberta would be fortunate through much of her recording career: almost until the end of the 1980s, she would never feel any pressure to deliver a hit and yet she would have five major hit pop and R&B singles between 1972 and 1977. As would be the case with so many of her contemporaries, she eventually had to deal with music industry's going corporate. For years, though, her relationship with Ahmet Ertegun, one of Atlantic's co-founders, allowed her a certain leeway and prestige. Over time, Roberta would end up dealing with others whose understanding of her art was relatively nonexistent and whose main interest and emphasis were generating profit for their corporate owners.

But back in 1970, the music business was all about making beautiful music, and *Chapter Two* was a wonderful showcase for an artist who was rapidly gaining a reputation as one of the most talented newcomers to arrive on the scene in a long time. Roberta had appeared more frequently than any other musical guest on "The David Frost Show"—a total of sixteen times, leading to a place in *The Guinness Book of World Records*—and had been seen on "The Merv Griffin Show," "The Tonight Show"; and a Bill Cosby television special. The relative success Roberta had gained meant she could afford to move into a new home in Alexandria, Virginia, which, as the 1972 *Blues & Soul* article noted, she shared ". . . with her husband, bass player Steve Novosel and four dogs."

Like so many other divas, Roberta said little about her private life. Only truly devoted fans knew she'd been married, and even fewer knew when the marriage ended. In interviews Roberta would focus entirely on music and on current projects and seldom make any reference to matters of the heart. Whatever might have been happening in her private life at the time, Roberta's career was in its ascendancy as 1971 began. She'd been in and out of the studios a few times, even laying down a seven-minute version of the Leon Russell song "Superstar" in March that remains unreleased to this day, as do recordings of "A House Is Not a Home," the Beatles' "Here, There and Everywhere," Marvin Gaye's "Save the Children," and the Five Stairsteps' 1970 hit, "Ooh Child." However, one recording date in March would have great significance for Roberta: apparently at the suggestion of Atlantic executive Jerry Wexler, who was responsible for signing Aretha Franklin to the label and producing so many of her early hits there, Roberta teamed up with Donny Hathaway for a session to record the Carole King song "You've Got a Friend."

Roberta needed very little convincing. The Chicago-born, St. Louis-raised Donny had met Roberta when they were both attending Howard University, and he'd gone on to work with Curtis Mayfield before he signed with Atlantic in 1970. Donny's aptitude as a keyboard player, composer, arranger, and producer made him one of the most important musical figures in contemporary 1970s R&B, and his role in Roberta's life would supersede that of merely being a collaborator. The two were true, soul-deep friends with an abiding and heartfelt appreciation for each other's musical skills. As such a recording union between the pair was an obvious and natural step, especially since Donny had worked so closely with Roberta on her *Chapter Two* album as an arranger, musician, and songwriting participant.

A few months would pass before the fruits of their first session together would hit the streets. Before that key event, Roberta became an even more frequent visitor to the Atlantic studios, although much of what she recorded in the spring of 1971 would never see the light of day. Most of an April 5 session was never used, nor was a May 24 date, leaving versions of tunes like "I Love You Porgy," "Let It Be," "For Your Precious Love," "Didn't We," Stevie Wonder's "Never Dreamed You'd Leave in Summer," and "She Will Break Your Heart" to languish unreleased in the tape vaults; along with a whole album of eighteen songs recorded at New York's Carnegie Hall.

Another live performance represented an emotional milestone for Roberta. A special "Soul to Soul" concert to mark the fourteenth anniversary of the nation of Ghana's independence was arranged. The show featured Ike and Tina Turner, Eddie Harris and Les McCann, the Staple Singers, the Voices of East Harlem, Wilson Pickett, Santana, Willie Bobo, and Roberta, "who recorded the moving 'Freedom Song' in a dungeon in one of the old slave cellars during her visit there with Les McCann." The whole event, along with various scenes of the artists hanging out in Accra, was captured on film and was shown on both sides of the Atlantic.

Fortunately, Atlantic Records captured the highlights for the 1971 *Soul to Soul* LP release. And when you listen to Roberta's deeply felt recording many years later, it is clear that it is one of the best performances she ever committed to tape. It is simply stunning. No doubt the emotionally charged setting inspired Roberta to go within herself to find the depth of feeling she expresses on the track.

Not too long after her return from Ghana, Roberta was back in the studio to put down more songs for what would be her third LP, and two days after she finished laying down six tracks, Atlantic released her first duet with Donny. "You've Got a Friend" finally gave Roberta her very first chart hit. Atlantic's faith in Roberta's talent had paid off, and the label was rewarded with a hit record on two of its most important artists.

To follow up its initial success, the team went back into Atlantic's studios, and, as was true of much of Roberta's early work at Atlantic, the lineup of musicians was outstanding. For this momentous event, it included guitarist Eric Gale, bassist Chuck Rainey, drummer Bernard Purdie, and master percussionist Ralph MacDonald. More often than not, the studio would be filled with the cream of New York players, such as guitarists David Spinozza and Hugh McCracken, organist Richard Tee, and drummer Ray Lucas. Recording artists in their own right, including drummers Grady Tate and Billy Cobham, and flautists Joe Ferrell and Hubert Laws, were also on other dates Roberta did that year. And she could always count on arrangers like William Eaton—who along with songwriting partner Ralph MacDonald penned Roberta and Donny's biggest hit "Where Is the Love"—or Arif Mardin to provide superb string charts for the sessions. Before "Where Is the Love" would become the third single from the LP, Atlantic released the team's soulful version of the Righteous Brothers' 1960s hit "You've Lost That Lovin' Feelin'" in October, just a couple of months after the sessions for the album ended with the wonderful instrumental "Mood," a Flack composition that featured Roberta on acoustic piano and Donny on electric keyboard.

The entire *Roberta Flack & Donny Hathaway* album, finally released in the spring of 1972, was magnificent. The duo's cover of "I (Who Have Nothing)" was chilling, the spiritual "Come Ye Disconsolate" was a fine tribute to both artists' church roots, and the Flack/Hathaway collaboration with songwriter Charles Mann on "Be Real Black for Me" was an amazing tour de force that rang true for many members of the audiences both artists had attracted. With Roberta on piano, Donny's ever-so soulful solo vocal on the standard "For All We Know" would forever more link him with the song, particularly among the primarily African-American record buyers who came to know and love his work.

As "You've Lost That Lovin' Feelin'" was finally ending its chart run, Atlantic was preparing to release Roberta's third LP, *Quiet Fire*. The critical factor was always the material, and this time around she was revisiting a couple of songs that had been longtime personal favorites.

For example, songwriter Van McCoy's "Sweet Bitter Love," a marvelous tune Aretha Franklin originally recorded toward the end of her years at Columbia Records, featured Roberta on piano and vocals with just a string section. She also took this approach on a reworking of the Shirelles' 1960 smash, "Will You Still Love Me Tomorrow." Roberta's version of this Carole King/Gerry Goffin-penned classic became the album's first single.

Another 1960 hit, the R&B chestnut "Let them Talk," had first been recorded by Little Willie John. As always Roberta added her own special magic to it, as she did to Simon and Garfunkel's "Bridge Over Troubled Water." In a rather interesting move, Roberta used Cissy Houston, the former leader of the Sweet Inspirations and background vocalist extraordinaire—and who had worked with and become good buddies with Aretha—for the track, along with the boys' choir from Cissy's Newark, New Jersey, church.

Roberta also tackled the Bee Gees' "To Love Somebody," which had given her good "friend" Nina Simone an international hit in 1968. Under Roberta's care, the song received a deadly slow, ponderous reading, which was sufficiently different from the Simone treatment to avoid any kind of comparison. Nina was apparently somewhat miffed at Roberta's rise to popularity—witness her outburst at a 1974 New York concert when she yelled, "I'm not singing no more. . . . You've got Roberta Flack. . . . What more do you want?" when the audience asked for an encore. Nina would have killed "Go Up Moses," an amazing five-minute, African-flavored, pulsating, percussive opus that Roberta had co-written with producer Joel Dorn and the Reverend Jesse Jackson. Simone would also have done a good job on "Sunday and Sister Jones," another epic from Gene McDaniels, who seemed to understand the kind of storytelling lyric that registered so well with Roberta.

Roberta's career seemed to be moving in the right direction when something strange happened. "The First Time Ever I Saw Your Face," one of the tracks from her first Atlantic album, was used in the Clint Eastwood movie *Play Misty for Me*, and as the film began to take off, the song suddenly took on a life of its own. Atlantic rushed it out as a single and, just three years after she'd recorded it, Roberta found herself sitting on top of the pop charts! The song went on to win two Grammy Awards, "Record of the Year" and "Song of the Year," and the sudden burst of interest in Roberta's back catalog resulted in gold status for her first three albums.

Atlantic wasted no time in releasing the Roberta Flack/Donny Hathaway project just as "The First Time Ever I Saw Your Face" reached the No. 1 spot on the charts and followed it up with the single "Where Is the Love," which became the duo's first R&B chart topper and a Top 5 pop smash. Within weeks, Washington, DC, proclaimed a special "Roberta Flack Day," and dedicated a whole weekend of celebrations to her, which ended with a forty-five-minute concert at the Lincoln Memorial. A month later, Roberta and partner Donny were in concert on the campus of the University of California in Los Angeles. Atlantic captured the momentous event on tape, but unfortunately for fans of both artists, the resultant recordings were never issued.

The Flack fire was also reaching across the Atlantic. In July, 1974, Roberta made her first trip to London and wowed audiences with a simple but stately, powerful performance. During the visit, she taped a concert for BBC-TV's "Sounds for Saturday" show, which *Blues & Soul* editor John Abbey reviewed, noting, "Perhaps the most convincing element to describe her true and total professionalism was the relaxed way she glided from song to song. . . ."

On the show Roberta also threw in "Fine and Mellow," a Billie Holiday classic. It is interesting to note that in a 1994 interview with Jacqueline Springer for *Blues & Soul*, Roberta said, "As human beings we are very affected by what we hear and live with—whether we like it or not—but when I first heard Billie Holiday I couldn't understand what the beauty was! But as I grew older . . . and experienced. . . ." Roberta never finished the thought, but I think that she was referring to realizations she had, in particular about love and relationships. But as usual, she was revealing little personal information, leaving curious people like me to speculate.

As Roberta went back into Manhattan recording studio Regent Sound toward the end of 1972, she was able to look back on a year of tremendous growth and accomplishment. She'd finally broken through to mainstream international recognition and acceptance as a recording artist. Her live performances were drawing critical raves, including a spot on Jesse Jackson's PUSH Expo in Chicago for the "Save the Children" concert, which Motown Records recorded and released. In this show Roberta sang on a segment with Quincy Jones that featured "On a Clear Day You Can See Forever" and "Killer Joe."

The following year, 1973, held plenty of promise. The only thing seemingly missing from the material Roberta had already recorded for a follow-up album to *Quiet Fire* was a song that could give her the kind of across-the-board success she'd enjoyed with "The First Time Ever I Saw Your Face." The story goes that during a plane ride, she was listening to the tape of a song that a relatively unknown singer/songwriter named Lori Lieberman had recorded. Written by Norman Gimbel and Charles

Fox, it supposedly described Lieberman's reaction to a performance by Don McLean of "American Pie" fame.

Roberta's version of "Killing Me Softly With His Song" was released as a single in February, 1973, and within weeks, it had reached the top of the pop charts and No. 2 on the R&B listings. The evocative ballad would eventually become the most recorded tune in the entire Flack catalog; it was covered by everyone from Luther Vandross, who served as a background singer for Roberta in the late 1970s, to new-jack singer Al B. Sure! Hip-hop superstars the Fugees revived the song in 1996 and featured Roberta in their video, which helped introduce her to a whole new generation of record buyers.

Just before the song's release, Roberta performed on a tribute to Duke Ellington, which aired as a CBS television special. She was in the company of Ray Charles, Sammy Davis Jr., Billy Eckstine, Aretha Franklin, Peggy Lee, Sarah Vaughan, Joe Williams, and gospel great Reverend James Cleveland. In many ways Roberta was the baby of the night in terms of the length of time she'd been a recording artist. But this didn't stop her from turning in an awesome version of "Lush Life," or from joining Lee, Vaughan, and Franklin in a blues medley.

Around the same time, Roberta hotfooted her way back to London to appear at the famous Royal Albert Hall with a full orchestra. The evening was magical. She'd brought along keyboardist Richard Tee, bassist Chuck Rainey, and guitarist Cornell Dupree. Her repertoire included tracks from all three Atlantic LPs, along with some songs that were obviously performance staples. These included "Ain't No Mountain High Enough"; "Somewhere"; a couple of Stevie Wonder songs, "Never Dreamed You'd Leave in Summer" and "Superwoman"; and one new tune, "Mister Magic," which would become a key track on her sixth LP, *Feel Like Makin' Love*.

I remember sitting in a box seat at the Royal Albert Hall, thoroughly enraptured by Roberta's voice. The venue was renowned for its great acoustics, and she was the perfect performer for the place; her clear-as-a-bell vocals resonating throughout the domed-shape hall, which traditionally was used for classical concerts. The purity of her sound and her clear enunciation fused with her skill as an emotive musical interpreter, putting Roberta in a class of her own. She wasn't a gospel-edged wailer, but someone who drew from her church training. Roberta was a trained musician who also knew the beauty of spontaneity.

Occasionally, this spontaneity was missing from some of her later 1970s recordings. *Killing Me Softly With His Song* "had its share of Flack gems, notably the songs "No Tears (in the End)," another Ralph

MacDonald collaboration; Leonard Cohen's "Suzanne," an incredible, almost ten-minute-long track; Gene McDaniels's "River"; and Janis Ian's "Jesse," a perennial favorite among Flack aficionados. But a campy, 1940s-like "When You Smile" seemed out of place.

An eighteen-month gap separated Roberta's fifth and sixth Atlantic albums, and from 1975 until the end of her Atlantic run twenty years later, her recording output was less than prolific. Much like one of her favorite singer/songwriters, Stevie Wonder, and unlike her then labelmate Aretha, Roberta would take two, three, and one time even six years in between album releases. It is worth noting that her relationship with Atlantic, as long as it had been, went through many changes. No doubt, the sale of the company to Warner Communications in the mid-1970s affected the musical direction the label was taking. In essence, Atlantic went from being one of the premier homes for black music of all kinds— from jazz, to R&B and soul—to being a haven for rock and pop.

By 1976 the roster of black artists at Atlantic dwindled to a mere handful of names including Roberta, Aretha and the Spinners, who were the main black moneymakers for the record company. To many outside observers, Atlantic had literally and figuratively lost its soul. And with the departure first of the Spinners and then Aretha—an event that seemed unimaginable—Roberta would be the lone holdout, the one black artist to have started her career with the company and still be there!

But rocky roads were ahead for both the label and an artist who had distinguished herself with five consecutive gold albums. Something had most decidedly changed between the release of *Killing Me Softly With His Song* and its successor, *Feel Like Makin' Love*, which finally hit the streets in March, 1975, an astounding *nine* months after the single's emergence as Roberta's very first pop *and* R&B chart topper. It was unheard of for a company to release a single so far ahead of an LP since any money to be made was in album sales. So it was no surprise that *Feel Like Makin' Love*, as strong as it was musically, failed to make the Top 20 and didn't achieve gold status.

Creative control of the recording process had shifted from Joel Dorn, who had been responsible for the first five albums, to Roberta herself. Under the pseudonym "Rubina Flake," a name she reportedly gave herself as a commentary on her own inconsistency or, as people would say, "flakiness," Roberta produced *Feel Like Makin' Love* with assistance from multitalented keyboardist Leon Pendarvis, Ralph MacDonald and songwriting partners William Eaton and Bill Salter, Gene McDaniels; on two standout tracks, "Some Gospel According to Matthew" and "She's Not Blind," musician Stuart Scharf helped out.

Overall the album sounded really strong: "Mr. Magic," originally done as a successful instrumental by saxman Grover Washington Jr., was exceptional. Stevie Wonder contributed "I Can See the Sun in Late December." "Nearly Ev'ry Midnite," written by Pendarvis and McDaniels, was a superb, haunting, bluesy ballad. "Old Heartbreak Top Ten," an untypically perky pop tune, added a degree of lightness, while the title track was just classic Flack. With its gentle, lilting groove, it boasted the kind of lyric most people could easily relate to. And with its memorable melody, the song earned a place of pride in the annals of 1970s contemporary popular music. For the project, "Rubina" had surrounded herself with some of the finest musicians and singers in the business, including Anthony Jackson, Alphonse Mouzon, Idris Muhammad, Bob James, Patti Austin, and Deniece Williams. But even with all the talent Atlantic had to work with, the album didn't fulfill sales expectations, and just one single, "Feelin' That Glow," crept into the Top 100.

I could tell that all wasn't quite well in the Flack camp when I saw one of Roberta's shows at Avery Fisher Hall in New York in the spring of 1976. I was unusually harsh in my critique of the performance, noting in my *Blues & Soul* review, "At a time when most other female performers are going to extraordinary lengths to glamorize themselves . . . Roberta has remained basically the same. No thrills and no frills . . . her total lack of banter, rap . . . with her audience leaves much to be desired. And our main bone of contention comes from the material. It comes off like Roberta Flack's 'Greatest Hits,' predictable, very pleasant but lacking a certain inspiration and fire." Although she performed a couple of new songs, "Why Don't You Move in With Me" and "This Time I'll Be Sweeter," I left the performance uninspired.

A year later, something had happened, and when I went to Smucker's, a wonderfully intimate club in Brooklyn, to see Roberta again, all my previous comments held no sway. The headline for my *Blues & Soul* review of this performance was "Roberta: better than ever . . ." and she was. "It was particularly significant," I reported, "that Ms. Flack should have chosen a nightclub as opposed to a concert hall for this first New York performance in a long while . . . and the obvious flow that developed between the performer and her audience suggests that it might not be a bad idea for her to do some more work in such settings because the effect is dynamic."

Roberta seemed to be in great spirits, working with a hot band that included James Mtume on percussion and Reggie Lucas on guitar, two men who would play a significant role in the months that followed. The song selection included a burning, slow-jam cover of the Spinners' "I'll Be

Around"; a new Gene McDaniels tune, "Why Don't You Move in With Me"; and my favorite, "God Don't Like Ugly," a song written by Gwen Guthrie, a background-singer-turned-songwriter, who would jump-start her own solo career in 1982.

I'd completely changed my viewpoint on Roberta in a year, even commenting on how the public should be more compassionate and patient with its favorite musical heroes: ". . . The whole performance was exhilarating and thoroughly enjoyable and proved once again that we shouldn't become impatient with our artists when they decide to take a hiatus from performing. If it means the kind of show that Roberta Flack put on, then no one should complain!"

In hindsight, I was very glad that I went to see Roberta's new show because she and I finally got to sit down for a *Blues & Soul* interview at the very start of 1978. Atlantic had released the single "25th of Last December" just before the end of 1977 as a prelude to Roberta's seventh album, *Blue Lights in the Basement*. Deejays across the United States were all over "The Closer I Get to You," a song that then-band members James Mtume and Reggie Lucas composed; Roberta did this heartfelt duet with Donny Hathaway, who had been away from the scene for a few years. It was an obvious hit single, and Atlantic obliged by putting it out in February, around the time Roberta and I got together.

The interview session gave me a chance to get answers to some of the many questions I'd pondered over the previous few years. As I made myself comfortable on the massive white sofa opposite a large grand piano in the living room, I asked Roberta about the gap between record releases. "That's quite simple," she explained. "We spent a long time going over material, trying to find the right combination of producers to work with. . . . You know, sometimes it's necessary to leave a project alone to be able to get a proper perspective on it. . . ."

Cognizant of the many changes that had occurred in the music industry over the ten years she'd been recording, Roberta had approached *Blue Lights* from a different viewpoint: ". . . with this particular album, I was really concerned with time . . . because previously, I felt that I could duplicate on record whatever I did in performance . . . . But now I'm hip to the fact that we've had to be more conscious . . . because, frankly, people won't get to hear those mammoth cuts. . . . Sure, that does restrict creativity—I must tell you! Take the cut 'The Closer I Get to You' . . . You should really hear that in its entirety! It's about eight or nine minutes long. . . . If you heard the whole thing, it would really blow your mind because the end is just incredible— the ad-libs and stuff that goes on between us."

Roberta mentioned that her next recording project would be another album with Hathaway: ". . . basically, it will include two or three songs that Donny and I will be doing separately and four or five duets together. After we finish that project, I'll be working on my next solo album. One thing I did learn from this one is that it really isn't good to allow as long a time gap between albums as we did just this last time." In between recordings, Roberta had in fact been a globe-trotter, making her first trip behind what was then the Iron Curtain, to Poland and Yugoslavia, and performing in Jamaica, Australia, New Zealand, and Japan.

Roberta and I discussed a few other matters during the conversation. These topics included her thoughts about honing her skills; she revealed, "I look at it the way a fighter looks at training. You've got to stay in shape, even if you're the greatest, right?". Roberta also explained how she chose material. ". . . I need to be able to relate to a song either through my own experience or through something that I can have empathy with," she said. She also talked about the challenge of being a public personality: ". . . it's so strange the way people see entertainers. They expect you to be dripping with furs all the time. Like one time when I went to a department store and the girl just refused to believe I was me because I wasn't in fur from head to toe! . . . I guess people need to dream and need to have their heroes but at the same time, they should really understand that entertainers are people [too]."

I realized that Roberta might have read my 1976 review because as we completed our warm and friendly chat, she mentioned that she had a new attitude about her performances: ". . . my stage show is going to be more visual. No phony theatrics now! But incorporating some new ideas. I feel a lot looser about music now, more sensuous about it. And I'd like to project some of that 'star' Flack on stage!" As I finally left what had been a good hour-long conversation, I knew that I'd made a connection, that I'd developed a new perspective on a woman whose music I'd been listening to since *First Take*. She certainly wasn't the egomaniac or aloof diva I'd been warned about. In fact, I looked forward to more opportunities to talk with her.

But several years would pass before we would meet again. In the meantime, Roberta's life and career would go through major changes and challenges. True to her word, the gap between albums lessened considerably: the gold album *Blue Lights in the Basement* was followed by a second 1978 release, a self-titled set that would be her least popular album of the decade.

Plans to work with Donny Hathaway were resurrected; however, at this stage in his life, he was dealing with some serious mental-health challenges. After a five-year absence from recording, Donny had returned to work with Roberta on "The Closer I Get to You," and he'd even done a one-off session that resulted in the 1978 Top 20 R&B hit "You Were Meant for Me." With great care and support from Roberta and manager/attorney David Franklin, who had worked with both performers for some time, Donny was coaxed back into the studios to record again. Only two songs were completed: "You Are My Heaven," a song co-written by Stevie Wonder and recording artist Eric Mercury, who at the time was Roberta's constant companion; and "Back Together Again," an Mtume/Lucas composition. The sessions were still ongoing, and on Monday, January 13, 1979, Roberta had dinner at her Manhattan home with Donny and David Franklin. Directly afterward, Hathaway returned to his hotel, the posh Essex House on Central Park South.

I received the call late that night from James Mtume. "Donny Hathaway just killed himself," he said in shock. I was shaken, unable to respond. "What?" I replied. "He jumped out of the 15th-floor window, man. Committed suicide. Listen, I gotta go. I wanted to let you know. I'll talk to you tomorrow." At the age of thirty-three, the father of two daughters, the brilliant music man behind six masterful albums and countless sessions as a superb keyboard player and arranger, and the writer of a six timeless classics, including "Tryin' Times" and "The Ghetto,") was gone. James confided in me that Donny's mental condition had rapidly deteriorated over the years, and in the liner notes for the reissue of *Extensions of a Man*, writer A. Scott Galloway had quoted Donny's widow, Eulalah, as confirming that toward the end of his life, her husband had been "very sick." He was on medication and required constant attention, but he seemed to be in good spirits the night he bade farewell to Roberta at her apartment. He died just a short time afterward. Understandably, she was completely devastated.

In conversations many years later, Roberta would mention to me just how Donny's death had robbed the world of such an amazing talent and in many ways, she felt she'd lost her musical soulmate. In 1984, she told me, ". . . Donny always had that belief, you know, that talent would win out in the end. It's just a shame that he's not around now, especially when the gaps are closing and people are really tuning into black music and respecting black artists on such a wide scale." In 1994, fifteen years after Donny's untimely passing, Roberta told British writer Jacqueline Springer, "He was the best thing: I don't know why he's gone. I was the one who had to identify his body . . . and I can assure you, that was not something I'd care to do again. It was very traumatic. . . ."

A year after Donny's death, Roberta seemed finally able to face the world. She'd produced some new material with Eric Mercury, and the results found their way onto *Roberta Flack Featuring Donny Hathaway*, which was released in March, 1980, and was preceded by the single "You Are My Heaven," a Top 10 R&B hit and surely one of the best sides she and Donny had ever cut. The punchy "Back Together Again" would be the their last release, and the back-to-back hits took Roberta's ninth album to gold status.

Other notable tracks on the LP include "Don't Make Me Wait Too Long," written by Stevie Wonder, and "Only Heaven Can Wait," written by Roberta and Eric. This was one of the tunes that Roberta recorded as a duet with soul stylist Peabo Bryson, who David Franklin also managed. The combination of Roberta and Peabo was powerful, and the two hit the road, recording a live album in the process. Some other studio tracks were added to the final package, which was called *Live and More* and released in December, 1980. The full potential of the Flack/Bryson duo wouldn't be realized until they recorded a second album, this time for Capitol (Peabo's recording affiliation at the time), three years later. *Born to Love* went gold, spearheaded by the beautiful "Tonight, I Celebrate My Love for You," which became a Top 5 R&B and Top 20 pop hit.

In between Roberta's first and second collaborations with Peabo, Roberta had been busy with other projects. She worked on the soundtrack for *Bustin' Loose*, a Richard Pryor movie. The album contained a Luther Vandross original, "You Stopped Loving Me," which became a Top 40 R&B hit in 1981. The following year, Roberta recorded the title track for the hit movie *Making Love*, a stunning ballad Burt Bacharach and Carole Bayer Sager wrote and produced. Three months later, in June, 1982, Atlantic released the album *I'm the One*, marking the beginning of Roberta's seven-year hiatus from working with the label.

In a 1984 interview Roberta and I did for *Blues & Soul*, she said that she felt the album hadn't reached its full potential. Fortunately, Roberta had rebounded with her second duet album with Peabo Bryson, and she'd also been busy working with one of her neighbors, Yoko Ono, on a tribute album to the late John Lennon. Roberta contributed a reggae-flavored treatment of the song "Goodbye Sadness," which became one of the standouts on the 1984 Casablanca LP *Every Man Has a Woman*.

Unusual as our telephone interview was, it was focused not around the release of any new product but on some advance publicity for an impending visit to the U.K. Our conversation was more like a chance for us to catch up. Roberta talked about the impact Tina Turner was having:

"I'm really inspired by the way she's just knocked everyone over. . . . She's just come on in and turned it out!" She was ready to talk about how she related to her own career, too: "I'm in this business because I want to reach people. It's not just about the artistic satisfaction I get as a professional musician. . . . I'm not particularly interested in waiting till I've been dead for a few years for people to find out I had talent." the interview went well, and since Roberta didn't have a new album out, the powers that be at *Blues & Soul* gave her the center spread rather than the front cover, which went to Stephanie Mills.

I went to see Roberta's concert at the Beverly theater later in 1984 and naturally, I wanted to go backstage to say hello. Her then-publicist, the late Fred Murphy, a good pal from my New York days when we'd been fellow journalists together, ushered me back. But he cautioned that she was mad with me! I was taken aback. "Why?" I asked incredulously. "I'll let Roberta tell you," he said with a twinkling grin.

"I can't believe you did that, David! I mean, you've known me for years, and I've been around for years. . . I can't believe you put Stephanie Mills on the cover of *Blues & Soul*!" I was embarrassed but had no reason to be. "Roberta, I'm really sorry. I had nothing to do with it, believe me. It's the editor of *Blues & Soul* who decides on that, honestly. And I thought it was going to be a cover story, too," I pleaded. "Well, I wouldn't have done the interview if I'd known it wasn't going to be the cover story," she replied before walking away.

So I finally got to see the other side of Roberta that I'd heard so much about, and it wasn't a pretty sight. I could understand her point completely. She was just making her point with the wrong guy, but it seemed nothing I said would appease her. I left feeling uncomfortable about the situation and relayed her upset to the editor of *Blues & Soul* magazine, who simply countered with a comment about Stephanie's then-hit status.

Five years would pass before Roberta and I talked again. She didn't release any new albums during this time. Atlantic Records had been through a number of executive changes during that period and for whatever reason, Roberta hadn't been inclined to finish a project until she was good and ready. Years later I would understand from talking with those in the know that she had a very tight contract with Atlantic. Unlike so many of her contemporaries, she had the final say on many aspects of her recording status with the label.

Roberta and I finally spoke in November, 1988, on the eve of the release of *Oasis*, an eleven-track album that clearly was her best work in the 1980s. Roberta had taken the reins as executive producer; had co-written four songs with, among others, her longtime friend and famous poet Maya Angelou, Brenda Russell, and bassist/producer Marcus Miller; and worked closely with a bevy of writers and producers, including Quincy Jones, Jerry Hey, Michael Omartian, Barry Miles, Ashford & Simpson, Siedah Garrett, Marvin Hamlisch, and Chaka Khan's brother Mark Stevens.

The result was spectacular. Roberta was understandably excited about the project and explained why it had taken five years to finish the new album: "If you try to churn out records on schedule, it just doesn't work. You can't rush the creative process. . . I've always had the same philosophy since I began recording nineteen years ago and that means taking my time. . . . There has to be a love affair between my mind, my heart, the melody and lyrics. I'm always listening to songs to see what gets the adrenalin going, what pulls me in." Roberta continued, "There is a method to this madness. If you can get just one song, just one tune that becomes a classic, it's worth waiting for. I understand how the record business works: it's a very thin line between the artistic and commercial aspects. You have a company putting up hundreds and thousands of dollars and you want to give them the best you can."

Fortunately, *Oasis* benefited from the presence of Sylvia Rhone as a key executive at Atlantic. Sylvia, who I'd first met back in 1975 when she was a secretary at Buddah Records in New York, had risen through the ranks to become the most powerful African-American woman at Atlantic. She made sure that Roberta was rewarded with a No. 1 R&B single even if the album didn't achieve the kind of sales it warranted.

For her part, Roberta was doing all she could to promote the album, still crisscrossing the globe. She told me with a laugh how her performing schedule could sometimes go out of whack: "I can remember not too long ago, I played a concert in Phoenix, left the next day for Barcelona, played one night there and was back playing in Pennsylvania the next night—but as you get older, it does get to be a little more stressful on the body so I don't do stuff like that anymore!"

Around this time, my relationship with Roberta began to have a more personal flavor. Always known for encouraging others to express themselves artistically, she had no problem listening to some songs I'd written. More than the songs, she was impressed with my smokey, bluesy voice. "Child, you can sing!" she whooped one time when I was visiting with her during a trip to New York. Much to my complete amazement, she even took the time to give me some vocal pointers, explaining to me the importance of finding meaning in a lyric. "Don't throw words away," she advised as I ran through the classic "Bewitched, Bothered and bewildered," before sitting down at the piano in her apartment to dissect my approach to "Strange Mood," one of my own songs. She continually encouraged me to pursue my musical interest as an avocation and couldn't understand my reluctance when I explained that my career as a journalist seemed to conflict with my desire to go full out into music. I treasured the support and warmth that Roberta expressed, and I thought that I'd found one diva, a fellow Aquarian, with whom I could have a genuine friendship.

Roberta and I did two more "official" *Blues & Soul* interviews in the 1990s. The first one was on the occasion of the release of *Set the Night to Music*, a 1991 album that her longtime Atlantic friend Arif Mardin produced. The title track, a duet with British reggae star Maxi Priest, became a Top 10 pop hit, but the rest of the album was a strange mixture of heavily synthesized tracks on an odd mix of songs. It didn't help that Roberta hadn't played keyboards on any of the tracks, which I felt meant that the special Flack musical touch was missing. When I asked her about that in our 1991 *Blues & Soul* interview, she explained, " . . . During the last eleven years, I've moved away from the necessity of doing both singing and playing. For a long time, I used sitting behind the keyboards as a security blanket . . . you're not nearly as distracted as when you have to face the audience. Believe me, it took a lot of courage for me to get up and do that. . . ."

It also took courage for Roberta to put together her 1994 self-titled album, a stunning collection of classic songs that many Flack fans agree was her best effort in many, many years—at least those fans who heard it. Even though the album contained some absolute gems, including covers of Al Green's "Let's Stay Together," Stevie Wonder's "Looking for Another Pure Love," and B.B. King's "The Thrill Is Gone," the heart of the record was her revival of jazz and blues classics like "Prelude to a Kiss," "In a Sentimental Mood," "Cottage for Sale," "Angel Eyes," and "My Romance." To cap it all off the album contained the brilliant original, "You'll Never Know ('Til You Let Go)."

Listening to a rough tape, I volunteered to do liner notes for the collection, and Roberta readily agreed. I ended up getting up out of bed one Sunday morning at 5:20 A.M. and coming up with the title for the piece: "She's Never Left, But Flack Is Back or . . . Way Past Due: When You Gonna Give It Up for the Diva You Forgot to Name . . . Yet Again." It was my contention that Roberta's musical contribution had never been fully appreciated or realized, and I waxed lyrical as I described her as "this musical icon, this American, nay African-American legend, proud, contributory, dignified, yet earthy, this woman with a passion for life, as wonderfully warm and giving as the sun in late December."

Roberta seemed genuinely touched by the notes, and when she performed in Los Angeles at the Greek theater, she dedicated the song "Let's Stay Together" to me with the words, "I love you, David Nathan!"—much to the surprise and amazement of my journalistic colleagues.

I was determined to do all I could to make sure people knew about the album, so in addition to the requisite *Blues & Soul* piece, I did a story for *Billboard* about how so many black pop pioneers were having a tough time getting airplay or, in some cases, new record deals. I mentioned James Ingram, Brenda Russell, Peabo Bryson, Dionne Warwick, Jeffrey Osborne, and Roberta. In keeping with *Billboard* magazine's policy, I was required to get current sales figures on any specific albums I mentioned, and the *Roberta Flack* set got a prominent place in the article. The album hadn't performed well, but I was obligated to supply the sales information, especially after interviewing Atlantic executives who claimed that they were still actively working the album.

After the *Billboard* story appeared in March, 1995, I tried calling Roberta, who I heard from the week after Phyllis Hyman, a good friend of mine, had tragically ended her life. Roberta left a message, I called her back, and she said she'd call me right back. Over a twelve-month period, I must have left seven messages but never heard a word back from Roberta. And whenever she has performed in Los Angeles in recent years, her office hasn't asked if I wanted to see the show. Although Roberta put out a fine Christmas album on Angel, I don't know how she has been doing since she left Atlantic Records in 1997. I saw her perform again at the Greek Theater in the summer of 1998 with Peabo Bryson and was taken a little aback with her Janet Jackson-styled red curls. I hoped we might finally get a chance to see each other in the green room after the show, but she never appeared. Certainly, the fact that she and I haven't spoken in three years in no way impairs my appreciation of her music and the many emotions it has stirred in me through the years. All that I've learned from the silence is that one of the greatest gifts you can bring to any relationship is unconditional love for the other person's essence, beyond personality and outward appearances. As Roberta herself says, "You'll never know 'till you let go!"

AN
BAK

good lov

sv

ITA
KER

e,
weet love

Whell Anita Baker first walked into a room in the relatively small offices that housed Elektra Records back in March, 1986, I expected a six-foot Amazon in her forties or, at the very least, a big-chested church diva, the kind that has people yelling "S-a-a-n-g, girl, s-a-a-n-g!" on Sunday mornings all over the United States. When a bubbly, petite woman in her late twenties, all of five-foot nothing, entered the equally tiny room Elektra had given us to talk in, I thought she was probably a secretary who had come to inform me that the subject of my interview, Anita Baker, was running just a few minutes late. When the woman chirped, "Hi, I'm Anita!" I almost fell over. "Oh," I stumbled, trying to compose myself. "Oh, pleased to meet you!"

Later on in the interview, which I conducted for the now-defunct British magazine *Street Scene*, I confessed that, based on having heard Anita's *Songstress* album but never having seen her perform, I'd formed a mental picture of her that was clearly at odds with the vibrant, young, and relatively tiny, woman I was meeting. She laughed when I told her that I couldn't believe such a big, booming voice could come out of such a small frame. Did anyone else ever have the same reaction? "Yes!" she grinned. "But that voice has been coming out me since I was fifteen, and I really get a kick out of the fact that people expect me to be this huge, big woman."

Neither of us knew that day that Anita would experience the kind of meteoric international fame or that she would be acclaimed as one of the most influential song stylists of the 1980s. Perhaps she hoped for some response from *Rapture*, her groundbreaking first album for Elektra, but she couldn't have imagined that it would go on to sell an astounding six million copies worldwide. She also couldn't have known that the follow-up, *Giving You the Best That I Got*, would sell another three million; that by 1995 she would earn eight Grammy Awards; and that in the world of contemporary music, she was an established, respected artist who could take her place of pride alongside the other divas included here.

Reaching this exalted plateau came with its share of challenges and bad press, and led to Anita's reputation as one of the more "difficult" women to work with in the music business. Over the years, since I first met

Anita, I've heard *all* the stories: yelling at sound people; snappy with airplane stewards; getting furious with record producers, angry with record executives, nasty with managers; and being a bitch to work with and a nightmare in the recording studio. Yes, I've seen or— more correctly—heard Anita Baker when she wasn't "feeling" it and didn't want to be bothered with me. I've seen her getting pissed with a sales assistant in a snooty Beverly Hills department store who looked at her as if she didn't belong there because she wasn't some rich, white bitch. Upon seeing Anita's platinum American Express card, however, that particular sales assistant changed her mind—especially when much to her amazement, it went through for the several hundred dollars Anita was paying for Christmas gifts. I can't defend Anita against all the comments I've heard because I wasn't there when many of these "incidents" occurred.

A fellow Aquarian, Anita, like Roberta Flack, is a woman of many moods. She has an overriding concern for giving her audiences her best, either onstage or on record, and her desire for perfection can cause her to be a pain in the ass for some of the people she has to work with. But I can only speak from my experience. I've hung out with her backstage in DC and Los Angeles and at Grammy and Soul Train Music Award shows, gone shopping with her, sat in her Grosse Pointe kitchen drinking a strawberry smoothie, written one of her tour programs, attempted to write a song with her—and always welcomed our conversations. I know her as a someone who: loves being at home with her husband, Walter, and her two sons; takes the time to pass on essential knowledge to up-and-coming artists; and is never reluctant to give props to other divas, such as Chaka Khan, Aretha Franklin, and Sarah Vaughan, all of whom influenced her. So, forgive me, but I am a little biased.

Undoubtedly possessed of one of the most instantly recognizable voices in contemporary music, Anita has been doing her musical thing for a good quarter of a century even though her recording career only started in 1979. Music has been an essential element in her life since her birth, January 26, 1958, in Toledo, Ohio. Only in recent years has she been willing to say much about her childhood and how she was raised. In a lengthy 1994 interview for *Blues & Soul*, she touched upon the subject when I asked about the inspiration for songs she writes. I didn't expect the answer I got. "I wish I could tell you that I consciously write in a particular way but how I write has to do with being a motherless child. No matter how wonderful the parents God gave me were, part of what I found out . . . when I was having my own children is the effect that being a motherless child had on my entire life," she replied.

346

Anita spent her early life in Detroit with her grandparents and after their death, with her aunt and uncle, Mary and Granville Lewis. "My aunt and uncle raised me like their own . . . and I've talked to everyone—from clergy, philosophers, from one end of the spectrum to the other—and my relationship with my birth mother has affected all that I do, from the way I carry myself to my relationship with my husband. He's come to understand but he used to ask me why he had to love me so hard, why he had to keep demonstrating that he cared. You see, I used to be able to walk away from anything or anyone—and I've always been that way. . . . In fact, until I started dealing with all of this [having my own children], the one thing I couldn't walk away from was *music*. . . ."

Anita's childhood was no walk in the park. "I was always having to make excuses for where my [birth] mother was," she said. She elaborated in 1994: "[It] could have taken me in other directions in my music. . . . I could have gone completely into fantasy-land. I remember, as a child, I always felt drawn to those great gospel songs like "God Will Take Care of You" because I needed to hear that. . . . But all of that early experience in life is what's made me who I am personally and musically and I wouldn't change it for the world. I've come to terms with what's happened and now there's a relationship with my birth mother that one can only have with that person. . . ."

As Anita explained in a 1986 *Street Scene* interview with me, she remembers hearing "Motown, Aretha, Chaka Khan, and jazz stylists like Sarah Vaughan, Ella Fitzgerald and Nancy Wilson" during her formative years, and at age twelve she was singing in a local Baptist church choir. Music seemed like a natural pathway, and in a 1986 interview with Mark Webster for *Blues & Soul*, she recalled the first time she got paid to sing: ". . . I was sixteen and I was playing this club called Henry's Cabaret Lounge—fabulous place! It was like this hole-in-the-wall bar, inner-city Detroit and there was a five-piece rhythm section and we got paid twenty dollars each . . . this first band I was with . . . was Humanity and we were just out of high school . . . I graduated in 1976 . . . and they had been members of the marching band and I was in the choir. . . ."

Not long after this first experience, Anita was playing gigs around Detroit with other local bands when bass player David Washington heard her and invited her down to audition for one of the city's most popular groups. "I had never had to audition before. I never had any problem getting work with groups," she told British writer Steve Bryant in 1986 for a *Blues & Soul* interview, "[although] Chapter 8 was *the* group in the city."

The group, which Washington and guitarist Michael J. Powell formed around 1971, had its genesis as the backing band for the Detroit Emeralds, popular 1970s recording artists. Anita's successful audition—at which she remembers singing "Smokin' Room," a Rufus & Chaka Khan chestnut, and the gospel classic "His Eye Is on the Sparrow—landed her the job.

Chapter 8 spent the next few years playing gigs in and around the Motor City, building a solid reputation for its heady brand of funk and straight-ahead R&B. It was only a matter of time before the group secured a record deal. Veteran record executive Otis Smith signed the group to Ariola, then distributed by Capitol. The group's first self-titled album hit the streets in the fall of 1979 and yielded two R&B chart singles, "Ready for Your Love" and "I Just Want to Be Your Girl."

Even though "I Just Want to Be Your Girl" did poorly on the charts at the time, the tune would go on to become something of a classic among R&B music collectors. Certainly, the song gave listeners a first real taste of Anita's sultry, velvet-toned, smoky alto sound even though it didn't exactly set the world on fire in terms of airplay or sales.

The group did tour, and as Anita recalled in a 1984 interview with *Blues & Soul* editor John Abbey, ". . . We'd worked just about everywhere—from major concert halls to little . . . clubs. I had tried to learn how to work any kind of an audience so I could get a reaction under any circumstances. I feel that the trick is for the artist to get involved in what's happening on stage so that the audience can feel involved, too. . . ."

But Ariola began running into problems with Capitol, and Arista bought the company. The sale didn't bode well for Chapter 8: Otis Smith was no longer with Ariola, and when it came time for the group's contract to be renewed, Arista didn't pick up the option. In 1986, Anita recalled how Arista executives ". . . told me I couldn't sing . . ." and used their opinion of the band's lead vocalist as one of the reasons they didn't renew Chapter 8's contract.

Chastened by the experience, Anita hightailed it back to Detroit. In 1984 she told Abbey what happened: ". . . I worked as a short order cook at first. Then I waited tables at a bar before I finally got a good job with a law firm downtown, as a receptionist. . . . Gradually, I found myself joining what I call the real world. I guess it really took me a full year to get [the music industry] completely out of my system. . . . For the first year or so that I was home, I would never even play the radio—and I didn't even own a stereo!"

After leaving Ariola, Smith took some time off before forming Beverly Glen Records in 1981. His first two signings were veteran soul men Johnnie

Taylor and Bobby Womack, with whom the company achieved considerable success.

Smith remembered Anita's distinctive vocal sound and got her telephone number from one of the members of Chapter 8. "When Otis first called me, I said *No!*" she told Abbey in 1984. "I was hesitant because it had taken me that long to settle in and become a responsible adult! I had a nine-to-five job, an apartment, Blue Cross [health coverage] and paid vacations. I wasn't going to just give it [all] up." Smith apparently offered Anita $10,000 to sign with Beverly Glen, but she was already earning that much from her day job. When he increased the amount, put it all in writing, and sent her an airline ticket, she reconsidered. ". . . Since I was working at a law firm, I had them look over the papers and they said it was fine . . . so I decided to give it a try," she explained.

In October, 1982, Anita moved to Los Angeles, into an apartment that was part of the Oakwood complex in Burbank. Years later, after we got to know each other, I was on my way to see her and told her I might be a few minutes late because I was catching the bus. "You don't drive?" she asked. "Well, when I first got to L.A., I didn't either. What bus do you use?" I told her that the good old 212 was just up the street from me on La Brea. She roared, "That's the same one I used to get when I lived in Burbank! Boy, I went on that 212 more than a few times!"

Once ensconced in Los Angeles, Anita began working on her first album with keyboard player/writer/producer Patrick Moten, who wrote or cowrote almost all the songs on what would be Anita's first solo LP . The only exception was the ultra-soulful "No More Tears," which Michael J. Powell, her former Chapter 8 buddy, had submitted. Beverly Glen spent some money on the album, using the services of noted arrangers Gene Page and Jerry Hey; such musicians as David T. Walker, Craig Cooper, and Paul Jackson; the famed Waters family as background singers; and notable session singers like Phil Perry, Jim Gilstrap, Clydene Jackson, Carmen Twillie, and Bunny Hall.

The result was an album that smoldered with Anita's sensuous, bluesy, mocha-flavored, distinctive vocal style pitted against a clean, smooth rhythm section. Recorded in Burbank and entitled *The Songstress*, the LP was ahead of its time. It was a masterful collection of songs that served as the perfect showcase for what I called "the rich tones, the deep yet warm timbre" of Anita's voice when I did liner notes for the CD Elektra reissued in 1991.

The album contained a number of standouts. "Angel," a superb, moody ballad, was the album's hit, and a Top 5 R&B smash that etched

Anita's voice into the consciousness of soul-music lovers everywhere—and a song that audiences still request, a good ten years after its release. "You're the Best Thing," the mellow "Will You Be Mine," and the wailing "Do You Believe Me" were all fine examples of Anita's ability to blend soul, jazz, and gospel in a way that made her a unique vocalist.

The album didn't happen overnight: Beverly Glen had relatively limited resources and distribution so its popularity spread across the country as R&B stations in different cities picked up on it. Although Anita was getting plenty of airplay in Los Angeles, she didn't have a band at the time the record first hit the streets. She didn't start doing live dates as a soloist until December, 1983, when Frankie Beverly chose her as an opening act for a show in Oakland with his group Maze. In the early part of 1984, Anita performed at the Beverly Theater before a packed house with a band whose line-up included former Rufus members Bobby Watson and Andre Fischer. East Coast dates followed, and by the spring of 1984 Anita had scored four chart hits from her first album, which came close to being a gold record.

In the first *Blues & Soul* interview Anita and I did together in 1986, she explained the response *The Songstress* had generated. "I don't know that anyone was doing the kind of music we included on that album. It was like returning to good ol' soul music, and I think we found that there was still a real audience for it. . . . I had my doubts, and I didn't think it would get any attention. Fortunately, I was wrong and people really got off into it." Of course, some creative issues cropped up, and as Anita mentioned in her second *Blues & Soul* interview in 1986, "I had a big hand in 'The Songstress' but all the creative input I was allowed, I had to fight for and [I] was not given proper credit for it." Nonetheless, the relative success of the album led Anita to believe there would be a second album on Beverly Glen: ". . . I worked solidly off that album for a year but people kept asking me when I was going back in the studios. I'd ask Beverly Glen and nothing happened. I felt stagnant, even though I knew something had to give."

Anita returned to Detroit and stayed there until she got work with the Crusaders back in Los Angeles at which point Sherwin Bash, her newly hired manager, let it be known that Anita was looking for a new deal. According to her comments to British journalist Steve Bryant for *Blues & Soul* in 1986, two companies expressed interest, Capitol and Elektra. Anita and Bash chose Elektra in part because the company was willing to handle the legal hassles that had arisen with Beverly Glen. "We obviously knew it was going to be a rocky road and Elektra was willing to do whatever was needed to secure me as an artist," she told Bryant.

"Also I liked the thought of going over [there]. . . . Starpoint was there, Peabo Bryson, but very few black female artists and they had the time to give us the proper attention we needed. . . ."

Anita was able to secure the right to be the executive producer for her first Elektra album. This was an unusual but, as it would happen, crucial move. It enabled Anita to have complete creative control and literally the last word on how the album would turn out musically. ". . . It was my job to come up with the songs and the producers. So you can imagine that I'm concerned about how people react to it," she told me in March, 1986, for a *Street Scene* article, on the eve of the *Rapture* album's release.

Anita had met with several well-known producers, including Maurice White of Earth, Wind & Fire fame (who mentioned their meeting to me) but, she said, ". . . I felt they were trying to lead me in some musical directions that I wasn't interested in pursuing." In the end, she asked Michael J. Powell, her old friend from Chapter 8, to handle the production for her all-important Elektra debut, with the exception of one track. "No One in the World," a song that Dionne Warwick had previously recorded, was produced by Marti Sharron and Gary Skardina. "Elektra . . . trusted me," she said in 1986. "They told me to go ahead and do some tracks, and they'd listen to what we came up with. I was pretty nervous . . . [and] it was four months into the project before they heard a thing—and they liked what they heard so Michael finished it off."

Elektra executives weren't the only ones who liked what they'd heard. Although the first single, "Watch Your Step," one of the three songs Anita contributed to the LP, made the R&B Top 30, it was the follow-up single that brought her mainstream success. With its languid, sensual groove, "Sweet Love" was an out-and-out smash. One of Anita's collaborative efforts, the song had an instant appeal, and within weeks of its release, it was perched in the nation's Top 10 and firmly entrenched in the upper reaches of the R&B charts. The *Rapture* album, which was released in April, spent an incredible three years on the Hot 200 LP listings, racking up four million domestic sales and, as the Baker magic spread throughout the world, another two million overseas.

There were many theories as to why the album exploded. First off, Anita didn't sound like anyone else on the airwaves. She wasn't the next Aretha, the next Patti, or the new Whitney Houston. Anita was her own woman with a sound that fused jazz and soul with ease, which was demonstrated so well on tracks like her own "Been So Long" and songwriter David Lasley's "You Bring Me Joy." All in all, the songs were strong, well constructed melodically with memorable hook lines. From the perky "Same Ole Love," to the atmospheric "Mystery," you could play the album from start to finish. Nothing jarred, and there were no starts and stops. The album was a solid piece of work, and people loved the fact that they could finally buy a whole album that flowed, rather than a collection of tracks put together by a bunch of different producers in search of hits—which was an increasingly common practice in the world of black music in the 1980s.

But more than anything else, beyond the songs and the fine production, it was Anita's vocals that captivated listeners. There was almost no one she could be compared to other than a "soul-ified" version of jazz great Sarah Vaughan, and certainly Anita hadn't denied the influence of jazz on her. In our interview in 1986, she said, ". . . my aunt has this great collection of Ella Fitzgerald and Sarah Vaughan—some wonderful stuff. If you listen to 'Been So Long' . . . you can get some idea of what I love and no doubt about it, I will get to doing a full-out jazz album at some point."

While it was obvious to music-industry pundits, members of the press, and record buyers alike that Anita was offering something new, she had her own theory as to why *Rapture* had taken off. She told me in a 1989 interview for *Blues & Soul*, "I didn't open *nothing*! Really, I feel as if it was Sade who busted it wide open for the type of music that I do. Why do I say that? Because three years prior to *Rapture*, I was doing the same kind of music and it fell on deaf ears. I know that when *The Songstress* came out, nobody heard it. When Sade came out with music with that jazz overtone, she was reaching people who were tired of the finger snap. I don't think my music would have been as successful, really, if her music hadn't been so well-received."

The British group Sade, which the stunningly beautiful Sade Adu fronted, had, in fact, sold millions of records with *Diamond Life*, its 1984 debut, and *Promise*, its 1985 follow-up. And while Anita's contention had some merit, it was also true to say that her own vocal approach was considerably different from that of her British counterpart. Unwittingly, by virtue of her success with *Rapture*, Anita had music-industry executives clamoring to sign other female vocalists who they thought could bridge the gap between jazz and R&B. Within a year, vocalists Regina Belle and Miki Howard were enjoying success with music that had a similar flavor, and even jazz divas like Dianne Reeves and later Rachelle Ferrell would find the musical climate far more receptive to their brand of fusion.

The success of *Rapture* also brought with it some new challenges for Anita. Before she could blink, she was on the road, initially doing some dates by herself and later that summer, opening as a special guest for legends like Smokey Robinson. The show with the Motown master was at the Greek Theater, and Anita wowed the audience with her warmth and charm. She was obviously having a ball, enjoying her newly found success, and several months later she did an astounding seven-night run at the Beverly Theater in Los Angeles and kicked ass! With an amazing band under the direction of keyboard wiz Bobby Lyle and the soul-searing Perri sisters providing background support, Anita put on a brilliant show. In addition to focusing on material from *Rapture*, she sensibly threw in "No More Tears" and "Angel," a couple of popular items from *The Songstress*, as well as a testifyin' version of the Emotions' classic "Blessed," which would have made a great recording if she'd ever put it on tape.

I can't remember if it was the show at the Greek or the one at the Beverly, but at one of the two Anita went off at the sound man. In between songs she berated whoever it was because she said she couldn't hear herself in the monitor, and basically, she wouldn't go on singing until the problem was fixed. It soon became common knowledge among press people, industry gossips, and even members of her audiences that Anita would give her sound people the business, as if she were never satisfied. The word got around that she was impossible to work with, a perfectionist who could turn into a raging tyrant in a moment. This kind of talk was the stuff from which myths evolved, and over the years further weight would be given to the popular contention that, in the true diva stakes, in regard to both temper tantrums and general disposition, she was vying for first place with the much-maligned Diana Ross!

In a *Blues & Soul* interview Anita and I did a year after *Rapture* began its rapid ascent to the top of the charts, she didn't deny that she'd been having a difficult time. She'd been on the road for almost ten months nonstop, and the mental and emotional wear and tear was beginning to show. As she explained, ". . . I'd have to be honest and say that I really needed to take time off now because I've begun to get a little *weird*! I mean, I've always been a perfectionist and now I feel that I've got something to live up to, something I have to prove. It was almost easier when no one was really watching my career like they do now! So just towards the end of touring, I felt like I had some real pressure on me."

Anita was taking time out to relax in Detroit and didn't expect to hit the road again until the summer of 1987. Satisfied that after a few bumps and bruises, she said, ". . . I've now got the perfect team to work with! It's taken about six months to get to this point and I've been through at least four different sound companies and more than a couple of production managers but I look at it as a process of elimination to get what you want. . . . I'm going to be honest and tell you that it had a lot to do with the right crew. Especially when it comes to the sound. If you don't have the right people supporting you, trying different things to make sure that the quality is great, you can have a real problem."

When Anita and I met up at a Beverly Hills hotel informally a few years later, she explained a little more about the reasoning behind her insistence on getting the best possible sound for her shows: "Look, people pay their hard-earned money to see me. If the sound isn't right, if the lighting isn't right, they don't go home and say, 'I saw Anita Baker and the sound man messed up!' No, they go home and tell their friends, 'I went to see Anita Baker and she sounded awful!' That's why I want the sound, the lighting, the music, my makeup and everything else to be right when I hit that stage!"

Fortunately, as 1987 began, Anita was experiencing some sweet relief from the pressures of performing. During a trip back home to Detroit in January, 1986, she'd met Walter Bridgforth Jr., an IBM marketing executive and real-estate developer. By November, when Anita was back in Detroit to receive the keys to the city, the pair got engaged, and Walter was dealing with Anita's success "just fine—because he knows that I'm a working girl and he relates to me that way. This is a two-income household. I'm real happy to have him in my life. . . ."

I met Walter myself not too long afterward. I was struck by his friendly manner, a certain sensitivity tempered with firmness. He obviously knew that Anita was no stranger to heartbreak, but he brought her the kind of assurance and comfort that made for a strong union. I saw them together several times in different settings—at the Grammy Awards, backstage, briefly at the couple's home in Grosse Pointe—and he was always easy to talk to and obviously aware of my ongoing admiration for his wife's impressive talent.

The impact Anita's music had on me and countless others in 1986 had made for a truly hectic year. Anita had made her first trip to Europe, performing at the Montreux Jazz Festival and in London to rave reviews and packed houses, repeating the success she'd started enjoying at home where she'd filled New York's Radio City Music Hall with adoring fans. She'd been forced to take a crash course on new-found fame. As she told me in 1987 for a *Blues & Soul* article, ". . . People stop me in the shopping malls now and ask for autographs and I don't mind. But I have to be constantly aware of how I dress now and folks have been turning up at my doorstep to say hello and give me tapes that they want me to hear!"

Although Anita had obviously made an adjustment from the years before when only staunch R&B listeners knew her music from her work with Chapter 8 and *The Songstress* album, she was adamant about cherishing those early believers: ". . . I'll never leave my R&B fans because they've been there forever and they'll be there when everyone else has written me off as a 'one hit wonder!' But seriously, I'm always going to be available to my black music fans because they are the base for any black recording artist and I'll never forget that."

As 1987 began, Anita was giving some thought to her next album, but she was in no rush. Although big-name producers were bugging Elektra to work with her, she felt that the team who had worked so well on *Rapture* would do the same for her all-important follow-up project. There was no shortage of songs to check out: "I have bags and bags of tapes to listen to—and I haven't even done any writing myself yet!" she stated in the spring of 1987 during a *Blues & Soul* interview. In reality, aside from a guest appearance with Detroit-based gospel greats the Winans (on the song "Ain't No Need to Worry," which became a Top 20 R&B hit that fall), Anita wouldn't spend enough time in the studio in 1987 to finish her second Elektra album until well into 1988.

In fact, instead of concentrating on the record, Anita spent much of 1987 on the road again because the demand for her performing services was so great. In a revealing interview with Mark Webster at *Blues & Soul* in 1988, just after the release of "Giving You the Best That I Got," the classic chart-topping title track for the new album, Anita expressed her concerns about the record. "You're not hearing the album the way I really want you to," she stated. "[It has] great songs but the wrong mix. . . ." She elaborated further when she and I talked in 1989: ". . . I'm accustomed to doing an album and then taking time to mix it. But everything got messed up, and I didn't feel comfortable about it. . . . With this album, I didn't even know that it was being mastered. We couldn't find [producer] Michael [Powell], and someone in my manager's office told me he was in the studio, mastering the album. I guess that's why I get the reputation for being crazy because I ran right over to the studio and asked them to stop and took my masters and put them in the car!"

Anita had plenty of good reasons to offer for the kind of behavior that had earned her the reputation of being a tough diva to work with. "I know a lot of people don't understand that—why an artist wants to be involved in every aspect—and I'm sorry that they don't understand. But the way I see it, the money that's being spent on my album, that's my money! It comes out of my royalties and all the record company did was lend it to you. Aside from that, I'm the one who has to perform the music for a long time and my ear is so sensitive that every time I hear something that disagrees with me musically, I almost feel physical pain. I feel like when I can't pay attention to every aspect of what happens with an album I'm doing, I'll give the role of executive producer over to someone else."

That said, *Giving You the Best That I Got* went on to sell four-and-half million copies worldwide and reinforced Anita's preeminence as one of the most innovative vocalists in contemporary black music. The moody "Good Love," which acclaimed L.A. songwriter Gary Taylor wrote, was a soulful masterpiece. "Good Enough," one of Anita's collaborations for the album, was a jazz-tinged gem. "Just Because," another No. 1 R&B hit and Top 20 single, and "Lead Me Into Love," a third R&B charted single were fine examples of Anita's skill at finding songs that were a perfect fit for her vocal style, delivery, and range.

In spite of Anita's reservations, the album proved to be a critical and commercial success, and she began including a couple of tunes from it when she hit the road on a much-anticipated tour with Luther Vandross in September, 1988. I was at one of the very first dates in a stadium just outside Washington, DC, to review the show for *Billboard* magazine, and I was greatly anticipating "The Heat" as it was called. In hindsight, the press, the industry, and the promoters should probably have called it "Dead Heat" or "The Fight" because the vibes between the two performers were poor—and bordering on awful.

I'd watched Anita's set, enraptured. She delivered, she sounded great, the band and the musicians were "on," and she ended the show with her just released new hit "Giving You the Best That I Got." I made my way backstage to say hello to her and to her backup group Perri, which I'd befriended through interviews we'd done. I was in the dressing room, laughing, joking, and congratulating Anita on her show when all of a sudden, the dressing room was being closed. "You better get out there!" one of the Perri sisters said. I squeezed through the door only to be told that I couldn't go any farther: a burly security man informed me, "No one can leave until Mr. Vandross is onstage." "Huh?" I shot back incredulously. "But you don't understand, I'm reviewing this show!" He reluctantly let me go to my seat. Rumor had it that Luther had given strict instructions that when he was about to go onstage that Anita's dressing-room area was to be sealed, presumably so they would have no contact. I was shocked! From what I saw, there was no doubt that these two superstars were having a tough time getting along. And when, onstage, Luther said, "Let's give a round of applause for my opening

act, Anita Baker," I knew that it was all-out war!

The final straw occurred when Anita canceled one of the multi-night dates at New York's Madison Square Garden. Of course, each performer would claim in retrospect that the other was responsible for the problems. Regardless of the backstage bitterness, the tour was easily one of the most successful ever conducted by two musical forces in the black-music world. It played before more than a million people and broke all kinds of box-office records.

When Anita was on the road with Luther, most people didn't know that she was pregnant. The stress and strain of the tour no doubt contributed to the miscarriage she suffered in 1989, and in the October, 1991, issue of *Upscale* magazine, she commented, "The good thing that came out of it was that people from all walks of life came forth to express their concern. . . ." Like Anita, Walter, her husband, was naturally devastated. But the couple, who had married on Christmas Eve 1988, was determined to create a family. Although she would endure a second miscarriage in 1991, Anita finally gave birth to a healthy son, Walter Baker Bridgforth, in January, 1993, five years after her marriage.

The years in between were filled with activity, but Anita was determined to take more control of her career choices. "I'll have a less hectic schedule and that's very important," she told me in an extensive *Blues & Soul* interview in the spring of 1989. "I don't think I realized just how much I was pushing myself before and when I had my miscarriage, I realized I should have stopped and sat down and given myself some time." In light of the multi-platinum success of her second Elektra album, Anita was more aware than ever of the pressures of the music business: ". . . I ask myself, how long can I sustain this—how long will it be before people say, 'She only sold a million this year'? I'm asking myself how I'm going to deal with it. It is inevitable—there's always a tapering off, the peaks and valleys—and I just want to keep myself in a place where, when there are valleys, I'm not so upset about [it]. . . . It's a question of realizing that when that happens, it's somebody else's turn and I have to be happy for them. . . . The way this business is, there's no middle ground unless you can take a year and figure out how to do exactly what you want. . . ."

By the time Anita and I talked in 1989, she and Walter had moved into a new home in Grosse Pointe, Michigan, which is about ten miles outside Detroit. She'd chosen the location "because when I was growing up, my grandparents would load up their station wagon and take us for a Christmas drive down Lakeshore [the thoroughfare that runs along Lake St. Clair]." Walter's family had the same tradition, so for the couple the move to the exclusive community had a great deal of symbolism.

Time at the new home gave Anita a chance to think long and hard about what she wanted to do for her next Elektra album. As she'd told Mark Webster at *Blues & Soul* in late 1988, "I'm beginning to feel the third album is the one I can experiment on—do things that aren't part of the package. Those jazz things that I kept talking about for this [second] album I feel I can include on the third. . . . "

During 1989 Anita and I got to spend more time together outside of the usual interview setting. When, she was in Los Angeles at Christmas, we got to hang out while she did some shopping. I remember distinctly asking her what she herself wanted as a gift. She opted for a rhyming dictionary because she intended to get more involved in songwriting for her third Elektra project. A mixup in schedules meant that she and Walter had to delay their flight back home, so she ended up driving me back to my apartment. On the way, I asked if we could stop off at a health-food store, and much to the delight of one of the sales clerks, she came into the store with me to browse for some vitamins.

In between stops, Anita played me roughs of some songs she planned to use for her next album. I was blown away. True to her word, she was going to move into a jazzier direction, and I sat enraptured as we listened to "Love You to the Letter," "Lonely" and a piece of "Fairytales," three songs that would end up on the album *Compositions*. She had another musical idea that she wanted me to check out, an idea for a song that she'd originally planned to produce on British singer Mica Paris. Anita had met Mica during her appearance in Britain at a special Nelson Mandela celebration in May, 1989, at London's giant Wembley Stadium.

For whatever reason the arrangement with Mica never panned out, and Anita was considering finishing off the idea and using it for her own upcoming album. Originally, she hoped to cut a rhythm track. When the musicians didn't have time to squeeze it in, she sent me a rough tape of herself singing at the piano in the first weeks of 1990. She had the basic phrasing for the song and just one line and asked me if I could come up with a lyric! I sweated and labored over it and finally came up with something I felt she'd like. Anita thought the lyric had some good lines, but in the end she had enough material for *Compositions*, so my lyrics were never used. Ultimately, Anita would come up with her own set of words and finish the song as "Wrong Man" on her fourth Elektra album, the 1994 set *Rhythm of Love*.

After this I truly felt that Anita and I'd crossed the line between journalist and interviewee. A certain comfort level existed between us. We laughed about both of us being Aquarians and the various quirks and eccentricities that went along with this horoscope sign. And just when I thought everything was cool . . .

Anita was in town to shoot a video for what would be the first single from *Compositions*, a song called "Talk to Me," which she'd written with Michael Powell and keyboard player Vernon Fails. Earlier in the week, she'd mentioned that I could stop by the video shoot. I left a couple of messages at her hotel in order to find out the time and location. Anita had originally said that Saturday would be a good day for me to check out the shoot, but when Saturday morning rolled around, I still hadn't heard from her. I called the hotel and was connected. "Hi," she answered curtly. "You know what? You're starting to bother me, David!" In all our dealings, I'd never heard that particular tone in her voice, and I was taken aback. "Look, I got your messages. If I wanted you to come by, I would have called you back," she continued.

I felt embarrassed and uncomfortable, and didn't quite know what to say other than that I was sorry. "I'm just under a lot of pressure," she offered as an explanation for her abruptness. "I've got this director on the video who wants to use interracial couples for everything. And I want some black couples. . . . " I listened and reminded her that this was *her* video and she needed to let her voice be heard on the matter. She took heart from my response. Sensitive to the fact that she was dealing with a delicate situation, I excused myself from the call.

That was the first and only time that I experienced the Baker attitude I'd heard all about from others. When I thought about this exchange later, I realized that Anita had a good point. As with any situation in life, you find out where people are coming from by their actions rather than their words. Yes, she'd originally invited me to visit the video shoot but she was entitled to change her mind, and by not calling me back she was sending me a message.

Fortunately, this incident didn't get in the way of our ongoing relationship. When *Compositions* was finally completed, Elektra paid for me to fly to Detroit to do an interview with Anita for *Billboard*. After an initial mixup, the result of a canceled flight, I finally arrived at the hotel in the city where we were supposed to do the interview. I learned that Anita and Walter had left after I didn't show up. I eventually got in touch with Anita through her L.A. publicist and found myself in a taxi going through the Motor City out to Grosse Pointe.

When I finally got to Anita's luxury home, she greeted me at the door. I apologized profusely for the confusion that had disrupted her day. We went out for a walk alongside Lake St. Clair in the clean, fresh air. As we walked, we talked about *Compositions* and how much of it had been cut live, the rhythm section playing as Anita sang, a throwback to the good old days of recording. She seemed really happy with the record, contributing her writing talents to seven of the nine tunes. Of all the albums she'd recorded, this one had a real personal stamp on it, and she was proud of what she'd accomplished with it.

Even though the sales of *Compositions* were dwarfed by the multi-million sales of her first two Elektra albums, the album was an artistic triumph and easily became my own personal favorite Baker recording. I loved the feel of songs like "Whatever It Takes," which she'd cowritten with Gerald Levert and his partner Marc Gordon. "Lonely" was a fine jazzy piece, and "Love You to the Letter" was a gorgeous, late-night torch song, the kind I loved. I couldn't stop playing "No One to Blame" because its lyrics spoke to so many situations I'd been in when I'd seemingly let potential love relationships remain just that—potential! And "Fairytales," a song that Anita had worked on with Nancy Wilson for one of her albums, was a poetic masterpiece, sung with just the right amount of bite and gutsy fervor, a story of unfulfilled expectations that had a universal ring to it.

"Talk to Me" was released in June, 1990, and made it to the Top 3 on the R&B charts, edging its way into the pop Top 50. Maybe it was just too artsy, maybe Anita's personalized phrasing made the lyrics hard to follow. Whatever the problem, I heard people comment that they couldn't understand all that Anita was saying on the song. It wasn't the first time that I'd heard people criticizing her style, claiming that because of her mannered approach she sometimes slurred or muffled her words. I never had a problem with that approach; in fact, I liked the fact that Anita had her own, incomparable style.

Certainly, as Anita's popularity had grown, her jazzy phrasing had made her the butt of some comedians' jokes. Perhaps the funniest reference was one that singer Patti Austin made. On a live GRP album, Patti did a skit on the vocal mannerisms of different artists, and she suggested that Anita and singer/songwriter Michael McDonald might in fact be one and the same person! "You've never seen the two of them together?" she asked the audience present for the recording. "Well, you know why? Because there's only one of them! You ever listen to Anita and then listen to Michael? I'm telling you, they're the same person!" Patti roared as she did a pretty good imitation of Anita's textured sound on a Michael McDonald song!

Another reason for the limited success of *Compositions* was that it might have been too eclectic for mainstream tastes. Nevertheless, this didn't stop Anita from picking up her seventh Grammy Award. And since I'd attended the announcement of the list of Grammy nominees in January, 1991, I called to tell her about it hours later. It seemed that no one had reached her before me, and she yelled out to Walter in disbelief, "Baby, I've got another Grammy nomination! I don't believe it!" She was genuinely happy because the album's slow sales performance had been disappointing, although she found that the public responded well when she did some of the songs during a 1990 tour that crisscrossed the country.

I saw the show at Irvine Meadows, just outside Los Angeles. Anita was better than ever. She genuinely seem to love the contact with the audience. In addition to the obvious hits, she did some of my favorites from *Compositions*, including "Fairytales," which—much to her surprise—got a rousing response. Afterward I went back to see her and watched as she patiently met with thirty winners of a radio contest, smiling, taking photographs, and signing autographs. Walter stood by, unobtrusive yet at the same time protective. The winners came in groups, and in between, she and I made small talk and caught up with each other.

Around the same time, Anita and I did an interview for *Blues & Soul* in which she talked about some of the issues facing black artists. She was typically candid in her comments: "The truth? The record industry is trying to kill R&B! What's happening in black music is the same thing that happened in the forties and fifties when black music was recorded by pop artists. . . . Today, R&B artists are at the forefront of the creative end of music but they are not necessarily getting the benefit of the sales. I want to stress that it's not just black artists who do R&B that I'm talking about. Look at Bonnie Raitt: she's been singing R&B for years but she just got her due last year. . . . I see great artists like Oleta Adams and Lalah Hathaway . . . I see how their records don't get anywhere near the exposure. Then there's someone like Mariah Carey—and this isn't personal about Mariah—who sounds black and she gets every available push while someone who is equally talented can't get arrested."

I assumed that as a multi-million-selling artist, Anita herself wasn't suffering from a similar lack of attention. I was wrong. ". . . I sell the records I do and work as hard as I do and I still have to beg for things that [Elektra artist] Linda Ronstadt doesn't even have to ask for. Again, it's nothing personal against Linda, it's just how this industry still operates. R&B is a much-loved genre throughout the world and it's exploited to the max and that hurts to the core," she explained.

Like few other black artists, Anita was committed to passing on information about the business. So she organized a seminar at a couple of black radio and music-industry conferences as a way of sharing what she called "the nuts and bolts stuff." The seminars included presentations by entertainment-industry accountants and attorneys. "I learned all this stuff the hard way," she confessed. "For instance, with paying people, especially when you're on the road. When my husband came along, he said, 'Where's the payroll checks?' and I said, 'I don't know!' I soon found out that when you're dealing with cash, all kinds of stuff can happen. People can puff up receipts, all kinds of things. . . . You make sure that everything is set up for you to take care of payroll checks yourself. You don't let anybody else have a signature card at the bank so that they can write checks on your account. You see, the attitude in this business is that if you're a creative person, stuff like paying people or dealing with accounts is too difficult for you to handle, that you should just concentrate on being creative. But the truth is you just need a few rules of thumb and some information. . . . I'm hoping that we can continue to do these seminars for people in the business and for just people just getting into it."

Finally off the road from a six-month tour in support of *Compositions*, Anita felt it was time to relax and take stock. She'd decided that her creative partnership with producer Michael J. Powell was pretty much over: ". . . by the time I'm ready to do my next album, I want to be able to come in and play the keyboards, to really do my own production. Michael and I have done some great work together—I love him but it's time to do some other things. I realized that after the last album: it's like we were making two different albums. I wanted to do the whole thing 'live' with musicians and that's not what he had in mind. The feeling between us now is kinda low: it's like my head is at the ceiling creatively and he won't let me out!"

Anita was hoping to turn her attention to doing production work on other artists, but the next few years would be about a more personal kind of production. After her second miscarriage in 1991, she stepped back from any active work in the music industry for a while, making just one exception when she participated in the sessions for Frank Sinatra's bestselling *Duets* project. Singing the standard "Witchcraft" with "Ol' Blue Eyes" was just one of a small handful of special guest spots she'd done over the years. In 1995, she did a duet with singer James Ingram on "When You Love Someone," a song she'd cowritten that was featured in the Billy Crystal/Debra Winger movie *Forget Paris*. Five years earlier, Anita was part of an all-star cast on singer Melba Moore's version of the black-nation anthem, "Lift Every Voice and Sing," along with Stevie Wonder,

Dionne Warwick, Stephanie Mills, Howard Hewett, and others. That same year [1990], she'd done a duet with Hewett, then also an Elektra artist, on the song "When Will It Be." This collaboration gave her a first chance to work with producer Barry Eastmond, known for his work with Freddie Jackson, Billy Ocean, and others. Anita's name also appeared on *Rubaiyat*, a special Elektra twenty-fifth-anniversary collection, singing the Carly Simon classic "You're So Vain"; Anita's cover of this song was produced by Arif Mardin, the man responsible for many hits by Aretha Franklin, Chaka Khan, and Bette Midler.

Both Eastmond and Mardin would play a role in Anita's fourth and final album for Elektra, but she wasn't focusing on recording in 1992. After five years of nonstop touring and recording, taking time away from the madness of the music business was the perfect decision for her: in the spring of 1992 she was pregnant again, and in January, 1993, little Walter was born. Unlike some other female performers whose significant others lived off their famous partners' incomes, husband Walter was financially self-sufficient. As Anita had mentioned to writer Jeff Lorez in a 1990 *Blues & Soul* interview, "[Walter] was formerly a sales rep at IBM for six years, then a year ago he left IBM to start his own business. He's also working on a few other real estate projects. . . ."

Five months after the birth of her first son, Anita took the first steps toward making a new record. "When I was pregnant my voice had pretty much left me," she told me during a lengthy 1994 *Blues & Soul* interview in conjunction with the release of the *Rhythm of Love* album. "I had no control over it. But I wasn't trying to rush anything. I was feeling a certain kind of euphoria and happiness and I just started working on new songs."

As Anita began putting together all the pieces for the new album, she and Walter did a little more personal production work. In May, 1994, Edward Carlton Bridgforth became the latest addition to the family. "I was in the studio up until the end of my eighth month," Anita grinned. "I came in waddling every night and would leave at three or four in the morning. . . ." Motherhood clearly agreed with Anita. She'd lost none of her special musical magic, and when *Rhythm of Love* hit the streets in 1994, Anita's many fans lost no time in hitting the record stores.

Anita had literally recorded a number of the tracks in her living room since she'd arranged for recording facilities to be set up at her home during her pregnancy with Eddie. Although producers Eastmond and Mardin contributed tracks to the album alongside famed jazzman Tommy LiPuma, well-known producer/musician George Duke, Gerald Smerek, one of Anita's main engineers, Anita produced most of the songs herself for her production company, named Female Trouble, Inc.

The album had more than its share of musical highlights: the self-descriptive title track, a groove written by Anita and old Beverly Glen buddy Patrick Moten; the atmospheric "Body and Soul," the first single from the album and a Top 5 R&B hit that managed to get enough pop play to sneak into the Top 40; a couple of nitty-gritty Baker compositions, "Wrong Man" and "Plenty of Room"; the standout, "I Apologize," a wonderful song written with producer Eastmond and Gordon Chambers, one of my former journalist colleagues. It was no surprise that the song won Anita her eighth Grammy in 1995. Although it wasn't as big a chart hit as "Body and Soul," the song resonated among Anita's fans, who showed how much they loved it when she began performing it in concert in 1994 and 1995.

In keeping with Anita's interest in the jazz arena, she covered the standard "My Funny Valentine" and was still considering the idea of doing a whole album of such songs. "What we did [with the song] was very special to me and we did the vocal in just one take. But I didn't feel I could do it until I had something to bring to it, since so many people have done the song before," she noted. "And that's how I feel about doing a whole album like that . . . I have to have honest interpretations of those kind of songs."

On the eve of the release of her new album, Anita was "excited, nervous, happy, scared . . . everything I could possibly be," she revealed, with a smile, as we wound down our interview at the posh Peninsula Hotel in Beverly Hills. After seeing a concert starring Whitney Houston at New York's Radio City Music Hall a few months before, she had the performing bug again. "I cried! I hadn't been to a concert since I stopped doing my own shows in 1991 and after I saw Whitney, I came back home and I was juiced! Do I miss touring? Hell, yeah. After seeing Whitney, I'm ready to get back out there."

By the end of 1994, after moving into a new fifteen-room lakefront mansion in Grosse Pointe, Anita was ready to hit the road again. This time the show was a little different: it was almost two hours long, and in addition to her hits and tracks from *Rhythm of Love*, Anita enjoyed doing hilarious impersonations of Diana Ross and Tina Turner! "I'm having a lot of more fun this time," she told me in our *Blues & Soul* interview in 1995, "and performing feels more like it felt when I first started out. You see, I'm no longer thinking that if I'm not perfect in everything I do onstage, my career will be over. My fans have shown me that I don't have to be 'perfect,' that they are really there for me. I'm not afraid all the time like I used to be and I have a different kind of confidence now. . . . It's like my fans all across the country reached out and gave me this really big hug. I'd get two or three encores a night and many times, I'd leave the stage in tears because it was just overwhelming to get the kind of response we got."

Anita had some initial fears as she took to the road: "You see, I'm still insecure behind that false bravado I put out there and what I call the 'suits' in the industry [executives, managers, and the like] play on that. But my fans have shown me that they're here for me through thick and thin. . . . They went out there and proved a point for me, that I can have a life and still have a career."

Anita would do battle with quite a few of the "suits" in the years that followed. Although her *Rhythm of Love* album sold two million copies, she felt that Elektra hadn't gone all out behind the project. She voiced her feelings to Sylvia Rhone, arguably the most powerful African-American woman in the music industry, who had replaced Bob Krasnow as the head of Elektra Entertainment. Krasnow was the visionary executive who had signed Anita to the label in 1985 and had given her the kind of creative freedom that enabled her to make albums that were an expression of her art rather than concessions to commercialism.

It was obvious to those who knew both women—independent, strong-willed women who knew how to get their respective jobs done—that the potential for conflict was there. Anita had cherished her relationship with Krasnow and had dedicated *Rhythm of Love* to him. When Rhone arrived from a successful stint at Atlantic, she had big shoes to fill since veteran executive Krasnow had developed a long-standing reputation for supporting artists in their desire for creative expression. While Rhone was also willing to take her share of creative chances, her mandate at Elektra was to make it into even more of a profit center for owner Time-Warner.

It didn't take long for Anita and Sylvia to disagree. In November, 1995, Anita asked for a release of her contract from Elektra, claiming that changes in the staffing at the label meant that she had to spend her own money for marketing, promotion, and publicity activities that were the label's duty to perform. Through her attorney, she claimed that there had been numerous breaches of contract. In December, Elektra had filed a suit to stop Anita from leaving the label. This suit was dropped in early 1996, and Anita subsequently joined the roster of Atlantic Records, another company that Time-Warner owned. In February, former manager Sherwin Bash had sued Anita for back payments; in May of the same year, Anita countersued him, his daughter Randy, and former attorney David Braun in an action that included a variety of claims, such as fraud, deceit, breach of contract, defamation and slander, and intentional infliction of emotional distress. In a statement she released to *Billboard*, Anita said, ". . . this all just boils down to what's happened to artists for many, many years. Management and large labels don't pay you. [Bash] thinks he should live off me the rest of my life. I hope for a total victory."

Lawsuits and countersuits weren't on Anita's mind the last time I saw her in the Washington, DC/Baltimore area in 1995. She was performing on a show with special guest Gladys Knight. What a great night it was! My good DC buddy Johnny Butler and I hooked up, and we agreed that the combination of the two soulful divas was "deadly!" When we went backstage after the performance, Johnny was thrilled to meet one of his all-time favorite singers. Anita, with Walter close by, was warm, welcoming, and witty. Gladys stopped by the dressing room at the end of the night, and the two women laughed and joked together. "Girl, you kicked it tonight!" Anita exclaimed. "Hey, you didn't do too bad either!" Gladys returned. "The both of you were brilliant!" I added.

As always, Gladys had given one of her so-good-it-hurts kind of performances, which peaked with her medley of "If You Don't Know Me By Now," "Love Don't Love Nobody," and Boyz II Men's "End of the Road." The mostly black audience members went nuts, and when Anita hit the stage, they were primed. Her show was pretty much the same one I'd seen in Los Angeles a few months before, but there was one big difference: both Anita and Gladys were performing in front of a crowd that bought their records, that stuck with them through career and personal challenges—the kind of audience whose hard-earned money paid their rent! Unlike the sometimes bourgeois L.A. crowd, invariably filled with industry "suits," wannabes, could-bes, has-beens, and never-bes, this was a paying crowd of loyal fans. And both performers fed off their energy.

Anita was in rare form that night. She sounded wonderful, she loved the audience, and they loved her back. Even though it wasn't part of the original show, she even slipped in the song "Angel" from her *Songstress* days and the crowd went wild. Through it all, through all the music-biz madness, Anita Baker hadn't forgotten her people, her roots, and the folks who had been in her corner from day one.

YOUNG
VAS

Chapter
15

, Janet,
nd Toni

Whitney Houston at the June,
1996 MTV Music Awards
Credit: Reuters/Sam Mircovich
Archive Photos

Luscious Janet Jackson in an
A&M records publicity shot
Credit: Patrick Demarchelier 8/95

Toni Braxton performing
in January, 1997
Credit: Archive Photos/
Scott Harrison

Honesty is the best policy, the expression goes, and if you're going to write about divas, you better tell it like it is. When I originally planned to write *The Soulful Divas*, I figured that a chapter on the three of the 1980s women most likely to stand the test of time—Whitney Houston, Janet Jackson, and Toni Braxton—would be appropriate. I also made a conscious choice not to include other 1980s and 1990s artists who others might consider to be candidates for longevity—such as Mariah Carey, Mary J. Blige, Faith Evans, and Erykah Badu—for the same reason I haven't included other qualified divas: I don't have any one-on-one material to draw from. This book was never meant to be a "Who's Who" on diva-dom. That said, I know that if I were writing this book ten years from now, it is likely that of the eighties divas I've met, Whitney, Janet, and Toni would make the cut.

I first met Whitney in 1977 when she was all of fourteen years old! She was singing behind her famous mother, Cissy Houston, one of the first soulful ladies I ever interviewed when I first moved to New York a couple of years earlier. Cissy, the former lead singer with the Sweet Inspirations—who had sung behind everyone from Elvis Presley to Aretha Franklin and had made some superb albums of their own—was in the midst of a career rejuvenation.

Cissy was performing at a swank New York cabaret club called Reno Sweeney's, a very intimate venue that enabled the audience to truly see a performer up close and personal! I saw Cissy on two different occasions in the space of a few months in the summer of 1977, and as I recall, Whitney was onstage for both shows. But it was during the second performance that mama Houston gave her little girl the chance to do a "step out." I also remember that Whitney sounded incredible, and Cissy made sure the audience knew that this was her baby. I reviewed the show for *Blues & Soul* magazine but didn't mention which song Whitney did. Memory is a strange thing: even though I don't recall what she sang, I can see her vividly as she stepped forward on a very crowded stage and got what was likely one of her first standing ovations.

Afterward I went backstage to say hello to Cissy and her husband,

John, and was introduced to Whitney. As always in after-show settings, the exchange was pleasant but brief. I was shocked that eight years later, when I met Whitney again at the Hyatt House Hotel on Sunset Boulevard, she remembered the meeting. When my good, good friend John Simmons, who was doubling as musical director for both Whitney and Stephanie Mills, reintroduced us, she smiled and said, "I met you with my Mom at Reno Sweeney's. You used to come and see her show a lot, didn't you?" That meeting took place in the spring of 1985. Whitney was in Los Angeles for her first show as an Arista recording artist, and her debut album had literally just hit the streets. None of us knew that within a year or so, that self-titled LP would sell a staggering nine million copies in the United States and several more million overseas, or that she would become one of the premier musical artists of the 1980s and 1990s, an international superstar, and a household name.

Watching Whitney's show at the Roxy, I was genuinely excited. Given her pedigree as the daughter of one of the most noted soul singers in the music business, I was hardly surprised that she sang her ass off. I didn't know all the details of what Whitney had been doing since her early years singing in the New Hope Baptist Church in Newark, New Jersey, where her mother was the choir director. But I did know that coming from a musical family that also included her cousins Dionne and Dee Dee Warwick, hanging out at historic recording sessions that her mother did with the woman Whitney would later call "Aunt Ree"—the illustrious Aretha Franklin—and just hearing the kind of harmonies that Cissy created on recordings with everyone from Luther Vandross to Chaka Khan, Whitney couldn't help but acquire some of the same potent soul power. I later found out that in addition to Whitney's early gigs doing backup for Cissy at Reno Sweeney's, she sang on sessions behind Lou Rawls, Chaka Khan, and the Neville Brothers, and even had a featured spot on an album by disco producer Paul Jabara in 1982. After seeing her face-to-face in 1985, I wasn't surprised that her stunning good looks had led to work as a model with spreads in magazines like *Glamour*, *Seventeen*, *Young Miss*, and *Cosmopolitan*.

All I knew that night at the Roxy was that I was seeing a singer I knew would be making a significant musical impact. Playing before a crowd of industry types—mostly press people like myself—Whitney was amazing. Even though her focus was mostly on cover tunes, I concluded a *Blues & Soul* review by stating, ". . . all Whitney needs now is some more original songs, which allow her the chance to use her dazzling vocal gymnastics and then, watch out for the emergence of a major star performer." I wasn't far off! About that night, I said, "Her live performances have plenty of punch, spirit and power." She started the evening with what I called "a stomping version" of Lionel Richie's "Love Will Find a Way." She also sang four songs from her Arista debut, "You Give Good Love," "Saving All My Love for You," "How Will I Know," and "The Greatest Love of All," a song George Benson previously recorded for the 1977 film *The Greatest*, about the life of prize fighter Muhammad Ali. Remarkably, all four songs provided Whitney with back-to-back No. 1 hit gold singles even though that night only audience members who had heard her album were even remotely familiar with the tunes.

Whitney did three duets with her brother Gary: "Take Good Care of My Heart" and "Nobody Loves Me Like You Do," which she'd recorded for her first album with then-labelmate Jermaine Jackson, and "Hold Me," which she'd cut with Teddy Pendergrass for his album *Love Language*, which had been a Top 5 R&B hit in 1984. Then came the highlight of the night: Whitney sang "I Am Changing" from the Broadway hit musical *Dream Girls*. As I noted in my *Blues & Soul* review, her cover of the song, which Jennifer Holliday first popularized, "resulted in a well-deserved standing ovation. When Whitney decides to pour her all into a song, she's clearly inherited the family tradition for inducing a spine-tingling reaction. . . ."

After seeing this show, which I described as "a spectacular performance," and hearing Whitney's first Arista album, I had no doubt about her potential for achieving success. *Blues & Soul* editor John Abbey conducted an interview with her in the summer of 1985, during which she explained that it had been her choice to pursue a career in music and that her first Arista album had been made without any direct input from her famous mother. "No, my mom let me do it for myself," Whitney commented. "In my life, she has been my inspiration but if I had wanted to venture into any other career, she'd have given me the same kind of support that she's giving me right now. . . . However, the fact that I chose this field is good because she's been through it all . . . [and] I've been in this business for ten years. I really have never considered following any other career. So, what my mom did was to help me—to teach and groom me. Where could I find a better teacher?"

Whitney had not only her mother and cousin Dionne in her corner, she also had one other secret weapon. His name was Clive Davis. As head of Arista Records, he had hands-on input into the recording output of practically all of the label's hitmaking artists, from Barry Manilow to Aretha Franklin, who had joined the company in 1980. Closer to home, Davis had helped rejuvenate Dionne's career as a bestselling artist when she signed to Arista in 1978. Even though Whitney claimed he didn't know she and Dionne were related when he offered her a contract with Arista, Davis knew that Whitney had many of the same star qualities. For one thing, she had all the ingredients to be a crossover artist. She could appeal to an R&B crowd, and she had enormous possibilities as a pop singer. Plus, it was impossible for him not to notice her appearance: young, svelte, and beautiful.

Time and time again, Davis had shown an uncanny skill for finding hit songs for his artists, and with Whitney, his talent as a man with a golden ear was given plenty of opportunity to shine. Even the process of making her first album had taken time: once aware of her potential after Arista A&R man Gerry Griffiths had invited him to check her out, Davis set out on a campaign to find the right songs for her label debut. He held showcases in New York and Los Angeles, inviting producers and writers to hear his new signing. The strategy worked. Whitney ended up in the recording studio with Michael Masser, Narada Michael Walden, Arista artist/musician/producer Kashif, and labelmate Jermaine Jackson.

But this wasn't merely a matter of matching Whitney with strong producers. For Davis, it was all about the songs. He was right on target: the first single, "You Give Good Love," with its slightly suggestive title, was the perfect vehicle for setting Whitney up with a solid R&B base. The fact that the song reached No. 3 on the pop charts was almost incidental. The follow-up, a song about the age-old dilemma of being the other woman, had an even greater pop feel. To those who knew Davis, it came as no surprise that "Saving All My Love for You" topped both the pop and R&B charts in the fall of 1985.

There was just one misstep. A third single, Kashif's "Thinking About You," got no pop response even though it was a Top 10 R&B hit. And from single number four, the upbeat "How Will I Know," a song produced by Narada Michael Walden that bore more than a passing resemblance to the Pointer Sisters' "He's So Shy," a 1980 hit, on to 1991's "Miracle," every single release by Whitney—with only one notable exception—was a Top 10 pop smash. The exception was "It Isn't, It Wasn't, It Ain't Never Gonna Be," a campy 1989 duet with labelmate "Aunt Ree" that might have been "too black" for pop stations to take.

Even though Whitney and I obviously had a little more of a personal bond than she likely had with too many other journalists, we didn't actually do a full interview until 1991, six years after she'd arrived on the international music scene. We did run into each other on a few occasions along the way, and one was particularly memorable. I happened to be in London when she was appearing at Wembley, a huge venue in London where all major acts performed. When I caught up with my friend John Simmons, who had given up his gig with Stephanie Mills to work full time with Whitney, after the show, he invited my sister Sylvia and me to hang out with him afterward at a private post-show party at the Hippodrome, which was a large nightclub in London's fashionable West End.

Whitney was seated in a special private area with her brother Gary; her father, John; her best friend and personal assistant, Robyn Crawford; and a few others, including the requisite security guards. The music was pumping, so some of us headed toward the dance floor—followed by Whitney! Before I could blink, Whitney was right there next to us, boogeying her feet off much to the despair of her security people who were horrified that she'd just taken off! When the deejay played "I Wanna Dance With Somebody," we all cheered and yelled and kept right on dancing until eventually, Whitney and company began to feel the effects of having put on a spectacular show at Wembley a few hours earlier. When she went back upstairs, he father commented to me that he'd never seen her having such a good time in public. "She just doesn't do that," he said, "but I guess she loves you guys here in London."

I next saw Whitney in Los Angeles when I went to visit my buddy John Simmons. As we were leaving the upscale West L.A. hotel, Whitney and Robyn Crawford were leaving, too, and we exchanged cordial greetings. Whitney and I didn't see each other again until I was backstage at a BeBe and CeCe Winans concert in Los Angeles. John had died suddenly not too long after that meeting in west L.A., and Whitney wanted to make sure I knew about his passing. I had no idea that John had in fact been ill for a while. When I saw him, I noticed only that he'd lost weight and that he had a bad cough. I was shocked when I heard from his brother about his death, but I was heartened to know that Whitney--and her mother, Cissy, who had introduced Whitney to John—had ensured that John received the dignified send-off he deserved. When Whitney and I saw each other after the Winans' show, during which she'd sung her heart out on "Hold Up the Light," we talked briefly about John; I sensed a genuine warmth in her.

In those six years between Whitney's first show at the Roxy in 1985 and my *Blues & Soul* chat with her, a great deal happened to her. Her first two albums had cumulative sales of way over twenty-five million copies worldwide. Whitney had broken record after record. She'd toured internationally and won the hearts of music lovers everywhere with her fusion of New Jersey gospel, old-school soul, and contemporary pop. When I heard Whitney's albums, I heard the vocal influences of her family: she had the vibrato of her mother, the grittiness of cousin Dee

Dee, and the lightness of cousin Dionne—a winning combination.

Ever since Whitney's debut album had taken off, Arista's Clive Davis became even more involved with her career. After all, Whitney had, hands down, become the label's hottest property, and Davis was concerned that his most important artist was properly promoted and publicized. Following her initial success, the job of shaping Whitney's public persona became no easy ride. Being in the glare of the public eye had also brought its share of personal challenges for Whitney. The rumor mill had gone on overdrive to find out more about her private life, and questions about her sexuality became a common subject for the press and public alike. Whitney brushed off the comments about her relationship with longtime friend Robyn Crawford. And when Whitney married former New Edition singer Bobby Brown in 1992, it looked as if the rumors would finally stop. But the marriage itself had more than its share of controversy. No matter how often Whitney would bring Bobby onstage with her—sometimes with their daughter Bobbi Kristina—and no matter how many times she would publicly state that the relationship was solid and declare her love for the singer with the bad-boy image, people still had their questions.

In addition some detractors said that Davis had too much input into her music and had taken away Whitney's soul. Critics charged that she'd abandoned her natural R&B roots and was now an out-and-out pop star with little interest in going back to her black fans. While it was true that her material had an unmistakably pop slant, her vocal approach still reflected her heritage. But those who viewed Whitney as an 1980s incarnation of Diana Ross—glitz, glamour, and all—weren't having it. No, they insisted, Whitney had sold out musically.

Whitney and I talked about this accusation during a telephone call in the summer of 1991, just a short while before she began shooting her first film, *The Bodyguard* with Kevin Costner. I asked her how she felt about the comments that she'd sold out musically. "I think it's funny," she replied, in a no-bullshit tone. "Instead of looking at my accomplishments, it's about whether I sing pop or whether my music isn't soulful anymore. Yes, I did have big pop success, and it took off very fast. I was singing real pop music, songs that were melodic and very catchy, but I was singing the you-know-what out of them! Was I supposed to be on just one level, one avenue? . . . I grew up with all kinds of music but the root of my singing is gospel, and it always has been, and you're a fool if you don't hear that in my music!" Well, okay!

To counter the criticism, Davis steered Whitney's third album, *I'm Your Baby Tonight*, in a slightly different direction. She'd hooked up with

Whitney Houston singing at
the White House during a state
dinner in honor of South African
President Nelson Mandela
in October, 1994
Credit: Reuters/Gary Cameron/Archive Photos

hotter-than-hot producers L.A. and Babyface, who worked on several cuts on the 1990 album. It contained a duet with Stevie Wonder and, overall had an R&B edge to it. Maybe Whitney's massive pop base didn't like it as much: in contrast to the approximately fifteen million copies the first two albums had sold, *I'm Your Baby Tonight* sold only about three million copies in the U.S.

When Whitney and I talked about the response to her third Arista album, she was blunt: "I'm not bitching about that at all. I know people who would die to sell 105 copies. I'm not complaining: I have a career based on three albums, and I'm truly satisfied with what God has blessed me with. . . . The truth is that I [have] had a lot of blessings. . . . People dream about [doing what I've done in five years] over a twenty-five-year period so I'm very thankful. . . . I recognize that no one's going to be on top forever, and, frankly, I don't want to be up there all the time!"

By the end of 1992 with three albums under her belt, Whitney clearly wanted to focus on the silver screen. Whitney's first film, *The Bodyguard*, was a box-office hit, the soundtrack spent months at the top of the charts, and her reading of Dolly Parton's 1974 hit "I Will Always Love You" was the No. 1 pop hit single for fourteen weeks, during which time it sold four million copies. Whitney walked away with three Grammy Awards, countless American Music Awards, and other accolades as a result of *The Bodyguard*. Even though critics contended that Whitney was simply playing herself on camera and that the character on screen was very much like the real-life diva, she would later counter that the role she played in the 1995 movie *Waiting to Exhale* was in fact far closer to her offstage personality.

While Arista kept releasing hit singles from *The Bodyguard*, Whitney paid attention to more personal matters. Her marriage to Bobby Brown took plenty of people by surprise, if only because Brown's rough-and-tough street image didn't jibe well with the notion that Whitney was a sophisticated, glamorous, if slightly aloof pop goddess. When the subject came up in private conversations, I said little. All I could do was remind those who couldn't figure out what the two had in common that Whitney had been brought up in Newark, New Jersey, not Beverly Hills. And even though her family was comfortable, she still knew more than a little about day-to-day street life.

As if to validate my own thoughts on the matter, Whitney herself made a comment in a 1996 interview with Jeff Lorez for *Blues & Soul*. Her remark said more than I ever could: ". . . I know bad girls, you know. Girls who are a lot tougher than I appear to be. I mean, I was born in Newark in the projects for the most part. My mother and father made a little money and we moved to East Orange [New Jersey] but I still went back to the projects and hung out there. I have two older brothers. No sisters, but my brothers were rough tumblers, you know, and I had to run with them and it taught me a lot about the streets. . . ." I concluded that Bobby and Whitney had more in common than people suspected and, as I've always done when people ask me about the private lives of those I interview, I couldn't comment on how "real" the marriage was. Like the musical team of Ashford & Simpson once wrote, "Nobody Knows the Inside," and this has been my modus operandi in regard to the real deal on my subjects' private lives, unless they choose to tell it themselves.

The birth of a daughter, named Bobbi Kristina, kept Whitney out of commission for a while, but in 1995 *Waiting to Exhale*, both movie and soundtrack, brought her back into the public eye. The film adaptation of Terry McMillan's bestselling book did exceptionally well. With its all-star cast and boosted by Whitney's chart-topping, million-selling single "Exhale (Shoop Shoop)," the soundtrack went platinum.

Whitney's third film, *The Preacher's Wife*, starred Denzel Washington. A "feel-good" movie, it received a relatively lukewarm response from critics and public alike. She ended 1997 on a better note: as one of the financial producers behind the top-rated ABC-TV musical version of "Cinderella," Whitney could proudly say she'd put her money where her mouth was. She appeared in the television movie playing the role of "Fairy Godmother," with singer Brandy. As I watched the show, I couldn't help but reflect on the almost fairytale-like nature of Whitney's early career. She'd started out as just another new female artist with a great pedigree and a whole lot of potential, and in the space of one decade, she'd become an international megastar.

But I also knew that all fairytales were just that. The last time I saw Whitney in concert at the Hollywood Bowl, I was for the most part unsatisfied. She sounded vocally just about okay and sang the usual hits, but I couldn't understand why she lumped songs like "I Loves You Porgy" and "I Am Changing" together. It just didn't make sense to me, any more than her insistence on bringing husband Bobby to the stage at the end of the evening.

At the time of this writing, Whitney's image has definitely undergone some changes as the result of her marriage. If you read tabloids, like sensational gossip, and listen to industry scuttlebutt, it would seem as if Whitney's career could use a boost. Personally, I have no doubt that she'll rebound from whatever negative publicity seems to have surrounded her during the last couple of years. You see, long before I met Whitney, I met Cissy. And before that, I met cousins Dionne and Dee

Dee. And somewhere in there, I met the Warwick sisters' mother [and Cissy's sister], Lee. And believe me, the Houston/Warwick clan is tough.

Beyond the glitz and glamour, Whitney Houston is the product of that family heritage. And these are women who survive the slings and arrows, who are unafraid to get "real"—strong, black women who almost dare you to mess with them. Don't be fooled. Whitney Houston comes from that kind of street-smart stock that knows how to rise from a fall in a New Jersey heartbeat!

I've interviewed Janet Jackson only three times. The first instance was at A&M Records, a week or two before the *Control* album turned her into an international superstar in 1986. The second occasion was on the telephone in 1990 after she'd just finished her first U.S. tour, and with a second multi-million seller, *Rhythm Nation 1814*, under her belt she was about to embark on her first European trek. And in 1993, we sat down for about two hours at her Malibu oceanfront home as *janet*, her first set for Virgin Records, hit the streets.

Janet was almost painfully shy, sitting down and signing autographs on copies of her then-brand new album as I walked in the room for our first interview in 1986. On the telephone in 1990, she was pleasant and easy to talk to. By 1993, she'd matured; she was confident, assured, aware, and perceptive. Unwittingly, over seven years, I'd seen Janet's transformation from a twenty-year-old, fresh from a short-lived, less-than-happy marriage and dealing with a lot of new challenges, to a woman who had a handle on her life and career. In the words of the title track of her breakthrough album, she'd taken control.

It wasn't always that way. Because Janet was a member of the Jackson family, having a career in the entertainment industry seemed inevitable. And sure enough, at the age of seven, Janet made her stage debut in her brothers' act at the MGM Grand; she did a brief, coy impression of legendary movie star Mae West, best known for her spicy double entendres and overall sassiness! This took place in 1975 when the Jackson 5 was on the verge of becoming simply the Jacksons, and was already on its way out of Motown Records, the group's recording home for the preceding six years.

Before Janet followed her brothers and became a recording artist, she veered off into television. Famed television producer Norman Lear had seen her on a Jacksons' television special, and in 1977 he cast her for the role of Penny Gordon Woods in "Good Times," one of the nation's favorite shows. She played the part for two years. In 1982, Janet was seen in "Diff'rent Strokes" as Charlene Dupree; she stayed on that sitcom about a year. A stint on the popular television show "Fame" followed, but by 1982 Joe Jackson, the ever-present patriarch of the Gary, Indiana, clan, felt that a recording career might be a timely move for his youngest daughter. In later interviews, Janet would claim that she had some reluctance to pursue music, and her first couple of albums for A&M Records reflected a certain vocal restraint.

Janet's first self-titled project included production work by R&B artists Rene & Angela, as well as Foster Sylvers of the family group the Sylvers, whose 1970s pop-and-soul concoctions bore some resemblance toward the recordings of the Jacksons. Although "Young Love" isn't a song that most people remember, this first single from *Janet Jackson* was actually a Top 10 R&B hit. The album did fairly well, so there was hope that the 1984 follow-up, *Dream Street*, might eclipse its predecessor.

Even though Janet's brothers Michael and Marlon both contributed to the album along with Giorgio Moroder, who was known for his work with Donna Summer, and Minneapolis funk man Jesse Johnson, *Dream Street* was a relative failure. The album spent all of six weeks on the charts, never cracking the Hot 100.

The lukewarm reaction to her first two albums only fueled criticism from industry pundits and music reviewers who claimed that Janet didn't have a strong vocal presence, range, or skill, and that she was simply trading in on her family name. This comment surfaced time and again as Janet's musical career began taking shape; in 1985, something had to happen to dull the criticism. The task of coming up with the right production hookup for Janet fell to John McClain, an A&M executive who had known the Jackson family since his own childhood days. McClain opted for the team of Jimmy "Jam" Harris and Terry Lewis, two multitalented music men whose industry career began when they were members of the Time, the 1980s band that toured with Minneapolis superstar Prince. From early hits with Klymaxx, the S.O.S. Band, Gladys Knight & the Pips, Cheryl Lynn, Thelma Houston, and Alexander O'Neal and Cherrelle, two artists they'd groomed musically, the longtime friends had established themselves as consistent hitmakers. In essence, the pair had created their own sound, which was a mix of strong melodies, catchy hooks, and ultra-funky grooves balanced with lyrically sound ballads. The combination was a winner. Before they met with Janet in 1985, Jimmy Jam and Terry Lewis were already considered in the first league of young, fresh producers who could deliver hits.

For Janet, her third album represented more than just an opportunity to make another record. She'd been going through some major personal changes. In August, 1984, she'd married James DeBarge of the Motown family group DeBarge. Press reports said that she'd defied members of her family by marrying the keyboard player, probably because some members of the DeBarge clan had gained something of a controversial industry reputation for alleged group fights and general abuse. As it was, the union didn't last. By March, 1985, the marriage had been annulled and Janet had moved back to the Jackson family's Encino complex.

During my first interview with Janet in April, 1986, which appeared in *The Los Angeles Herald Examiner* and Britain's now-defunct *Street Scene*, she made a fleeting reference to the marriage, noting, "The last few years—what with my marriage and all—weren't easy for me. See, I don't think it has to do with my age. People say that when you're young, you don't know. But it's all about experience and I found out that the maturing process isn't always fun." In a *Blues & Soul* interview around the same time, she told editor Bob Killbourn, "The simple truth was that I just wasn't ready for marriage and the commitment that it requires. I was totally unprepared for marriage and the responsibility. . . . I was working from five in the morning until eight or nine at night on the 'Fame' [show's] set and James was just beginning his work at the studios when I arrived home. With that type of situation, it's pretty difficult to make any relationship work, let alone one which had two inexperienced kids as principals. We simply didn't have the time to work out the problems."

Janet's marriage had come during a period when she'd left home, ostensibly to do the "Fame" show. "I was living away from home and I was doing the show while the family was preparing for the [national] 'Victory' tour. I got the chance during that time to see life in the raw and it was good for me to have that kind of experience," she told me. "Like I said, I've led a pretty sheltered life. . . ."

Janet's union with musical risk-takers Jam and Lewis came at the perfect time. As she told Killbourn, "I suppose there comes a time in everyone's life when they shed the child in themselves and adopt an adult attitude to life. I couldn't continue to present an image which I knew to be false and not representative of the person behind it. The early Janet Jackson was innocent, was naïve. . . . I'm not knocking that period of my life and career. . . . I know the fact that my surname was Jackson certainly didn't harm my career but you cannot lean on others' talent or reputation for an entire career. . . I had known for some time that it was necessary for me to break the image and present the real Janet Jackson if I was to be taken seriously. There is only one Peter Pan— the rest of us have to grow up!"

Finding an authentic way of expressing herself musically was Janet's mission for her crucial third A&M album. After executive McClain suggested Jam and Lewis, she did her homework by listening to the music they'd been making for the past five years. After finally meeting with the team in Minneapolis, she knew she'd found the right partners for her musical coming of age. "I think people are surprised, even shocked at this [new] album," she told me as we sat face-to-face in the international conference room at A&M's Hollywood office. "I know that I've always been perceived as this innocent young girl. I mean, people were still pinching my cheeks when I was eighteen!"

Janet's third album, released during on March 2, 1986, was aptly named *Control*. As she explained for *The Los Angeles Herald* and *Street Scene* articles, ". . . I decided it was time for me to make more of my own decisions, to be responsible not just for my personal life but also for my career. . . . I was there for everything [on the album]—the rhythm tracks, the mixing, every part of this. . . ." In fact, Janet ended up coproducing all nine cuts on *Control*, cowriting all but two songs, and playing keyboards on eight of the tunes. "I studied piano when I was six for a month along with my brother Randy and then I gave it up. Eventually, I started playing by ear and although I played on demos for songs . . . I never played on record until now. I was fooling around in the studio one day when Jimmy heard me and he said, 'Hey you can play.' I was kind of shaky about it then, but I'm happy that I did it now," she said.

Beyond the music contained on the new album, Janet decided what she would wear for the cover and how her hair and makeup would look; she also had final say over which photographs would be used for all the materials that would surround the release of the album. Janet wanted her personal stamp on all aspects of the record and had resisted the temptation to include any other members of her family on the album. As she told *Blues & Soul* editor Killbourn, ". . . I wanted to stand or fall on my own terms. Any appearance by my family would have been a compromise on my part and I've stopped compromising! I'm aware that this is a departure from what I've done before but I think—I hope—that people will recognize the honesty in the album. . . ."

Janet needn't have worried. *Control* hit the top spot on the charts. In all, it sold in excess of five million copies domestically with several more million worldwide. The album was a legitimate bestseller for two full years and spawned not one but six R&B Top 3 hit singles, five of which went to No. 1. The pop charts reflected a similar story: five singles went into the Top 5, the first four singles went gold, and "When I Think of You" made it to No. 1. Aided by eye-catching, adventurous videos, Janet had fully and completely arrived on the international music scene, her success as a young, black, female artist rivaled only by the impact Whitney Houston had begun making on the scene just a year earlier.

The two women were quite different even though plenty of music fans were buying albums by both performers. Though they were only three years apart in age, they came from different worlds. Exactly how different was even more evident on Janet's fifth album. *Rhythm Nation 1814* was a harder, tougher record than *Control*." And as adventurous as she'd been on that album, with tunes like "Let's Wait Awhile," a plea for abstinence from sex; "What Have You Done for Me Lately," a no-nonsense demand for reciprocity; and the self-descriptive "Nasty," Janet, Jam, and Lewis began stretching the musical and lyrical boundaries on her fifth album. While the multi-platinum Whitney Houston was telling the world she was "So Emotional" and asking "Where Do Lonely Hearts Go," Janet was gathering her young troops for universal togetherness via "Rhythm Nation," commenting on "The State of the World," planning an "Escapade" with a potential new lover, and dealing with a game-playing liar who liked to live on the edge on "Black Cat."

Rhythm Nation reflected a whole new level of musical exploration, heavy and industrial in places, and with a much darker feel than *Control*. It also outsold *Control* domestically, racking up more than six million sales, and was a global smash. If anyone was in doubt, *Rhythm Nation* made it clear: Janet Jackson was no longer a little girl. She'd evolved into a mature young woman who understood that when she looked out into the world, she saw a lot of challenges for her own generation. Her attitude and approach bore some comparison to that taken by her megastar brother Michael: in much the same way that he'd created a niche as a musical adventurer, Janet was making her own mark.

When Janet and I spoke over the telephone in the fall of 1990, she was fresh off the road from her first nationwide tour and preparing for her first European dates. She was happy to comment on *Rhythm Nation*: "I wanted to do this; I chose to because there is a responsibility I feel as a young entertainer. I started to realize that I had become a role model for young people and I said, 'If this is what I am to people, I might as well do something positive.' I actually wanted to do this kind of album when I was doing the *Control* LP but it's all a matter of timing. . . . [And] the response from the public has been great. . . . I feel that we are getting the message on the album to the kids. They are our future, and I feel that the only way anything can be resolved or solved is by our joining hands, coming together, uniting. No matter what the problem, whether it's illiteracy or gang violence, it's going to take time: we have to work together as a group, we have to be strong and very patient."

The 1990 tour had been grueling but incredibly successful. For the

Janet Jackson as
depicted on the
cover of a Virgin Records
promotional folder
Credit: Virgin Records

most part, Janet had silenced those who wondered if she was simply the product of the visual age of video and the advance technology of studio production. I saw her at the Los Angeles Forum, and the placed was packed to capacity. After an opening set from Janet's musical director Chuckii Booker—at the time, a recording artist in his own right—the air was heavy with anticipation as a video clip surrounding the song "Alright" preceded Janet's entrance. She started out with "Control," and with a couple of exceptions—the ballads "Let's Wait Awhile" and "Come Back to Me"—the show was high energy all the way.

Janet sang hard, but it was her almost nonstop dance moves that blew the audience away. I almost felt breathless myself as I watched her clamber up the stairs of a specially built structure and move from one groove to another. As I noted in my *Blues & Soul* review, ". . . It was non-stop action and boundless energy from Ms. J. who was clearly dedicated to giving the crowd value for money. . . . She seems to have unlimited energy and one can't help but wonder quite how she's able to keep the pace going night after night."

The next day, A&M hosted a luncheon for Janet. She walked around, smiled, and posed for photographs, in the process providing me with one of the centerpieces of the photo display in my living room. To date, I can't think of anyone who has visited my humble abode for the first time without commenting on the picture of us together, Janet wearing what was then her trademark cap and neo-military outfit and me grinning like a Cheshire cat!

During a telephone chat a few months later, she told me that the "Rhythm Nation" tour had challenges. "It's been a lot of fun . . . not as grueling as people told me it would be. It's all about the people you have around you that affects how the tour goes," she said. The secret to her boundless energy? "Well, a lot of groups who tour may go out and party and more power to them! Right after my show, I go back to the hotel . . . and I go straight to sleep. I just get a lot of rest. I don't need to exercise because dancing every night is the right exercise—I used to work out with a trainer every day but I got so big. . . . I take a lot of vitamins, and I've had B12 vitamin shots. In fact, one time I felt my energy was kind low during a show so I went offstage for a moment to take some B12 through my nose. When I got back on-stage and started dancing, it started running out of my nose! It looked like I had blood coming out of my nose. . . . I'm sure some people were wondering about whether I was sniffing drugs or something!" she revealed.

For all the attendant ups and downs of life on the road, the "Rhythm Nation" tour had brought Janet directly to her adoring audience, a crowd that was primarily under forty and mostly under twenty-five, of every color, race, creed, and persuasion. Latino gays mixed with Asian couples; black and white girls barely into puberty stood alongside hand-slappin' black and white homies; African-American queens, male and female alike, were up on their feet next to strictly-from-the-Valley married couples. It was a circus, a celebration, a melting pot—people curious to see exactly what Janet had to offer. After completing the worldwide portion of the tour, Janet took time off to reevaluate her career. Another two years would pass before her name would grace the charts again. A Jam and Lewis-produced duet with singer Luther Vandross on "The Best Things in Life Are Free" from the film *Mo' Money* became a No. 1 R&B hit and Top 10 single in the summer of 1992.

During the four years between *Rhythm Nation 1814* and Janet's next album, her contract with A&M came up for renewal. In fact, as she told me in our lengthy interview at her Malibu home, the deal had ended the day she completed *Rhythm Nation*. As a free agent, she was looking at different options. By 1991 all the bids had come in, and Janet made her choice. She decided to sign with Virgin Records, a global company that had started in the U.K. and had begun its U.S. operations in the late 1980s. The label had been successful with acts like singer/dancer Paula Abdul, British retro group Soul II Soul, English pop musician Steve Winwood, and New Age group Enigma, among others.

Although Janet wouldn't reveal the exact terms of the deal when she and I spoke, it was rumored that Janet had signed on the dotted line for a cool 32 million dollars. She did, however, explain her rationale for doing the deal with Virgin: ". . . I had a lot of offers. . . . A lot of times, I know, new kids coming along are so impatient to get a deal that they'll sign with the first company that's interested. But it has to be right. I decided to sign with Virgin Records because I felt it wasn't all about suits and ties. It was cool. It had more of a family atmosphere. Jeff Ayeroff and Jordan Harris (then-heading up Virgin's American operations) are real cool. They'd call and say, 'We gotta get this shit done!' but really there was no pressure. There's *another* reason I signed with Virgin—but I can't get into that. . . ."

Janet didn't rush into the recording studios once she'd signed the deal in 1991. Her focus was on the silver screen. She'd agreed to star in the John Singleton film *Poetic Justice*, appearing with rap star Tupac Shakur. Janet talked about the film during our telephone conversation: "I think doing *Poetic Justice* was a big turning point for me. I was very shy before I did the movie. I'm not anymore. It opened me up. The character I play is very real. When I read the script, I saw there was a lot of cursing. . . . I thought, 'Oh. . . .' [But] I loved making the movie. . . . It was a lot of hard work. . . . I prepared for the film . . . although I know a lot of people wondered how this girl from Encino could play someone from South Central. . . . I used to go down to South Central when I was in high school. I had a friend who lived there. During the making of the movie, I hung out at the Fox Hills Mall. But I didn't have a big bodyguard next to me. . . . I was just hangin' out. . . . I met these girls at a club one night, and we ended up spending two months together, hanging out. That brought a certain reality. . . . They were kinda standoffish to begin with. I asked them why. They said, 'We thought you'd be some stuck-up bitch.' People have a certain perception. People might think I'm a prima donna . . . knowing my public life. . . ."

In 1993 I had my own perceptions when I arrived at the oceanfront mansion Janet shared with companion and best friend Rene Elizondo. I wasn't sure what to expect when Rene opened the door. We chatted on the patio, which afforded a spectacular view of the Los Angeles coastline as the sun was going down late one afternoon. Rene and I talked about the ocean and the Hawaiian island of Kauai until Janet joined us. She smiled, apologized for not being ready when I arrived just minutes before, and ushered me up to her office to talk about *janet*, her latest album, an ambitious record with twenty-seven tracks, musical interludes included.

With Jam and Lewis, and on one track, musician/producer Jellybean Johnson, Janet had created an album that would once again alter the public's perception of her as an artist. "If," a funky, gritty track, talked about her fantasies. "The Body That Loves You" was a jazzy tune with a slight Caribbean flavor; "Funky Big Band," a celebration of African-American music and culture; "This Time," a striking tune that featured opera star Kathleen Battle; "New Agenda," a straight-up piece about pride, respect, and dignity with participation from Chuck D. of Public Enemy fame; and the hypnotic, chart-topping first single, "That's the Way Love Goes."

I noticed that Janet had an air of confidence without being arrogant or aloof when we spoke. She seemed genuinely pleased to talk about her work and explained that the album was definitely a lyrical departure from her last record. "[It's] about love, falling out of love, about being in love. Even after I finished *Rhythm Nation*, I knew I wanted to take that route with the next album, to deal with love as the main subject matter. The album's about what's happened in my life, past, present, and what I'd like to have happen in the future. Women will really relate to this album—but not to the exclusion of men," she said. The conversation went on in more detail to talk about the songs on the record and Janet's sense of responsibility as a public figure: "I feel like, with entertainers, our life is a gift from God. . . . We do have a duty in sharing our music . . . being someone that kid can look up to . . . being able to tell kids about drugs, like 'Don't touch that shit!' I've always felt like that. . . ."

I instinctively knew when it was time to stop and as we were winding down, Janet and Rene invited me into what he jokingly called the "liposuction room," so named because it was actually a room filled with equipment Janet used to work out with, countering press comments that she'd undergone surgery to remove excess fat. When I asked to use the telephone so I could call for a taxi, Janet offered to give me a ride home! With two of her dancers in tow, Janet, Rene, and I headed back to my apartment in a black Jeep with incredible speakers. On the way, we listened and sang along with her brother Michael's *Off the Wall* album. When I arrived at my home, I thanked Janet and Rene and resisted the urge to yell to all my neighbors that Janet Jackson was in the Jeep that was pulling away.

About a week after the interview appeared in *Blues & Soul*, a messenger with a huge bouquet of flowers and a note knocked on my door. The note said, "Thank you for restoring my faith in journalists. Love, Janet." I was floored. In all my years of writing, I could remember getting only a couple of such gifts. In 1985 I received a Christmas hamper from Aretha Franklin, and another year I got a Christmas food spread from Anita Baker. But I'd enjoyed relatively long-term relationships with both of those divas, so getting flowers from Janet was particularly unexpected.

I've seen Janet only twice since the interview, once in 1997 at a lavish party held for the release of her second Virgin album, *The Velvet Rope*, and once in the spring of 1998 when she was attending the Los Angeles launch of Jam and Lewis's new company, Flyte Tyme Records. Both exchanges were very brief, and although I reminded her—specifically on the second occasion—of our long interview at her home in Malibu five years earlier, she was polite but I couldn't tell if she *really* remembered it! I wasn't that concerned because I realized that over the ensuing years, she'd surely done more than a few more interviews and met a slew of other journalists in the process.

I didn't get to interview Janet for *The Velvet Rope* release, but that didn't stop me from considering it, in many ways, to be her boldest work. I found a good deal of irony in the fact that, at the big bash Virgin Records held at the Sony film lot in Culver City, the chances of seeing Janet face-to-face were almost zero. This was because she was closeted in a room within a room, and the only way to gain access was to literally go behind a velvet rope—and if you didn't have the right tag, you didn't stand a ghost in hell's chance of saying hello to her! But I knew that rather than having much to do with Janet's own reluctance to meet people, this setup was typically the work of zealous, way-too-protective record executives who feared their coveted superstar would somehow be less super if she mingled with the multitude of "invited" guests.

The seeming hypocrisy on the part of label personnel didn't diminish my appreciation for Janet's work on the album. I loved "Got Til It's Gone," with its Joni Mitchell sample even if it wasn't a major hit. I thought "What About That," a no-shit slab of funk that cast Janet in the role of a woman confronting her man on his two-timing around, hit the spot for realism and honesty. And although I, along with several of my more critical journalist friends, probably read more into it than I should, I loved the fact that she didn't change the gender of the object of her affection on her cover of Rod Stewart's "Tonight's the Night"! The record-buying public seemed to like *The Velvet Rope*. Although initially it didn't sell as strongly as its predecessors, the album picked up steam as Janet hit the road in 1998. I saw her at the Los Angeles Forum, and she was amazing. Her energy was upbeat, and she truly performed for an adoring audience. Even though *The Velvet Rope* might have been too bold lyrically for some radio stations, the crowd responded with much enthusiasm when Janet performed songs from the album. Certainly, from an artistic standpoint, Janet Jackson has shown, once again, that she is unafraid to use her music as a vehicle to express herself fully and completely. And in a musical climate that remains producer-driven, that spirit and approach are refreshing. Janet's success just goes to show what happens when a diva takes control.

Funny the changes that life brings. The first full interview I ever did with Toni Braxton for *Blues & Soul* in 1993 sported the heading, "The First Lady Of LaFace." My third interview with her, conducted in 1996 upon the release of her second album, mentioned the same phrase. The April, 1998, issue of *Billboard* contains a news story detailing the latest developments in a round of legal action that began in December, 1997. That was when Toni, through her attorneys, filed a suit claiming that she was no longer bound by her contract with LaFace and its joint-venture partner Arista Records. The lawsuit cited a California statute commonly known as the "seven year rule," which automatically puts an end to personal services being rendered to a company. Luther Vandross and Don Henley had filed lawsuits against their respective labels years before as a way of renegotiating original contracts—and had been successful.

In January, 1998, LaFace and Arista countersued and, according to the *Billboard* story, a spokesperson for both companies reported that in October, 1997, Toni had been offered a $10 million advance, a recording fund of $4.5 million for her third album, an increased royalty rate of 19 percent on new projects and 18 percent on her two previous albums—and through her representatives had rejected it. In January, 1998, Toni also filed for Chapter 7 bankruptcy amid allegations that she was doing so as another tool to enable her to leave LaFace and Arista. She went on "The Oprah Winfrey Show" and explained she hadn't personally kept track of her expenses and bills, hadn't signed all her own checks, and had debts of more than a million dollars. Oprah was less than thrilled about it all, reminding Toni—and the viewing audience of several million—that she always maintained total control over her business dealings and strongly urged other performers to do the same.

The last legal action came from Toni when she asked the bankruptcy court in Los Angeles to declare her LaFace contract unenforceable, alleging that a former attorney, business managers, and personal managers hadn't been working in her best interests in her relationship with LaFace, leading to her financial disarray. Her new manager, Gladys Knight's ex-husband Barry Hankerson, went on record stating that excessive charges by the label had resulted in Toni's money woes.

As I read the *Billboard* stories, I was stunned. Their contents were a far cry from the conversations Toni Braxton and I had since we met in 1992 when LaFace hired me to work with her as a media coach; I was to train her in how best to handle interviews with the press. The need had arisen as a result of the popularity she was achieving through two duets she'd recorded with Kenny "Babyface" Edmonds, the cofounder of LaFace with Antonio "L.A." Reid, for the Eddie Murphy hit movie *Boomerang*.

During my initial meeting with Toni, I found her to be quite shy and nervous. She'd never been exposed to the press before, and she wasn't sure what questions might be asked of her. It wasn't so much that she had anything to hide; it was more a desire that she come across as articulate and smart. She needn't have worried. Yes, Toni was a little timid to start out with, but she was clearly no dummy. She was most concerned about personal questions, but I assured her that until her first album came out, she probably wouldn't be asked too much about that side of her life.

Toni's arrival at LaFace had followed a somewhat circuitous route. The Maryland-born daughter of a minister, Toni had only limited exposure to secular music because of her family background. During our first "proper" interview in 1993, she mentioned how she had to sneak to watch "Soul Train" when her parents weren't around: "I remember the thing that really inspired me to want to sing. I was watching the television program 'Good Times,' and I had a crush on J.J. Walker. I saw a very young Janet Jackson singing to him, and I figured that if I grew up and became a great singer, he'd fall in love with me, too!"

Practicing with perfume and ketchup bottles as pretend microphones, Toni stole away to the bathroom--"the one place I knew I could have some privacy"—so she could imagine what her stage act might be like. Even though her strict upbringing prevented Toni from initially hearing much secular music, her family didn't stop her from entering local talent contests. At one such competition she met songwriter/producer Bill Petteway, whose claim to fame was writing "Girl You Know It's True" for Milli Vanilli. In 1989, Petteway introduced Toni to Ernesto Phillips, a member of the R&B group Starpoint. Phillips also auditioned Toni's four younger sisters, Tamar, Trina, Towanda, and Traci, and signed all five to his production company, subsequently signing a deal for the Braxtons with Arista Records.

The label released just one single, "Good Life," in 1990. And although it only did moderately well, it served as an introduction for Toni to producer/label owners L.A. and Babyface. The team had created LaFace in 1991 and was actively looking for a female vocalist when it heard "Good Life." An audition at which Toni sang and played piano led to an offer to Starpoint's Phillips, and once she'd checked in with her sisters, Toni became a LaFace artist. As she explained in 1993, "Since they're all younger than me, they were either in junior high or high school and they really wanted to complete their education," Toni said of her siblings. "They felt this was a big opportunity for me . . . they were fully behind me and [felt] I should go ahead."

Toni's only concern when she started working with L.A. and Babyface had to do with her own confidence level. "My first reaction when I realized I was going to work with them directly was, 'I hope I'm up to the caliber of artists they work with.' I really wanted them to be proud of me as the first female artist at LaFace." She had little to worry about. With a distinctive voice that had power and range, reminiscent at times of Anita Baker's sultry contralto or Whitney Houston's gospel-edged soprano, Toni could really sing—unlike some of the other young female vocalists who had gained popularity as the new decade began.

It was fortuitous for Toni that L.A. and Babyface were working on their first LaFace soundtrack, and that it was for a film with strong potential. *Boomerang*, a comedy starring Eddie Murphy, Halle Berry, and Robin Givens, was a box-office hit. The soundtrack was a bestseller, racking up three million sales after its release in June, 1992. The soundtrack's success

Radiant beauty
Toni Braxton in
December, 1996
Credit: Popperfoto/
Archive Photos

had more than a little to do with Toni. Her duet with label head and star-in-his-own-right Babyface on the song "Give U My Heart" was not only a No. 2 R&B hit, but also a Top 30 pop success. With a grin, Toni said, "I decided I'd help him with his recording career!"In reality, the duet was her launching pad, and LaFace followed it with Toni's solo effort for the soundtrack, the wistful "Love Shoulda Brought You Home Tonight."

Even before Toni's first album for LaFace was complete, she found herself with a No. 2 R&B and Top 40 pop hit. This was an unusual occurrence, and because she had two back-to-back hits, the anticipation for her solo debut grew among both industry insiders and the public. But it would be a while before *Toni Braxton* would hit the streets: L.A. and Babyface wanted to ensure that the launch of their first female vocalist would get the attention it deserved.

The industry scuttlebutt had it that Clive Davis, the head of Arista, LaFace's joint venture partner, was less than impressed with Toni's singing style. Of course, he already had his own share of divas, the young superstar Whitney Houston—by this time six years into a monumental career—and the legends Aretha Franklin and Dionne Warwick. That put even more pressure on the LaFace principals to deliver, which they did.

Toni Braxton included seven tunes that the two hitmakers had produced themselves with then-partner Daryl Simmons. The album was filled with standout performances like "Seven Whole Days," a smoldering jazzy ballad that had critics convinced that Toni was the "young" version of Anita Baker, and "Best Friend," a song Toni had cowritten, coproducing it with Ernesto Phillips of Starpoint. But beyond the album cuts were the hits, five tunes that jumped out of the album and onto the pop and R&B charts. Three achieved gold status: the instantly memorable "Another Sad Love Song," the acoustic ballad "Breathe Again," and "You Mean the World to Me." A fourth single, "I Belong to You," ran its course on the charts when it was flipped, and "How Many Ways," with a remix by R. Kelly, ran right back up the list of bestsellers.

Apart from Toni's obvious musical skills, she looked fine—slim, hip, and very pretty. For Toni, the album was all about lyrical honesty: "The songs on this first record are real!" she emphasized when we spoke in 1993. "They're about things that people experience in relationships, with love, heartbreak, and all that goes along with dealing with everyday situations. . . . [The song] "Best Friends" is very personal. It's something that happened to me: I was breaking up with this guy, and my best friend started dating him straight away. . . . It was like, 'You've finished with him, so I'm having him for myself'. . . and that hurt!"

Toni felt that the album reflected her personality, which she described as ". . . kinda witty, aggressive at times, and sometimes real shy and reserved. Musically, the album is R&B with a little pop feel and a hint of jazz." She wasn't too hung up on what might happen with it: "It's not so much about whether it goes gold or platinum. It's more about wanting people to love the music for itself." Toni had nothing to worry about. In all, the album sold eight million copies domestically and a few more worldwide, making it a close second to the debut of Arista's Whitney Houston. Any rumored initial concerns that Arista's Davis might have held privately were lost in the sales figures. L.A. and Babyface had once again demonstrated their ability to find and nurture new talent.

Toni's arrival as an artist with potential for longevity was reaffirmed in March, 1994, when she walked away with two Grammy Awards, one for "Best R&B Female Performance" for "Another Sad Love Song," and another for "Best New Artist." Toni would break the occasional jinx that dogged "Best New Artist" Grammy recipients like Arrested Development and Christopher Cross, achieving further multi-platinum success with her all-important follow-up album. But Toni wasn't too focused on the contents of her second LaFace LP when we spoke in the spring of 1994, just after she'd received the Grammys. She was too busy dealing with the sudden rush of fame and the aftermath of a great tour as the opening act for R&B veterans Frankle Beverly and Maze. She explained, "It feels like a wonderful dream. I definitely never expected to have this kind of success, and when the album sold over three million copies, that was a real turning point. It was hard for me to realize that just a year and half ago, I was singing "Love Shoulda Brought You Home"—I didn't expect to have success this early in my career, honestly!"

Toni had experienced changes and adjustments: "Right now, it's all exciting. Sure, my body's tired and I could use a day off or two, but I realize that what I'm doing now is creating the fundamentals for a career and that's a lot of responsibility." In our 1994 *Blues & Soul* magazine interview, Toni confessed that she had little time for romance: "Guys? It's funny because they haven't been knocking down doors! In fact, I've been telling people I'm interviewing for the position [of boyfriend] and one guy actually sent me an application and another gave me a resume!" A joking remark made during an appearance on "The Arsenio Hall Show" had started the rumor mill turning with hints of bisexuality. And Toni's sometimes tomboy-like appearance only fueled the comments. By the 1996 release of her sophomore album, that look was long gone: long tresses and a decidedly feminine wardrobe had replaced her short haircut, jeans, and tank tops.

In the wake of our interview, Toni was off to the Far East and Australia before tackling Europe for the first time and then heading back into the studios for work on her second LaFace project. LaFace and Arista had a lot riding on the success of the album, ultimately known as *Secrets*. The Atlanta-based company had been through publicized legal action with its other mainstay best-selling act TLC, which filed Chapter 11 bankruptcy in 1995 amid allegations, counter-allegations, and general bad feeling between the rap/hip-hop trio and the LaFace principals.

There had been some other separations as well. L.A. Reid and his wife, singer/songwriter Pebbles, had split up. Babyface was no longer based in Atlanta; he was now living with Tracy Edmonds, his new bride, in Los Angeles, fueling word that the two longtime friends had been through some major changes in regard to their business dealings.

Meanwhile, Arista's female megastar Whitney Houston hadn't had a non-soundtrack album release in four years, even though the multi-platinum success of both the *The Bodyguard* and *Waiting to Exhale* soundtrack albums had more than made up for the void. The label's other reigning diva, Aretha Franklin, was still two years from delivering a new record. Toni Braxton could, and ultimately would, help bring home the bacon for both labels in 1996.

By virtue of the first single, "You're Makin' Me High," with its overt reference to masturbation and semi-steamy video, people knew that the cutesy Toni Braxton they'd discovered through her debut album had an image makeover with her sophomore set *Secrets* The lead-off song was about the most controversial tune on the album, although "Talking in His Sleep," one of the two tunes she cowrote for the project, was lyrically strong in dealing with infidelity. Toni confessed in our 1996 interview just before the album's release that ". . . the song was based on a true story! You see, some stupid people do talk in their sleep. . . ."

Toni also explained that "You're Makin' Me High" was intentionally included on the album as part of a strategy: "There's nothing like [it] on the first album. I think we went for something that would work for young and old, a little bit of everything. . . . The main thing is that this record sounds younger." And the song itself? "[It] lets people see another side of me. The song is more about what I'm thinking about, my sexual fantasies, rather than what I'm acting out. I guess it's another dimension of me—and it fits in with the whole idea of "secrets" as the title we gave the album. You know, I do have my own little secrets!" she concluded.

Secrets ended up selling six million copies and spawned major hits like "Unbreak My Heart" and "How Could an Angel Break My Heart," earning her two more Grammy Awards, for a grand total of five in just three years. Toni was once again riding the crest of a wave. But it turned slightly tidal when she appeared on the cover of *Vibe* magazine in the summer of 1997 with a towel strategically placed over her otherwise apparently nude body! The preacher's daughter talked about sex amidst provocative photographs that showed nipples and all. Certainly, the image that had been created for her first album—petite, cute, girl-next-door—was gone. She was now a steamy seductress on the prowl!

I last saw Toni at a release party for *Secrets* at a fashionable restaurant in Los Angeles. She was very friendly, and we posed for a photograph that had us so tightly wrapped in each other's arms that the Arista publicist who helped set up the event never sent it to me— probably for fear of it appearing in print! Yes, I did get her telephone number with my request for us to hang out sometime. But we never did because within months, Toni was preparing for a national tour with superstar saxophone player Kenny G. I was left with my fantasies—which were destroyed incidentally after I read the *Vibe* article!

Toni and I never talked about the business and how she was coping that day. But during two of our interviews, she made what in retrospect would be relevant comments given the lawsuits and bankruptcy in 1998. Back in 1993, during our *Blues & Soul* interview, she'd said, "You do have to get adjusted to the business aspects of the music business and really, no one can tell you about that. There are just some things you have to learn through experience. I'm fortunate because I do have two great teachers in L.A. and 'Face but honestly, you can never be ready for what you might have to deal with in this business." Then in 1996, Toni said she'd learned "[the importance] of being hands on with my career. Nothing happens unless I say it's okay, and you know, as a new artist, I didn't know the business too well [at first]. But I've learned a lot, and I've had some great teachers. Patti LaBelle has been very supportive in terms of input, and I make it a point to know about contracts, about budgets, and about any decision affecting my career . . . and L.A. and Babyface have made it a point to include me in on everything that's happening in my career. No, there are no dumb artists around here!"

Toni Braxton definitely isn't dumb. But after seeing how events have unfolded in the first few months of 1998, I'm left wondering whether the advice she has been getting has always been that sound. Certainly, her talent is intact: the two albums and the live performances I've seen leave no question about her natural ability. New York audiences seem to agree: Toni began appearing in the Broadway musical version of *Beauty and the Beast* in the fall of 1998 to rave reviews. Unlike a whole bunch of other young women purporting to be vocal queens, Toni really can sing—the invariable qualification for a true soulful diva!

INDEX

Photo credits, page 400 (left to right, top to bottom):

Ron Wolfson/London Features International; Michael Ochs Archives; Popperfoto/Archive Photos; Promotional shot; Michael Ochs Archives/Venice, CA; Michael Ochs Archives/Venice, CA; Archive Photos; Archive/Frank Driggs Collection

RECOMMENDED LISTENING LIST

THE SOULFUL DIVAS
Volume 1: Pop'n' Soul Sirens (Hip-O)
Volume 2: Dance Queens (Hip-O)
Volume 3: Softly With a Song (Hip-O)
Volume 4: Bold Soul Sisters (Hip-O)
Volume 5: Ladies of Jazz'n'Soul (Hip-O)

DIONNE WARWICK
Hidden Gems (Rhino)
From the Vaults (Ichiban Soul Classics)
The Dionne Warwick Collection (Rhino)
Dionne Sings Dionne (River North)

NINA SIMONE
The Colpix Years Anthology (Rhino)
The Best of Nina Simone (Philips)
The Very Best of Nina Simone:
Sugar in My Bowl (RCA)
Baltimore (Sony/Legacy)

ARETHA FRANKLIN
From Jazz to Soul (Sony Legacy)
The Queen of Soul (Rhino)
Greatest Hits 1980-1994 (Arista)
Aretha Arrives (Rhino)
Amazing Grace (Atlantic)

ESTHER PHILLIPS
The Best of Esther Phillips
1962-1970 (Rhino)
The Best of Esther Phillips
(Epic Associated)
From a Whisper to a Scream
(Sony Legacy)

DORIS TROY
Just One Look: The Best of Doris Troy
(Ichiban Soul Classics)
Doris Troy (Apple-Capitol)

DIANA ROSS
Surrender (Motown)
The Boss (Motown)
Forever: Musical
Memoirs (Motown)

GLADYS KNIGHT
Gladys Knight & The Pips
Anthology (Motown)
Just For You (MCA)

CHAKA KHAN
The Best of Rufus Featuring Chaka Khan (MCA)
Epiphany: The Best of Chaka Khan (Reprise)
Come 2 to My House (NPG)

PATTI LaBELLE
Over the Rainbow: The Atlantic Yearsqs
(Ichiban Soul Classics)
Nightbirds (Epic)
Greatest Hits (MCA)

MILLIE JACKSON
Totally Unrestricted! The Anthology (Rhino)
Caught Up/Still Caught Up (Hip-O)

NATALIE COLE
The Best Of Natalie Cole (Capitol)
Unforgettable (Elektra)

PHYLLIS HYMAN
Phyllis Hyman (The Right Stuff)
The Legacy of Phyllis Hyman (Arista)
Forever With You
(Philadelphia International)

ROBERTA FLACK
The Best of Roberta Flack (Atlantic)
First Take (Atlantic)
Roberta (Atlantic)

ANITA BAKER
The Songstress (Elektra)
Rapture (Elektra)
Compositions (Elektra)

WHITNEY HOUSTON
Whitney Houston (Arista)
I'm Your Baby Tonight (Arista)
The Bodyguard (Arista)

JANET JACKSON
Control (A&M)
janet (Virgin)
The Velvet Rope (Virgin)

TONI BRAXTON
Toni Braxton (LaFace)
Secrets (LaFace)